Backpacking in Michigan

Other books by Jim DuFresne

Isle Royale National Park: Foot Trails & Water Routes

50 Hikes in Michigan

Porcupine Mountains Wilderness State Park

Best Hikes for Children: Michigan

Michigan State Parks

Michigan: Off the Beaten Path

Michigan's Best Campgrounds

The Complete Guide to Michigan Sand Dunes

Road Trip: Lake Michigan

Tramping in New Zealand

Glacier Bay National Park

Alaska

Hiking in Alaska

Wild Michigan

Backpacking in Michigan

Jim DuFresne

Ann Arbor   **The University of Michigan Press**

2010   2009   2008   2007   4   3   2   1

A CIP catalog record for this book is available from the British Library.

U.S. CIP data applied for.

ISBN-13: 978-0-472-03268-6 (pbk. : alk. paper)
ISBN-10: 0-472-03268-2 (pbk. : alk. paper)

To Troop 1261,
for that first step down the trail,

and Greg,
who always knew that the adventure, not the
rank, is what matters.

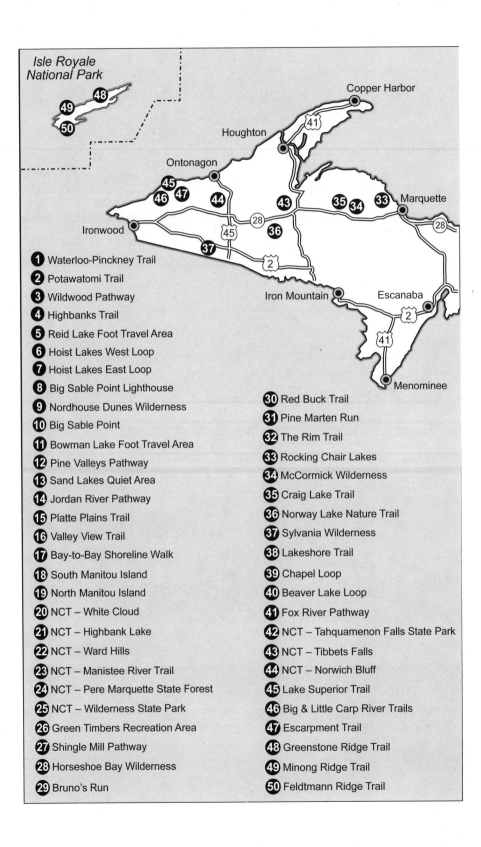

Isle Royale
National Park

Copper Harbor

Houghton

Ontonagon

Marquette

Ironwood

Escanaba

Iron Mountain

Menominee

1 Waterloo-Pinckney Trail
2 Potawatomi Trail
3 Wildwood Pathway
4 Highbanks Trail
5 Reid Lake Foot Travel Area
6 Hoist Lakes West Loop
7 Hoist Lakes East Loop
8 Big Sable Point Lighthouse
9 Nordhouse Dunes Wilderness
10 Big Sable Point
11 Bowman Lake Foot Travel Area
12 Pine Valleys Pathway
13 Sand Lakes Quiet Area
14 Jordan River Pathway
15 Platte Plains Trail
16 Valley View Trail
17 Bay-to-Bay Shoreline Walk
18 South Manitou Island
19 North Manitou Island
20 NCT – White Cloud
21 NCT – Highbank Lake
22 NCT – Ward Hills
23 NCT – Manistee River Trail
24 NCT – Pere Marquette State Forest
25 NCT – Wilderness State Park
26 Green Timbers Recreation Area
27 Shingle Mill Pathway
28 Horseshoe Bay Wilderness
29 Bruno's Run

30 Red Buck Trail
31 Pine Marten Run
32 The Rim Trail
33 Rocking Chair Lakes
34 McCormick Wilderness
35 Craig Lake Trail
36 Norway Lake Nature Trail
37 Sylvania Wilderness
38 Lakeshore Trail
39 Chapel Loop
40 Beaver Lake Loop
41 Fox River Pathway
42 NCT – Tahquamenon Falls State Park
43 NCT – Tibbets Falls
44 NCT – Norwich Bluff
45 Lake Superior Trail
46 Big & Little Carp River Trails
47 Escarpment Trail
48 Greenstone Ridge Trail
49 Minong Ridge Trail
50 Feldtmann Ridge Trail

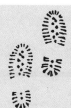

Backpacking in
Michigan

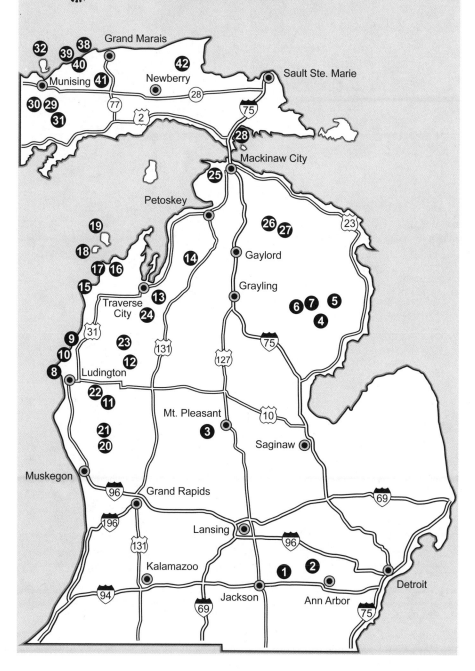

Grand Marais

32 39 38

40

Munising 41

Newberry

42

Sault Ste. Marie

28

30 29

31

77

2

75

28

Mackinaw City

25

Petoskey

19

18

17 16

15

14

Gaylord

26 27

23

Traverse
City

13

24

Grayling

6 7 5

4

9

31

23

10

12

8 Ludington

131

127

75

22

11

Mt. Pleasant

10

21

20

3

Saginaw

Muskegon

96 Grand Rapids

69

196

Lansing

131

96

Kalamazoo

1 2

Detroit

94

69 Jackson

Ann Arbor

75

For many backpackers scenic Munising Falls is the end of the Lakeshore Trail, a four-day walk from Grand Marais to Munising.

Contents

Isle Royale National Park

Map Legend

The 70 maps in the following sections use these symbols:

Described trail

Other trail

Paved or gravel road

Two-track or forest road

Drinking water

Campsite or camping area

Trailhead with parking area

Restrooms or vault toilets

Scenic viewing point

Park office or museum

Rental cabin or structure

High point or peak

Trail post or numbered junction

Free-use shelter

Lighthouse

Boat launch

Modern campground

Old-growth trees

Waterfall

Historic mine

Shipwreck

Swimming beach

Covered bridge

Cemetery

Wetlands

Trails at a Glance: *Lower Peninsula*

Trail	Distance	Days	Difficulty
1. Waterloo-Pinckney Trail	38.5 miles	4	Moderate
2. Potawatomi Trail	17.5 miles	2	Moderate/Challenging
3. Wildwood Pathway	3 miles	2	Easy
4. Highbanks Trail	14 miles	Overnight	Easy/Moderate
5. Reid Lake Foot Travel Area	9 miles	2	Moderate
6. Hoist Lakes West Loop	6.4 miles	2	Moderate
7. Hoist Lakes East Loop	5 miles	2	Easy
8. Big Sable Point Lighthouse	4 miles	Overnight	Easy
9. Nordhouse Dunes Wilderness	6.1 miles	2	Moderate
10. Big Sable Point	15 miles	2	Moderate
11. Bowman Lake FTA	4 miles	Overnight	Easy
12. Pine Valleys Pathway	4.1 miles	2	Easy
13. Sand Lakes Quiet Area	7.4 miles	2	Moderate
14. Jordan River Pathway	18.7 miles	2	Moderate/Challenging
Sleeping Bear Dunes National Lakeshore			
15. Platte Plains Trail	7 miles	2	Easy
16. Valley View Trail	3 miles	Overnight	Easy
17. Bay-to-Bay Shoreline Walk	36 miles	3	Moderate
18. South Manitou Island	12 miles	3	Moderate
19. North Manitou Island	16.6 miles	3	Moderate
North Country Trail			
20. NCT – White Cloud	24.8 miles	2	Moderate/Challenging
21. NCT – Highbank Lake	12 miles	Overnight	Moderate
22. NCT – Ward Hills	21.6 miles	3	Moderate
23. NCT – Manistee River Trail	21.5 miles	3	Moderate/Challenging
24. NCT – Pere Marquette SF	19.6 miles	3	Moderate
25. NCT – Wilderness SP	23.4 miles	3	Moderate
Pigeon River Country State Forest			
26. Green Timbers RA	8 miles	Overnight	Moderate
27. Shingle Mill Pathway	10 miles	2	Moderate

Nearest Town	Page	Highlights
Chelsea	29	Rolling hardwood forests and numerous lakes
Pinckney	41	Lakes, walk-in campsites and a rental yurt
Mount Pleasant	47	Walk-in campsites, covered bridge
Tawas City	51	Numerous overlooks of the AuSable River
Curran	57	Walk-in campsites overlooking small lakes
Glennie	63	Scenic vistas and lakeshore campsites
Glennie	67	Fishing in Hoist Lakes, walk-in campsites
Ludington	71	Beautiful beaches and a historic lighthouse
Manistee	75	Scenic vistas, sand dunes, uncrowded beaches
Manistee	81	A beach walk past dunes and a lighthouse
Baldwin	87	Walk-in campsites on an undeveloped lake
Baldwin	90	Spend a night on a protected little lake
Traverse City	94	Walk-in campsite and off-trail fishing
Mancelona	98	Scenic overlooks and great fall colors
Empire	107	Lake Michigan beach; uncrowded and beautiful
Glen Arbor	111	Walk-in campsites in a hardwood forest
Empire	115	Spectacular shoreline scenery and dunes
Leland	123	Towering dunes, giant cedars, and shipwrecks
Leland	133	Sunsets, remnant farms, backcountry camping
White Cloud	143	White River and schoolhouse lodging
Baldwin	149	A series of small, isolated lakes
Baldwin	152	Camping on remote McCarthy Lake
Mesick	159	The mighty Manistee River and a small waterfall
Traverse City	167	Old growth forest, lakes and walk-in campsites
Mackinaw City	173	Wetlands, French Farm Lake, rental cabins
Vanderbilt	183	Sturgeon River Valley, free-use shelters
Vanderbilt	187	Pigeon River, overlooks, lakeshore campsites

Trails at a Glance: *Upper Peninsula*

Trail	Distance	Days	Difficulty
28. Horseshoe Bay Wilderness	6 miles	Overnight	Easy
29. Bruno's Run	10 miles	2	Moderate
30. Red Buck Trail	2 miles	Overnight	Easy
31. Pine Marten Run	16.5 miles	3	Moderate
32. The Rim Trail	21.8 miles	3	Moderate
33. Rocking Chair Lakes	2 miles	Overnight	Moderate
34. McCormick Wilderness	6 miles	Overnight	Moderate
35. Craig Lake Trail	8 miles	2	Moderate/Challenging
36. Norway Lake Nature Trail	1.2 miles	2	Easy
37. Sylvania Wilderness	9.2 miles	2	Easy/Moderate

Pictured Rocks National Lakeshore

Trail	Distance	Days	Difficulty
38. Lakeshore Trail	42.4 miles	5	Moderate/Challenging
39. Chapel Loop	10.4 miles	2	Easy/Moderate
40. Beaver Lake Loop	11.5 miles	2	Moderate
41. Fox River Pathway	34.7 miles	4	Challenging

North Country Trail

Trail	Distance	Days	Difficulty
42. NCT - Tahquamenon Falls SP	15 miles	2	Moderate
43. NCT - Tibbets Falls	3.6 miles	Overnight	Easy
44. NCT - Norwich Bluffs	12.9 miles	2	Challenging

Porcupine Mountains Wilderness State Park

Trail	Distance	Days	Difficulty
45. Lake Superior Trail	17.1 miles	3	Moderate/Challenging
46. Big & Little Carp River Trails	27 miles	4	Moderate/Challenging
47. Escarpment Trail	4.3 miles	Overnight	Moderate

Isle Royale National Park

Trail	Distance	Days	Difficulty
48. Greenstone Ridge Trail	42.4 miles	5	Moderate
49. Minong Ridge Trail	31.6 miles	6	Challenging
50. Feldtmann Ridge Trail	29.8 miles	3	Moderate/Challenging

A backpacker uses an umbrella hat during a rainy day on the North Country Trail in the Pere Marquette State Forest.

Backpacking in Michigan

How to Escape Our Hectic World
and Find Your Way Back Home

Lace up the boots. Hoist a backpack. Take a hike. Spend the night.

In a world as chaotic, loud, and busy as ours, where life seems to be moving at a fast forward speed, where we're always connected to everybody via cell phones, pagers, and instant messaging, the solution to slowing down and getting away is surprisingly simple and affordable; go backpacking. Load up your pack with just the essentials – and nothing more – and take a walk in the woods. Simplify your needs and let the physical exertion of following a trail and the spirit of being outdoors refresh and relax you. It's cheaper than a day at the spa and far less complicated to plan than a retreat to a monastery in the mountains.

Dayhiking is also a fine escape, but for the effort of carrying a small load on your back, you can greatly extend the amount of time spent away from rush-hour civilization and enjoy that rare experience of drifting off to sleep at night to the rustle of leaves above or the gentle roll of an endless surf. The next morning, you'll be invigorated by the knowledge that your only deadline of the day is to pitch the tent before dark.

For many of us, this simple path to solitude is the best way to purge the mind and lift the soul.

The outings don't have to be long or difficult. A common misconception is that backpacking has to be a week on a trail lugging around a 45-pound backpack. No so. Many of the 50 treks covered in this guide are overnight adventures; some are a walk of only a mile or two, making them ideal for families with young children. What they have in common is a scenic spot to end the day, often designated walk-in campsites. Some sites are near Great Lake beaches; others are on an inland lake or a trout stream; a few are even perched on a high ridge with a million-dollar view.

All are away from the road.

Michigan's classic backpacking trails are also covered. They include such great routes as the Greenstone Trail, a five-day walk across Isle Royale National Park; the Lakeshore Trail, a four-day walk from Grand Marais to Munising along the famed Pictured Rocks; and a three-day trek around North Manitou Island in Sleeping Bear Dunes National Lakeshore. These and other long-distance trails require pre-trip planning, additional time off, and a certain level of backcountry expertise and fitness.

But don't put away the backpack after your trip to Isle Royale. In between those grand adventures, use weekend excursions to take advantage of Michigan's extensive network of foot trails and the fact that there's more of the North Country Trail here than in any other state. The trailhead doesn't have to be that far Up North; the hike in doesn't have to be long; the pack certainly doesn't have to be that heavy. Just carry in a little bit of food, some coffee for the morning, a flask of brandy for the evening. If you're confident about the weather, skip the tent and sleep under the stars.

Just leave your car behind and enter the woods to spend a night with nothing around you but what nature intended. This is the essence of backpacking; a simple and easy escape from our urbanized world at home.

When to Backpack

The traditional backpacking season in Michigan is June through August. The days are long, the weather is warm, and the kids are out of school. In the summer, temperatures can range from a chilly and rainy 60 degrees on the shores of Lake Superior to a blistering 90 degrees or even hotter elsewhere in the middle of August. Sunny weather and blue skies are the norm, but always pack along the raingear as the weather can change quickly at this time of year, with thunderstorms and heavy rain suddenly blowing in from the Great Lakes.

Depending on the winter, both the length of it and the snow accumulation, there can be good hiking beginning in late April in the Lower Peninsula and early May in the Upper Peninsula. Streams may be swollen and trails a bit muddy, but wildflowers are often in full bloom while birds and waterfowl will be migrating north. Expect temperatures in the 50 and 60 degrees, depending on how far north you are, and frequent rain showers. Also be prepared for mosquitoes by mid-May in the Lower Peninsula while the Upper Peninsula's dreaded black fly season usually occurs for seven to 10 days in late May. Avoid the U.P. at all costs during black fly season.

Mosquitoes will be around through early August and deer flies for much of the summer. If bugs are something you'd like to avoid at all costs, plan major backpacking trips in mid-to-late August. It's even better in September and October, which, in my opinion, is the best time to be in the woods in Michigan.

During the fall, daytime temperatures are pleasantly cool, 70 degrees or lower. Showers are common but so are those glorious Indian summer days when the sky is a deep blue, the forest is dry, and the temperature peaks in the mid-60s. And then there are the fall colors. At Isle Royale and the Porcupine Mountains in the western Upper Peninsula the hardwoods reach their peak color in the third week of September. In the northern tip of the Lower Peninsula and around Traverse City the best colors occur in the first week of October, and along the Waterloo-Pinckney Trail in southeast Michigan you can enjoy flaming reds and burnt yellows at the end of October.

The unofficial end of the backpacking season is November 15, the first day of the firearm deer season. By the time the 16-day season is over, many areas of northern Michigan will have already received their first snowfall.

Packing the Pack

Backpacking does require specialized gear that will allow you to stay warm, dry and pleasantly comfortable at night when there are few if any amenities. To carry that equipment you'll need a backpack. The overwhelmingly popular choice today is internal frames that feature a frame built inside the pack, making them extremely adjustable and thus enhancing your comfort, balance, and freedom of movement.

Whatever you choose – internal or a pack with an external frame – make

Backpackers & Bears

It's possible while you're backpacking in the wilds of Michigan to encounter a black bear in the northern third of the Lower Peninsula or anywhere in the Upper Peninsula. But not likely. Bears are normally afraid of people, and when a bear encounters hikers they usually leave the area in a hurry.

There are two areas – Porcupine Mountains Wilderness State Park and Pictured Rocks National Lakeshore – where backpacker-bear encounters were so frequent that bear poles were erected in most of the backcountry campsites. At night, you simply use a long hook to hang your pack, with all your food in it, on the top of one. No more bruins raiding your dinners.

If you are in any other area and worried about bears entering camp, place all food and scented items like toothpaste in a bag (sleeping bag stuff sacks work well) and suspend it 12 feet above the ground and far enough from the trunk of a tree to prevent a bear from reaching or jumping on it. You might have to suspend the bag from two trees or use multiple ropes to accomplish this.

If you see a bear near the trail, move away from it or turn back. Give sows and cubs plenty of room. Do not confront or feed a bear. Never take food into your tent at night and keep a clean campsite to reduce the chances of a wandering bruin visiting you in the middle of the night.

The park staff at the Porcupine Mountains has developed a code called *Understanding Bear Behavior*:

A bear is studying you if it...
- Stands on its hind legs to get a better view.
- Waves its nose around smelling the air.
- Makes low, non-aggressive grunting sounds.

A bear may be getting upset if it...
- Clicks its teeth.
- Gives a loud blowing sound.

A bear is telling you to leave when it...
- Blows loudly.
- Makes short lunges and hits the ground or nearby objects.
- Gives a bluff charge that stops short of you.

sure it is a high-quality pack with a waist belt, padded shoulder straps, and a chest strap. For overnight outings, you'll need a pack with a capacity of 2,500 to 3,000 cubic inches. For treks that last three days or longer, most people need a pack that holds 4,000 cubic inches. Avoid glorified day packs or backpacks that are designed to be converted into a piece of luggage. Also bring a pack cover, for protection against the rain, or store everything in the pack in plastic bags.

Footwear: One of the most important pieces of equipment on the trail is your footwear. In Michigan most backpackers opt for lightweight nylon boots made by sport-shoe companies like Merrell, Vasque, or Lowa. These "lightweight hiking boots" are designed for easy terrain and carrying moderate loads, which covers nearly all the treks described in this book. For week-long treks in rugged areas, such as Isle Royale and the Porcupine Mountains, the traditional leather hiking boots are a better choice. Such boots offer more support with a stiff leather upper, a more durable sole and protective shanks. Both styles can be purchased with Gore-Tex linings that make them waterproof, something to consider seriously.

You should also have a spare pair of shoes to wear once you're in camp. A growing number of hikers now pack along rafter sandals such as Tevas. These heavy rubber-soled sandals, held onto your foot by straps, are lighter to carry, dry quicker, and can be just as comfortable as running shoes.

Clothing: The only way to survive weather that changes as often as it does in Michigan and to accommodate the many exertion levels of backpacking is to dress in layers. Generally, you will have three layers – underwear, insulating layer and shell layer – and will remove or add layers according to the conditions.

Begin with a set of lightweight underwear of polypropylene or some other high-tech synthetic fabric. Synthetic underwear, as opposed to wool, silk, or cotton, will do the best job of "wicking" moisture away from the skin to the surface of the garment. The insulating layer provides essential warmth. For that layer, many hikers use a jersey of pile or fleece fabric such as Polartec rather than a wool sweater. Like wool, the pile will keep you warm when wet, but it dries much faster. Avoid cotton at all costs.

The final layer – parka and overpants – must protect you against wind, rain or, heaven forbid, a freak snowfall in October. Waterproof but "breathable" garments will provide the most protection and comfort. Gore-Tex is the best-known of the breathable materials, but others are available.

Tent: The most popular tent by far is the dome tent. They're light, and the curved design and crisscrossed poles provide plenty of room. More importantly, these tents are freestanding, so they don't have to be staked out to be set up. Tunnel tents are an elongated variation of the dome tent. They usually require two or three stakes and are lighter than dome tents and are far more stable in strong winds or heavy storms. Bivy or solo tents are extremely small units, often weighing less than three pounds, that provide shelter for one person.

The Minnesota ferry, Voyageur II, *unloads backpackers at McCargoe Cove Campground in Isle Royale National Park.*

Your choice of a tent will depend on how much space you need and your budget. Whatever you spend, the tent should have a good rain fly and netting around the doors and windows that is bug proof, so you aren't a nightly smorgasbord for any mosquito that passes by.

Sleeping Bag: Many backpackers have spent the night debating the qualities of natural down versus synthetic fibers. When wet, down will clump, while synthetic will keep you warm even if it's soaked. But nothing compresses as tightly or is as light as down, which can greatly reduce the weight of your pack. You just have to keep it dry.

A three-season bag, which usually suits temperatures between –10 degrees and 40 degrees, is the best overall choice for Michigan. A mummy bag will fit closer to your body. If you like to roll around in your bag, the slightly wider

Backpacking When I'm 64 (and Older)

I met my hero on Isle Royale, a backpacker named Jim Preish. The North Carolina hiker didn't carry the heaviest pack on the island nor did he have the fastest pace on the trail. Far from it. But Preish captured my admiration because at the age of 65, he was still out there backpacking and I had no reason to believe he wouldn't be when he turns 70.

Who says senior citizens can't go backpacking? Not Preish. He did have some suggestions for those of us who hope to keep trekking long after we've received the gold watch:

• Lighten the load. This is critical for anybody, young or old. Always perform a shakedown before every trip and evaluate every piece of gear in your pack. Do you really need a trailside espresso maker or that bulky solar shower?

• Even with required equipment, you can lighten your load. Down sleeping bags are up to half the weight of synthetic bags. If you're sleeping alone use a solo tent instead of a two-man dome. Measure your food carefully in advance and repackage it. Hauling uneaten food for four or five days is a cardinal sin.

• Invest in gear that will make you more comfortable on the trail. For many of us, it's the extra thick, self-inflatable Thermarest pad for a better sleep at night. For Preish it was a small, folding stool so he didn't have to sit on the ground after a long day on the trail.

• Reduce your daily mileage. Plan your trip so you're only covering 5 miles a day instead of the 10 or 12 miles you did in your youth.

• Then slow up the pace and stop often. The breaks don't have to be long, just more frequent to give your legs a chance to recover throughout the day.

• When faced with a particularly hard day, take ibuprofen in the morning before you head out. Preish believes ibuprofen is much more effective in preventing sore muscles to begin with than relieving the pain of them in the evening.

modified mummy bag is more suitable but weighs more.

Along with a bag, you'll want to pack along an insulated sleeping pad to reduce the ground chill. For comfort, consider investing in a self-inflating pad, such as the Thermarest.

Camp Stove: Cooking dinner over a crackling campfire may be a romantic notion while you're planning your trip, but it is an inconvenience and often a major headache when you're actually on the trail. Rain, strong winds, and a lack of available wood will hamper your efforts to build a fire, and some places, like Isle Royale, don't even allow campfires in the backcountry. Bring a reliable stove and make life simple in the woods. Many stove brands are on the market today, but stoves like the MSR WhisperLite, which can be "field repaired," are the most dependable.

Water Filter: In Michigan, water from all lakes, streams, and rivers must be treated before you drink it to avoid the dysentery caused by Giardia lamblia. In the backcountry, unless it comes from a hand pump, consider it unsafe to drink. The simplest way to purify water is to pump it though a giardia-rated filter. Models such as the Katadyn Mini Filter or MSR's Waterworks are designed to take out whatever you shouldn't be drinking. You can also boil water for a full minute to purify it, but consider the time and extra fuel boiling requires. Packing along a filter makes life easier on the trail.

Other Gear: In the summer, you will want to carry along insect repellent, sunscreen, sun glasses, and a wide-brimmed hat, especially when hiking trails in dune country. In the spring and fall, mittens and stocking cap are often needed at night or to avoid chilling when you stop for a break or lunch. No matter what season it is, always pack a small first-aid kit that contains items (moleskin, bandages) to take care of blisters that suddenly develop 3 miles from the trailhead.

Finding Your Way Back Home

The maps included in this book are intended to complement the text, not to be used when you're on the trail. In the description of every hike, the best possible maps are listed and in many cases they are the US Geological Survey (USGS) topographical maps. Known simply as a "topo" or "quad," these maps come in a variety of scales, but the smallest scales available (1:24,000 or 1:63,360) are the most useful ones to backpackers.

One source of customized USGS quads is MyTopo (877-587-9004; *www.mytopo.com*). From the Montana-based web site you can create and order online a 1:24,000 scale map of the area you will be hiking in. The waterproof maps are 24 by 36 inches and cost $14.95.

If you plan to go backpacking in Michigan regularly, a digitized, interactive mapping program is an excellent investment. Digital maps are more than just a topo on the screen of your computer. The base map that has been digitized is often the USGS quad while the accompanying software, called a "map engine," makes the program interactive and allows you to customize a map for any upcoming hike. You can highlight your route, mark places where you plan to camp, even add notes such as times and distances, and then print it out to take on the trail. The maps are also seamless, meaning you can print exactly the coverage you need even if it is split between four quads. Companies that sell complete sets of maps to Michigan include Maptech (800-627-7236; *www.maptech.com*) and National Geographic (800-962-1643; *www.ngmapstore.com*).

Even if you pack a GPS unit, always carry a small compass into the wilderness and know how to use it correctly.

Using This Guidebook

The 50 treks covered in this book were chosen for their interesting scenery and the fact they all feature backcountry camping. Thus, they are described in a day-by-day format. An "overnight" outing is simply a hike to a walk-in campsite and then returning to your vehicle along the same trail the next day. A two-day hike is also a single night in the woods but following a different segment of trail each day. A three-day outing would be two nights on the trail; a four-day hike would be three nights on the trail, and so on.

Many of the treks are along point-to-point trails, where you start here but end up over there, sometimes 20 or 30 miles away. The best way to handle such walks is to drop off a vehicle at one end and then shuttle back to the beginning, a logistic ordeal that requires two cars. In many cases there is public transportation available that will return you to the starting point or help shuttle a vehicle. These have been well covered in the text. When all else fails, there are suggestions on which segments of the trail are best for an overnight outing so you can backtrack to where you left the car.

Difficulty, Distances & Elevation: Each trail is rated according to difficulty in the fact box at the beginning of the section:

Easy trails are well maintained and frequently used, with planking and foot bridges over wet areas and plenty of directional signs. These tracks are extremely level, present few, if any, navigational difficulties and can be attempted by families and visitors with just day-hiking experience.

Moderate trails are well cut and usually well marked but more strenuous than easy trails and generally longer, averaging 4 to 7 miles a day. They also feature greater changes in elevation and thus require better physical stamina and map-reading skills.

Challenging trails are usually lightly marked paths in rugged areas that results in considerable climbing of ridges and bluffs. These trails are usually four or five-day outings with some days as long as 10 miles or more. Such hikes might also involve other special considerations, such as following unmarked ridges, crossing unbridged streams, or camping in bear country.

Trail distances are provided for both the overall trip and day-by-day stages, but I have avoided listing hiking times. An average hiker with a 30-pound pack will cover a mile of well-marked and somewhat level trail in 30 to 40 minutes. But that is only an "average" as some speedsters will cover that distance in half the time while others, constantly stopping to look at wildflowers or to enjoy another handful of trail mix, will need twice as long. Using the mileage in the text, it's important for you to determine early on what your hiking speed is with the load that you are carrying, the terrain you are covering and the party you are with (you can only hike as fast as the slowest person in the group). Then apply that to the rest of the trek.

Elevation is provided in feet in the description of the walk and on the

Michigan's Top Ten Treks

All the trails in this guidebook are walks worth doing, but here are Michigan's best backpacking adventures, in my humble opinion:

1. The Lakeshore Trail (*Pictured Rocks National Lakeshore*) A four- to five-day walk through impressive sand dunes, past shipwrecks, and along the famed Pictured Rocks. This is our most stunning trail, a pilgrimage that every Michigan backpacker needs to make at least once in their life.

2. Big & Little Carp River Trails (*Porcupine Mountains Wilderness State Park*) Follow the Big Carp River from its beginnings in the mountains to its end at a freshwater sea. Plan this trek in advance, and you'll be able to hike from cabin-to-cabin.

3. The Greenstone Trail (*Isle Royale National Park*) Michigan's classic five- to six-day walk from one end of the largest island in Lake Superior to the other.

4. North Manitou Island (*Sleeping Bear Dunes National Lakeshore*) A three-day hike around this wilderness island in Lake Michigan, featuring sandy beaches and brilliant sunsets.

5. Jordan River Pathway (*Mackinac State Forest*) In early October the brilliant fall foliage on this two-day trek along the pristine Jordan River will leave you color blind.

6. Minong Ridge Trail (*Isle Royale National Park*) The toughest trail in Michigan. Hike it – or simply survive it – then add a notch on your walking stick.

7. Manistee River Trail (*Manistee National Forest*) Combine this easy trail with the rugged segment of the North Country Trail opposite it and you have a three-day loop along the scenic Manistee River.

8. Grand Island Recreation Area (*Hiawatha National Forest*) A three-day hike around an island that has cliffs and bluffs almost as impressive as Pictured Rocks.

9. North Country Trail (*Wilderness State Park*) You begin near one of the finest beaches in the Lower Peninsula; you end three days later at the fudge shops of Mackinaw City. In between you traverse a state park called Wilderness.

10. Waterloo-Pinckney Trail (*Waterloo* and *Pinckney Recreation Areas*) This walk is amazing if for no other reason than it's a three-day backcountry escape in the most urbanized region of Michigan.

How much gear is too much? A backpacker finds out while setting up camp in Isle Royale National Park.

maps as contour lines. In the fact box of each trail the Highest Elevation Gain is listed and represents the hardest climb of the entire walk. There could easily be others almost as high.

Responsible Backpacking

Be thoughtful when you are in the wilderness; it is a delicate environment. It's best to hike and camp in small groups that have less impact on wildlife and terrain. Please forgo the boomboxes and radios.

Carry in your supplies and, more importantly, carry out your trash. Never litter or leave garbage to smolder in a fire pit. Always put out your fire and cover it with natural materials, or better still, don't light a fire in heavily traveled areas. It's best to use a camp stove and leave the axe at home. Either pitch the tent in designated campsites or select a level area with adequate water runoff. Use a plastic ground cloth to stay dry rather than a ditch around the tent. Position the tent so that it blends in with the environment, and never set up camp within 200 feet of natural water or the trail. Wash, brush teeth, and clean dishes well away from all water sources. Never use soap or clean up directly in streams or lakes.

In short, practice low-impact, no-trace camping and leave no evidence of your stay. Only then can these areas remain true wilderness.

Lower Peninsula

A backpacker pauses briefly at the top of Sackrider Hill to enjoy the view before continuing the Waterloo-Pinckney Trail, a four-day walk through the Waterloo and Pinckney recreation areas.

Waterloo-Pinckney Trail
Waterloo and Pinckney Recreation Areas

Counties: Jackson and Wastenaw
Nearest Towns: Chelsea and Pinckney
Distance: 38.5 miles
Hiking Time: Three to four days
Highest Elevation Gain: 208 feet
Difficulty: Moderate
Highlights: Rolling hardwood forests, numerous lakes and walk-in campsites

When looking for a backpacking trip, many Michigan hikers head Up North to the long trails in the Upper Peninsula. Or south to the Appalachian Trail in Tennessee or east to the White Mountains of New Hampshire. Few consider what lies in their backyard.

Yet only an hour's drive from Detroit or less than 30 minutes from Ann Arbor and Jackson is the Waterloo-Pinckney Trail, a 38-mile trek through a mix of rolling oak-hickory forests, wetlands and small farms with faded red barns. Despite being practically encompassed by the mushrooming growth of Southeast Michigan, this walk is anything but urban. In the three to four days required for the entire route you pass 10 inland lakes, climb surprisingly rugged ridges and stand on top of three scenic vistas to gather in the view.

Experience this slice of wild in late summer or fall and you'll witness deer bounding through the woods, ducks and geese migrating south or possibly Michigan's largest and most stately bird, sandhill cranes, resting in a field. You'll also skirt small pastures, pass rows of shoulder-high corn and occasionally hear cattle calling. This trail is as much about Southeast Michigan's surviving farms as it is the preservation of woods and wetlands.

The landscape you'll hike through includes numerous marshes and ponds, along with grassy meadows, that were farmed in the early 1900s but were abandoned by hard-luck families during the Great Depression of the 1930s. The land eventually reverted to the federal government, which handed it over to the state in 1943. Waterloo and Pinckney recreation areas were created the following year, and trail development followed, with much of it laid out in the late 1960s.

But it was 20 years before Waterloo-Pinckney became a journey for backpackers. In 1984, land purchases funded by the National Resources Trust Fund and Washtenaw County allowed a trail to be built through the county's Park Lyndon. This final two-mile link connected the 22 miles of trail in Waterloo with the equal-sized network in Pinckney that included the 17.5-mile Potawatomi Trail. Waterloo-Pinckney was dedicated in 1986, and there have been hikers on it ever since.

lly the route was marked with a variety of symbols, blue DNR angles and even mile posts. Numerous bridle paths and old roads ation areas also added to the confusion in the woods and it was mon for backpackers to lose the trail and have to backtrack to again. But in recent years the trail has been improved greatly by the two recreation areas and now is well posted and much easier to follow.

The Waterloo-Pinckney begins at Big Portage Lake in Waterloo Recreation Area and ends at Silver Lake in Pinckney. You have to walk the route from west to east due to mountain bike/hiking regulations implemented in Pinckney. These regulations require walkers to cover a 6.5-mile segment of the Potawatomi Trail, the last stretch of the long route, in a counterclockwise direction. In Waterloo Recreation Area hikers share some portions of the path with equestrians and will occasionally encounter a horse or two. In Pinckney, you will encounter numerous mountain bikers any day of the week and hundreds of them on the weekend. The best way to avoid the two-wheelers is to end this hike in the middle of the week and get an early start that final morning.

Although the Waterloo-Pinckney is 35.5 miles from end to end, this hike is 38.5 miles because backcountry camping is not allowed along the trail. The most common way to cover the route is to hike to the modern Sugarloaf Lake Campground the first night, a walk of 15 miles. The following day you hike 10 miles to Green Lake Campground and then 6.5 miles to the walk-in campground on Blind Lake in Pinckney Recreation Area on the third day. Because Blind Lake is a half mile from the trail, the final leg would be a 7-mile hike to Silver Lake Dayuse Area where a drop-off vehicle can be left.

Stronger backpackers will often shorten the trek to three days by hiking from the Green Lake Campground to Silver Lake, a 13-mile walk. If 15 miles is too much for one day, begin from the Equestrian Campground in Waterloo for a 9-mile trek to Green Lake. The second night could then be spent at Blind Lake. Overall I found the most scenic stretches of the trail to be from Clear Lake Road to Mill Lake in Waterloo, from Green Lake to Hadley Road and the final stretch on the Potawatomi Trail. But there is a tremendous sense of accomplishment that motivates people to complete the entire route and to be able say later, to the astonishment of many, they backpacked 35 miles through Southeast Michigan.

Trip Planner

Maps: The area is covered by the USGS topos *Chelsea*, *Grass Lake*, *Gregory*, and *Pinckney* but the maps do not show most of the trail. Both recreation areas have a *Waterloo-Pinckney Trail* map but it is not entirely accurate. The most accurate maps of the route are the park maps for Pinckney Recreation Area and the Waterloo Recreation Area.

Getting There: The Waterloo-Pinckney Trail parallels I-94 between Jackson and Ann Arbor. The Big Portage Lake Dayuse Area and Campground is the western trailhead and is reached by departing the interstate at Race Road (exit 147) and heading north to Seymour Road. The lake entrance is just a mile east (right) on Seymour, and you'll find the trail posted by the boat launch. Depart I-94 at MI-52 (exit 159) and head north to reach the Silver Lake Dayuse Area. Within 6 miles, turn east (right) on North Territorial Road and then north (left) again on Dexter-Townhall Road, where the park entrance is posted.

There are pull-outs, however, on many roads that the trail crosses. Good places to leave a car include the parking area to Sackrider Hill on Mt. Hope Road, at Waterloo's horsemen campground just off Loveland Road, near Clear Lake, across McClure Road from Waterloo headquarters, at Green Lake Rustic Campground and at the Pickerel Lake boat ramp off Hankerd Road in Pinckney Recreational Area.

Fees & Reservations: Backpackers must stay at the Sugarloaf Lake Campground, if it is open. The modern facility costs $19–21 per night and sites can be reserved through the state park reservation system (800-447-2757; *www.midnrreservations.com*). After the campground closes in mid-October, backpackers can stay at the nearby Equestrian Campground which is first-come-first-serve and $10 a night. The other option is to rent one of the two Burns Cabins, located in the Equestrian Campground. The rustic cabins have 20 bunks each, wood stoves for heat and are $80 per night plus a $5 reservation fee. The cabins are reserved and rented through Waterloo Recreation Area (734-475-8307).

Rustic Green Lake Campground is $10 a night and sites can not be reserved in advance. Blind Lake walk-in sites can be reserved in advance through the state park reservation system (800-447-2757; *www.midnrreservations.com*) and are also $10 per night.

Hikers also need to have a state park vehicle permit ($6 daily, $24 annual) and call the Pinckney Recreation Area (734-426-4913) in advance if they are staying at Blind Lake or leaving a drop-off car at Silver Lake.

Information: The headquarters for Pinckney Recreation Area (734-426-4913) is located on Silver Hill Road, just before you enter Silver Lake Dayuse Area. The headquarters for Waterloo Recreation Area (734-475-8307) is on McClure Road. Both offices are open Monday through Friday, 8 a.m. to 5 p.m. Another source of information and maps is Waterloo's Gerald E. Eddy Discovery Center (734-475-3170) just off Bush Road and reached from Pierce Road, exit 157 on the interstate. From June through October the center is open Tuesday through Saturday from 10 a.m. to 5 p.m. and Sunday from noon to 5 p.m.

Trail Guide

Day One (15 miles) The trail begins near the Big Portage Lake boat launch and is marked by a large display sign and map. You begin by skirting a ridge and viewing the lake below, then swing south, staying in the woods except to cross an old gravel pit road at 0.6 mile. You come to the first climb of the trip, a 40-foot ascent, just before crossing paved Seymour Road at 1.2 miles.

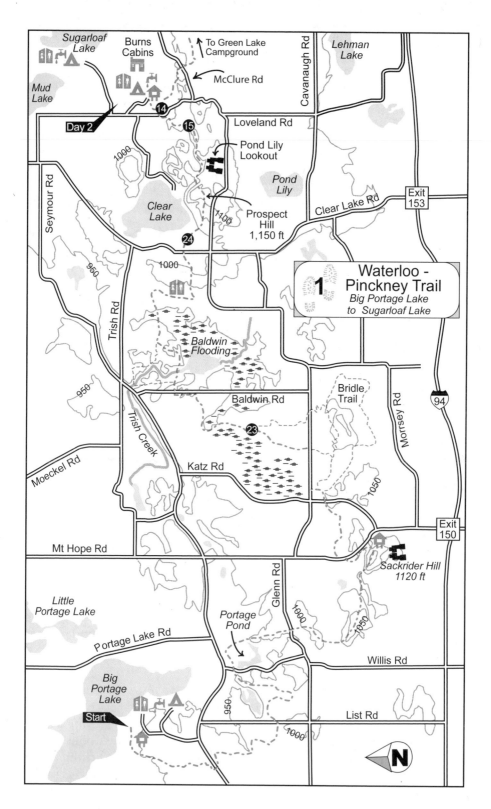

South of Seymour, the trail quickly crosses a small grassy area and powerline right-of-way, then re-enters the woods. For the next mile you climb low hills and ridges and descend to pass a marsh, pond, and other low-lying wet areas. This area is interesting, even though it can get a little buggy in late June or early July.

List Road is crossed at 2 miles and a half mile later the trail arrives at an old and very overgrown road. Signs direct you to swing north (left), where you move out of the forest and into a grassy clearing. You veer to the right when the trail splits and arrive at Willis Road within 0.7 mile of the old road or 3.2 miles from the start. There's a parking area along Willis Road while on the other side is Portage Pond, the largest body of open water seen since Portage Lake. A footbridge crosses the north end of the pond over the dam, and from there you climb back into the forest.

Just after 4 miles you descend to a large marshy area and use a boardwalk to cross it and return to the forest to descend to Glenn Road. On the other side of the dirt road the climbing gets serious. You top off on a 1,050-foot ridge and follow the crest of it while staring down into a forested ravine. At 5 miles, the trail makes a sharp descent off the ridge, breaks out of the trees, and then begins its climb of Sackrider Hill.

The view gets better with every step, and by the time hikers reach the cross (at 5.5 miles) that marks the 1,128-foot top, many are a little stunned. There are finer panoramas in Michigan, in the Upper Peninsula no doubt, but for those who just climbed 208 feet from Portage Pond, this one is remarkable. From the observation deck you can see 360 degrees, but the view to the southwest is the best. Below are miles of Michigan, including rolling farm fields, other ridges, barns, and, of course, I-94, humming with traffic if it's late in the day. It can be a strange feeling, looking at rush-hour traffic while shouldering a backpack.

The trail quickly drops off the hill to a parking lot where a trail marker directs you to head north to skirt Mt. Hope Road. Within a half mile you pop out of the woods at the paved and often busy Mt Hope Road, follow it north for 20 yards and then pick up the trail on its east side where it's marked by a "Welcome Foot Travel" sign. Here the trail cuts across a field before swinging south (right) into the woods and reaching Katz Road 6.7 miles from the start. On the east side of the dirt road you remain in the woods but quickly merge into a bridle/mountain bike trail. With the well-known Potawatomi Trail practically next door I doubt if many mountain bikers use this trail but it's obvious from the hoof prints that many horseback riders do.

Trail signs have you heading north (left) at the junction and at 7 miles from the start you arrive at Glenn Road for the second time. Head east and follow the dirt road for 0.3 mile to pick up the trail as it departs north (left) as a wide, eroded path in the woods. After passing a bridle trail junction marked with post No. 23, the trail swings east and breaks out of the woods and crosses an extensive, grassy field. Most of the open areas are old farm fields from when settlers arrived in the early 1800s with plows and axes in hand. The glaciers that created the ridges and lakes also left a topsoil of predominantly sand and gravel that hindered the effort of farmers in the region. Eventually many families became part of a relocation relief measure, a Great Depression program in which the federal government moved them to more productive land.

You skirt a farm with a red barn and a classic brick farmhouse before emerging at Baldwin Road at 9 miles. Head north on the paved road for a quarter mile and then east on a two-track that is gated. You immediately come to a junction with the bridle trail heading north. Here the Waterloo-Pinckney Trail is posted in both directions but by remaining on the two-track and continuing east you'll follow the shortest route and within a quarter mile arrive at Baldwin Flooding.

The flooding, a joint project between the state and Ducks Unlimited, is where Trist Creek has been impounded for waterfowl. Keep an eye out for ducks and other winged wildlife in the wetlands. You re-enter the woods on the other side of Trist Creek and within a half mile rejoin the bridle path. The terrain remains mostly wooded and eventually you pass a vault toilet before the trail swings east and emerges at Clear Lake Road at 11 miles from Portage Lake.

The trail resumes directly across the paved road. Within a half mile of the road, you cross a Y-junction with a pair of dirt roads and then begin climbing. It's a steep climb of almost 150 feet; at one point, there are even switchbacks in the trail, making it probably the sharpest ascent of any trail south of Lansing. Eventually you reach the top, known as Prospect, a 1,150-foot highpoint with a USGS marker. There is no view here, but after you descend slightly and climb a ridge, the trees clear to allow a scenic vista of the farm fields to the southwest as well as Pond Lily Lake to the south. This spot is Pond Lily Lookout. From here, you begin a rapid descent to reach Loveland Road, 14 miles from Portage Lake.

On the east side of Loveland Road is a huge sign announcing that Green Lake is another 9 miles and that horses are banned further east in the park. The Equestrian Campground is a half mile north and Sugarloaf Lake Campground a mile. The modern campground has 180 sites in an open, grassy area near the large lake. There are modern bathrooms with showers and a small swimming area. The campground is reached by heading north (left) on Loveland, then east (right) on an entrance drive.

The horsemen's campground is a rustic facility with vault toilets, a hand pump for water, and 25 sites in a wooded setting. Within the campground are Burns Cabins, two twenty-bunk structures hemmed in by woods and featuring wood-burning stoves, tables, chairs, and mattresses.

Day Two (10 miles) For many the second day is a 10-mile walk to Green Lake Campground but stronger hikers will push on to the Blind Lake Campground in the Pinckney Recreation Area, a 16.5-mile trek.

Backtrack to where the trail crosses Loveland Road and head east. The trail quickly swings southeast and climbs a wooded ridge before breaking out at McClure Road and resuming on the south side of the dirt road. You remain in the rolling woods but within a half mile or 2 miles from Sugarloaf Campground cross McClure Road a second time and soon arrive at a junction and post No.13. This is where the Waterloo-Pinckney Trail merges into Hickory Hills Nature Trail, a mile-long loop with 20 numbered posts that correspond to an interpretive brochure. You can follow the loop either to the north (left) or south (right).

To the south you'll descend a stairway of railroad ties and quickly cross McClure Road a third time. On the south side the trail descends to Crooked Lake where a bench has been placed overlooking its scenic north end. Just beyond the bench is a stone foundation, the remains of a pump house that provided water for the Sylvan Estates Country Club before it went bankrupt during the Great Depression. The trail then climbs steeply away from the lake and through open meadows that were once fairways.

Post No. 12 is reached 2.9 miles from Sugarloaf Campground and marks where the Waterloo-Pinckney Trail departs from Hickory Hills Nature Trail. There is a parking area here along with a vault toilet while just across McClure Road is the Waterloo Recreation Area headquarters, a source of maps and drinking water.

The Waterloo-Pinckney Trail continues east, crosses Ridge Road, merges into Lakeview Trail at post No. 10 and then leaves the 1.5-mile loop at post No. 9. You remain in the forest and head south to reach post No. 8 within a half mile or 4.2 miles from Sugarloaf Campground. The post marks where the Waterloo-Pinckney merges into the Oak Woods Trail, a 1.3-mile loop from the Gerald E. Eddy Discovery Center. By heading north (left) at this

The Largest (and Loudest!) Bird in Michigan

Of all the wildlife spotted while hiking the Waterloo-Pinckney Trail the most impressive, if you're lucky enough to spot one, is the sandhill crane, Michigan's largest and loudest bird. Although often confused for a great blue heron, the crane is considerably larger, with an adult standing three to four feet tall, weighing in at around 10 pounds and possessing a wing span of more than six feet. They are also louder with the crane's trumpet-like call a result of the bird's long windpipe coiled in the resonant breast bone. When in flight cranes fly with their necks outstretched, herons with their necks in an s-curve.

Cranes pair off in the spring and travel to their nesting site and then in late summer meet in a staging area where hundreds of them gather to make the trip south. During the summer they spend their time nesting, often in large marshes with open water, roosting and feeding on insects, worms, frogs, snakes and grubs but also plants, rootlets and berries. On the Waterloo-Pinckney Trail look for them in shallow marshes, sedge meadows and open bogs as well as agricultural fields.

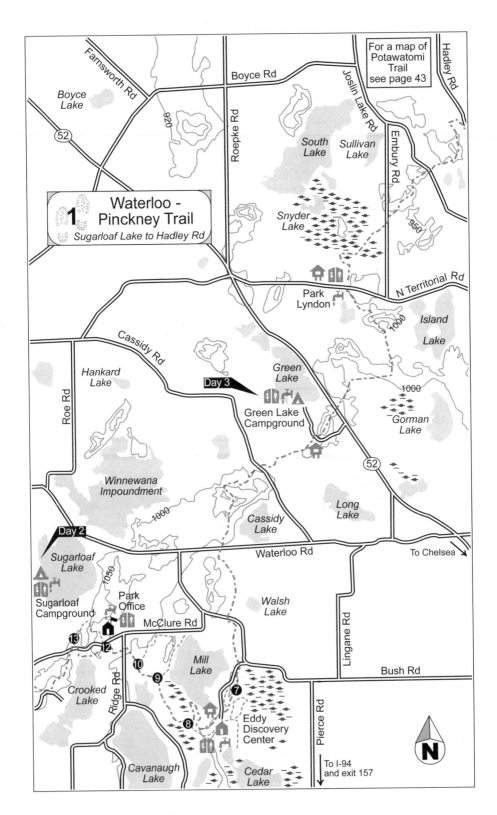

For a map of Potawatomi Trail see page 43

Waterloo -
Pinckney Trail
Sugarloaf Lake to Hadley Rd

Boyce Lake

Boyce Rd

Farnsworth Rd

920

52

Roepke Rd

Joslin Lake Rd

Hadley Rd

South Lake

Sullivan Lake

Embury Rd

Snyder Lake

950

N Territorial Rd

Park Lyndon

Island Lake

1000

Cassidy Rd

Hankard Lake

Roe Rd

Day 3

Green Lake

Green Lake Campground

Gorman Lake

1000

Winnewana Impoundment

1000

52

Cassidy Lake

Long Lake

Day 2

Sugarloaf Lake

1050

Waterloo Rd

To Chelsea

Sugarloaf Campground

Park Office

McClure Rd

Walsh Lake

Lingane Rd

Bush Rd

13

12

10

Ridge Rd

9

Mill Lake

7

Pierce Rd

Crooked Lake

8

Eddy Discovery Center

To I-94 and exit 157

Cavanaugh Lake

Cedar Lake

N

junction you'll traverse a ridge that parallels Mill Lake and enjoy several views of the water before arriving at the interpretive center.

The Gerald E. Eddy Discovery Center is reached 5 miles from Sugarloaf Campground and marks the halfway point of the day. The facility was extensively renovated in 1989 and renamed as a tribute to Gerald Eddy, a former director of the Geological Survey Division and then the Department of Conservation, the forerunner to the DNR. The center reflects Eddy's career with an exhibit room devoted to Michigan's geological history and another to the natural history of the state recreation area. There are also restrooms, drinking water and a picnic pavilion, making this an ideal spot for an extended break or lunch.

To continue onto Green Lake pick up Old Field Trail in the center's lower parking lot. In less than a half mile you arrive at post No. 7, marking where the Waterloo-Pinckney Trail departs the nature trail to first head east (right) and then north. You quickly cross the center's paved entrance drive and then in a half mile cross the entrance to the former Mill Lake Outdoor Center, which is no longer operated by the park. The trail swings close to Bush Road and then, a mile from Eddy Discovery Center, crosses the road and begins climbing. This ridge is steep, but quickly tops out and you follow the crest of it to a view of a scenic marsh to the west. The trail eventually descends and crosses Waterloo Road, passing a "Prison Zone" sign, indicating that nearby is the Cassidy Lake Correctional Facility.

The trail then swings east, climbs a few hills, some steep, and leads you across Cassidy Lake Road. On the other side you cut through rolling, grassy fields to the dirt entrance drive to Green Lake Rustic Campground, reached 5 miles from Eddy Discovery Center, 10 miles from Sugarloaf Campground and 23 miles from the start of the trail. The campground is 0.3 mile north along the entrance road and has 25 sites in a lightly shaded, grassy area. Five sites are on a low bluff overlooking the lake and make for a splendid place to end the day. The facility also has vault toilets, fire rings, water, and a boat ramp to the lake.

Day Three (6.5 miles) If your destination is only the walk-in sites at Blind Lake, then this is a short but very interesting day. Have a leisurely breakfast, linger on the trail, soak in the scenery.

The Waterloo-Pinckney Trail continues on the other side of the entrance drive to the campground and immediately ascends Riley Hill, a climb of almost 80 feet to the top. You descend the east side and within 0.3 mile from the campground road pop out at busy M-52. By crossing the state highway you finally leave the Waterloo Recreation Area. On the east side you begin by following a private driveway before trail signs lead you back into the woods.

Soon the trail becomes an old road, straight and wide that heads due east while skirting a wetland, the first of many for the day. The trail swings north off the overgrown road and a mile from Green Lake passes a pothole marsh.

If it's early in the morning, pause to look for wildlife here. Within 0.3 mile you're climbing a 1,040-foot high ridge, passing a sign that announces you've entered Park Lyndon, a 205-acre Washtenaw County park. It's almost a 100-foot climb before you top off but somebody has thoughtfully placed a bench along the way. Ahhhh! Take a load off your feet.

The Waterloo-Pinckney Trail merges into the park's trail system but remains well marked and 1.7 miles from Green Lake you arrive at the entrance to Park Lyndon South, where you'll find a picnic pavilion, restrooms and drinking water. Cross North Territorial Road to Park Lyndon North where there are more picnic tables, restrooms and nature trails. There is also a large picnic pavilion and behind it the Waterloo-Pinckney Trail departs the county park for good and immediately climbs a wooded ridge. You follow the crest of the ridge and enjoy views on both sides of it through the trees before descending to an extensive marsh 2.5 miles from Green Lake. Not to worry. Two long boardwalks keeps your boots dry as you cut through the middle of this huge wetland, an interesting place to linger if the bugs don't have you running down the trail.

You re-enter the woods on the east side of the marsh and at 2.8 miles pop out at Embury Road. The trail is posted directly across the dirt road and soon leads you through grassy meadows. Just before arriving at Joslin Lake Road at 3.3 miles from Green Lake you pass the crumbling stones of an old fireplace, all that remains of a cabin that once stood here as part of Camp Crile.

On the east side of Joslin Lake Road, you hike underneath the crackling hiss of a towering set of power lines and then re-enter the woods. The trail skirts a wetland area known as Sullivan Lakes, often missed by hikers due to the heavy foliage in the woods, and then swings north and climbs another ridge. You descend this wooded hill to another wetland area that requires three boardwalks to cross it before you arrive at Hadley Road at 4.2 miles.

Trail signs lead you up a grassy hill on the east side of the paved road and eventually back into the woods. You skirt the south end of an unnamed lake, which is hard to view until the trail swings north and descends sharply to the bottom of the ravine. You get a better glimpse of the marshy lake here before climbing away from it into open meadows. The trail then skirts a parking area off Goodband Road before crossing the road itself 5.5 miles from Green Lake.

On the east side of the dirt road you make a gentle climb up a ridge. Its 980 feet of elevation is just high enough to provide the third spectacular vista of the trip. To the southwest, you look over the rugged terrain of Waterloo Recreation Area and can see no fewer than 10 forested ridges in different shades of green. The trail descends sharply off the ridge and arrives at post No. 12, marking a junction with the Potawatomi Trail, a 17.5-mile loop that lies totally in Pinckney Recreation Area.

Less than a half mile to the west (left) are the Blind Lake campsites reached 6.5 miles from Green Lake. This walk-in facility includes five sites with fire rings and tables, drinking water and a vault toilet. Site No. 1 is right on the shoreline and makes for a tranquil spot to spend an evening if there are not too many mountain bikers blasting through or jet skiers buzzing the lake. There is a one-night limit at Blind Lake and you must reserve a site in advance. If you're packing a cell phone and credit card you can do it that day from the trail by first calling the state park reservation system (800-447-2757) and then the Pinckney Recreation Area (734-426-4913).

Day Four (7 miles) The final leg to Silver Lake Dayuse Area is another scenic one but keep in mind that mountain bikers will be riding towards you on the trail. An early start is the best to avoid as many bikers as possible. The map of this section is with the Potawatomi Trail (page 41).

From Blind Lake backtrack to post No. 12 and continue east (left) on the Potawatomi Trail. You return to a thick hardwood forest and then follow the contour of a series of hills. At one point the trail follows the crest of a narrow ridge with a steep ravine on both sides of you. You skirt isolated Dead Lake 1.5 miles from the Blind Lake and then resume climbing hills before emerging at Hankerd Road in another mile.

The trail follows paved Hankerd Road briefly to the south (right) and then swings east (left) resumes just onto Pickerel Lake Access Road. You follow the access road and then leave it to skirt the south end of the scenic lake from a high bank. You can see a popular fishing pier at the lake's west end. At post No. 4 you arrive at the junction with the Silver Lake Trail, reached 3.5 miles from Blind Lake. If you're eager to get back to your car, follow this short loop to the left. Within a mile, you'll be in the parking lot of the Silver Lake Dayuse Area. The Silver Lake Trail is actually a more scenic walk than the final stretch of the Waterloo-Pinckney Trail, and you'll clip off more than 2 miles.

Purists, however, will want to finish the remaining 3.5 miles. This last leg heads southwest and weaves its way along the edges of numerous marshy areas and ponds before rejoining the Silver Lake Trail. From there, it's a half mile to the eastern trailhead in the Silver Lake Dayuse Area, where there are picnic tables, restrooms, water and even a beach to lie out on after four days on the trail.

A pair of sandhill cranes strut through a farm field near the Potawatomi Trail. The cranes are Michigan's largest and loudest birds.

Potawatomi Trail
Pinckney Recreation Area

Counties: Washtenaw and Livingston
Nearest Town: Pinckney
Distance: 17.5 miles
Hiking Time: Two days
Highest Elevation Gain: 128 feet
Difficulty: Moderate to challenging
Highlights: Numerous lakes, walk-in campsites and rental yurt

The Potawatomi is one of Michigan's legendary trails but not because it was the first backpacking route developed in the southeast corner of the state. It was mountain bikers who made the "Poto" a legend and easily the most popular trail in Michigan.

The 17.5-mile loop was constructed in the mid-1960s by backpacking-minded Boy Scouts with most of the troops coming from the Ann Arbor Council. In the early 1980s, the Poto was known as a unique two-day walk, the only long-distance route with walk-in campsites near Detroit. Then the new sport of mountain biking arrived in Michigan, particularly in cycle-crazy Ann Arbor, and within five years off-road cyclists outnumbered hikers.

Thanks to the two-wheelers, the Potawatomi is the most heavily used trail in the state, attracting close to 120,000 users annually. Many bikers arrive as far away as Ohio, Indiana and Illinois, attracted by Potawatomi's widespread reputation for being a hilly and challenging long-distance ride through the woods.

Although the Potawatomi is possibly the most famous mountain bike trail in the Midwest, it still clings to its roots as a destination for backpackers. To encourage walkers and reduce conflicts with cyclists special regulations have been implemented on most trails in the Pinckney Recreation Area. Mountain bikers must follow the Potawatomi, Crooked Lake and Silver Lake Trails in a clockwise direction while hikers must follow them counterclockwise.

Backpackers can undertake the full loop or use the Shortcut spur to reduce the walk to 14 miles. They can also overnight at the walk-in campsites on Blind Lake or utilize a new rental yurt. Opened in 2007, the Mongolian-style tent sleeps four and is equipped with propane heat, eliminating the need to carry a tent or sleeping pads.

The traditional itinerary for backpackers is to undertake a 10.5-mile trek the first day to Blind Lake followed by a 7-mile hike the next day to the Silver Lake Dayuse Area. By utilizing the shortcut and reserving the yurt you could lighten your load and shorten the first day to 4.5 miles and finish the outing with a 9.5-mile walk the second day.

The key to an enjoyable experience on the Poto and avoiding as many bikers as possible is to hike mid-week and begin each day early. You'll also encounter few cyclists in late April. Some backpackers reserve the yurt and walk the trail in the winter when there is little snow accumulation in Southeast Michigan, a frequent occurrence in recent years. The worst time to hike the Potawatomi is on weekends in the summer or after 3 p.m. midweek.

Also keep in mind that this area is mushrooming with development and sprawl and it's impossible, even on the Potawatomi, to escape it. You'll pass private homes, hear traffic rumble by or spot motorboats on many of the lakes. But if you plan it right, there also will be moments when the trail plunges into a thick oak forest, seemingly miles from anywhere, or skirts a small, undeveloped lake without a soul on it. It's moments like this that makes it hard to believe you're so close to home.

Trip Planner

Maps: The area is covered by the USGS topos *Gregory* and *Pinckney* but the maps do not show large stretches of the trail. The *Pinckney Recreation Area Biking And Hiking Trails* map is the best one available at the park.

Getting There: To reach the Silver Lake Dayuse Area from US-23 depart at exit 49 and head west on North Territorial Road for 12 miles. Turn north (right) onto Dexter-Townhall Road for a mile to the posted entrance of the state recreation area on Silver Hill Road. The park headquarters is a half mile up the road where you can pick up maps. Just beyond the office are the parking lots for Silver Lake.

Fees & Reservations: Blind Lake walk-in sites and the rental yurt should be reserved in advance through the state park reservation system (800-447-2757; *www.midnrreservations.com*). The walk-in sites are $10 per night. Hikers also need to have a state park vehicle permit ($6 daily, $24 annual) and call the Pinckney Recreation Area (734-426-4913) in advance if they are staying at Blind Lake for the night or leaving a car overnight at the Silver Lake Dayuse Area.

Information: The headquarters for Pinckney Recreation Area (734-426-4913) is located on Silver Hill Road, just before you enter Silver Lake Dayuse Area and is open Monday through Friday, 8 a.m. to 5 p.m.

Trail Guide

Day One (10.5 miles) A large display map marks the trail at both the lower and upper parking areas, marking the directions of travel mountain bikers and hikers must follow. Hikers head in a counterclockwise direction so they begin with the Crooked Lake Trail from the upper lot trailhead. The trail begins by skirting Silver Lake, using a long boardwalk to weave between low-lying wet areas and young stands of trees, and within a quarter mile passes post No. 2. This junction marks where Silver Lake Trail heads to the southwest (left).

Head right and within a half mile from the start, the Crooked Lake Trail

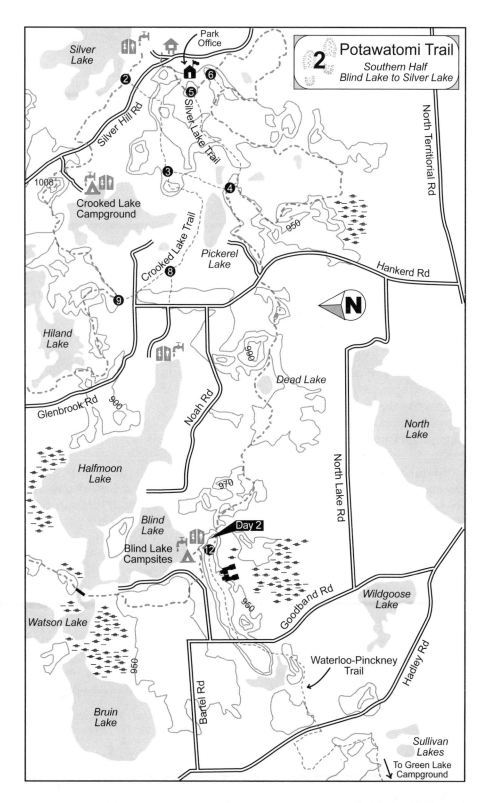

swings west and begins a long ascent away from the lake and into the woods. Silver Hill Road, a dirt road, is crossed followed by a steep climb. The trail then descends to cross Crooked Lake access road and then climbs again, this time to a 1,008-foot high point. The first mile of the journey ends on the top of this hill where there is an excellent view of Crooked Lake and the surrounding ridges and a bench to enjoy it from.

The trail begins a long descent, bottoms out at a bridged creek, and then climbs to a post No. 9, 2.7 miles from Silver Lake. At this junction Crooked Lake Trail departs south (left); the Potawatomi heads north (right) to swing past two marsh areas and cross a huge wooden bridge over the channel between Halfmoon Lake and Hiland Lake at 3.7 miles. Just beyond that, you come to the dirt access road that leads east to Hiland Lake.

Side Trail: By heading east (left) on the access road you'll quickly cross Glenbrook Road at post No. 10 and pick up the start of the Shortcut that reduces the Potawatomi to a 14-mile loop. The rental yurt and a water pump are reached in less than a half mile along the Shortcut and within a mile you will return to the Potawatomi at post No. 11.

From the Hiland Lake access road the Potawatomi continues north and within a mile or 4.8 miles from the Silver Lake Dayuse Area crosses Patterson Road. Another way to shorten the first day by almost 3 miles is to simply follow Patterson Road 0.2 mile west (left) to where the Potawatomi recrosses the paved road heading south. North of Patterson Lake Road, the Poto is a 3-mile loop that skirts Goslin Lake and crosses Doyle Road to the edge of the state park (a towering fence marking the boundary) before swinging back south.

Within a half mile after re-crossing Patterson, the trail passes post No. 11, marking west end of the Shortcut, and then begins a long descent to skirt around a marsh pond. You emerge at a dirt road between Patterson and Halfmoon lakes 9 miles from the start and in less than a half mile you arrive at the large wooden bridge over the channel between Watson and Halfmoon Lakes. This is a scenic spot, a good place to linger and rest. From the bridge you ascend to the most level stretch of the day through a semiopen area of scattered trees around Blind Lake.

The first day ends with you passing the posted junction to the Boy Scout Camp Mumhacke, descending to cross a dirt road, and emerging at an overgrown four-wheel drive track. Head east (left) and you'll soon be among the walk-in sites on the south shore of Blind Lake, reached 10.5 miles from Silver Lake trailhead. Blind Lake has five sites with fire rings and tables but only one that overlooks the lake. Grab it if you can. There is also a pump for drinking water and a vault toilet. There is a one-night limit on the walk-in campground and sites should be reserved in advance.

Day Two (7 miles) The Potawatomi passes through the Blind Lake campground and then heads south to reach post No. 12 in less than a

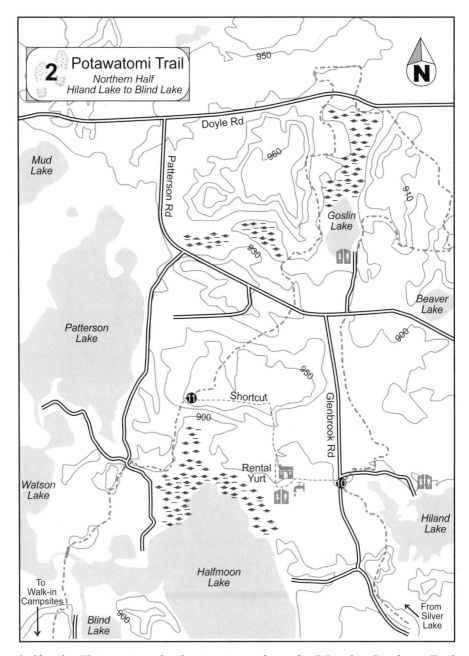

N

950

Doyle Rd

960

Mud
Lake

Patterson Rd

910

Goslin
Lake

930

Beaver
Lake

Patterson
Lake

900

950

11 Shortcut

900

Glenbrook Rd

Rental
Yurt

10

Watson
Lake

Hiland
Lake

To
Walk-in
Campsites

Halfmoon
Lake

900

Blind
Lake

From
Silver
Lake

half mile. This post marks the junction where the Waterloo-Pinckney Trail merges with the Potawatomi. To reach the Silver Lake Dayuse Area you head east (left). But if you have the time, consider heading west on the Waterloo-Pinckney Trail, which climbs a ridge to a scenic viewing point on top.

The final leg of the Potawatomi Trail, a 6.5-mile walk from post No. 12 to Silver Lake Dayuse Area, is covered in Day Four of the Waterloo-Pinckney Trail.

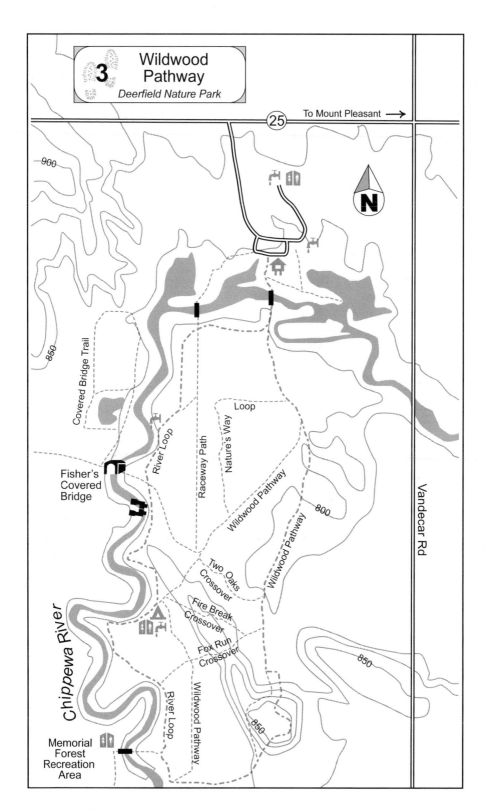

Wildwood Pathway
Deerfield Nature Park

3

To Mount Pleasant →

25

900

850

N

Covered Bridge Trail

Loop

Nature's Way

River Loop

Raceway Path

Wildwood Pathway

Wildwood Pathway

800

Fisher's
Covered
Bridge

Two Oaks
Crossover

Fire Break
Crossover

Fox Run
Crossover

850

Chippewa River

River Loop

Wildwood Pathway

850

Vandecar Rd

Memorial
Forest
Recreation
Area

Wildwood Pathway

Deerfield Nature Park

Counties: Isabella
Nearest Town: Mount Pleasant
Distance: 3 miles
Hiking Time: Two days
Highest Elevation Gain: 50 feet
Difficulty: Easy
Highlights: Walk-in campsites and covered bridge

First impressions can be misleading, even for backpackers. Pull through the entrance gates and Deerfield Nature Park appears like any other county park scattered across Michigan. There are picnic tables and grills, a swimming area, shelters and play equipment, volleyball courts and horseshoe pits. But cross the swing bridge to the south side of the Chippewa River and you'll discover that vast majority of this Isabella County park is a quiet backcountry area. No roads here. Access is via an 8-mile trail system that skirts the Chippewa River, swings past 10 walk-in campsites and includes a scenic covered bridge.

Established in 1973, Deerfield is 591 acres of lightly rolling hardwood forest split in half by 3 miles of the Chippewa River and located only 6 miles from Mount Pleasant. This far upstream, the Chippewa is a small but scenic river that gently flows and swirls over a gravel bottom, making it popular with canoeists. Thanks to the river and the backcountry, Deerfield is a haven for wildlife, especially whitetail deer, which are often sighted in early spring or mid-September. You might also encounter wild turkeys here, along with ruffed grouse, while the Chippewa supports a healthy fishery of smallmouth bass and northern pikes.

The main loop within the park is the Wildwood Pathway, a 2.6-mile route that was designated a National Recreational Trail in 1980 by the U.S. Department of Interior because of its forested beauty. By combining a portion of the pathway with the River Loop, you can enjoy a overnight adventure of only 3 miles with a night spent at the walk-in campsites overlooking the Chippewa River. This is an ideal backpack outing for children, even as young as four or five. But keep in mind that the park is open to mountain biking and, due to its close proximity to Central Michigan University, a moderate number of off-road cyclists use the trails.

Trip Planner

Maps: The area is covered by the USGS topo *Winn* but the map in the *Deerfield Nature Park* brochure is more than adequate for this easy hike.
Getting There: Deerfield is west of Mt. Pleasant or about an hour's drive from Lansing on US-27. There are two entrances to the park. The main one is

off of M-20 (Remus Road), 6 miles west of Mount Pleasant. The trail network can also be reached from the west entrance, which is reached from M-20 by heading south 1.6 miles on Winn Road.

Fees & Reservations: The Deerfield walk-in campsites are $12 a night for county residents and $15 a night for non-residents and can be reserved through the Isabella County Parks and Recreation Commission. A vehicle permit ($5 daily) is also required to enter the park.

Information: For more information contact the Isabella County Parks and Recreation Commission (989-772-0911, ext. 340; *www.isabellacounty.org/parks*) or call Deerfield Nature Park (989-772-2879).

Trail Guide

Day One (1.1 miles) The trailhead is in the parking area near the river and from the display sign a wide, wood chip path heads south to quickly arrive at the impressive and somewhat bouncy swingbridge over the Chippewa River. From the bridge you head south briefly on Wildwood Pathway to reach a junction with River Loop. Head west (right) to follow River Loop as it skirts the low bluffs above the Chippewa. In late fall, when the leaves have fallen, the trail provides a view of the river's gentle current almost every step of the way. Within 0.7 mile of the trailhead you come to an artesian well where the cold, clear water spills down the bank. Fill up the canteen; this water is safe to drink. Nearby is a bench with a view of the park's famous bridge.

It's a quick walk along the bluff to Fisher's Covered Bridge. The bridge was first built in 1968 with a railroad trestle from the Coleman to Mont Pleasant Line by a local businessman. It became such a beloved part of the park that it was quickly rebuilt in 1996 after portion of it was destroyed by fire. The crossing is the only covered bridge in Michigan that has to be reached on foot and is listed with the National Society for the Preservation of Covered Bridges. On the other side of the bridge is a picnic table, a grill, and Covered Bridge Trail, a mile-long loop around a former walleye rearing pond.

Continuing south along River Loop, you remain on the edge of the bluff and quickly come to the best view of the day. From this point, you overlook a bend in the Chippewa in one direction and the bridge in the other. Another bench is located here and it's hard not to sit for a spell. River Loop continues along the bluff, eventually descends to the water, passes a short spur to Wildwood Pathway and 1.1 miles from the trailhead arrives at the walk-in campground. There are ten sites here and most provide a great view of the river from the door of your tent. Facilities include fire rings, vault toilets, and a hand pump for water. Since the campground can only be reached on foot or by canoe, it's rarely filled.

Day Two (1.9 miles) For a slightly longer route back, begin the day by continuing south on the River Loop. The trail remains above along the bluff, passes another viewing point, and then swings inland where, in 0.4

Fisher's Covered Bridge in Deerfield Nature Park can only be reached on foot or by bike.

miles from the campground, comes to a posted junction to a second swing bridge. This bridge leads to a picnic area (tables, grills, and vault toilets) in the Memorial Forest Recreation Area on the west bank of the Chippewa. Just beyond the spur junction, the River Loop merges with the south end of the Wildwood Pathway.

You can return on either segment of the Wildwood loop, but the western (left) is mostly an old vehicle track while to the east the pathway is a true footpath that winds over a more interesting terrain. The eastern route begins with a scenic stretch of hardwoods and then comes to a split in the trail. The right-hand fork is posted with a "Steep Hill!" warning, a sign meant for skiers and bikers, not hikers. The spur over the steep hill spur is a climb of 50 feet followed by a quick descent of its backside. The other fork bypasses the hill and the two merge together a mile from the campground, just before the junction with Fire Break Crossover, one of three crossover spurs to the west side of Wildwood Pathway.

The pathway continues north, passes Two Oaks Crossover in a quarter mile and then enters a low-lying stretch of the forest that can often be muddy and wet during the summer. Wildwood Pathway merges into one trail 1.7 miles from the campground. Just a quarter mile to the north is the swing bridge over the Chippewa River and a return to civilization...at least from a young backpacker's point of view.

Lumberman's Momument is a 14-foot statue of three loggers. The bronze lumbermen have watched over this stretch of the Au Sable River since 1932.

Highbanks Trail

Huron National Forest

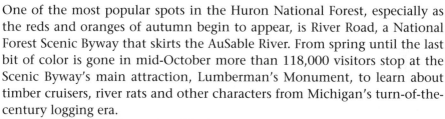

County: Iosco
Nearest Towns: Tawas City and Oscoda
Distance: 14 miles
Hiking Time: Overnight
Highest Elevation Gain: 159 feet
Difficulty: Easy to moderate
Highlights: Lumberman's Monument, numerous overlooks and the AuSable River

One of the most popular spots in the Huron National Forest, especially as the reds and oranges of autumn begin to appear, is River Road, a National Forest Scenic Byway that skirts the AuSable River. From spring until the last bit of color is gone in mid-October more than 118,000 visitors stop at the Scenic Byway's main attraction, Lumberman's Monument, to learn about timber cruisers, river rats and other characters from Michigan's turn-of-the-century logging era.

Want to avoid the packs of leaf peepers? Then park the car and hit the trail.

Traversing the steep river bluffs that lie between the AuSable and the asphalt of River Road is the Highbanks Trail. The linear footpath stretches 7 miles from Iargo Springs to Sid Town and allows you to enjoy the spectacular scenery while escaping the crowds.

After River Road was designated a Scenic Byway in 1989, the U.S. Forest Service turned its attention to upgrading the trail and began by building a series of barriers to eliminate off-road vehicles from the area. In the mid-1990s, the stairway, decks and boardwalks at Iargo Springs were rebuilt and in 2000 new interpretive displays were installed at Lumberman's Monument.

But the most significant change took place the following summer when the east end of the Highbanks Trail was re-routed from a hill above a cluster of cottages known as Sid Town. The trail was extended a half mile northeast to Sawmill Point, where the U.S. Forest Service maintains 17 primitive campsites and a boat launch. The new trailhead not only provides easier access and better parking but allows hikers to turn the trek into an overnight adventure with an evening spent on the banks of the AuSable River.

Highbanks Trail is easy hiking. There is very little elevation gain – with the exception of sidetrips to the AuSable River at Iargo Springs and Lumberman's Monument – and plenty of overlooks and benches along the way to take extended breaks. Only the mileage makes it a moderately hard trek. If a two-day, 14-mile outing is too much for you, than plan to overnight at Monument Campground at Lumberman's Monument, reducing the entire walk to 7 miles.

Trip Planner

Maps: The area is covered by the USGS topos *Loud Dam* and *Sid Town* but the maps do not show the trail. The Huron National Forest has a free *Highbanks Trail* information sheet that includes a map that is available online.

Getting There: The western trailhead is located in the Iargo Springs parking lot, a mile east of M-65 along River Road. The eastern trailhead is in the Sawmill Point parking lot, along Cooke Dam Road, 1.7 miles north of River Road and 1.5 miles east of Lumberman's Monument. In between are two more places to pick up the path; the Canoe Race Monument and, farther east, the Lumberman's Monument.

Fees & Reservations: There are 17 sites at Sawmill Point that are $5 per night plus a $10 service fee for each site. You can reserved them in advance through the National Recreation Reservation Service (877-444-6777; *www.recreation.gov*). Monument Campground is $8 per night and sites can not be reserved in advance.

Information: Call the Huron Shores Ranger Station (989-362-8961) in Oscoda or check the Huron-Manistee National Forests web site (*www.fs.fed.us/r9/hmnf*).

Trail Guide

The westrern trailhead is at Iargo Springs, where along with parking, there are vault toilets, picnic shelters, and drinking water. Most people begin their walk with a 300-step, 159-foot descent to the AuSable River. At the bottom of the bluff a quarter mile of boardwalk winds through towering cedars to eight observation decks; half of them perched above the gurgling springs, the rest overlooking the AuSable.

Iargo is the Chippewa word for "many waters" and it's believed that Native Americans gathered here once for tribal pow-wows where they would drink the cold, clear water for medicinal powers. Today Iargo is still a tonic. No matter how many leaf peepers are zipping along River Road, the springs are always a quiet and tranquil spot that soothes the soul.

From the Iargo Springs parking lot, Highbanks Trail heads east where it follows the edge of the bluffs briefly, skirts a gully, and then merges into the powerline corridor. You follow this man-made intrusion for a quarter mile until you come to another panorama of the river, at which point blue diamonds mark where the trail and electrical lines part company. The trail continues to hug the forested edge of the banks for another mile, providing you glimpses of the AuSable River valley between the trees.

You break out in the parking lot for Canoer's Monument, 1.75 miles from the start. The stone monument, topped by a pair of giant paddles, was originally built as a memorial to Jerry Curley, who died training for the Au Sable River Canoe Marathon. Today it stands in honor of all racers who attempt the annual 150-mile event from Grayling to Oscoda, often cited as the toughest canoe race in the country.

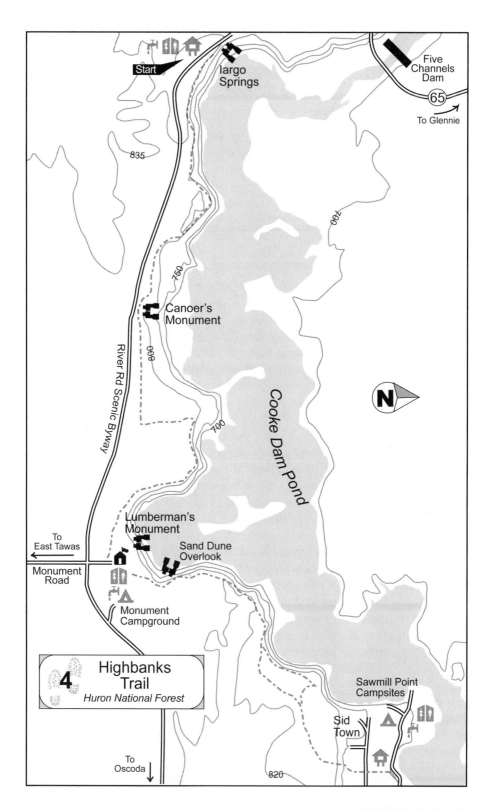

Start

Iargo
Springs

Five
Channels
Dam

65

To Glennie

835

780

750

800

Canoer's
Monument

700

Cooke Dam Pond

N

River Rd Scenic Byway

Lumberman's
Monument

Sand Dune
Overlook

To
East Tawas

Monument
Road

Monument
Campground

Highbanks
Trail
Huron National Forest

4

Sawmill Point
Campsites

Sid
Town

To
Oscoda

820

For years this spot was also known as Eagle Nest Overlook because an active nest was located nearby. But the eagles have since rebuilt their nest on the other side of the river. Still observant hikers, especially those packing along binoculars, will often spot the impressive birds soaring over the river from here.

Beyond the monument, Highbanks Trail again skirts the powerlines for a half mile through a terrain that is very sandy and rolling. Eventually the trail swings north to return to the edge of the bluff and 2.5 miles from the start you arrive at one of the best overviews of the AuSable River in the first half of the hike. Standing from the edge of a high bluff, you gaze down at the Cooke Dam Pond, a simply spectacular sight in the fall.

You stay close to the edge for the next half mile and then breakout again at the powerlines before passing underneath them. The final half mile is a level stroll through a red pine plantation before arriving at Lumberman's Monument, 3.5 miles from Iargo Springs.

The monument itself is a 14-foot bronze statue of a timber cruiser with his compass, a sawyer with his cross-cut saw and a river rat using a peavey to turn a log. The bronze lumbermen have watched over this stretch of the Au Sable since 1932. Surrounding them is a dayuse area with picnic tables, restrooms, drinking water nature and the Lumberman's Monument Visitor Center that is open from 10 a.m. to 5 p.m. daily until the colors fade away in the third week of October.

The adjacent outdoor exhibit area features replicas of a rollway and logjam while a hands-on peavey display lets you try your skill at being a river rat turning a log. There is also a small video theater where you learn that the lowly logger, viewed by many as a colorful Paul Bunyan-like character, was in reality cheap labor. In the middle of the winter, he made $2 for a 12-hour day spent pulling a saw while cold water and snow sloshed in his boots. Little wonder that by the time most loggers turned 35 years old they were too worn out or too sick to continue being a logger.

Nearby are observation decks along the edge of the bluffs and a stairway that descends 260 steps to the shores of the AuSable. Tied up at the bottom of the stairs is a replica of a wanigan; the cook's raft that followed the log drives and kept the river rats well fed. Step aboard and see how one man and his assistance fed an army of lumberjacks.

A side trail leads to nearby Monument Campground, a U.S. Forest Service facility with 20 rustic sites in a red pine plantation. Amenities include fire rings, picnic tables, drinking water and vault toilets.

From the Lumberman's Monument the Highbanks Trail heads northeast, passes underneath the powerlines and then comes to a junction with the Forest Discovery Trail, a fully accessible interpretive trail, and Sand Dune Overlook, a viewing point that puts you almost 200 feet above the AuSable River. Highbanks Trail stays near the edge of the forested bluffs and passes more viewing points before swinging southeast and returning yet again to the powerlines, 1.5 miles from Lumberman's Monument.

An overlook with a sweeping view of Cooke Dam Pond at Lumberman's Monument.

Here you have a choice of either following the powerline corridor or continuing on to hike along an old two track. The blue diamonds of the Highbanks Trail mark both routes. The powerlines remain close to the edge of the bluffs providing more panoramic views but it can be a strange end to a hike. At one point you're standing beneath a steel tower with a red sign that says "Danger High Voltage Wires" but enjoying the best view of the day. Perched high above the AuSable River, you can see almost the entire length of Cooke Dam Pond, including most of the bluffs you walked that day.

Within a half mile the two routes merge and then you make a steady descent before crossing the paved access road to Sid Town, a cluster of cottages and a store. Just beyond it to the north you arrive at the eastern trailhead of the Highbanks Trail in the Sawmill Point Parking Lot, reached 2.8 miles from Lumberman's Monument or 6.3 miles from Iargo Springs. It's a little more than a half mile along the gravel road to the end of the point and the AuSable River, where many of the campsites are located. Facilities at Sawmill Point include vault toilets, fire rings and drinking water, while most of the sites overlook the river. This is a great spot to spend the evening before backtracking to your vehicle the next day.

Scattered around Reid Lake are a handful of fishing docks where an evening can be spent casting for bluegills and other panfish.

Reid Lake Foot Travel Area
Huron National Forest

County: Alcona
Nearest Town: Curran
Distance: 9 miles
Hiking Time: Two days
Highest Elevation Gain: 130 feet
Difficulty: Moderate
Highlights: Walk-in campsites overlooking small lakes

Tap. Tap-tap. Tap-tap-tap.

We had just pulled into the parking area for the Reid Lake Foot Travel Area when we spotted our first wildlife; deer flies were bouncing off the windows of our car. It was almost enough to make us drive off in search of a motel room. But we stayed and before the day was over we also sighted several whitetail deer, a blue heron, bluegills that were still on their beds in Reid Lake, a porcupine that waddled towards us on the trail. And the animal most responsible for this haven of wildlife, a beaver.

Pack the *Deep Woods Off* and take a hike.

This lovely little lake was privately owned until 1966, and some of the surrounding land was still being farmed in the early 1960s, as is evident by the open fields and even a small orchard. Eventually the U.S. Forest Service purchased 3,700 acres, designated it non-motorized in 1975 and assisted the Youth Conservation Corps in developing a 6-mile trail system.

In 1991 the USFS added Little Trout Lake to increase its acreage to more than 4,000 acres and in 2002 began expanding the trail system and series of backcountry campsites. Today the Foot Travel Area includes 12 miles of trails, eight backcountry campsites, two charming lakes and numerous wetlands, marshes and bogs. It is this mix of marshes intermingled among rolling hills of hardwood forests that attracts and supports an abundance of wildlife.

And that, of course, includes mosquitoes and deer flies if you arrive in June or July. Wait until late August when the bugs begin to thin out or, better yet, arrive in early October when there are none and the hardwood forests are burning with fall colors.

Reid Lake experiences its heaviest use on weekends during the winter when skiers arrive to tackle a 2.5-mile loop from the M-72 trailhead to the lake. But this could change in the future with the area's newly expanded trail system. The Foot Travel Area is now the destination of an ideal weekend backpack, an overnight trek of 9 miles to a remote, lakeshore campsite, the outing that is described here.

Trekking is not hard at Reid Lake. The trails are well marked with blue blazes, the junctions are marked with locator maps, and the gently rolling terrain contains few climbs of any significance. Even when trails wind around low-lying wet areas, they are surprisingly dry thanks to the old two-tracks that many follow and a series of new boardwalks.

The rustic campsites feature fire rings and benches with half of them located at Reid or Little Trout Lake. Several, but not all, have wilderness privies and those at Reid Lake have a source of safe drinking water nearby.

If the trek to Little Trout Lake is too much mileage, then simple hike into Reid Lake for an evening. The shortest trail to the lake is from M-72 to post No. 2, a mile walk. Campsites lie on the north side of the lake, or 0.4 mile to the southeast along the shoreline trail to the south side.

Trip Planner

Maps: The USGS topo *Bucks Pond* shows the northern half of the trail system but not those around Little Trout Lake. For this trek the U.S. Forest Service *Reid Lake Foot Travel Area* map is adequate and usually available from a map box at the M-72 trailhead.

Getting There: The main trailhead is reached from Harrisville by heading 19 miles west on M-72 to the posted entrance. From Mio, head east on M-72 for 21 miles to its junction with MI-65 near Curran, then continue along MI-72 for another 10 miles to the entrance on the south (right) side of the state highway.

A second trailhead was built in 2003 that provides direct access to Little Trout Lake. Continue east of the main trailhead and then turn south (right) on Stout Road. Within 2 miles turn right on Fowler Road and follow it 2 miles west to the posted trailhead at the intersection of Fowler Road and Forest Road 4433.

Fees & Reservations: Camping is free but a vehicle pass to the Huron-Manistee National Forest is required to hike the trail. The pass is $3 a day or $5 a week and can be purchased at the M-72 trailhead.

Information: There are U.S. Forest Service offices in both Mio (989-826-3252) and Oscoda (989-739-0728). You can also obtain a trail map and additional information from the Huron-Manistee National Forests website (*www.fs.fed.us/r9/hmnf*).

Trail Guide

Day One (3.5 miles) This day begins at the M-72 trailhead and heads south to Little Trout Lake for the night. Begin by heading east (left) at the display board along a wide trail that follows the gently rolling terrain to post No. 8. Along the way you pass through the perfect rows of a red pine plantation and then break out at your first marsh, crossed via a stretch of boardwalk that keeps the boots dry. From here, the trail makes an ascent to post No. 8, 1.3 miles from the start and marked by a locator map sign. Reid Lake is only 0.3 mile to the west (right), but head east (left) to reach Little Trout Lake.

In the beginning the trail to post No. 9 resembles a former railroad bed

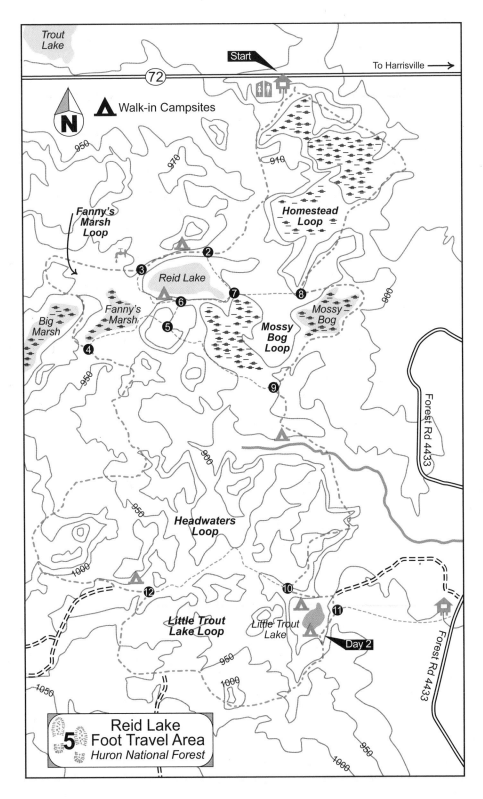

Trout Lake

Start

To Harrisville →

72

N

▲ Walk-in Campsites

950

970

910

Homestead Loop

Fanny's Marsh Loop

2

3

Reid Lake

7

8

990

6

Big Marsh

Fanny's Marsh

5

Mossy Bog

Mossy Bog Loop

4

950

9

900

Forest Rd 4433

Headwaters Loop

950

1000

12

10

11

Little Trout Lake Loop

Little Trout Lake

Day 2

Forest Rd 4433

950

1050

1000

950

1000

5 Reid Lake Foot Travel Area
Huron National Forest

before swinging south into a rolling terrain of hardwoods. Eventually you break out at Mossy Bog and tiptoe along a narrow foot path between two open marshes. This is an interesting area in the spring with peepers croaking and wildflowers blooming but buggy in the summer. The trail ascends away from the bog to return to the woods and arrives at post No. 9, just over 2 miles from the trailhead.

The trail to post No. 10 heads south as an old two-track and within a quarter of a mile arrives at a backcountry campsite. This one is perched on a low ridge above a grassy marsh and features a wilderness toilet nearby. The trail departs from the campsite and dips to cross a stream on a foot bridge and then makes a long gentle climb onto a ridge. From there you continue following the old two-track that can be so overgrown at times you'll have to stop to look for the next blue blaze. At 1.1 miles from post No. 9 or 3.2 miles from the start you arrive at post No. 10 and a sign indicating the next campsite. This site is at the northwest corner of Little Trout Lake where there is a fire ring and spot to pitch a tent or two in a stand of red pine.

Head east (left) at post No. 10 and follow the two-track as it skirts Little Trout Lake and crosses an earthen dam that was rebuilt in 2003 to stabilize the lake's water levels. Just across the dam you arrive at post No. 11. At this junction a well defined two-track, looking like a dirt road, heads 0.7 mile east to the Fowler Road trailhead. This trek continues along the Little Trout Lake Loop by picking up the overgrown two-track that veers sharply to the southwest. It's easy to miss this trail and more than one backpacker has mistakenly continued on to Fowler Road.

Within a hundred yards of post No. 11 you arrive at the backcountry campsite with a fire ring on the south side of Little Trout Lake, reached 3.5 miles from the M-72 trailhead. This is a great place to set up for the night as you can position your tent with a clear view of the lake. If any wildlife pauses at this oasis in the evening or early morning, you'll spot them.

Day Two (5.5 miles) The second day continues with the Little Trout Lake Loop following an old two-track through the woods that is overgrown at times with a carpet of ferns. Keep an eye out for the blue diamonds on the trees. You climb to an elevation of 1,020 feet where the trail swings to the north and makes a long gentle descent to post No. 12, a junction reached 1.5 miles from post No. 11. Here a pair of two-tracks merge at the edge of a grassy bog, a place to look for wildlife. Head west (left) at the post to quickly reach another backcountry campsite, featuring a wilderness toilet.

You're now continuing north along the back side of the Headwaters Loop that within a half mile swings to the northeast and stays in the woods until it descends to the edge of an open meadow. The trail can be hard to follow here but it swings west (left) and follows the fringe of the forest to skirt the edge of the meadow. Eventually you'll see a well-defined path enter the woods and quickly pass a trail sign for another backcountry campsite. This site is 2.5 miles from Little Trout Lake or 6 miles from the M-72 trailhead and

Reid Lake: Beavers, Dams & Wetland Wonders

The trail system in the Reid Lake Foot Travel Area winds past numerous ponds, marshes, bogs and the tract's crowning jewels, Reid Lake and Little Trout Lake. Each bit of water and wetland was either created by beavers or at the very least supports a lodge or two.

Beavers are master engineers. They are extremely good at building dams to block moving water, creating wetland habitats that support a variety of other wildlife, from waterfowl and herons to fish, frogs and turtles. When hiking in the area keep an eye out for telltale signs of active beavers; peculiar pointed stumps, chewed and toppled trees, dams made of branches and mud, stick lodges surrounded by water.

Other wetlands in the tract are man-made, many intentionally. At Little Trout Lake you hike across a water control structure installed by the U.S. Forest Service to replace an old beaver dam that had collapsed. The structure was responsible for restoring the lake's level and saving the wetlands the dam created.

is tucked away in the trees along with a wilderness toilet.

Within 0.8 mile, or 3.3 miles from Little Trout Lake, you reach post No. 4 where Headwaters Loop merges into Fanny's Marsh Loop. Head west (left) as the trail descends to Big Marsh, which can be more like a small lake during a wet spring, and then climbs over a low ridge before swinging east.

A mile after leaving post No. 4, you reach the northwest corner of beautiful Reid Lake and the junction at post No. 3. Just before the junction, you pass a spur to a hand pump for drinking water. If you're not in a hurry to head home there are four campsites on Reid Lake. The more scenic ones are along the south side of the lake and reached by heading south (right) at post No. 3. The pair of sites are shady spots that sit on a bluff overlooking the lake and a fishing dock below. Head east (left) at post No. 3 to reach two more sites, which also sits above the lake and features a wilderness toilet nearby.

In all, there are three fishing docks on Reid Lake, one on the south shore and two on the north shore. At one time Reid was stocked annually with rainbow trout and still supports a population of the fish. Other species include panfish, especially bluegill, largemouth bass and some perch. The trout and bass are most often caught by anglers who have hauled in a canoe, but the panfish can easily be landed from the docks on the north side. For either one, anglers usually turn to leaf worms rigged on a small hook and split shot to entice the fish into striking. Add a bobber if you're dock fishing for bluegill.

From the north shore campsite, the trail continues east to quickly reach post No. 2. Here you can continue to skirt the lake, a walk of almost a mile, or return to the M-72 trailhead by heading north (left). This final leg is a wide path through the woods and, for the most part, a gentle, mile-long descent to the parking lot.

A backpacker enjoys an early morning cup of coffee in his walk-in campsite on Byron Lake in the Hoist Lakes Foot Travel Area.

Hoist Lakes West Loop
Hoist Lakes Foot Travel Area

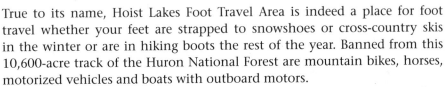

County: Alcona
Nearest Town: Glennie
Distance: 6.4 miles
Hiking Time: Two days
Highest Elevation Gain: 140 feet
Difficulty: Moderate
Highlights: Scenic vistas, numerous lakes, walk-in campsites

True to its name, Hoist Lakes Foot Travel Area is indeed a place for foot travel whether your feet are strapped to snowshoes or cross-country skis in the winter or are in hiking boots the rest of the year. Banned from this 10,600-acre track of the Huron National Forest are mountain bikes, horses, motorized vehicles and boats with outboard motors.

From spring through fall Hoist Lakes is a place backpackers can call their own.

Set up in 1976 to provide a quiet oasis from our motorized society, Hoist Lakes is large enough to contain more than 20 miles of trails and a handful of walk-in campsites, making it the destination for two ideal backpacking outings for the weekend. One begins from the eastern trailhead (Hike 7) and the other, which is described here, is a 6.4-mile loop from the western trailhead. Both are overnight treks where a spare day can be spent exploring more of the trail system or enjoying a little wilderness fishing in the lakes where you'll be camping.

The tract can be surprisingly rugged in places with many hills topping 1,200 feet in elevation and a couple providing panoramic views from the top. Hoist Lakes is covered by forests of pine, aspen, and other hardwoods that are broken up by seven named lakes and numerous ponds, marshes and beaver-flooded streams. Opportunities to observe wildlife are very good. Perhaps the most famous residents of the area are the least encountered ones: black bears. There are also red fox, mink, and coyotes, but more often than not the wildlife that hikers spot are wild turkeys, ruffed grouse, whitetail deer, beavers, porcupines, and a variety of waterfowl and birds.

Backcountry camping and campfires are allowed anywhere in the tract as long as you're at least 200 feet from an open body of water, swamp, or foot trail. But why bother? Some of the most beautiful walk-in campsites in the Lower Peninsula are located at Hoist Lakes and are usually so lightly used you won't have to worry about snagging a spot to pitch your tent. Although there is a hand pump for water a mile from Byron Lake, it's good practice always to carry in water since the pump is not always working.

Trip Planner

Maps: The area is covered by the USGS topo *Curran* but as is so often the case the trail is not on it. The Huron National Forest has a free *Hoist Lakes Foot Travel Area* information sheet that includes a map and is available online.

Getting There: Hoist Lakes is east of Mio, 22 miles west of Harrisville, or a good three-hour drive from Detroit. If heading north, take M-65 through the town of Glennie, then in 5 miles turn west onto Sunny Lake Road. Follow Sunny Lake for 5 miles, then turn north on Au Sable Road. The first junction is where De Jarlais Road (also known as Forest Service Road 32) splits off. Continue north (left) on De Jarlais, and in a half mile you'll arrive at the western trailhead and parking area.

Fees & Reservations: Camping is free but a vehicle pass to the Huron-Manistee National Forests is required to hike the trail. The pass is $3 a day or $5 a week and can be purchased at the trailhead.

Information: Call the Huron Shores Ranger Station (989-362-8961) in Oscoda or check the Huron-Manistee National Forests web site (*www.fs.fed. us/r9/hmnf*).

Trail Guide

Day One (1.7 miles) It is a short walk to the Lake Byron campsites, ideal if you're driving up after work on Friday. Most backpackers can be at the sites with their tents set up in less than an hour.

You'll find a vault toilet and a large information board at the western trailhead and a trail that departs east into a forest of mixed pines and hardwoods. Blue diamonds will keep you on track and in less than a half mile you'll climb a small hill and gently descend to the first junction, marked by post No. 6.

Head south (right) and through the trees you'll spot Carp Lake on the east side of the trail. You pass the small, roundish lake from above and then swing east to arrive at post No. 8 where one of the two hand pumps in the Foot Travel Area is located. You continue east, with the trail passing through a stand of predominantly maple that is magnificent in the fall, and then climb a ridge to gain more than 60 feet in elevation and top out in paper birch.

From here you begin a long but gradual descent back into hardwoods, finally bottoming out 1.6 miles from the start at post No. 9 at the north end of Byron Lake. One of the largest lakes in the area, Byron has panfish, perch, and a population of smallmouth bass but is tough to fish from the shoreline. Carry in a float tube along with your rod-and-reel if you are intent to spend a day catching dinner.

An unmarked path follows the west bank, while the main trail heads around the north end and quickly comes to post No. 10, a junction with a

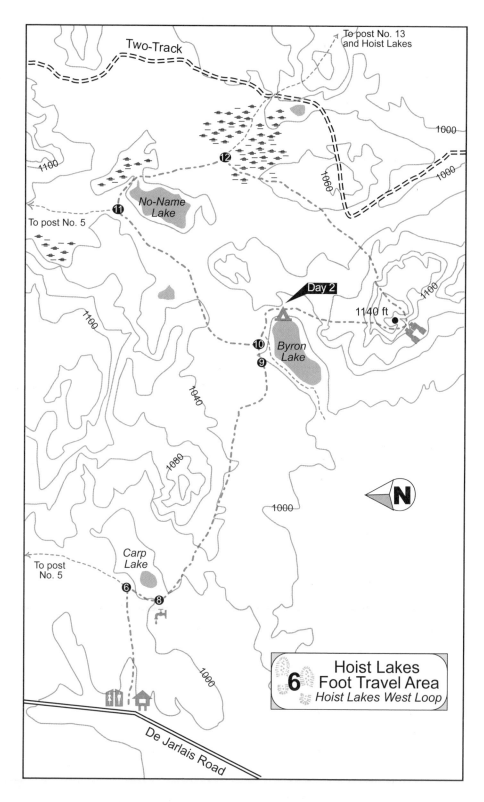

Two-Track

To post No. 13
and Hoist Lakes

1000

1100

12

1060

1000

No-Name
Lake

11

To post No. 5

Day 2

1100

1140 ft

10

Byron
Lake

9

1100

1040

1080

1000

Carp
Lake

To post
No. 5

6

8

N

**Hoist Lakes
Foot Travel Area**
Hoist Lakes West Loop

6

1000

De Jarlais Road

"Campsites" sign. One trail veers north (left). Follow the other to the east (right), quickly passing the first of three official campsites and many unofficial ones. Campsite No. 3 provides a tent pad, fire ring, and a bench, and a long stairway leads down the sandy bluff to the water. This is an excellent spot to spend the night as you'll enjoy a view of Byron Lake in its entirety along with forested ridges behind it. Cross your fingers that nobody else is there when you arrive.

Day Two (4.7 miles) This day is set up so you can leave the tent and gear at your campsite and follow a 3-mile loop past a scenic highpoint and No-Name Lake without the burden of your backpack. You return to post No. 10 where you can quickly gather up your equipment and back track to the western trailhead. You could carry your equipment with you and even follow a 6-mile route out via post No. 5 to post No. 6, but who says backpacking has to be a grunt? Enjoy the day without any weight on your shoulders.

From the campsite No. 3, the trail continues to follow the ridge along the east shore, passing a sandy beach at one point and then two more posted campsites. Eventually you descend past an unmarked vehicle track, climb a hill as the trail swings away from the lake and begin climbing once more after a short but steep descent.

This is the longest climb of the trek, a gain of 140 feet in elevation, but as you near the top, the first views begin to appear. You top off at 1,140 feet, a highpoint reached 2.4 miles from the western trailhead, where there is a clearing among the trees and a 180-degree view. Along with the rugged ridges that enclose the AuSable River Valley, you can see the famous river itself which lies only 2 miles to the southwest.

The trail skirts the top of the hill before making a sharp turn and beginning a steady half mile descent. You bottom out at a clearing, where you pass a pond and marshy area and then follow a level route to post No. 12. At this junction head north (left) for No-Name Lake. The shallow lake is quickly reached, and if it's a dry summer, there will be, not water at its north end, but an extensive mud flat. You leave the lake with no name, climb 60 feet and reach post No. 11, 2.6 miles from Byron Lake.

Head south (left) to pick up the easy cutoff spur to Byron Lake. To the north (right) is the trail to post No. 5, 0.8 mile away, and the longer loop to the western trailhead. The cutoff spur passes a couple of small ponds and wetlands where there are signs of beaver activity all around, particularly gnawed tree stumps.

Within a half mile you return to post No. 10 and the Byron Lake walk-in campsites. Pack your gear and backtrack the 1.7 miles to the western trailhead if your schedule is so demanding you can't stay for another night.

Hoist Lakes East Loop
Hoist Lakes Foot Travel Area

County: Alcona
Nearest Town: Glennie
Distance: 5 miles
Hiking Time: Two days
Highest Elevation Gain: 60 feet
Difficulty: Easy
Highlights: Hoist Lakes, walk-in campsites

Hoist Lakes Foot Travel Area is named after a cluster of three small lakes that make for a delightful spot to spend a night. The U.S. Forest Service agrees. USFS officials have placed two of the tract's three walk-in camping areas here, one on the shore of North Hoist Lake, the other on South Hoist Lake.

Although large swaths of the northern half of the foot travel area were clear-cut in the late 1980s, particularly between post No. 5 and post No. 3, this 5-mile loop was spared the heavy hand of commercial logging. For the most part you stay in the woods unless you're skirting a marsh, pond or those scenic little pothole lakes.

There's no scenic ridge-top view on this trek that is the highlight for many walking the West Loop (Hike 6). But a dayhike to that high vista south of Byron Lake is possible and a great reason to spend another night camping at Hoist Lakes – or to pack along your rod-and-reel and a handful of Mepps or other small spinners. Byron has populations of smallmouth bass, perch, and panfish, while South Hoist Lake is stocked annually with rainbow trout.

The hike into the South Hoist Lake walk-in sites is a 2.4-mile trek from the eastern trailhead with an equally long return, backtracking only a half mile of trail. For those looking for more mileage and more scenery, consider continuing past Hoist Lakes to spend the night at the Byron Lake campsites. This would be a 12-mile loop that would include the high vista and skirting five lakes before returning to the eastern trailhead.

Like the West Loop, you can set up a backcountry campsite anywhere as long as you stay at least 200 feet from a lake, stream, or foot trail. The trail system is extremely well marked with blue diamonds and locator maps at every junction but you will encounter a number of old two-tracks and logging roads that cut through the area.

Trip Planner

Maps: This hike is also covered by the USGS topo *Curran* but the trail is not shown on it. The Huron National Forest has a free *Hoist Lakes Foot Travel Area* information sheet that includes a map and is available online.
Getting There: To reach the eastern trailhead from I-75, exit onto US-23

near Standish and then, in 15 miles, head north on M-65. Follow the state road as it curves east and then sharply north as it crosses the AuSable River and passes through the town of Glennie. The trailhead will appear 40 miles from US-23 just south of the junction with M-72.

Fees & Reservations: Camping is free but a vehicle pass ($3 daily, $5 weekly) to the Huron-Manistee National Forest is required to hike the trail. The pass can be purchased at the trailhead.

Information: Contact the Huron Shores Ranger Station (989-362-8961) or the Huron-Manistee National Forests web site (*www.fs.fed.us/r9/hmnf*).

Trail Guide

Day One (2.6 miles) The posts along the East Loop are numbered counterclockwise and the route will be described in this direction. At the eastern trailhead you'll find ample parking along with vault toilets and a large information sign. Just south of the display sign the trail departs west and immediately comes to a metal gate, a barrier to motorized vehicles, with a three-way junction just beyond it.

Three wide tracks depart into the woods here, with one clearly a logging road and the other two posted as trails. Head north (left) on the trail, the scenic route to post No. 14. Follow the wide path through a rolling terrain of lightly forested hills and a pine plantation. Within a half mile the trail veers left and 0.7 mile from the trailhead you reach post No. 2 where there is a hand pump for water and two benches. At this junction a logging two-track appears from the south, while trails head north (right) to post No. 3 and straight to the west for post No. 14 and Hoist Lakes.

The trail to Hoist Lakes immediately skirts two low-lying wet areas. The one to the north is an open marsh ringed by an impressive stand of paper birch. If it's late in the day, pause here and search for any sudden movements as this area attracts a variety of wildlife. The trail skirts the marsh from above and then makes a 60-foot ascent to the top of a hill. On the far side of the hill, you swing past a small lake partially covered by a mat of cattails and plants where the gnawed stumps along the trail are indications that beavers have been active here in the past.

Just beyond the pond, or 1.7 miles from the trailhead, post No. 14 is reached, marking the junction with the other trail from M-72. Head west (right) and you'll soon be enjoying a view of a valley and its surrounding ridges through the trees. After a half mile and a gentle climb, the trail comes to a posted junction with the campsites spur. One trail heads south (left) to follow a ridge around South Hoist Lake and then descends to post No. 13.

The other, marked by a "Hoist Lakes Campsites" sign, departs to the west and within 0.3 mile arrives at the lake's north shore. The campsites are located on a low bluff overlooking a bend in the lake. They feature a fire ring, benches, and an excellent view of the entire lake. At night you'll know if any trout are rising to the surface to feed.

Just west of these campsites is a junction with a trail heading north

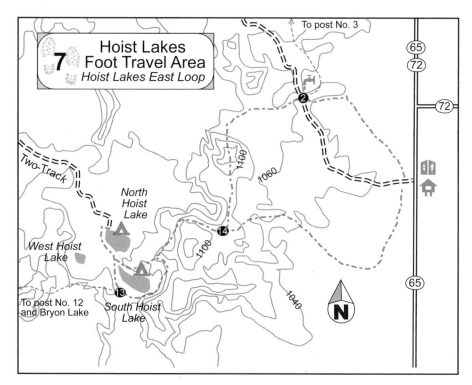

(right) a quarter mile to North Hoist Lake. The walk-in campsites are also on the north side of this lake where you can pitch your tent on another high bank overlooking the water. Also nearby is smaller West Hoist Lake, but it's not seen from the main trail system. To reach it, you must follow one of a number of paths that head west from the campsites' spur trail.

Day Two (2.4 miles) To avoid backtracking, something most backpackers detest, begin the day at the junction to North Hoist Lake. Head south (left) and follow the trail as it skirts South Hoist Lake and arrives at post No. 13. For those continuing on to Byron Lake via the high vista south of it, a hike of 4 miles, head west (right).

To return to the eastern trailhead head east (left) and climb away from the junction as the trail skirts the south side of South Hoist Lake, providing a peak through the trees of the small lake below. Within a half mile you arrive at the junction with the campsites spur. Head east (right) and backtrack to post. No. 14, reached 1.1 miles from the campsites on South Hoist Lake.

This time continue east by heading straight at the junction to follow the southern route to the trailhead. You're only 1.3 miles from your car but this segment is not quite as scenic as the one to the north. After passing a small wetland, you climb a low ridge and then make a gradual descent first through hardwoods and then into an old clear-cut where match-stick aspen have taken over. Eventually you arrive at the three-way junction where the parking area is just to the east (right).

Big Sable Point Lighthouse is the highlight on an easy, overnight hike to Jack Pine Campground in Ludington State Park.

Big Sable Point Lighthouse

Ludington State Park

8

County: Mason
Nearest Town: Ludington
Distance: 4 miles
Hiking Time: Overnight
Highest Elevation Gain: None
Difficulty: Easy
Highlights: Walk-in campsites with quick access to Lake Michigan beaches and a historic lighthouse

Ludington State Park, the largest state park along Lake Michigan at almost 5,300 acres, has four campgrounds. Three of them are modern facilities whose 347 sites are so popular during the summer that they must be booked months in advance.

But backpackers, looking for an easy escape from the bustling crowds, can bypass them for Ludington's newest campground. Opened in 2006, Jack Pine Campground is a walk-in facilities of 10 sites, located a mile from the park entrance and halfway to the historic Big Sable Point Lighthouse. Stunning beaches that border Lake Michigan are a mere five-minute walk from the campground.

The campground makes for a short hike and a great spot from which to further explore this beautiful park. Located between Hamlin Lake and Lake Michigan, Ludington includes open sand dunes, 5.5 miles of shoreline along the Great Lake, ponds, marshlands and forests. The park's backcountry is extensive and is laced by eight loops that total almost 20 miles of foot trails which are easily accessed from Jack Pine Campground.

This is an excellent and easy family adventure. There is no elevation gain on this trail unless you count the 112 feet to the top of the Big Point Sable Lighthouse, a climb that kids are usually more than happy to undertake.

Trip Planner

Maps: The *Ludington State Park Hiking Trails* map is more than adequate for this trek.
Getting There: The park is 8.5 miles north of the city of Ludington at the end of M-116.
Fees & Reservations: A daily vehicle entry fee of $6 or a state park annual pass of $24 is required to enter the park. Sites in Jack Pine Campground are $16 per night from May to October and $10 a night the rest of the year. You can and should reserve sites in advance during the summer by calling (800) 447-2757 or online at *www.midnrreservations.com*.
Information: Call the Ludington State Park headquarters (231-843-2423).

Trail Guide

Park in the lot just north of the main gate and begin by walking through the Pines Campground to the lighthouse service road, marked by a locked gate. Keep in mind there is no parking in the campground nor is the service road open to motorized traffic other than an occasional park vehicle.

The service road is a sandy two-track that heads north towards the lighthouse through terrain of open dunes, juniper and stands of jack pine. Within 0.7 mile you pass a signposted junction where the Coast Guard Trail heads east to the rest of the park's trail system and eventually reaching Beechwood Campground in a mile. To the west a spur leads to Lake Michigan.

The service road continues north and in less than a quarter mile reaches Jack Pine Campground. Scattered along a loop in a stand of jack pine and juniper are 10 sites with site A through D fairly close together and the rest scattered for a bit more privacy. Facilities include a hand pump for drinking water, vault toilets and a table and fire ring at every site.

Just to the west, across the service drive and over a low dune, is Lake Michigan and miles of undeveloped beach. Continue north on the service drive and in less than a mile you arrive at Big Sable Point. At the tip of the sandy point is Big Sable Point Lighthouse, whose black-and-white tower is the park's distinctive trademark.

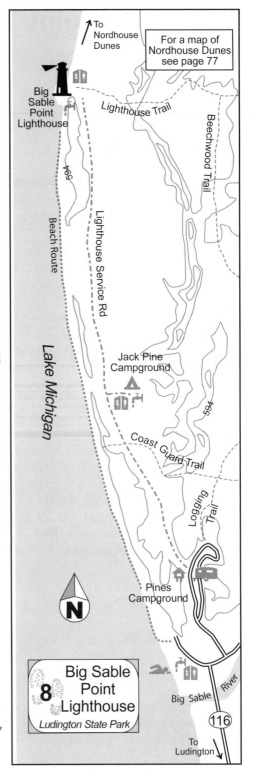

Hikers explore the open dunes in Ludington State Park.

The classic structure was authorized by President James Buchanan in 1858 after the barge *Neptune* sank off the point and 37 people drowned. Actual construction began in 1866 and a year later its light was illuminated by Burr Caswell, Mason County's first resident and the first caretaker of the lighthouse.

The light was placed on the National Register of Historic Places in 1983 and today is an interesting maritime museum that can only be reached on foot, a perfect complement to Jack Pine Campground. The attached lightkeeper's residence contains furnished rooms, historic displays and a gift shop. You can then climb a circular iron stairway of 130 steps to the top of the tower and step outside. The view is worth every step as Ludington State Park lies to the east and the blue horizon of Lake Michigan to the west.

Big Sable Point Lighthouse (231-845-7343; http://bigsablelighthouse.org) is open from 10 a.m. to 5 p.m. daily from May through October. Admission is $2 for adults and $1 for children. Outside there are picnic tables while nearby is the marked Lighthouse Trail that heads east to the heart of the park and the rest of the trail system.

Hikers enjoy a stroll along the beach in the heart of the Nordhouse Dunes Wilderness in the Manistee National Forest.

Nordhouse Dunes Wilderness
Manistee National Forest

9

County: Mason
Nearest Town: Manistee
Distance: 6.1 miles
Hiking Time: Two days
Highest Elevation Gain: 90 feet
Difficulty: Moderate
Highlights: Scenic vistas, sand dunes, beautiful beaches

When the Michigan Wilderness Act was passed in 1987, the Nordhouse Dunes of the Manistee National Forest was designated a federal wilderness, the only one in the Lower Peninsula. Already a Foot Travel Area, the U.S. Forest Service proceeded to remove signs and markers from the trails and the names of trails from the maps. One of the foot paths was called the Michigan Trail. It was a lofty title for a trail in the Great Lakes State and this walk easily lived up to it. Lying like a thread between the roar of the Lake Michigan surf and the quiet interior of the forests, the Michigan Trail is one of the most scenic hikes in the state and a wonderful start to an overnight adventure. Even if it doesn't have a name.

The trail stretches 1.9 miles above the shoreline between the southern observation platform in the Lake Michigan Recreation Area to a stretch of open dunes. You then camp on the edge of the dunes, just above a beautiful beach, and the next day complete the 6.1-mile loop by following a trail to the Nurnberg Road trailhead, where you pick up another path to the campground. Or if you were overwhelmed by the scenery of the first day's hike, then simply backtrack or follow the beach 3 miles back to your car.

For an even shorter overnight hike, many backpackers begin at the Nurnberg Road trailhead parking area where two trails depart into Nordhouse Dunes. The most popular route begins furthest to the west and leads 1.4 miles to the open dunes along the shoreline and the south end of the former Michigan Trail.

Although designated a wilderness, Nordhouse Dunes is relatively small, only 3,450 acres, fragile and popular. The Lake Michigan Recreation Area, a large rustic National Forest campground and dayuse area at the north end, will be filled most of the summer. At the same time you will encounter other people on the beach during the day and a handful of campers in the backcountry at night.

Regulations prohibit camping on the beach as tents must be at least 400 feet from the Lake Michigan waterline. Due to its heavy usage, camping and campfires are also discouraged in the open dunes. The best places to set up camp for a night are just inside the pines and hardwoods of the forested dunes where you will be protected from the wind and won't have to contend with blowing sand. Carry in all your water and a backpacker's stove to make life easy in the woods, and carry out your trash.

Trip Planner

Maps: The USGS topo for this trek, *Hamlin Lake*, includes most of the trails. The USFA also has *Nordhouse Dunes Wilderness* handout with a map on the backside.

Getting There: The Lake Michigan Recreation Area is located almost halfway between Manistee and Ludington. From M-55 in Manistee, head south on US-31 for 10 miles and then turn west (right) on West Forest Trail (also labeled Lake Michigan Road on some maps) for 8 miles to its end. From US-10 turn north on US-31 at Scottville, 7 miles east of Ludington. West Forest Trail is reached in 11.5 miles. The Nurnberg Road trailhead is reached from US-31 by heading 3 miles west on West Forest Trail and then a mile south on Quarterline Road.

Fees & Reservations: A National Forest vehicle permit ($3 daily, $5 weekly) is required to hike in the Nordhouse Dunes. Camping at Lake Michigan Recreation Area is $14 a night.

Information: More information and maps can be obtained at the Manistee Ranger Station (231-723-2211) at 412 Red Apple Road just off US-31 and south of the town of Manistee or online at *www.fs.fed.us/r9/hmnf*.

Trail Guide

Day One (2 miles) This trek begins at the Lake Michigan Recreation Area, a rustic campground of 99 wooded campsites well spaced along four loops. There are hand pumps for water, fire rings, and picnic tables, but no electricity or showers. There is also a dayuse area and access to the beach, a lovely stretch of sand split in half by Porter Creek.

The recreation area lies just outside of the designated wilderness and is flanked by two observation decks perched high on top of the dunes like a pair of sentinels guarding Lake Michigan. The hike begins with a scramble up 122 steps to the southern observation platform. Catch your breath and admire the view of Lake Michigan. Right behind the platform is a trail post and map sign for the Arrowhead Trail, the start of the network. The left path heads inland, the trail to the right towards the water, the reason most hikers head right. The trail actually follows a dune ridge high above the shoreline and is surprisingly level and easy walking for the first mile. You quickly pass a pair of trails that descend to the beach and 0.3 mile from the platform arrive at the junction of the Arrowhead Trail. This junction is posted because the entire Arrowhead Trail, a loop of less than a mile, lies outside the designated wilderness. In another 0.3 mile you pass a sign announcing you are entering the Nordhouse Dunes Wilderness.

Here the trail hugs the steep edge of a wooded dune. On one side are dunes forested in hardwoods, pines, and an occasional paper birch. On

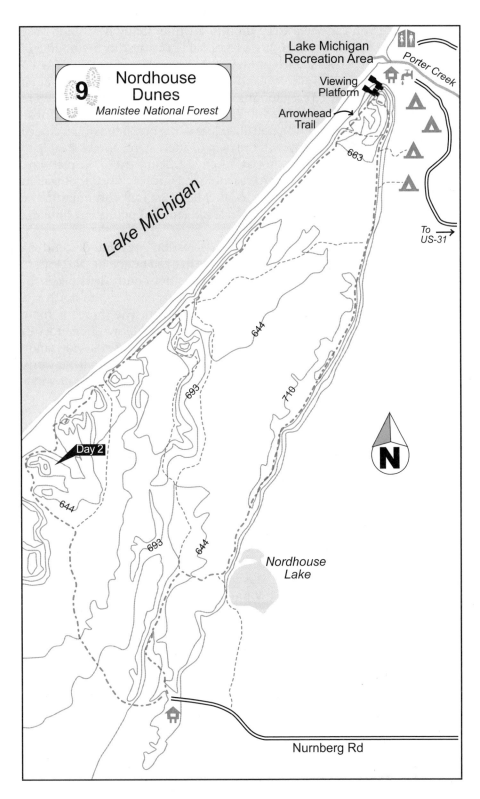

Lake Michigan
Recreation Area

Porter Creek

Nordhouse
9 Dunes
Manistee National Forest

Viewing
Platform

Arrowhead
Trail

663

To
US-31

Lake Michigan

644

693

710

N

Day 2

644

693

644

Nordhouse
Lake

Nurnberg Rd

the other side you can see a steep drop to a white, sandy beach and Lake Michigan blue on the horizon. It's a remarkable contrast in the middle of the summer; from a cool shaded forest you look at a strip of hot sand. At 1.1 miles you pass through a scenic stand of paper birch and then arrive at an unmarked junction that's easy to miss if you're mesmerized by the views to the north. The spur east (left) leads 0.7 mile to the return route of this trek.

Continue south (right). The trail dips close to the beach to skirt an eroded section of the bluff and then, with the help of a few steps, climbs steeply to top off at the third junction of the day, reached 1.2 miles from the platform. The trail that heads due south (left) reaches the Nurnberg Road trailhead in 1.7 miles. The route former known as the Michigan Trail continues to the southwest (right) and stays close to Lake Michigan by dipping and climbing along the shoreline bluff.

At 1.6 miles from the Lake Michigan Recreation Area you descend via steps to the fourth junction of the day, this one marked by an old "No Horses" sign lying on the ground. The trail that departs due south (left) heads for the Nurnberg Road trailhead while just a few steps away to the north is a beautiful beach and the rolling surf of Lake Michigan. The shoreline route continues southwest (left). You cross a tongue of wind-blown foredunes in a quarter mile and then return to the woods before arriving at a wide sandy path that heads inland. This is the southwest edge of the trail network, reached 1.9 miles from the platform. What lies beyond is an area of wind-blown dunes, beach grass, and woody patches of juniper and stunted jack pine surrounded by open sand.

The best camping in this area is in the hardwoods tucked behind the shoreline bluff between the last two junctions. By no means try to camp on the beach or in the open dunes; you'll never get the sand out of your tent or sleeping bag. But in the evening do retreat to the beach or an open dune for spectacular sunsets that dissolve into the dark blue of Lake Michigan.

Day Two (4.1 miles) Return to the wide and sandy path that marks the southwest corner of the trail system and head south into the forest. Within 0.3 mile, you arrive at the junction. The trail to the left ends at the fourth junction you past the day before. Stay to the right. You'll quickly skirt a few small marshes and then arrive at a V-junction where an old two-track climbs steeply up a hill. The foot trail veers right here as a sandy path and begins a long but easy ascent of its own. This is followed by an equally long descent, after which the trail curves around a large marsh with an open pond in the middle. From the trail, you can look down into the entire wetland, an excellent place to look for deer early in the morning.

Eventually you swing to the east and descend to the Nurnberg Road trailhead, reached 1.4 miles from Lake Michigan. Pick up the next segment by crossing the parking area to the path marked by a "No Motorized Vehicles" sign. Beyond the barrier you enter the woods and gently climb along the back side of a dune. Within a half mile from the parking area you come to a

A backcountry campsite in the Nordhouse Dunes Wilderness.

junction. Head south (right). Shortly you'll come to another junction near the edge of a ridge with a trail that descends south (right) off the bluff for Nordhouse Lake.

To return to the Lake Michigan Recreation Area head to the northeast (left) along the trail that continues to skirt the ridge. You'll be rewarded with views of Nordhouse Lake, a large, shallow lake surrounded by marshes, and then climb a 740-foot knob where there will be views to the southeast of the marshy interior of the Nordhouse Dunes Wilderness. The trail continues to traverse this crest of forested dunes, and 2.1 miles from the Nurnberg Road trailhead or 3.5 miles from the start of the day, you arrive at a junction. Here a trail descends the ridge to the west (left) to reach Lake Michigan in less than a mile.

Continue north (left) from the junction and a gray water tower looking totally out of place quickly pops up, a sign that you have officially left the federally designated wilderness. The campground now lies below you. Before returning to the observation deck you pass two stairways, the first leading down to the sites along the Oak Loop and the second to the Hemlock Loop. The observation deck is reached 2.7 miles from the Nurnberg Road trailhead or 4.1 miles from Lake Michigan.

A backpacker pauses in front of the Big Sable Point Lighthouse during a two-day walk from Manistee to Ludington.

Big Sable Point

*Manistee National Forest
and Ludington State Park*

Counties: Manistee and Mason
Nearest Town: Manistee
Distance: 15 miles
Hiking Time: Two days
Highest Elevation Gain: None
Difficulty: Moderate
Highlights: Beautiful beaches, sand dunes, historic lighthouse

Most people travel from Manistee to Ludington in their car via US-31. But backpackers are lucky. They can take the slow and scenic route by walking the shoreline and spending the night in a pristine wilderness. This adventure is another of Michigan's wonderful long-distance beach walks, a 15-mile overnight trek along Lake Michigan between the two cities and around Big Sable Point.

In the beginning a portion of this walk crosses private beaches. Not to worry. In 2005, the Michigan Supreme Court ruled that the state's Great Lakes' shorelines is a public easement from the ordinary high water mark to the waterline, open to walkers, beachcombers and, yes, backpackers hauling a tent and a sleeping bag with visions of spending a night in the wilds.

The rest of the trek is public shoreline through a pair of parks that preserve Big Sable Point. The first is the Nordhouse Dunes Wilderness, a 3,450-acre preserve where forested dunes raise 140 feet above Lake Michigan, and open dunes surround patches of trees like islands in a sea of sand. The federally-designated wilderness (see Hike 9) is open to backcountry camping and its location is ideal, allowing you to set up camp along a remote stretch of beach almost halfway between Manistee and Ludington.

Where the federal wilderness ends, Ludington State Park begins. The 5,200-acre unit in Mason County is the largest state park along Lake Michigan and includes 5.5 miles of Great Lake shoreline. It's also one of the most popular. In its southern half, Ludington contains 355 sites in three adjacent campgrounds that are usually filled daily from late June through August. There are also paved trails, an interpretive center and other amenities, the reason more than 700,000 visitors arrive annually. But its northern half, almost 1,700 acres, is a state designated Wilderness Natural Area; a trail-less, undeveloped area of open and forested dunes bordered on one side by Lake Michigan and on the other by Hamlin Lake.

Together the two parks create a unique route through Michigan's dune country for backpackers. There's backcountry camping opportunities in Nordhouse Dunes, a walk-in campground in Ludington, a historic lighthouse to visit and wonderful beaches from one end to the other. What more could you ask for when shouldering a pack?

The 15-mile walk begins at Magoon Creek Natural Area just south of Manistee and stops at the developed area of Ludington State Park. Being a point-to-point hike does complicate transportation for those who arrive with only one vehicle. If that's the case, begin at the Lake Michigan Recreation Area, a Manistee National Forest campground. The trek down the shoreline to the Jack Pine Walk-in Campground at Ludington State Park is a round-trip of 16 miles.

Trip Planner

Maps: The USGS topos that cover the route are *Manistee NW* and *Hamlin Lake*. There is also the Ludington State Park trail map and the Nordhouse Dunes Wilderness map from the Manistee National Forest.

Getting There: The hike begins at Magoon Creek Natural Area, just south of Manistee. From US-31 turn onto Fox Farm Road where the natural area is posted. Head west for 3 miles and then north on Red Apple Road for a half mile to the entrance of the park. Parking and a trailhead are located near the entrance gate. The hike ends at Ludington State Park, which is 7 miles north of Ludington at the end of M-116.

Fees & Reservations: There are no fees for backcountry camping in the Nordhouse Dunes. A vehicle entry permit ($3 daily or $5 weekly) is required to enter Ludington State Park. If you stay in Jack Pine Campground sites are $16 per night from May to October and $10 a night the rest of the year. You should reserve sites in advance during the summer by calling (800) 447-2757 or online at *www.midnrreservations.com*.

Information: For more information call the Manistee Ranger District of the Manistee National Forest (231-723-2211) or Ludington State Park (231-843-8671).

Trail Guide

Day One (9 miles) The northern end of this hike is Magoon Creek Natural Area, a 97-acre preserve maintained by Filer Township. The park has a picnic area with toilets, water, and a pavilion on a bluff overlooking Lake Michigan and almost 2 miles of hiking trails with 38 interpretive posts spaced along the paths. It's best to park outside the entrance gate and follow the trail system to access the shoreline.

A wood chip path on the north side of the entrance gate will lead you past posts No. 1 through No. 8 and then break out of the woods to reach the picnic area in 1.5 miles. Here the dune bluffs are so steep and high that a wooden rail fence has been erected to keep park users from taking one step too many. The view of Lake Michigan and the beautiful beach below is spectacular to say the least. Pick up the posted Beach Trail as it descends to the mouth of sluggish Magoon Creek. Cross it and 2 miles after leaving your car you're hiking south along the Lake Michigan shoreline.

From the park it's a walk of 3.2 miles along the beach before you enter the Manistee National Forest. Along the way you pass beneath two stretches of homes. You rarely see a house or cottage. For the most part they're hidden high above the beach at the top of shoreline bluffs. The only indication that homes are nearby are the long staircases leading from the bluffs to the beach.

When you ford Cooper Creek, the first stream along the way, you enter the national forest and after the next one, Porter Creek, reached 6 miles from the start, you enter the Lake Michigan Recreation Area. This popular campground has 99 rustic sites along four loops along with flush toilets, a picnic area and drinking water. The beach here is stunning and a long wooden boardwalk leads from the beach to the dayuse area. Both the campground and the dayuse area have drinking water. The next source of drinking water is 7 miles away at Ludington State Park.

Here you have a choice for the final stretch of the day; trail or shoreline. On the south side of the recreation area is an observation deck on top of a dune, reached via a stairway of 122 steps. Behind the platform at the top is a trail that skirts the shoreline bluff and leads 2 miles south into the Nordhouse Dunes (see Hike 9).

But most backpackers prefer to follow the beach into the heart

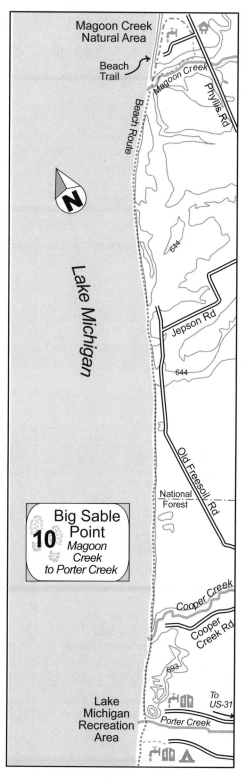

of this wilderness. It's roughly a 3 mile walk along the shoreline before you arrive at the forested edge of a vast expanse of open dunes. The best backcountry camping spots are found here. Hike into the woods on the back side of the shoreline bluffs where you'll be protected from wind and blowing sand. Regulations mandate that you pitch your tent at least 400 feet from Lake Michigan.

Day Two (6 miles) Return to the shoreline and head south for another day of beachcombing. At this point you're traveling through some of the most remote stretches of Lake Michigan shoreline in the Lower Peninsula. Most times you see more wildlife tracks than foot steps. Packing along a field guide to animal prints is useful here.

Most of the scenery will be sand and dunes to the left and water to right as only two man-made landmarks are passed along the shoreline. The first is a small Nordhouse Wilderness sign making the border between state and federal land, reached 2 miles from where you camped or 5 miles from Porter Creek. The second is quite large; the distinctive white and black tower of Big Sable Point Lighthouse. Sharp eyes will pick it up more than a half mile before reaching it 7 miles from Porter Creek or 13 miles from the start.

Completed in 1867, the

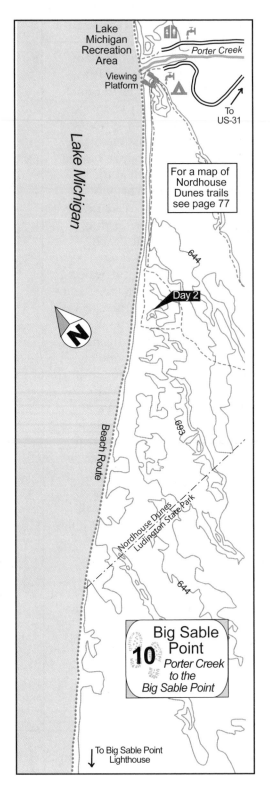

For a map of Nordhouse Dunes trails see page 77

Big Sable Point

10 Porter Creek to the Big Sable Point

A backpacker heads up the beach in Nordhouse Dunes Wilderness. The federal wilderness area is the highlight of a walk around Big Sable Point from Manistee to Ludington.

lighthouse sits at the rounded tip of Big Sable Point. Today the structure serves as an interesting maritime museum, one that can only be reached on foot.

It is staffed by volunteer lightkeepers. From May through October the Big Sable Point Lighthouse (231-845-7343; *http://bigsablelighthouse.org*) is open from 10 a.m. to 5 p.m. daily. For a small fee you can visit the lightkeeper's restored residence and then climb a circular iron stairway of 121 steps to the top of the tower for a grand view of what you just covered on foot.

From the lighthouse, there are two ways to reach the developed area of Ludington State Park. You can follow the Lighthouse Access Road, a sandy two-track closed to motorized vehicles. Within a mile the access road passes the Jack Pine Campground, a set of walk-in sites with water and toilets and in 2 miles it ends in Pines Campground.

But since you began on the beach you might want to end on the beach. If that's the case just continue south along the shoreline until you arrive at the Big Sable River within the state's park's developed area.

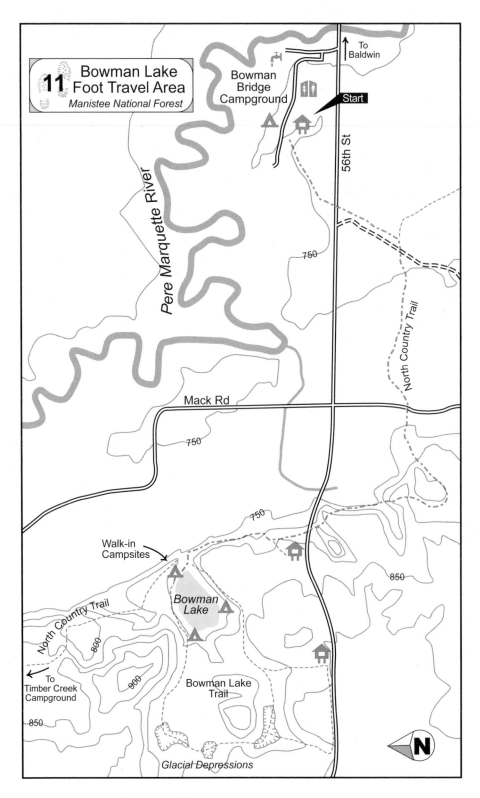

Bowman Lake
11 Foot Travel Area
Manistee National Forest

Bowman
Bridge
Campground

To
Baldwin

Start

56th St

Pere Marquette River

North Country Trail

750

Mack Rd

750

750

Walk-in
Campsites

Bowman
Lake

850

North Country Trail

800

To
Timber Creek
Campground

900

Bowman Lake
Trail

850

Glacial Depressions

N

Bowman Lake Foot Travel Area

Manistee National Forest

11

County: Lake
Nearest Town: Baldwin
Distance: 4 miles
Hiking Time: Overnight
Highest Elevation Gain: 89 feet
Difficulty: Easy
Highlights: Walk-in campsites on a secluded lake

At times during the summer the Bowman Bridge Campground on the Pere Marquette River is like a three-ring circus. There will be RVers running their portable generators, youth organizations setting up camp in the group sites, paddlers pulling out of the Pere Marquette, others putting in and canoe livery trailers whipping through like luggage carts at Detroit Metro Airport.

This is get-away-from-it-all camping? If not, then your walk-in sanctuary is just to the west at Bowman Lake.

Bowman Lake and Bowman Bridge are practically next door to each other and are even connected by the North Country Trail, but they are a world apart. Bowman Bridge is one of the most popular campgrounds in the Manistee National Forest. Bowman Lake is a "Semi-Primitive Non-Motorized Area," a 1,000-acre tract of rolling wooded terrain and a few wet areas that is split north to south by almost 3 miles of the NCT.

Bowman Lake is a glacial depression that filled with water when the ice melted. Its shoreline of steep ridges gives you the feeling of northwoods seclusion even though you're only a half mile from a paved road. The tract also contains several more depressions that were carved by glaciers 10,000 years ago but never filled with water. Today they appear as treeless pits.

You can camp anywhere in the tract but the vast majority of visitors never venture much beyond Bowman Lake where there are a series of walk-in campsites. Encircling the lake is the Bowman Lake Trail, a 2.5-mile foot path that is separate from the NCT and marked by a series of gray diamonds.

This overnight trek is described from Bowman Bridge Campground and is a one-way hike of 2 miles to Bowman Lake. But you can easily shorten it to just a half mile by beginning at the Bowman Lake Trailhead on 56th Street west of Baldwin. That would make Bowman Lake an excellent adventure for young children or anybody who wants a quick and easy get-away from that busy national forest campground.

Trip Planner

Maps: The Bowman Lake Trail is shown on the USGS topo *Townsend Lake* but not the NCT. The best map is the Bowman Lake handout from the Manistee National Forest that is available online.

Getting There: To reach Bowman Lake from M-37 in Baldwin head west on Seventh Street and follow it as it curves and becomes 56th Street (also labeled Carrs Road). Within 6 miles you cross the Pere Marquette River and pass the entrance to Bowman Bridge Campground. The main trailhead and parking lot for the foot travel area is 1.5 miles farther west on 56th Street. A second trailhead is another 0.5 mile farther west.

Fees & Reservations: A Huron-Manistee Recreation vehicle pass ($3 daily, $5 weekly) is required to park at Bowman Bridge Campground or the Bowman Lake trailhead. Sites at Bowman Bridge Campground are $13 a night and can be reserved in advance through Recreation.gov (877-444-6777; *www. recreation.gov*). Camping is free in the Bowman Lake tract.

Information: For a map of the area call the Baldwin Ranger District office (231-745-4631) or go online at the Huron-Manistee National Forest web site (*www.fs.fed.us/r9/hmnf*).

Trail Guide

Day One (2 miles) Bowman Bridge is a large campground with 24 sites, including four of them set up as walk-in for tent camping, ideal for backpackers who arrive on a Friday evening with plans to hike into Bowman Lake on Saturday. A spur for the North County Trail departs from the campground, immediately crosses 56th Street and then parallels a two-track briefly before arriving at a posted junction with the NCT a half mile from the start.

Head west (right) to follow the NCT as the trail swings around a wet area and in a half mile crosses Mack Road. On the other side of the gravel road you begin climbing, almost 90 feet in a quarter mile before the trail swings north to follow a ridge. Within 1.5 miles from Bowman Bridge Campground you descend to re-cross 56th Street and then come to a posted junction with the spur from the Bowman Lake Trailhead.

Continue north as the trail skirts the base of a steep ridge and within a half mile from 56th Street reaches another posted junction. This is where the North Country Trail continues north (see Hike 22), while Bowman Lake Trail heads left (west) over a low point in the ridge. Just on the other side is Bowman Lake, a serene body of water where there isn't a cottage in sight.

At the east end of the lake there are two backcountry campsites, each being basically a fire ring and a level spot to pitch a tent with a view of the lake. Two more are located at the west end and reached by the Bowman Lake Trail.

The lake's muddy bottom makes swimming less than desirable, even on the hottest afternoons, but it's good for the fish. Occasionally you'll see anglers portage in a canoe or a belly boat and then work the lake for bass, bluegill or redear, another species of panfish. If you have packed in a rod and reel you can easily fish from shore as a path skirts the entire lake.

Bowman Lake Foot Travel Area features a handful of walk-in campsites overlooking the small, undeveloped lake.

Day Two (2.5 miles) Looping to the west around the lake is Bowman Lake Trail, a 2.5-mile pathway that is well marked by a series of blue diamonds. From the campsites head northwest (right) to continue along the Bowman Lake Trail as it follows the northern shore, passes another campsite and then climbs away from the lake. It doesn't take long to reach the first of three glacial depressions, marked by wooden pillars in the path.

In the third depression is a junction, with one fork heading southwest to the second trailhead on 56th Street; the main trail continues at the east end of the depression and leads you back into the trees. It's another 0.5 mile through the forest before you descend into view of the lake again. Here the trail follows the south side of Bowman Lake before returning to the campsites and the junction with the North Country Trail.

Pine Valleys Pathway

Pere Marquette State Forest

County: Lake
Nearest Town: Baldwin
Distance: 4.1 miles
Hiking Time: Two days
Highest Elevation Gain: 69 feet
Difficulty: Easy
Highlights: Secluded lake

Before even hoisting your pack for an overnight trek to Lost Lake, you might think you're already lost. At the trailhead parking lot there are signs for snowmobiles, off-road vehicles, and cross-county motorcycles, leading many hikers to ponder whether they might have taken a wrong turn somewhere.

But half hidden in the back of this staging area for motorized activity is what you're looking for, the start of the Pine Valleys Pathway. Before there were snowmobilers and four-wheelers racing through this section of the Pere Marquette State Forest, there were hikers and skiers.

Pine Valleys was built in the mid-1970s when Nordic skiing was booming in Michigan and the Forest Management Division was building trail systems to accommodate skinny skis. But at Pine Valleys planners also added a walk-in camping area at Lost Lake and soon this pathway became as popular for backpackers looking for an easy outing as for cross-country skiers.

Located 13 miles north of Baldwin, the pathway is a system of three interconnected loops that total 8.2 miles. The southern loop was heavily clear cut in the late 1980s and today still resembles a match stick forest of aspen. The northern loop is bisected by two-tracks, snowmobile routes and the Little Manistee Trail used by ORVs.

The middle loop, however, is a gem, a forested path that leads you on a 4.1-mile hike to the lake and back. Here you are isolated from the nearby motorized activity and can enjoy a quiet evening camped along the shores of Lost Lake. While this portion of the pathway does attract an occasional mountain biker or horseback rider from a camp on Stewart Lake, chances are good that you will have the trail as well as the lakeside campground to yourself throughout most of the summer.

Trip Planner

Maps: The Lost Lake area is covered by the USGS topo, *Stewart Lake,* but the trail is not on it. The Forest Management Division has a free Pine Valleys Pathway map that can be picked up at the DNR Baldwin Field Office
Getting There: The pathway is in the northern portion of Lake County,

A backpacker relaxes in a walk-in campsite on Lost Lake, reached by the Pine Valleys Pathway.

13 miles north of Baldwin or a half-hour drive west of Cadillac. From M-55, head south for 9 miles along M-37, then turn east onto 7 Mile Road, The trailhead and parking area is a large, grassy area on the south (right) side of 7 Mile Road, a quarter mile from M-37.

Fees & Reservations: Camping is free at Lost Lake.

Information: the DNR Baldwin office (231-745-4651) is located just north of town on M-37 and is open 8 a.m. to 4:30 p.m. Monday through Friday. Maps can be picked up at information display outside after hours.

Trail Guide

Day One (1.6 miles) In the trailhead parking area you'll find a display board, vault toilets and post No. 1 half hidden in the back, marking a narrow, overgrown path. Head east (left) to reach post No. 2 in a quarter mile. This is the junction where the northern loop splits off to the north (left), reaching Lost Lake in 2.3 miles.

The middle loop continues to the east (right) and becomes a wider trail to handle skiers in the winter. The hike also beomes more hilly as you gain elevation on the way to post No. 3, reached 0.8 miles from the parking area. This post marks a short crossover spur south to the return trail for Pine Valleys Pathway. At this point, the middle loop follows an old vehicle track before veering to the right to cross the dirt road to Stewart Lake. The pathway is clearly posted on both sides.

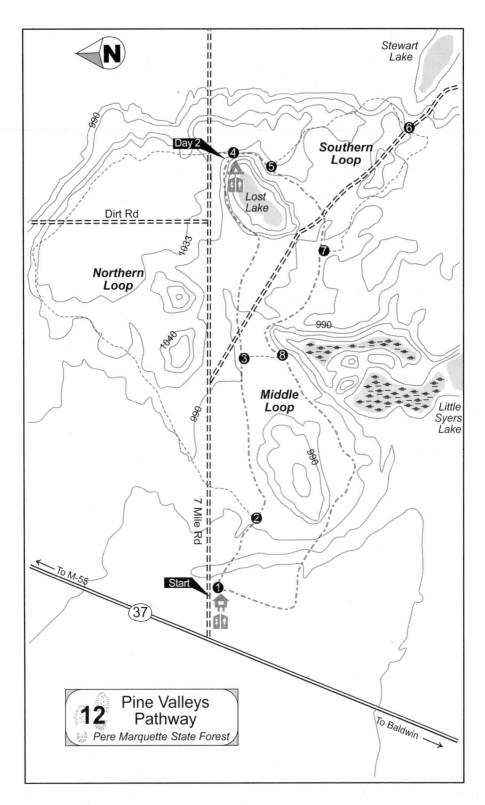

Stewart Lake

N

Day 2

Southern Loop

④

⑤

⑥

Lost Lake

Dirt Rd

Northern Loop

⑦

990

③

⑧

Middle Loop

990

Little Syers Lake

7 Mile Rd

②

Start

①

To M-55

37

To Baldwin

12 Pine Valleys Pathway
Pere Marquette State Forest

After crossing to the east side of the road, the pathway swings to the southeast and 1.5 miles from the start you climb a bluff for your first view of Lost Lake. The trail skirts the bluff high above the lake briefly before arriving at a pair of vault toilets. From here a path descends to the five lakeshore sites. The vault toilets are the campground's only amenities as the hand pump that once existed here has been removed. Pack in water or filter what you use from the lake.

Despite the lack of luxuries or even toilet paper in the outhouses (pack that in too), Lost Lake is a wonderful spot to spend a night. The small lake is less than 1,000 feet in length but enclosed by 60-foot-high bluffs forested in a variety of hardwoods. Even when there is a wind, the lake is usually quiet and still, its lightly rippled surface often reflecting those shoreline colors. In the morning you'll want to linger at Lost Lake, watching the sunrise spread across its surface while savoring a second cup of coffee.

Go ahead and linger. The return trip to your car is a walk of only 2.5 miles.

Day Two (2.5 miles) From the campground, backtrack to the trail at the top of the shoreline bluffs. The pathway continues to skirt Lost Lake from above, with many unofficial trails leading down to the water either made by hungry beavers or anglers. You soon skirt 7 Mile Road, seen through the trees, and within a quarter mile arrive at post No. 4, where the northern loop re-enters. The trail continues to traverse the lakeside bluffs, and a half mile from the campground, arrives at post No. 5.

The fork heading south (left) is the start of the southern loop, which leads in 0.6 mile to Stewart Lake, a small body of water with cottages and a church camp on it. The southern loop then returns to the middle loop at post No. 7, though you have to stomach some clearcuts.

To remain on the middle loop head west (right) from post No. 5. It immediately begins a nearly half-mile descent bottoming out at the dirt road to Stewart Lake. From there, it remains a forested walk, reaching the locator map at post No. 7, a mile from the campground or 0.6 mile from post No. 5. You'll find a skier's bench here, too high off the ground for most hikers.

Post No. 8, one hill and a quarter mile away, is quickly reached and then the trail swings southwest to arrive at what appears to be a flooded pond. Actually, it's an arm of Little Syers Lake that has been heavily dammed up by beavers and now attracts a variety of wildlife, especially birds and waterfowl. The trail swings away from the lake on an old logging track that arrives at a wildlife project. The grassy clearing is a planting of rye grass for the benefit of deer (and thus hunters), which feed in such open areas. The trail never crosses the clearing but rather skirts the edge of it.

Keep an eye out for trail markers as the pathway crosses three logging roads and cuts through a second rye grass clearing during the next half mile. Eventually the trail swings near M-37, where at times it's possible to hear the traffic rumble by, then returns to post No. 1 in the trailhead parking area, reached 1.5 miles from post No. 8.

Sand Lakes Quiet Area
Pere Marquette State Forest

County: Grand Traverse
Nearest Towns: Traverse City and Kalkaska
Distance: 7.4 miles
Hiking Time: Two days
Highest Elevation Gain: 69 feet
Difficulty: Moderate
Highlights: Secluded lake

You don't have to go far to replace the traffic, summer crowds, or the relentless commercialization of Traverse City with woods and a bit of quiet. A short drive – but a world away – from northwest Michigan's largest urban area is the Sand Lakes Quiet Area, five small lakes surrounded by rolling hills of oak and pine. This 2,500-acre tract does not possess the stunning scenery of nearby Sleeping Bear Dunes but it is quiet, thanks to a ban on motorized activity. It is also a great overnight escape from the city as one of the lakes features walk-in campsites, vault toilets, and even a well for drinking water.

Part of the Pere Marquette State Forest, Sand Lakes was designated a non-motorized "quiet area" in 1973. There are actually 12 lakes and ponds within the tract that can be accessed by maintained trails or unmarked fire lanes. The five Sand Lakes are marl lakes, glaciated-created body of waters that contain a high percentage of calcium carbonate in the sediments at the bottom, the reason some of them feature an unusual greenish color. Several of the lakes are more than 40 feet deep and Sand Lake No. 1 is managed for rainbow trout while Sand Lake No. 2 has brook trout.

The tract's maintained trails form a 6.2-mile loop, with eight trailheads providing access from four different roads and the Guernsey Lakes State Forest Campground. The trails are wide, well marked with locator maps, and generally easy to follow. The posts are numbered in a clockwise direction, with post No. 1 located at a parking area on the corner of Sand Lake and Broomhead roads. From this trailhead it's only a 1.25-mile trek to the walk-in sites on Sand Lake No. 1.

But this description begins at the trailhead in Guernsey Lakes State Forest Campground, for an overnight adventure that includes covering the entire loop. You begin with a 4.6-mile walk the first day and then conclude the outing with an easy 2.8-mile hike the second day.

The North Country Trail (NCT) utilizes 3.5 miles of the Sand Lakes trail (see Hike 24, page 167) which resulted in many of the trail posts being re-numbered in 2007. The map in this book shows the updated numbers but older maps will display the original system of posts for years to come.

Keep in mind that mountain biking is allowed on the trails and the area does attract a fair number of them, mostly after work or on the weekends. But you'll find that most mountain bikers arrive at Sand Lakes looking for a leisurely ride to enjoy the scenery. Hard-core mountain bikers head over to the much more challenging VASA Single Track that is only 2 miles away.

Trip Planner

Maps: Sand Lakes is covered by the USGS topo *South Boardman*, but the map does not include the trails. The DNR Forest Management Division has a Sand Lakes Quiet Area map which doesn't have contour lines but is sufficient for most hikers.

Getting There: From Kalkaska turn west on Island Lake Road just north of the McDonalds on US-131. Within 5.5 miles you pass Island Lake then veer to the left on the dirt road and follow it 1.5 miles to Guernsey Lake Road (also known as Campground Road). Although Guernsey Lake Road is not posted, there is a state forest campground symbol here. Turn south (left) and the campground entrance is reached in a mile.

To reach the trailhead from Traverse City, take M-72 23 miles east to Cook Road. Turn south (right) here, swinging east and then south again and ending up on Broomhead Road. After 4 miles, turn left on Sand Lakes Road, then right on Guernsey Lake Road to the trailhead parking area.

Fees & Reservations: There are no fees for hiking or camping in the quiet area. Camping at Guernsey Lake State Forest Campground is $10 per night

Information: Call the DNR Kalkaska office (231-258-2711) for a map.

Trail Guide

Day One (4.6 miles) Small lakes abound in this part of the Pere Marquette State Forest especially around Guernsey Lake State Forest Campground. Surrounding the entrance of the campground are Little Guernsey Lakes, three small bodies of water within view of Guernsey Lake Road. The campground is 30 sites on a pair of loops, all of them sites on a bluff above the Guernsey Lake with stairways leading down to the water. Facilities include tables and fire rings as well as a hand pump for water, and vault toilets.

On the entrance drive to the campground is a parking area with post No. 15 and a map box across from it. This is the spur to post No. 13 on the main loop. The spur begins as a level path through a stand of red pine before descending to post No. 14, marking a junction with the North Country Trail. To the east (right) the NCT winds past several small ponds, one visible from the junction, on its way to Kalkaska. You head west (left) where the trail follows an old logging road around what used to be the northern inlet of Guernsey Lake.

In 0.7 mile from the start of the day you gently descend to post No. 13. Head south (left). This stretch of the main loop is another old dirt road through a forest of pines, oaks, and maples. You quickly pass Pit Lake, a small, round body of water marked with a sign but not labeled on maps.

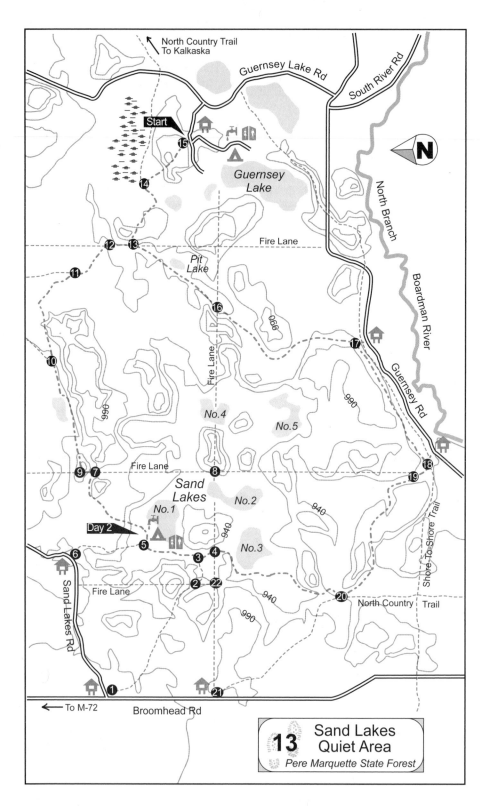

North Country Trail
To Kalkaska

Guernsey Lake Rd

South River Rd

Start

Guernsey
Lake

N

Fire Lane

Pit
Lake

North Branch

Boardman River

Sand Lakes Rd

Fire Lane

No.4

No.5

990

Fire Lane

Sand
Lakes

No.1

No.2

No.3

940

940

Day 2

940

990

North Country Trail

Shore-To-Shore Trail

Guernsey Rd

Fire Lane

To M-72

Broomhead Rd

13 Sand Lakes
Quiet Area
Pere Marquette State Forest

From the lake, the trail continues in a growth of pine and in 1.1 miles from the campground reaches post No. 16. The post marks a junction with an old fire lane that heads west to Sand Lake No. 4. You continue south to post No. 17, passing more unmarked trails that head west presumably for Sand Lake No. 5. This spot might be a little confusing, but the main loop is marked with blue blazes on the trees. Eventually the trail straightens out, and you can see the yellow trailhead gate just off River Road.

Just before the gate is post No. 17, where the loop swings west (right) and soon begins to follow the edge of a low ridge. The forest here changes to a stand that is dominated by oaks, maples, and other hardwoods. You skirt River Road from above, though you rarely see the dirt road, then descend to post No. 18. Head north (right) to reach post No. 19 less than a mile from the last post and 2.8 miles from the state forest campground.

The trail returns to following an old logging road and eventually descends to an opening of tall shrubs and saplings, a good area to look for deer, especially near dusk. Post No. 20 is where the North Country Trail merges with the Sand Lakes trail system from the west. Also at this junction is a path that heads northwest (left) to reach a trailhead on Broomhead Road in 0.75 mile. The main loop swings to the north (right) and continues to follow the logging road. Within a quarter mile the old road ascends a forested ridge while the main loop veers off to the left.

You skirt a bog area, re-enter the woods, and emerge at Sand Lake No. 3, a clear body of water that can be fished for bass and panfish. The trail skirts the lake for a good view of it, then arrives at post No. 4, a 4.2-mile walk from the state forest campground. Continue north (right) at the junction to reach post No. 3 and then post No. 5 in a half mile. The walk-in campground is a short walk beyond post No 5. The facility is on the edge of Sand Lake No. 1 and has a pair of vault toilets and a water pump near the lake. It's a shady area with enough space for a half-dozen tents. The lake is oblong shaped, shallow in most places, and surprisingly green at times.

Day Two (2.8 miles) The day begins by backtracking to post No. 5 and then at the junction continuing northeast (right) for post No. 7, reached in a half mile. At the junction the main loop swings north (left) to follow a fire lane briefly, quickly ascending to post No. 9. Here the main loop leaves the fire lane and swings to the east (right) for a scenic stretch. In the next half mile you skirt a small, unnamed lake where on a still day its surface is a perfect mirror for the shoreline trees. From the west end of the lake the trail then ascends to post No. 10, reached 1.2 miles from the walk-in campsites.

The main loop continues east and weaves its way through the gently rolling terrain, forested in hardwoods and pines. You reach post No. 11 within a half mile and then follow the crest of a low ridge before emerging at another fire lane, a junction marked by post No. 12. Head south (right) on the fire lane and post No 13 quickly pops up, 2.1 miles from the start of the day and 0.7 mile from your vehicle at the state forest campground. Head southeast (left) and backtrack the first leg of your journey.

Jordan River Pathway
Mackinac State Forest

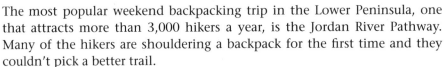

County: Antrim
Nearest Town: Mancelona
Distance: 18.7 miles
Hiking Time: Two days
Highest Elevation Gain: 218 feet
Difficulty: Moderate to challenging
Highlights: Blue-ribbon trout stream, scenic overlooks, walk-in

The most popular weekend backpacking trip in the Lower Peninsula, one that attracts more than 3,000 hikers a year, is the Jordan River Pathway. Many of the hikers are shouldering a backpack for the first time and they couldn't pick a better trail.

Located north of Mancelona, this 18.7-mile trek is a loop, eliminating complicated transportation arrangements, and features a walk-in campground near its halfway point. The fact that it is a two-day walk makes it an ideal weekend outing for backpackers from southern Michigan. It has enough climbs, especially on the second day, to give anybody a sense of accomplishment while many find its logging history an interesting aspect of the hike. Most of all, the Jordan River Pathway is a scenic walk where much of the day is spent either skirting the cedar banks of blue-ribbon trout stream or climbing to overlooks for views of the valley below.

The Jordan River Valley is an 18,000-acre block of the Mackinaw State Forest, protected from future logging or gas development. Most of it is centered around the Jordan River, Michigan's first National Wild and Scenic River and a popular destination for anglers fishing for brook trout. The area was heavily logged in the early 1900s with lumberjacks leaving behind their telltale trademark, a sea of stumps. But since then the forest has recovered and now is proposed as an old growth forest area.

The tract's best wildlife viewing opportunities are for beavers, raccoons, mink, otters, herons, and waterfowl seen along the river corridor. Most of the land is forested in hardwoods, home to many species of woodland songbirds and raptors. The other wildlife you'll encounter are insects. Because of the low, wet nature of the Jordan River, spring flooding is common and black flies, deer flies, and mosquitoes can be extremely numerous in spring and early summer. On the other hand fall colors are spectacular in early October, a great time to hike the pathway.

Part of this pathway doubles up as the North Country Trail. The NCT follows 11.2 miles of the pathway, mostly along the river. This section of the NCT begins at the Warner Creek Pathway, along M-32, and then splits off to join the Jordan River Pathway to the south. The Warner Creek trailhead could be an alternative starting point from the traditional one at Deadman's Hill

The Pinney Bridge State Forest Campground is a walk-in facility for backpackers hiking the popular Jordan River Pathway.

that is described here. Keep in mind that backcountry camping is not allowed along either pathway, only at the Pinney Bridge walk-in campground.

It's also good to remember that the Jordan River Pathway is not an easy trek. You must be prepared to haul a backpack almost 10 miles each day and are constantly climbing in and out of the valley. If you include a side trip to visit the Jordan River Fish Hatchery then it's almost a 20-mile hike. This one, however, is well worth the sore knees afterwards.

Trip Planner

Maps: The Jordan Valley Pathway is covered by four USGS topos – *Deadman's Hill, Chestonia, Alba* and *Mancelona* – of which none of them shows the trail. Your best bet is the *Jordan River Pathway* brochure from the DNR Forest Management Division, which includes the trail but not contour lines.

Getting There: The main trailhead for the Jordan River Pathway is Deadman's Hill, a scenic overlook posted along US-131, 11.5 miles north of Mancelona or 6 miles north of Alba. From US-131, turn west on Deadman's Hill Road and drive 2 miles to the parking area and trailhead at the end. If driving north on I-75, depart at exit 282 and head west of Gaylord on M-32.

Fees & Reservations: There are no fees for hiking the Jordan River Pathway.

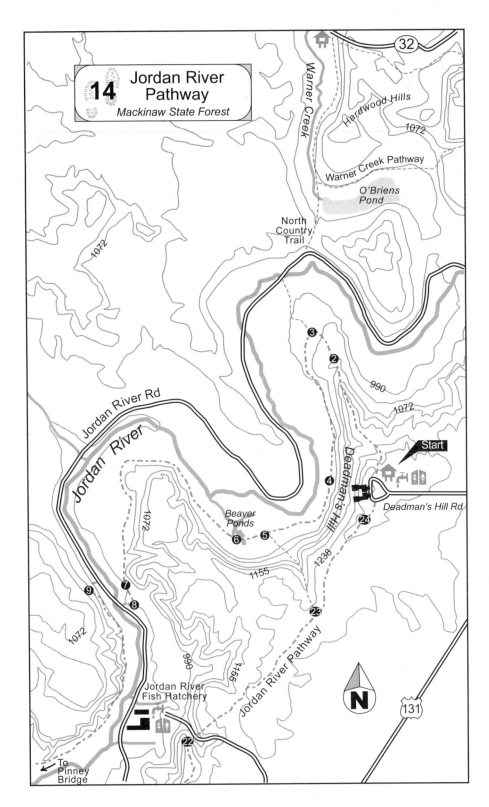

Jordan River Pathway
Mackinaw State Forest

14

Warner Creek

Hardwood Hills
1072

Warner Creek Pathway

O'Briens Pond

North Country Trail

Jordan River Rd

Jordan River

1072

1072

Beaver Ponds

Deadman's Hill

Start

Deadman's Hill Rd

990

1072

Jordan River Pathway

1238

1155

1072

990

1155

Jordan River Fish Hatchery

N

131

To Pinney Bridge

Sites at the Pinney Bridge State Forest Campground, a walk-in facility, are $15 a night and can not be reserved in advance.

Information: Just west of Gaylord on M-32 is the DNR regional headquarters (989-732-3541) where you can call or pick up a trail map.

Trail Guide

Day One (8.7 miles) One of the Lower Peninsula's most popular overlooks during fall colors is Deadman's Hill. The 1,237-foot high ridge was named after "Big Sam" Graczyk who was run over by an overloaded "Big Wheel" in 1910 on the day the logger was to be married. Or so the story goes. From the steep edge of the ridge you can gaze over the river valley and see nothing but ridges and trees.

Within the dayuse area are vault toilets, drinking water and a trailhead with an intentions box on the north side of the parking lot. From there the pathway quickly descends from Deadman's Hill, following a northwest arm spur of the ridge and descending almost 300 feet in the first half mile. Eventually you bottom out in a small meadow on the valley floor where the trail makes a sharp 180-degree turn at a posted junction. This is where the North Country Trail merges with the pathway. Head north (right) on the NCT and you reach the Warner Creek Trailhead on M-32 in 2.4 miles.

The pathway heads south (left) and re-enters the woods as it skirts the base of Deadman's Hill. The next mile is an interesting stretch as the ridge towers above you on one side while occasionally you catch of a glimpse of creeks headed for the Jordan River on the other side. Within 1.4 miles or 2 miles from the start you reach another posted junction. The trail to the south (left) is the 3-mile loop that will take dayhikers back to the top of Deadman's Hill. To continue on to Pinney Bridge Campground head west (right).

Just pass the junction the pathway arrives at the first evidence of its logging past; a wide, dry, and arrow-straight path through a wetland area. The raised railroad bed was built in 1910 by the White Lumber Company so its flat-bed cars could haul out the freshly cut timber to East Jordan. Now it keeps the boots of backpackers dry despite the beaver ponds on either side of the trail. In the first two miles of the trail the terrain changes from forest to wetlands to beaver ponds to grassy meadows. But no Jordan River. Not until 3.5 miles into the hike is the river seen for the first time when the trail descends to post No. 8 on the banks of it.

Designated Natural Scenic in 1972, the Jordan River flows from the northeast corner of Antrim County to the south arm of Lake Charlevoix in Charlevoix County, forming a watershed of 101,800 acres. The outstanding feature of the river is the clarity of its water; it derives 90 percent of its flow from springs gurgling out of the hills and bluffs surrounding you.

At post No. 8, you spill out onto Jordan River Road, use a vehicle bridge to cross the river and then follow the dirt road north briefly before picking up the trail on the west side of the road. From here the trail climbs into the forest, swings south, and returns to the river in less than a mile from Jordan

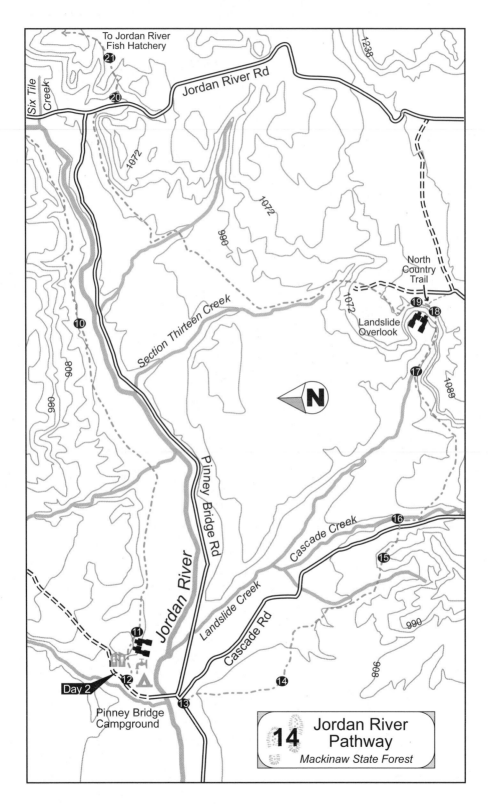

River Road. You hug the banks of the Jordan for more than a mile for one of the most scenic stretches of the pathway. The clear and cold current of the Jordan swirls and weaves its way through a maze of grassy humps and islands, some supporting huge cedars, others little more than a bouquet of wildflowers in the spring.

At 5.5 miles from the Deadman's Hill trailhead, the pathway merges onto another old railroad grade, this one built by the East Jordan Lumber Company in 1918. You climb to a spectacular overlook at almost 900 feet and then descend to emerge at Pinney Bridge Campground. In 1915 the campground was the site for Logging Camp Number 2 of the East Jordan Lumber Company. More than 60 men lived in the camp's barrack-type homes mounted on 60-foot-long flatcars so they could be easily moved. Later the site served as a Civilian Conservation Corps camp.

Today an open meadow remains. Although the campground is listed as having eight sites, on any summer weekend there can easily be twice as many parties setting up tents. Amenities include fire rings, vault toilets and a hand pump for water. There is also a payment pipe to drop in your nightly fee. From the campground a wide trail heads south to quickly arrive at Pinney Bridge, a lovely spot to watch the Jordan River flow past you.

Day Two (10 miles) This day is longer, a 10-mile walk back to Deadman's Hill or 11 miles if you include a visit to the fish hatchery. It is also more rugged with much of it spent climbing in and out of the ravines carved by spring-fed creeks. Cascade, Landslide, and Section Thirteen are the creeks that make the Jordan River so clear and pristine.

From the campground you head south on an old two track and cross the Jordan on Pinney Bridge and from there quickly arrive at Pinney Bridge Road near its intersection with Cascade Road. On the south side of Pinney Bridge Road the trail is marked with post No. 13. You then begin your first climb of the day, ascending through beech-maple forest before leveling out to cross through several small clearings and ford a couple of streams in the first mile. Following another steep climb, you descend to post No. 15 and then arrive at Cascade Road, 2 miles from the campground. Be alert in this first stretch as you pass many overgrown forest roads and two tracks that can mislead hikers at times. The trail is marked by blue blazes.

On the east side of Cascade Road is post No. 16 and from there you descend to Cascade Creek, a scenic little creek with a split-log foot bridge. The trail briefly follows the creek and then climbs out of the ravine the stream has cut. Post No. 17 is reached 3 miles from the campground or a mile from Cascade Road and is followed by more up-and-down walking in hilly terrain before the trail finally descends to Landslide Creek.

This is another scenic stream, especially in the spring when the additional water volume gives it some strength and size. The trail skirts the cedar-banks of the creek briefly, an area that can be wet at times, and then begins a steep climb out of the Jordan Valley. You gain more than 200 feet, enough elevation for a bench halfway up and another one near the top at the edge of the bluff. The bluff is skirted briefly before the trail arrives at post No. 18 and post No. 19 at Landslide Overlook, a 4-mile trek from the campground.

This spectacular vista features a bench and railing and provides a panoramic view of the valley. Below you can hear, but usually not see, Landslide Creek rushing towards the Jordan River. Two trails depart from the overlook. One is the North Country Trail that heads south to a parking area at the end of Harvey Road and then follows Harvey Road to US-131.

The Jordan River Pathway departs the overlook to the northeast, though you might have to search for the trail and its blue blazes. It continues to skirt the bluff briefly then swings away. You cross three two-tracks and skirt a small meadow before finally descending to Section Thirteen Creek a mile from the overlook or 5 miles from Pinney Bridge.

The creek is a delightful stretch to walk as the trail skirts its bank, passing many pools along the way. After a half mile, the trail swings away but reaches a second stream, this one featuring a bench, 6 miles from Pinney Bridge. After leveling out, the trail emerging from the woods at post No. 20 on the east side of Jordan River Road, 3 miles from Landslide Overlook.

On the other side you follow a two-track up a hill and then continue on a wooded trail, reaching post No. 21 within a half mile and the paved entrance drive of the Jordan River National Fish Hatchery in a mile.

Side Trip: Head left on the entrance drive to reach the hatchery, an 8.8-mile hike from the campground. The federal facility is an interesting place to take an extended break. Constructed in 1962, the hatchery is used primarily for the production of yearling lake trout that are used to stock Lake Michigan and Lake Huron. Two million yearlings are raised annually beginning as eggs in incubation jars and later as fry and fingerlings in indoor tanks and outdoor raceways.

The hatchery (231-584-2461) is open 7 a.m. to 3:30 p.m. Monday through Friday but has a 24-hour visitors center onsite. The center has interpretive displays and viewing windows along with bathrooms and drinking water. Even on the hottest day in the middle of the summer, this room is delightfully cool due to the 23,000 gallons of water in the building that's always kept at a constant 46 degree temperature. Ahhhh.

To return to the pathway you backtrack along the entrance drive, a half-mile walk uphill. From here the trail departs north (left) into a beech-maple forest and remains a level walk for the next mile. At 10 miles from Pinney Bridge (including a side trip to the hatchery), you arrive at the posted junction with the three-mile loop.

Head right and the final mile will remain as a level walk through the forest until you break out at the parking area on Deadman's Hill. Along the way keep an eye out for post No. 24 to see if the crosscut saw is still embedded in a trunk of a tree. A logger broke the saw and stuck it in the crotch of a young tree more than 60 years ago. The maple continued to grow, encasing the piece of iron that has been eroding ever since.

Sleeping Bear Dunes National Lakeshore

Thanks to the high vistas and open country created by the dunes, Sleeping Bear Dunes National Lakeshore features the best dayhiking south of the Mackinac Bridge through scenery that rivals anything you see north of the bridge. Mixed in with all those fine hikes are a handful of backpacking opportunities, including two island adventures and a beach walk along an undeveloped stretch of Lake Michigan.

All this hiking is located in a national park that stretches 72,000 acres between Frankfort and Leland and includes 35 miles of shoreline on the mainland, two remote islands in Lake Michigan, and the largest dunes in the Midwest. The park maintains a dozen trails that total 60 miles on the mainland and extensive trail systems on South and North Manitou islands.

You can enjoy easy overnight outings on Platte Plains or Valley View Trails, staying at walk-in campsites. Or for a longer walk, there's the 36-mile beach hike from near Point Betsie to almost Glen Arbor. Backpackers looking for a remote and wilderness-like adventure jump on a ferry in Leland and head to North Manitou Island, a wild place without cars or any development other than a ranger station and a campground.

The best place for information and maps is the Philip Hart Visitor Center (231-326-5134), at M-22 and M-72 in Empire. Its distinct 50-foot tower is modeled from the U.S. life-saving stations that served the Great Lakes during the late 1800s. Inside the center is a large relief map along with exhibits devoted to the natural and human history of the area, a video theater, an information counter with trail maps and a bookstore. The park also maintains an excellent web site (*www.nps.gov/slbe*).

Platte Plains Trail in Sleeping Bear Dunes National Lakeshore offers backpackers out-standing coastal scenery, a variety of loops, and a walk-in campground.

Platte Plains Trail
Sleeping Bear Dunes National Lakeshore

15

County: Benzie
Nearest Town: Empire
Distance: 7 miles
Hiking Time: Two days
Highest Elevation Gain: 33 feet
Difficulty: Easy
Highlights: Beautiful Lake Michigan beaches, walk-in campsites

My son was 11 years old when I gave him his first backpack and a new pair of hiking boots for Christmas. That August he joined me on a trip to go hiking in Alaska. That meant in between the two events we needed a shakedown, an early season outing in which we tested his pack, broke in those boots, and eased into what was shaping up to be a summer of backpacking.

Platte Plains is exactly what we needed.

Stretched out along serene Platte Bay, this slice of the Sleeping Bear Dunes National Lakeshore offers outstanding coastal scenery, 14.7 miles of trails, a variety of loops and, best of all, a walk-in campground, the reason to hoist a backpack. With its easy hiking and ban on mountain bike use, Platte Plains is one of the best destinations in the Lower Peninsula for anybody's first overnight adventure in which all that's needed is strapped to their back.

The Platte Plains trail system is accessed from four trailheads – Platte River Campground and at the west ends of Esch Road, Trail's End Road and Peterson Road. There are three main loops in the trail system. The Otter Creek Loop is a 4.6-mile walk around the creek and Otter Lake. The Bass Lake Loop is a 3.5-mile trek from Trail's End Road past Bass and Deer lakes.

The longest loop, the one described here, is Lasso Loop, a 7-mile trek that begins at Platte River Campground and includes skirting the beautiful beaches along Platte Bay and passing through White Pine Backcountry Campground. While this hike can be covered by most people in three to five hours, spending a night at White Pine is a very enjoyable experience and a great way to escape the summer mobs that cluster in this section of the national lakeshore.

Ideally located halfway along the Lasso Loop in a ravine between two forested dunes, White Pine Campground is a gem. Wind-blown dunes, panoramas of the Manitou Islands, and beaches free of crowds and coolers are within a short walk of your site. If planning to spend a night, pack in water or a filter. There's a community fire ring in the campground, but cooking is best done on a backpacker's stove. And don't forget the bathing suit. The swimming is excellent in Platte Bay.

Trip Planner

Maps: Most of the trail system is on the USGS topo *Beulah* but the *Platte Plains Hiking Trail* map from the National Park Service is more than adequate.

Getting There: From the Philip Hart Visitor Center in Empire, head south on M-22 to reach Platte River Campground in 9.5 miles, the start of this hike. Other Platte Plains trailheads include the west ends of Esch Road 4 miles south of Empire, Trail's End Road 6 miles south of Empire, and the west end of Peterson Road 10 miles south of Empire.

Fees & Reservations: A vehicle park pass ($10 weekly, $20 annual) is required for Platte Plain trail and can be purchased from the Philip Hart Visitor Center. Campsites at White Pine are $5 a night and can not be reserved. You must, however, pick up a permit at the Platte River Campground office (231-325-5881) in advance to hike to White Pine.

Modern sites at Platte River Campground are $21 a night, rustic sites are $16, and walk-in sites are $12. You can reserve these sites in advance through ReserveUSA (877-444-6777; *www.recreation.gov*).

Information: For more information contact the Philip Hart Visitor Center (231-326-5134; *www.nps.gov/slbe*), which is open daily.

Trail Guide

Day One (2.7 miles) Spending the night before your trek in the Platte River Campground is a great way to turn this hike into a weekend outing. This facility features 179 sites, including those with hook-ups for recreational vehicles and 25 walk-in sites that are secluded in the woods at the north end. There is also a picnic area, water, showers, restrooms, a contact station with information and interpretive programs during the summer.

There are actually several places in the campground to enter the trail system. At the back of Loop 1 through Loop 4 are short spurs that connect to the Old Railroad Grade. This hike begins from the walk-in camp area where a trail leads directly to Lake Michigan and is marked by blue tipped posts. In less than a half mile, you break out of the trees and enter the low dunes along the Lake Michigan shoreline. Here the trail swings east to follow the shoreline and provide views of the water and then 0.8 mile from the campground swings south to arrive at post No. 9.

Continuing south is what is labeled on many maps as the old railroad grade. The narrow gauge line was built in the 19th century between a logging town on the west end of Platte Lake called Edgewater and docks on Lake Michigan, where ships carried the cut lumber to cities like Chicago. The railroad bed is a level path – because workers filled in every dip and flattened every rise of sand before laying the tracks.

To reach White Pine, head east (left) to enter a forest that provides more solid footing than the dunes but remains a level walk. You break out in a grassy clearing and arrive at post No. 8, reached 1.3 miles from the start and marking where the trail crosses Peterson Road. A short walk down the road

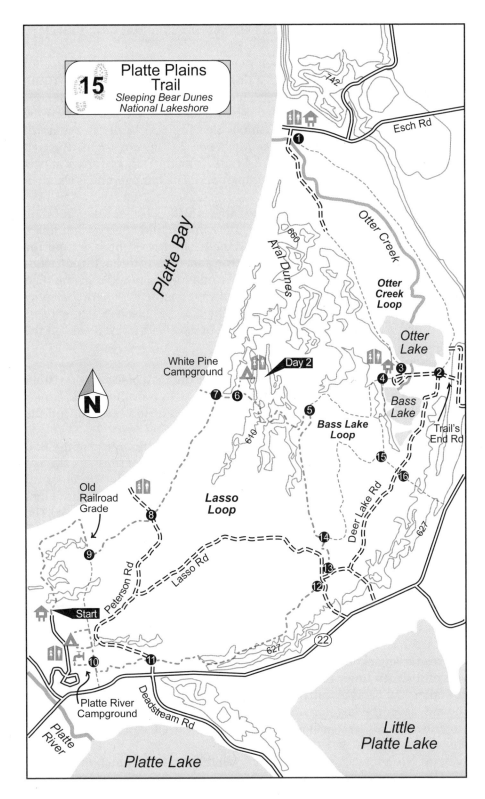

Platte Plains Trail

15

Sleeping Bear Dunes
National Lakeshore

Platte Bay

Esch Rd

Otter Creek

Otter Creek Loop

660

Aral Dunes

Otter Lake

White Pine Campground

Day 2

N

Bass Lake

3

4

2

Trail's End Rd

5

Bass Lake Loop

7 6

610

15

16

Old Railroad Grade

Lasso Loop

8

Deer Lake Rd

627

9

Lasso Rd

14

Peterson Rd

13

12

Start

22

10 11

Platte River Campground

627

Deadstream Rd

Platte River

Little Platte Lake

Platte Lake

to the left is a parking area, vault toilet, more beautiful beach, and sweeping views of the bay.

East of Peterson Road, the trail remains in the lightly forested area for a half mile and then moves into a thicker stand of oak and pine. Within 2.4 miles from Platte River Campground you reach post No. 7. To the west (left) a path leads into an area of wind-blown dunes, where you can view the entire Platte Bay along with the famous Sleeping Bear Dunes to the north and South Manitou Island in Lake Michigan. To the east (right) the trail follows a gently rolling terrain and 2.5 miles from the start you arrive at post No. 6 and the spur to White Pine Campground. The campground is less than a quarter mile away.

White Pine is located in a narrow ravine, with wooded ridges running along both sides of the secluded sites. The campground offers a vault toilet, a community fire ring, and six sites. There is no view of the lake from the campground, but near site No. 6 a path wanders west through the woods and quickly breaks out into an area of wind-blown dunes. From the high perch of the dunes, you are rewarded with an immense view of the Sleeping Bear Dunes and South Manitou Island. The Lake Michigan beach, with its clear waters and sandy bottom, is just a 10-minute walk away. Break out the bathing suit.

Day Two (4.3 miles) For most people the second half of Lasso Loop, from White Pine to Platte River Campground, is a two- to three-hour trek. Unless you're in a hurry to leave this paradise, there's no reason not to spend the morning on the beach.

From White Pine Campground, backtrack to post No. 6 where the trail continues due east and quickly enters the hilliest section of the loop. Marked by black-tipped poles to warn cross-country skiers in the winter of an "Advance" section, these ridges and hills are ancient shoreline sand dunes that mark the position of Lake Michigan after each glacial ice melt. The steepest climb is at the beginning, and after topping off, the trail follows the crest of the ridge around a pond filled by cattails. You descend, climb again to skirt another pond, and then drop quickly to the base of that dune. The trail levels out somewhat to wind through an impressive stand of pines, and 0.8 mile from White Pine, comes to post No. 5.

This post marks the junction where the Lasso Loop and Bass Lake Loop merge. To the north (left) is the mile-long spur to a trailhead at Trail's End Road. Lasso Loop continues south (right) along a level stretch that is marked by green triangles. Here's another interesting change of scenery, as on one side of the path tower pines, with their thick understory of ferns, while on the other, you pass one cattail marsh after another. The largest marsh is seen 0.4 mile from the last junction, and often in June wild iris can be spotted from the trail. Other marshes follow for almost the entire 1.1-mile length of this stretch.

Post No. 14, reached 2 miles from White Pine, is the junction with the second trail to Trail's End Road. To reach Platte River Campground, head south (right). In 0.3 mile, you come to Lasso Road at post No. 13. Turn left on the road and watch for where the trail continues on the right, marked by post No. 12. The terrain remains level and is forested for a mile; then the trail begins skirting more of those ancient lakeshore sand dunes. At one point, there are forested ridges towering over you on both sides of the path.

After swinging so close to M-22 that in the summer you can hear the traffic, the trail climbs a ridge and skirts more marshy areas. You descend to cross Peterson Road a second time at post No. 11. On the other side of the road, the trail swings north and, in 0.3 mile, merges into the old railroad grade. Turn north (right) here and follow the old line. The first posted spur to a campground loop appears on the left in less than a quarter mile.

Valley View Trail
Sleeping Bear Dunes National Lakeshore

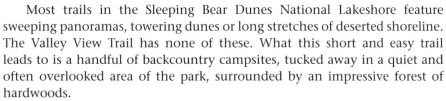

County: Leelanau
Nearest Town: Glen Arbor
Distance: 3 miles round trip
Hiking Time: Overnight
Highest Elevation Gain: 247 feet
Difficulty: Easy
Highlights: Walk-in campsites in a beautiful forest

Most trails in the Sleeping Bear Dunes National Lakeshore feature sweeping panoramas, towering dunes or long stretches of deserted shoreline. The Valley View Trail has none of these. What this short and easy trail leads to is a handful of backcountry campsites, tucked away in a quiet and often overlooked area of the park, surrounded by an impressive forest of hardwoods.

The Valley View Trail offers an overnight escape into a region of Michigan that is often overrun by tourists in the middle of the summer. When Platte River and D.H. Day Campgrounds are filled to capacity with motorhomes, humming generators and sun-burnt families, Valley View is a peaceful oasis where you can pitch your tent and sip your morning coffee in the shade of hardwoods while watching a whitetail meander through a small meadow. The price for such tranquility is carrying your necessities 1.5 miles from a parking lot. And then carrying them out when you're ready to head home.

Such a small price in today's congested world.

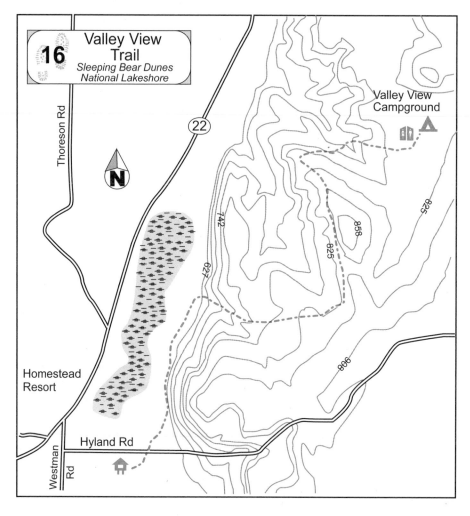

The best time to arrive is from late September through mid-October when the beech and maples that form much of the canopy are burning with fall colors. Without the heat, bugs or crowds and with such autumn splendor overhead, this relatively obscure trail becomes a priceless weekend getaway.

Your necessities should include water as there is neither a source for safe drinking water here nor a stream or lake nearby to filter water.

Trip Planner

Maps: Trail maps are available at D.H. Day Campground Office or from a box at the trailhead. The maps are very simplistic but more than adequate to lead you to the backcountry campsites.

Getting There: From Glen Arbor head north on M-22 for 2 miles. Across from the main entrance of the Homestead Resort, turn right (south) on

Westman Road and then quickly turn east (left) on Hyland Road. The posted trailhead is 100 yards east on Hyland Road.

Fees & Reservations: Campsites are $5 per night and can be paid at D.H. Day Campground just west of Glen Arbor or the park's Philip A. Hart Visitor Center in Empire. You'll also need a park vehicle pass ($10 weekly, $20 annual).

Information: Contact the Sleeping Bear Dunes National Lakeshore Visitor Center (231-326-5134; *www.nps.gov/slbe*) or the D.H. Day Campground Office (231-334-4634).

Trail Guide

Valley View Trail begins next to the information sign in the parking lot and immediately crosses Hyland Road. On the north side the trail enters that beautiful forest and you remain in it until you reach the campsites. Nearby is M-22 and you can hear the traffic rumbling by until the trail swings sharply east and begins steadily climbing a ridge. You gain more than 240 feet in the next half mile, topping off on the forested dune where the trail swings north and then follows the rounded crest of it.

The largest beech and maple are located here and will dazzle you in the fall. In 1.25 miles from the parking lot, the trail swings east again, descends off the dune, climbs a smaller one and then descends gently into a small open meadow. Welcome to Valley View! Not spectacular, not like places on South Manitou Island, but quiet and more than likely all yours.

The small meadow is encircled by hardwoods and sumac. On its east side are five numbered campsites, two of them with fire rings, all of them just inside the trees. Sites three and four indeed have a view of the valley from the makeshift benches other backpackers have created. Also located nearby is a wilderness toilet.

A family climbs the steep shoreline dunes north of North Bar Lake. This is the most impressive stretch of the Bay-to-Bay Shoreline Walk.

Bay-to-Bay Shoreline Walk

Sleeping Bear Dunes National Lakeshore

17

Counties: Benzie and Leelanau
Nearest Towns: Empire and Glen Arbor
Distance: 36 miles
Hiking Time: Three days
Highest Elevation Gain: None
Difficulty: Moderate
Highlights: Michigan's most spectacular shoreline scenery and dunes

Someday park officials at Sleeping Bear Dunes National Lakeshore would like to develop a Bay-to-Bay Trail that would lead backpackers from the south end of the national park to the north. They would follow a trail through the wooded dunes as they leapfrog from Platte Bay to Sleeping Bear Bay to Good Harbor Bay, spending each night at secluded walk-in campsites.

Until that trail is built, this trek is an ideal substitute. The Bay-to-Bay Shoreline Walk is a stunning three-day backpack along the Lake Michigan shoreline, beginning at Old Indian Trail in Benzie County and ending at D.H. Day Campground just west of Glen Harbor in Leelanau County. Along the way you skirt the most impressive dunes on the Michigan mainland, towering hills of sand that dwarf anybody traversing the beach below.

In between the dunes are some of the state's best beaches. If you arrive in July or August, pack a suit and a tube of sunscreen to linger in the sand and surf. This is not a trek to rush through. Plan on an extended afternoon break each day where you do nothing more than watch the waves roll in on a deserted stretch of beach you can call your own.

This outing is also a lesson in maritime history that the proposed inland trail will never be able to match. The shoreline from Empire to Glen Haven is often referred to as the "Shipwreck Trail" due to the large number of vessels that sank in the wicked Manitou Passage it borders. During the heyday of Great Lakes shipping from the 1850s to 1920 almost 50 boats sank in the passage, including 22 less than 400 yards from the shoreline.

When the lake levels are low or the water extremely calm, hikers often spot two wrecks from the shoreline; the *Jennie and Annie*, a schooner that sank in 1872, and the *James McBride*, a brig that went down in 1857. When the weather is rough and the waves are powerful, pieces of shipwrecks will break loose from their underwater graveyard and wash ashore. Eventually you hike right past the Sleeping Bear Point Maritime Museum where you can stop and learn why there were so many shipwrecks and how the U.S. Life-Saving Service rescued the distressed sailors.

Although this is a beach walk with virtually no elevation gain, this trek should not be taken lightly. It's a 36-mile, point-to-point walk that includes covering 15 miles the final day. Soft sand can be tiring after a few hours, especially if you're hauling a pack, while trying to stay on the hard sand near the waterline often results in wet boots or blisters from the uneven slope of the beach.

Camping is permitted only at Platte River Campground, White Pine Backcountry Campground and D.H. Day Campground, each posted and accessible from the shoreline. But to break up the days more evenly, this description includes spending the second night in the quaint town of Empire at a lodge or a bed-and-breakfast. Some backpackers might recoil at the notion of bedding down anywhere but in their small tent, but in the middle of a 36-mile walk, I find a hot shower, a soft bed and a cold beer a rather inviting thought.

Trip Planner

Maps: It would require four USGS topos to cover this route (*Frankfort, Beulah, Empire,* and *Glen Haven*), a lot of paper that is really not necessary. A better alternative is the *Sleeping Bear Dunes National Lakeshore Map & Trail Guide* from Michigan Maps, Inc (231-264-6800; www.MichiganMapsOnline.com), which covers the entire walk on a single sheet.

Getting There: This walk begins with Old Indian Trail and ends at D.H. Day Campground. To reach the Old Indian trailhead from the Philip Hart Visitor Center in Empire, head south on M-22 for 12 miles and look for the entrance to the trailhead parking lot, which is posted on the north (right) side of the road. To reach the D.H. Campground head north on M-22 from the visitor center and then veer left on M-109. Within 5 miles you'll swing right toward Glen Arbor and pass the campground entrance just before reaching the town.

Fees & Reservations: A vehicle park pass ($10 weekly, $20 annual) is required for this walk and can be purchased from the Philip Hart Visitor Center. Campsites at D.H. Day are $12 per night, at White Pine $5 per night, and at Platte River Campground $16 for regular sites and $12 for walk-in sites. You can not reserve sites at D.H. Day or White Pine but can at Platte River (877-444-6777; *www.recreation.gov*).

For lodging in Empire there is the Lakeshore Inn (231-326-5145) with 11 rooms at the corner of M-72 and M-22, a half mile from Lake Michigan. There is also a number of bed-and-breakfasts in town with the closest to the beach being the Cottonwood Inn (231-326-5535; *www.cottonwoodinnbb. com*). Also in Empire are restaurants, coffee shops, a supermarket, and Joe's Friendly Tavern.

Information: For more information contact the Philip Hart Visitor Center (231-326-5134; *www.nps.gov/slbe*), which is open daily.

Trail Guide

Day One (13 miles) This trek begins with the only trail you'll follow for three days. From the trailhead a level path immediately enters the woods and quickly reaches a posted junction. Stay to the right (north) at this junction and the next one to follow the trail marked by black triangles indicating an "Advanced" route for cross-country skiers. This route is by far the most interesting of the three as it winds over a series of low dunes, forested in mixed hardwoods and pines, and passes small marshes.

In 1.5 miles from the trailhead, a third junction is posted where you head right (north) to quickly enter an area of open dunes and then arrive at Lake Michigan in a quarter mile. This is a scenic spot, even though a couple of cottages are visible to the west. To the east you view nothing but beach, while out in Lake Michigan is South Manitou Island, its perched dunes clearly visible.

Begin your beach walk. To the right (east) the shoreline is a strip of sand usually 20 to 30 feet wide, depending on the lake level, and bordered by low grassy dunes. Eventually the beach curves to the northeast and begins rounding Platte River Point. Here the beach widens considerably until you reach the river itself after 5 miles of beach walking or 6.5 miles from the Old Indian trailhead. At the mouth of the Platte River the water is rarely more than ankle-deep most of the summer and usually a traffic jam of colorful inflatables and inner tubes whose owners have just floated downstream.

Cross the river and head right (west) a short distance along the shore to reach Lake Township Park, where there are restrooms, drinking

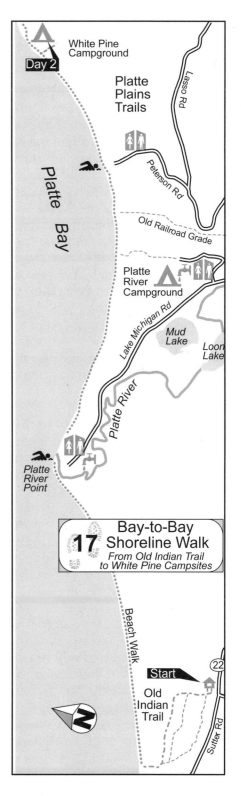

water, picnic tables and a very busy parking lot. Head left (east) to continue to Platte Plains and White Pine Backcountry Campground. Within 2.5 miles you pass the first of several blue-tipped poles along the beach. This one is the path that heads south a quarter mile to Platte River Campground, where there are restrooms, drinking water, and walk-in sites for backpackers. In another half mile is another post marking the end of the Old Railroad Grade Trail that also heads south to the campground. Still another half mile east, or 4 miles from the mouth of the Platte River, you pass the end of Peterson Road, the reason for the sunbathers on the beach. Just down the road are vault toilets.

Beyond Peterson Road, the narrow beach will most likely be deserted again for the next 2 miles. The scenery is stunning as the water is often calm, and on the horizon you cannot only see South Manitou Island, but also the towering Sleeping Bear Dunes on the mainland. Keep one eye on the low dunes along the beach, however. Within 6 miles from the mouth of Platte River or 12.5 miles from the start of the day, you'll spot a "White Pine Campground" sign, marking the trail that heads south to the walk-in sites.

White Pine is a short walk from Lake Michigan and has six sites, a fire ring and a vault toilet located in a narrow ravine. Even when Platte River Campground is bustling with summer tourists, these secluded sites are a quiet escape well worth the hike in. In the evening you can return to the beach and watch the sun melt into Lake Michigan. The perfect way to end the first day.

Day Two (8 miles) Return to the shoreline and head right (north). The beach remains narrow, and the dunes low for the next 2 miles. It's easy to tell when you near the Esch Road access. You cross Otter Creek and the beach suddenly becomes a wide and sandy spot with usually a number of sunbathers scattered about. The swimming here is excellent, while a path leads into the woods to a parking area and vault toilet but no source of drinking water. Esch Road marks the north end of the Platte Plains hiking area of the park, and from 1880 to 1911 was the site of a bustling lumber town named Aral. The town included a sawmill, stores, homes, and a wharf at the mouth of Otter Creek, but when the nearby trees disappeared, so did Aral.

Heading north from the Esch Road access, the beach quickly narrows, and in a half mile the dunes begin to close in. Within a mile of the road the dunes are towering over you. Here you are most likely alone again, looking at the mesmerizing waves of Lake Michigan or South Manitou Island floating on a blue horizon. Eventually you round Empire Bluffs Point, almost 4 miles from Esch Road or 6 miles from the start of the day. The famous perched dunes now rise almost 500 feet above while popping back into view is Sleeping Bear Dunes to the north.

What is also visible for the first time is the Manning Lighthouse, overlooking Empire's Lake Michigan Park and South Bar Lake, the end of the second day. The park is a quick 2-mile walk away and just before you arrive, you pass through a private beach that is posted. Even if you're not stopping for the day, Lake Michigan Park is a good spot for an extended break. Facilities include restrooms, drinking water, a picnic pavilion, and two beaches, one on the Great Lake and the other on South Bar Lake, which is usually the warmer of the two.

Empire, named after a schooner that was icebound there in 1865, was a site of a lumber mill by 1873 and an incorporated town by 1895. At one point the Empire Lumber Company operated one of the largest hardwood mills in the area. Today, Empire is a sleepy little hamlet that serves as the gateway to Sleeping Bear Dunes National Lakeshore. The supermarket and taverns are on Front Street, a quarter mile away; the Philip Hart Visitor Center and Lakeshore Inn are a half mile from the beach. While this day is short, it's easy to while away an afternoon in Empire, which includes a wonderful museum complex of four buildings.

Day Three (15 miles) Return to Lake Michigan Park and continue heading north along the shoreline. You'll quickly pass a number of "Private Beach – Shoreline Walking Permitted" signs, acknowledging the State Supreme Court decision in 2005 that beach walking is a traditional right in Michigan. The largest cluster of cottages on this hike are passed in the first mile. Along this stretch is the *Jennie and Annie*, a two-masted schooner that sank during a November storm in 1872 with seven crew members

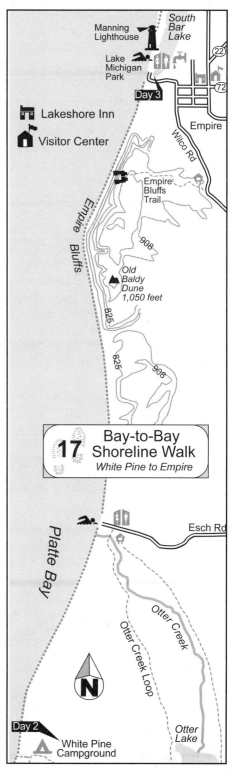

perishing when they tried to swim to safety. The vessel ran aground close to shoreline, and during calm conditions is occasionally spotted from the beach between South and North Bar lakes.

Within 3 miles you cross the outlet stream from North Bar Lake, and through a gap in the dunes you can see and easily reach this beautiful, long narrow lake. The area is designated the North Bar Lake Nature Preserve as it is home to several rare and endangered species including Pitcher's thistle, Michigan monkey's flower, and the prairie warbler. A trail around the lake and a series of wooded steps over the dune that separates the two lakes will lead you to a dayuse parking area with toilets but no drinking water.

A few more cottages to the north are passed as you head toward a large wooded slope that marks the south end of Sleeping Bear Dunes, the park's trademark perched dunes. Within 1.5 miles from North Bar Lake or 4.5 miles from Empire the trees quickly give way to slopes of loose sand and clumps of grass. You'll immediately spot a large observation deck near the top of them, reached from Pierce Stocking Scenic Drive and during the summer filled with visitors waving down at you.

Once beyond it, you begin the best part of this three-day walk. For the next 4 miles the dramatic dunes tower above, at times more than 400 feet, while a feeling of wilderness-like solitude descends on you. This is also the best area for beachcombing and hunting for Petoskey stones. After a storm the debris that washes ashore is amazing at times; sunglasses, flip-flops, cans of soda, dead fish, bits of shipwrecks. The beach is very narrow here, and at one point you'll reach a half-mile stretch of large rocks and little sand. Those who decided to do this walk in running shoes will pay a painful price here.

Eventually the high dunes lose their lofty elevation while trees begin

Looking for Shipwrecks in Sleeping Bear

Looking for shipwrecks? This is the trek to do it, say park officials who have put together a brochure entitled *Beachcombing for Shipwrecks*.

Most of the ships ran aground close to shore, often within 400 yards of the beach. That makes the wrecks susceptible to storms, waves and shoreline ice. Sometimes a hard blow will uncover a huge section of a hull. But more times than not, the forces of nature break off small pieces of the wreck and toss them ashore for hikers to puzzle over them.

Timber from ships often is white oak – black when wet, whitish when dry – with rounded edges or corners. The best telltale signs that the piece is from a wreck are iron rings, spikes, pegs or fasteners attached to the wood.

Keep in mind that a lot of wood you'll see will be from docks, breakwalls, steps and boathouses. If the wood has straight edges and square corners, it's most likely a land structure. Shipwreck wood is often curved with metal fasteners every few inches.

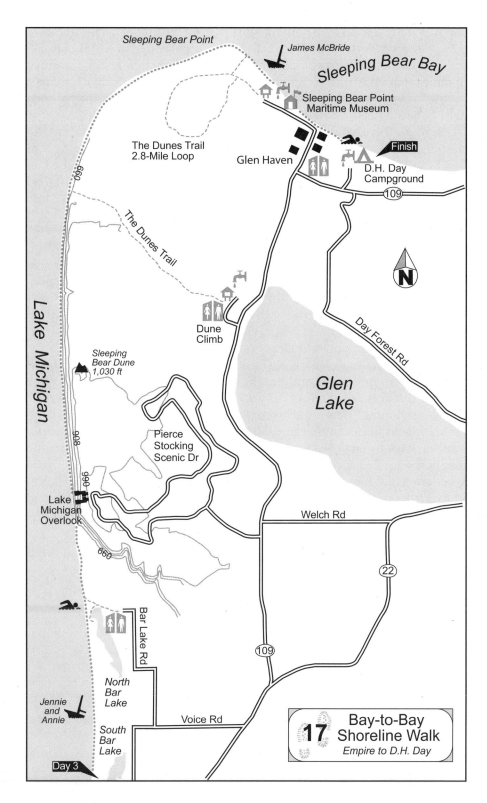

Sleeping Bear Point

James McBride

Sleeping Bear Bay

Sleeping Bear Point
Maritime Museum

The Dunes Trail
2.8-Mile Loop

Glen Haven

Finish

D.H. Day
Campground

109

The Dunes Trail

Lake Michigan

Dune
Climb

Sleeping
Bear Dune
1,030 ft

Day Forest Rd

Glen
Lake

Pierce
Stocking
Scenic Dr

990

660

Lake
Michigan
Overlook

Welch Rd

22

660

N

Bar Lake Rd

109

North
Bar
Lake

Jennie
and
Annie

South
Bar
Lake

Voice Rd

17 Bay-to-Bay
Shoreline Walk
Empire to D.H. Day

Day 3

popping into view up the shoreline. Just past the first set of cottonwoods or 6.25 miles after leaving North Bar Lake you spot a blue tipped post that marks the west end of the Dunes Trail. This trail is a 2-mile trek across a number of dunes that ends with a romp down the park's famous Dune Climb to a dayuse area with restrooms, drinking water, and a small store that is open during the summer.

Beyond the Dunes Trail, the shoreline begins curving east around Sleeping Bear Point, reaching the point in 3 miles and entering Sleeping Bear Bay. Keep an eye out for shipwreck pieces here. Most of them are washed up from the *James McBride*, a two-masted brig bound for Chicago with a load of lumber when she was forced ashore near the point in 1857 and sank. Timber and iron fittings from the ship have been appearing on the beach since 1988.

Within a half mile of rounding the point you pass a blue-tipped post, marking the beach trailhead to the park's Sleeping Bear Point Loop, a 2.8-mile trail through the dunes. In another half mile you reach the Sleeping Bear Point Maritime Museum. This U.S. life-saving service station was built in 1901 on the point itself to assist the growing number of wrecks in Manitou Passage. When a dune threatened to engulf the buildings in 1931, the station was moved east to its present location.

Today the station is a maritime museum that includes one room outfitted as a steamer wheelhouse and another as surfmen's quarters. During the summer the museum stages a daily reenactment of U.S. life-saving service rescue techniques. There are also restrooms and drinking water here, making the station an ideal spot for an extended break. The museum is open daily from late May through September, including 10:30 a.m. to 5 p.m. during the summer.

Beyond the museum it's a mile to the historic village of Glen Haven, whose red cannery boat museum is clearly visible from the beach, and another half mile to D.H. Day Campground.

South Manitou Island
Sleeping Bear Dunes National Lakeshore

18

County: Leelanau
Nearest Town: Leland
Distance: 12 miles
Hiking Time: Two to three days
Highest Elevation Gain: 125 feet
Difficulty: Moderate
Highlights: Spectacular shoreline dunes, great beaches, shipwrecks

During the summer South Manitou Island is a tropical-like paradise with crescent-shaped beaches, calm, turquoise water and a slow, idyllic pace to it. The 5,260-acre island is laced with 17 miles of trails and old roads but, like tropical islands everywhere, the shoreline is too beautiful for most visitors to stray very far from.

That's why one of most popular trips among backpackers who step off the boat here is simply to follow the beach. This trek is a mix, hiking old two-tracks and trails 3.7 miles to South Manitou's most remote campground the day you arrive, followed by a 7-mile beach walk on the second day. On the third day you return to the ferry wharf by either trail or beach.

This 12-mile trek can easily be done as an overnight hike, arriving on the ferry at 11:30 a.m. and being back at the wharf the next day well before it leaves at 4 p.m. But why rush? South Manitou, a place free of vehicles and rush-hour traffic, is one of Michigan's most interesting islands and those who have never been here before often regret having to leave after only two days.

Located 7 miles off Sleeping Bear Point on the mainland, South Manitou is the southernmost island of a Lake Michigan archipelago that stretches northeast to the Straits of Mackinac. The island's west side features perched dunes that rise more than 400 feet above Lake Michigan while old farms, a schoolhouse and other remains of the island's agricultural past are scattered inland.

Like its sister island, North Manitou, the vast majority of campers and hikers reach the island on a ferry that departs from Leland's Fishtown. It's a 90-minute trip, and along the way you will view Sleeping Bear Bluffs, North Manitou's scenic west shore, and North Manitou Shoal Light in the middle of the Manitou Passage.

Unlike North Manitou, where backcountry camping is allowed anywhere, you can only camp in three designated campgrounds on South Manitou: Weather Station, Bay, and Popple. All three overlook a stretch of Lake Michigan beach and have toilets, while Weather Station has a pump for drinking water. You must arrive at South Manitou fully equipped as there are no stores for food, supplies, or a forgotten tent peg. You will also need a filter or the ability to boil water at Popple Campground as the nearest pump is 2 miles away.

For a shorter backpacking adventure, an ideal one for kids, hike to Weather Station Campground, an easy 1.3-mile walk from the ferry dock. The next day you can leave the packs behind and continue west to explore the perched dunes and the old growth cedars known as the Valley of the Giants before returning to the wharf to catch the ferry.

Trip Planner

Maps: The USGS topo *South Manitou* covers the entire island, showing the roads, campgrounds, and most of the trails. The National Park Service also puts out a small reference map that is inadequate once you're on the trails.

Getting There: Manitou Island Transit (231-256-9061 *www.leelanau.com/ manitou*) provides passenger ferry transportation to South Manitou Island from Leland, a small resort town on the west side of the Leelanau Peninsula 24 miles north of Traverse City. From a wharf in Leland's Fishtown, a ferry departs daily from mid-June through August at 10 a.m. and reaches the island at 11:30 a.m., where it docks until its departure at 4 p.m. From June 1 to June 15 there is no service on Tuesday and Thursday, and in May, September, and October service is reduced even further. The round-trip fare is $29 for adults and $15 for children.

There are approximately 3 miles of dirt road on South Manitou, and Manitou Island Transit runs a motorized tour past sights such as the old schoolhouse, farms, and the main cemetery. The company also offers a lift to hikers to where the trail swings close to the road, which shaves off the first mile of the walk. Check with transit officials for details, drop-off spots, and prices.

Fees & Reservations: A vehicle park pass ($10 weekly, $20 annual) is required to visit South Manitou as well as a backcountry permit ($5 per night for up to four people) to camp there. You can purchase vehicle permits and backcountry permits from the Philip A. Hart Visitor Center in Empire, or during the summer from a ranger stationed at Fishtown from 8:30 to 10 a.m. During July and August, advance reservation is strongly recommended for the ferry, especially on the weekends.

Information: The best place for information is Philip Hart Visitor Center (231-326-5134; *www.nps.gov/slbe*) in Empire. There is a ranger station (231-334-3976) on the island during the summer with limited staff.

Trail Guide

Day One (3.7 miles) After stepping off the ferry, head up the dock to the boathouse that was built in 1901 as part of the U.S. life saving station established here. The surf boat that was used to rescue sailors still sits inside the boathouse, but of more interest to many visitors is the three-dimensional

South Manitou Island includes several shipwrecks, including the Francisco Morazan, *a freighter that ran aground in 1960.*

map that shows the rugged contour of the island. Rangers conduct a brief orientation for both hikers and campers in the boathouse and then hand out backcountry permits. The cluster of buildings surrounding the boathouse at the east end of Burdick Road are known as the Village and include restrooms, drinking water, the two-story lightkeeper's home that now houses the ranger station, and a small museum.

There are two ways to reach the trail to Popple Campground on the north side of the island. You can head west on Burdick Road for a mile and then north on Ohio Road for 2 miles, passing the restored schoolhouse and a water pump along the way and ending at Johann Hutzler's farm. Keep in mind this is also the route the motor tour follows.

Beach lovers and others will want to head west on Burdick Road but then quickly veer right onto the road posted with a sign for Bay Campground. This road stays close to the shoreline of Crescent Bay and in a half mile reaches the camping area. Bay is the largest campground on the island with 25 sites, a toilet, and fire rings. Half of the sites are tucked among the trees offering some protection from the sun and lake breezes. The rest of the sites are in the open with views of the water. All of them are only a few steps from a stunning beach.

From Bay Campground a trail continues north along the shore, passing side trails to the ruins of the Burdick General Store and the Bay Cemetery. You reach the east end of a wide trail known as Old Chicago Road, 0.6 mile from the campground or 1.2 miles from the boathouse. South Manitou's first village was located here, clustered around a lumber mill and Burton's Wharf, the principal pier on the island until the 1920s. Remains of the wharf can still be seen in the bay.

Old Chicago Road is ruler-straight and extends to the heart of South Manitou. Within 0.7 mile you arrive at the intersection with Ohio Road where a half mile south (left) is the school house and a pump, the nearest source of safe drinking water to Popple Campground. West of Old Chicago Road is what is commonly referred to as the Farm Loop, a 1.75-mile loop past a pair of restored farmhouses and the ruins of a third.

To reach Popple Campground you head north (right) on Ohio Road passing South Manitou's main cemetery and then entering the woods to arrive at a junction 0.7 mile from the intersection or 2.7 miles from the boathouse. The cemetery is well preserved and contains several rows of headstones, most from the longtime families that homestead and farmed South Manitou. One of the homesteaders was the Hutzler family. By heading left at the junction and staying on the old road, you arrive at the farm of Johann Hutzler within 0.3 of a mile. The site includes a small barn built in the 1800s and the Hutzler farmhouse that was erected in the 1920s.

A trail continues north from the barn into the woods and within a quarter mile comes to a junction. Head north (left) and follow the trail as it climbs a wooded dune then descends to Popple Campground, 0.7 mile from the Hutzler Farm or 3.7 miles from the boathouse. Popple has seven

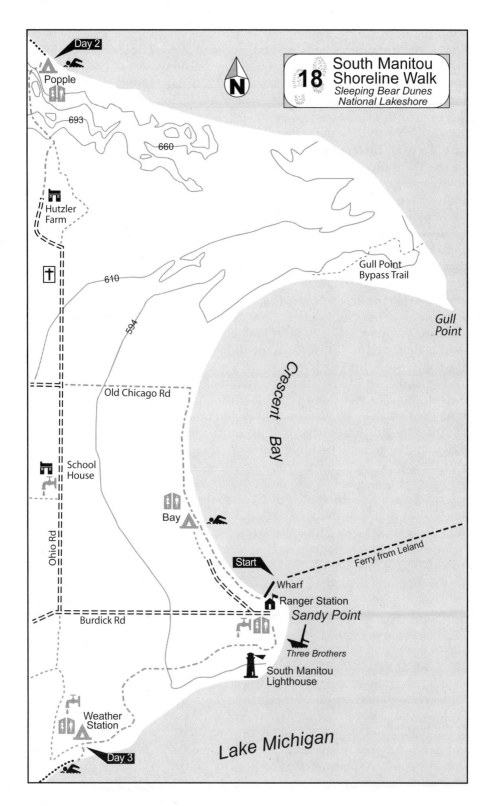

Day 2
Popple
693
660

N

18 South Manitou
Shoreline Walk
*Sleeping Bear Dunes
National Lakeshore*

Hutzler
Farm

610

594

Gull Point
Bypass Trail

*Gull
Point*

Old Chicago Rd

Crescent Bay

School
House

Bay

Ferry from Leland

Ohio Rd

Start

Wharf
Ranger Station
Sandy Point

Burdick Rd

Three Brothers

South Manitou
Lighthouse

Weather
Station

Day 3

Lake Michigan

campsites from most of which you can see Lake Michigan through the trees. It's the island's most secluded and isolated spot to spend a night but beware: *There is a lot of poison ivy in this area!* From the sites you can descend a low sandy bluff to another beautiful beach with a magnificent view of North Manitou Island, less than 4 miles away. The large blowout on the south shore of North Manitou is Old Baldy.

Day Two (7 miles) From Popple Campground hit the beach for a day on the shoreline. In the past hikers occasionally had to climb up a bluff or enter the water to skirt an obstacle like a fallen tree. But the low lake levels of recent years have made this easy shoreline walk even easier, and you shouldn't have any problem keeping your boots dry.

To the west (left) you immediately begin to round the island's most northern point and within a half mile, South Manitou's perched dunes are already towering more than 150 feet above you. You sidle this steep fortress of sand for the next 4 miles. At one point the perched dunes rise 425 feet from Lake Michigan. These spectacular dunes make up the entire west shore of South Manitou. Only Sleeping Bear Bluffs across the Manitou Passage on the mainland are higher and more dramatic. Those perched dunes, however, are crawling with tourists most of the summer. Out here, you're by yourself, in what feels like the edge of the world. Or at least the edge of Michigan.

For the adventurous, when you near the southwest corner of the island you can drop the packs and scale the steep dunes, a knee-bending climb of more than 300 feet. From the top of the dunes, the views of Lake Michigan and the mainland are extensive, while further inland are ghost forests, trees that were buried and killed by the migrating sand only to be uncovered later.

Back on the shoreline the sandy beach becomes rockier as you round South Manitou's southwest corner. Eventually you swing east for the first time all day and spot the shipwreck. It takes another half mile or 5.2 miles from Popple Campground to arrive at a beach directly across the grounded *Francisco Morazan*, the middle third of which still stands above the water less than 100 yards offshore.

The freighter departed Chicago on November 27, 1960, and was bound for Holland with 940 tons of cargo, a crew of thirteen, its captain, and his pregnant wife. The next day it ran into 40-mile-per-hour winds, snow, and fog that made a virtual whiteout. The captain thought he was rounding Beaver Island, more than 70 miles away, when he ran aground. A Coast Guard cutter and helicopter rescued the 15 persons, but the wreck was left behind to be forever battered by Lake Michigan. Now it's probably the most popular destination for hikers on the island.

The wreck moves out of view when you round the next point south. In the middle of this bay is Theo Beck's farmhouse, built in the late 1800s and one of the many abandoned buildings still remaining on the island. The farmhouse is often referred to as "The Lodge" ever since two Detroit

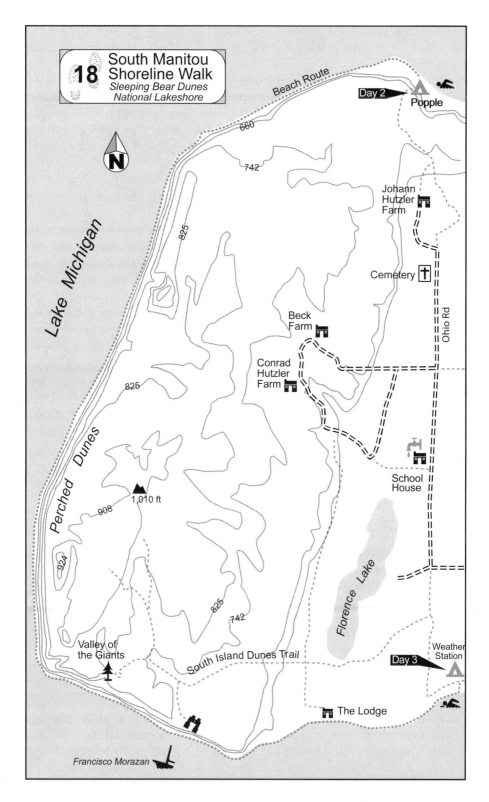

18 South Manitou Shoreline Walk
Sleeping Bear Dunes National Lakeshore

N

Beach Route

Day 2
Popple

660

742

Johann Hutzler Farm

Cemetery

Lake Michigan

Beck Farm

Conrad Hutzler Farm

Ohio Rd

825

825

School House

Perched Dunes

908

1,010 ft

924

Florence Lake

742

825

Valley of the Giants

South Island Dunes Trail

Day 3

Weather Station

The Lodge

Francisco Morazan

businessmen purchased it in the 1940s and briefly operated it as a retreat for Rotarians. For the first time since leaving Popple Campground, you can leave the beach and pick up a trail near the farmhouse. From here you can head north 0.3 mile to reach the South Island Dunes Trail.

Stay on the beach and around the next point is the beach below Weather Station Campground, 1.8 miles from the shipwreck or 7 miles from Popple. The campground is up on the bluff and has 20 sites, a pump for drinking water, toilet, and fire rings. Five sites are near the edge of the bluff and give way to a dramatic view of Lake Michigan and Sleeping Bear Bluffs 7 miles away on the mainland. In the summer, you can sit on this bluff and watch freighters slowly steam their way through the Manitou Passage, the reason these sites are always the first to go.

Day Three (1.3 miles) To reach the boathouse and ferry wharf, you can follow the trail east out of Weather Station for a walk of 1.3 miles that pops out of the woods near the South Manitou Lighthouse. Or you can return to the beach.

The beach is actually the shorter route to Sandy Point and a more scenic one. For most of the way, you can see the top of the lighthouse sticking out above the trees. Built in 1871, the lighthouse featured a Third Order Fresnel

South Manitou Island in Its Heyday

When the Erie Canal was opened in 1826, commercial shipping increased dramatically on the Great Lakes. The Manitou Passage quickly became a crucial shortcut for vessels traveling between Chicago and Buffalo, with South Manitou Island becoming an important fueling stop for steamers. The island's Crescent Bay was the last deep harbor on the voyage until boats reached Chicago 220 miles to the south. From 1860 to the early 1900s, so many ships sought its protection that it was often referred to as the "Forest of Masts."

To help guide captains through the narrow passage, a small light was erected on a house here in 1840, the first navigational light on Lake Michigan. But the shipwrecks continued to mount, so it was replaced by a two-story brick building with a 35-foot tower in 1858. Finally in 1871 the island's third lighthouse, featuring a 104-foot tower, was constructed and then manned by a string of 17 keepers and 32 assistant keepers until its 87-year operation ended in 1958.

By the time the current lighthouse was lit, South Manitou already had a well-established community of self-sufficient farmers. The isolation of the island provided an ideal environment for growing prize-winning rye, beans, and peas, while passing ships carried off the surplus crops to mainland markets. At its peak in the 1880s, South Manitou had a year-round population of almost 100 people, including 13 farmers, two fishermen, a wood merchant selling fuel to steamers, and a grocer.

A pair of backpackers relax on the beach at South Manitou Island while waiting for the ferry to arrive from Leland.

lens from Paris that on a clear night was visible 18 miles away. It could well withstand the violent winds of Lake Michigan. The walls of the tower are five feet thick at the base and taper to less than three feet at the top, and they are hollow inside, allowing them to sway in the wind. The spiral staircase inside is not attached to the walls, which allows it to move as well.

It's 117 steps to the top platform, but the view is worth every one of them. The lighthouse is usually locked, but several times a day rangers give a presentation about the light that ends with a climb to the top. Times are posted on the tower door.

A boardwalk leads from the lighthouse back to the boathouse or you can continue along the beach to reach the wharf via Sandy Point. Along the way you'll pass another shipwreck. The *Three Brothers* ran aground in 1911 and now lies on the steep slope just off Sandy Point. Because her bow is in fairly shallow water, it has since become Michigan's most popular wreck for snorkelers.

At North Manitou, backpackers pass numerous buildings, tools, and other leftover remnants from when the island was home to farmers and loggers in the early 1900s.

North Manitou Island
Sleeping Bear Dunes National Lakeshore

19

County: Leelanau
Nearest Town: Leland
Distance: 16.6 miles
Hiking Time: Three days
Highest Elevation Gain: 231 feet
Difficulty: Moderate
Highlights: Beaches, remnant farms, backcountry camping

Wild, isolated, and remote, North Manitou Island offers backpackers a completely different experience than its smaller sibling just to the south. Or practically anywhere else in the Lower Peninsula. On this 14,753-acre island the trails are longer, the possible itineraries more numerous, and day visitors rare. The places where you can pitch your tent are almost limitless because, unlike South Manitou, there are few restrictions on backcountry camping.

In short, many arrive at North Manitou to escape. They want to spend their days hiking and their nights camped on a bluff overlooking Lake Michigan at a place where there are no cars or city lights. Just the stars overhead and the roar of the surf on deserted beaches below. These are such rare qualities that North Manitou Island is the only slice of the Sleeping Bear Dunes National Lakeshore that the National Park Service manages as a wilderness. Among the strict rules the NPS enforces is a ban on motors, off-road vehicles, mountain bikes, and pets.

North Manitou is 7.7 miles long, 4.2 miles wide, and laced with more than 22 miles of designated trails that are posted with directional and mileage signs. Even more unsigned trails exist, and all paths are either old roads or railroad grades. The trails wind through impressive stands of maple and beech, through clearings that used to be farm fields, past serene Lake Manitou, and over the open dunes at the southern end of the island. The highest point on North Manitou is 1,001 feet, a rather remote spot in North Manitou's rugged northwest corner. But overall, the hiking is level and the trails are not difficult to follow.

North Manitou also had a history of residents farming, logging and saving sailors. But unlike South Manitou, the building and leftover remnants are not as numerous or as well-preserved. The lack of a natural harbor delayed the first woodcutter arriving at North Manitou until 1850 or 10 years after they began cutting on South Manitou. Farming soon followed and in 1860 North Manitou recorded its largest population: 269 residents with almost a dozen families maintaining farms. In 1877, a U.S. life saving station, including a lighthouse on Dimmick's Point, was built on the island. For 23 years the North Manitou Light was the only source of guidance for ships in the treacherous Manitou Passage until stations were established later at South Manitou and Sleeping Bear Point.

Even summer cottages began appearing on the island at the turn of the century and many are still standing today in the Village, where the NPS maintains a ranger station and backpackers step ashore from the ferry. But by the 1920s most of North Manitou was under single ownership, and used primarily as a private hunting preserve until the park acquired control in 1984. To improve the hunting, nine whitetail deer were released in 1927, and the small herd, without any natural predators, exploded to more than 2,000 by 1981. The state of Michigan began staging special deer hunts on the island in 1985, and today the herd numbers less than 100.

Other wildlife that might be seen includes garner snakes and especially chipmunks, which are encountered too frequently to be natural. Chipmunks have become so troublesome to backpackers since they invade packs and food supplies that rangers urge visitors to hang their food in the trees, almost as if you were in bear country.

Even more so than South Manitou, the vast majority of visitors arrive at North Manitou onboard the ferry from Leland. On this island the ferry merely arrives, unloads and departs, the reason for the lack of day visitors.

A park ranger meets all ferries and gives a brief orientation on the island's special rules. That includes a ban on all fires other than the community fire ring in the Village Campground. Either bring a backpacker's stove or feast on cold meals. There are no stores here. You must be totally self-sufficient when you arrive and pack all trash out when you leave. The only source of safe drinking water is at the ranger station; all other water should be treated. You can camp anywhere on the island except:

- Within sight or sound of a building, a major trail, or another camper.
- Within 300 feet of an inland water source such as a lake or stream.
- On the beach along Lake Michigan.

After arriving many backpackers hike to the west side of North Manitou where they set up camp for two or three days in some of the most scenic backcountry campsites found in Michigan. Then they explore the rest of the island – without the burden of backpack – before returning to the Village to catch the ferry home.

This trek is the classic walk around the island and is described in a counterclockwise direction from the Village, the easiest direction to walk it, with nights spent at two of the most scenic areas: Lake Manitou and Fredrickson Place. This makes for a short, 2.6-mile walk the first day and a 5-mile trek the third day. To be on the ferry when it departs at 11 a.m. you either need to be on the trail by 7:30 a.m. or plan to spend a third night in the Village Campground.

Trip Planner

Maps: The USGS topo, *North Manitou Island*, covers the entire island and shows the major trails. The National Park Service's North Manitou Island

As on many islands in Lake Michigan, the lack of predators has made North Manitou a home to a large population of garter snakes.

brochure has a map with mileage and the major farms listed.

Getting There: Manitou Island Transit (231-256-9061; *www.leelanau.com/manitou*) also provides ferry transportation to North Manitou from Leland, a small resort town reached from Traverse City via M-22 and M-204. From a wharf in Leland's Fishtown a ferry departs daily from mid-June through Labor Day at 10 a.m. and reaches the island at 11:10 a.m. *It immediately loads* *and departs North Manitou!* Don't be late at the dock or you'll be spending an unplanned night on the island. In May, September, and October service is reduced and you'll need to call the ferry company for a current schedule. The round-trip fare is the same as it is for South Manitou, $29 for adults and $15 for children.

Fees & Reservations: The park fees are also the same as on South Manitou. A vehicle pass ($10 weekly, $20 annual) is required as well as a backcountry permit ($5 per night for up to four people) to camp on North Manitou. You can purchase vehicle permits and backcountry permits from the Philip A. Hart Visitor Center in Empire or during the summer from a ranger stationed at Fishtown from 8:30 a.m. to 10 a.m. During July and August advance reservations are strongly recommended for the ferry, especially on the weekends.

Information: For more information contact the Philip A. Hart Visitor Center in Empire (231-326-5134; *www.nps.gov/slbe*).

Trail Guide

Day One (2.5 miles) From the ferry dock you head into the Village that is surrounded by a 27-acre clearing, much of it an old airstrip. The ranger station is a former lightkeeper's residence and on the side of it is a water faucet while nearby is a pair of vault toilets. Just to the south is the original boathouse for the U.S. life-saving station, the oldest building on the island dating back to the 1870s. On the north side of the trail you pass another water faucet, trash containers, and a small visitors center where rangers hold their camper orientation. The beach near the Village, like throughout most of the island, is a beautiful stretch of sand littered with small pebbles and bleached driftwood.

Just west of the Village is a posted four-way junction. A short walk to the north (right) is the Village Campground, where you'll find eight numbered sites, two community fire rings, and a toilet. To the south (left), Fredrickson Place lies 5.1 miles away, while due west is the trail to Lake Manitou.

The trail to the serene lake begins with a gentle climb across the old airstrip and then returns to the woods. Within a mile from the dock, it passes the old apple orchard of the Frank Farm. At one point North Manitou supported more than 3,000 apple trees as well as pear and cherry trees scattered in small orchards across the island. Just beyond Frank Farm you re-enter the woods and pass a side trail that departs southwest (left) to a spot on Lake Manitou known as the Boathouse. The actual boathouse is no longer there, but the area is still a pleasant place to camp.

The main trail heads northwest (right) from the Boathouse junction and in a mile or 2.2 miles from NPS dock arrives at the clearing known as Bennon's Place. To the west is the lake, reached by a side trail that passes through a small clearing closer to the lake known as Fiskes just before reaching the water. Most backpackers set up camp at Bennon's or Fiskes and then explore the lake by following a rough trail along the shoreline.

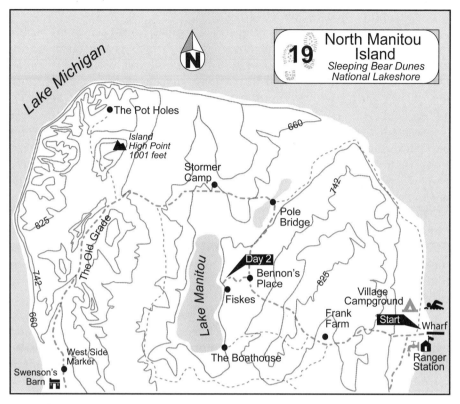

Lake Manitou has healthy populations of smallmouth bass and perch that experience little fishing pressure. The most successful anglers haul in a belly boat, an inflatable raft, or even a pair of waders to get away from the shoreline and reach deeper sections of the lake.

Day Two (9 miles) Return to Bennon's Place and head north (left) on the main trail through two more clearings. In 1.2 miles from Lake Manitou, you reach a junction called the Pole Bridge, which isn't a bridge at all, but rather a culvert over a stream in a large swamp. One trail departs north (right) to loop back to the Village, a walk of 2.8 miles.

Another trail heads west (left) and is posted "West Side." This trail (left) begins as a level walk and within 0.6 mile reaches Stormer Camp. The camp was the site of a logging operation that operated until 1950, and today a handful of old cars and even a set of wagon wheels can still be seen along the edge of the grassy clearing. The trail remains level for another half mile until Davenport Camp, the site of a second logging camp, and then you begin a steady ascent.

Eventually you top off at a side trail that leads north (right) to the gullies in the northwest corner of the island known as the Pot Holes. The main trail begins to curve south (left) here as it passes through the most rugged section of North Manitou. The route is actually an old railroad grade dating back to 1910, and it's easy to envision the tracks running through the hills to a logger's camp known as Crescent City.

Three miles from the Pole Bridge or 4.2 miles from Lake Manitou the former railroad grade begins a rapid descent, which is the rationale for walking this stretch from east to west. Within a mile you lose more than 250 feet in elevation and break out into a long, narrow clearing. At the south end of the clearing, you re-enter the woods briefly, then arrive at Swenson's, a huge field.

Swenson's is more than a half mile long, and a popular spot for backpackers to spend the night. You can see glimpses of Lake Michigan even from the trail, but if you cut across the field to the bluffs above the beach, you'll be greeted with an excellent view of South Manitou Island and the perched dunes on its west side.

In the middle of the clearing is the "West Side" marker, while at the south end are the ruins of the Swenson's farm, including a very impressive barn. All around are wild strawberry plants and raspberry patches. Camping spots abound here, and a pleasant afternoon can be spent hiking the beach north to view the steep bluffs in the northwest corner of the island and climbing the dunes that cut into them.

Just before Swenson's barn, the main trail enters the woods, heading south along what is obviously the raised bed of the old railroad line, and within a half mile reaches a posted junction. To the east (left) is Centerline Trail that cuts across the middle of the island to reach the ranger station in 5.1 miles.

You head southwest (right). Within a quarter mile, the trail swings to the south and then comes to an unmarked junction with two trails, 1.6 miles from Swenson's clearing or 6.8 miles from Lake Manitou. These two side trails veer to the east towards Tamarack Lake, a small lake that is hard to find. The main trail continues due south and is easy to identify. Within a half mile, views of Lake Michigan open up between the trees as the trail arrives on a bluff above the lake.

You remain on the bluff until the trail descends to the Johnson Place, reached 2.6 miles from the Swenson's clearing or 7.8 miles from Lake Manitou. Johnson Place is a small clearing with easy access to the beach below, making it another popular camping area. Unlike Swenson's, all that remains of this homestead are small remnants of an old apple orchard.

The trail departs the clearing, enters the woods, where dunes are pouring down between the trees, then swings inland. From the Johnson Place it's 1.2 miles to Fredrickson Place via the foot trail. An alternative route and an easier hike is to simply follow the beach from one clearing to the next, beginning from Swenson's.

There are also no buildings at Fredrickson Place, a homestead farm that was settled in the 1840s, but there are some beautiful spots in which to pitch a tent. Here you can set up camp on a grassy bluff high above the lakeshore and have an incredible view of South Manitou Island and the mainland. After setting up camp, give serious consideration to hiking south along the

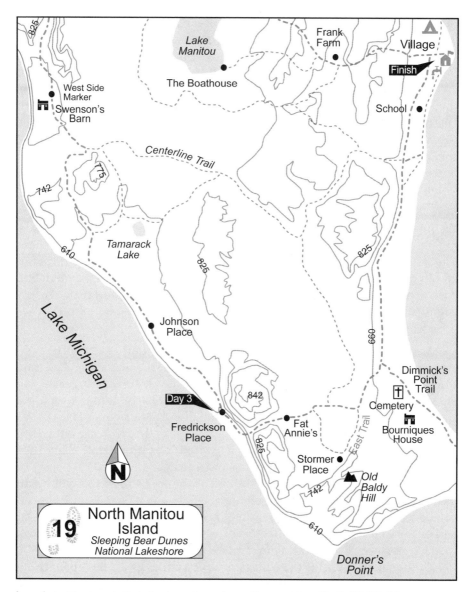

Lake
Manitou

Frank
Farm

Village

Finish

The Boathouse

West Side
Marker

Swenson's
Barn

School

Centerline Trail

Tamarack
Lake

Johnson
Place

Dimmick's
Point
Trail

Cemetery

Day 3

842

Fredrickson
Place

Fat
Annie's

Bourniques
House

Stormer
Place

Old
Baldy
Hill

N

19 North Manitou
Island
*Sleeping Bear Dunes
National Lakeshore*

Lake Michigan

East Trail

Donner's
Point

beach to Donner's Point, stopping along the way to climb Old Baldy, an open dune that rises almost 140 feet above Lake Michigan. It's a 2-mile beach walk to Donner's Point.

Day Three (5.1 miles) Get an early start if you want to catch the 11 a.m. ferry. The hiking is not hard but plan on at least three hours for the 5.1-mile trek to the Village. Better yet, plan on overnighting at the Village Campground so you have plenty of time to explore the ruins at Stormer Place and Bourniques Place.

The main trail departs Fredrickson Place and makes a short climb to Cat Hole clearing and then gently descends to Fat Annie's, a posted clearing, reached 0.7 mile from Fredrickson Place. After reaching the clearing, the trail levels out and the next 1.3 miles to the junction with Dimmick's Point Trail is a pleasant, wooded hike. Along the way, you pass two unmarked trails that form a loop south to Stormer Place. The first, the west trail, is very hard to spot and then even harder to follow. Those interested in the ruins should use the east trail, which is located 0.3 mile before you reach the junction with Dimmick's Point Trail. The Stormers were a German family that moved to the island in 1859 to farm, but left after only five years. In 1908 the oldest son, Peter Stormer, returned as a logger and built his home at the south end of the island here. Among the ruins that remain are the foundations of his home, a log barn, and farm equipment.

Side Trip: A 0.3 mile after the east trail to Stormers homestead, you reach the junction to Dimmick's Point. Turn south (right) if you want to make a mile-long side trip to see the cemetery and farm house at Bourniques Place. The trail to Bourniques quickly enters a clearing and in a quarter mile passes an old cemetery. There are 22 people here with the oldest headstone dating back to 1885 and the newest only to 2005. A half mile beyond the cemetery is Bourniques Place, a picturesque weathered farmhouse and barn that are in a clearing.

At the posted junction to Bourniques, the main trail heads north (left) as a wide, unmistakable path towards the Village 3.1 miles away. The walk through the beech-maple forest is surprisingly level, considering that you are skirting the base of a 70- to 300-foot-high ridge. The trail does make a short climb, though, 1.3 miles from the junction to Bourniques Place or 3.3 miles from Fredrickson Place. Just before ascending the ridge, an unmarked trail veers off to the northeast (right). This trail is an alternative route back to the Village and occasionally passes views of Lake Michigan.

The main trail meanwhile breaks out of the forest after the climb and passes through the south cherry orchard, where a few of the old trees can still be seen. The next posted junction is around the bend and marks the east end of the Centerline Trail, which heads west across the center of the island to reach the Swenson's clearing in 4 miles.

To the north (right) is the Village, only 1.1 miles away. Before reaching the ferry dock, you pass an unmarked and hard to find spur that leads to a former one-room school. One of only two on the island, the school opened in 1907 and included grades one through eight. The ruins are a short walk off the main trail and amount to little more than a pile of lumber and a few bricks on a stone foundation. In a half mile farther north, you break out of the woods into the clearing that surrounds the Village.

North Country Trail

Someday the North Country Trail will be completed, a continuous foot path spanning 4,600 miles through seven states from Crown Point in upper New York to Lake Sakakawea on the Missouri River in North Dakota. Michigan will be in the middle, containing more of the North Country Trail – 1,150 miles – than any other state. The trail will wind across almost the entire length of the Upper Peninsula, then hop across the Straits of Mackinac via the Mackinac Bridge and traverse the Lower Peninsula.

Someday … but why wait? Already the NCT offers backpackers numerous opportunities to hit the trail overnight, for a few days, or even a week.

In this section six segments of the NCT are described as backpacking opportunities. They begin as far south as White Cloud and extend into Wilderness State Park near Mackinaw City. Some portions allow mountain bikers, but all are lightly used, and even on the weekends only a handful of other hikers will be encountered.

The drawback of the NCT is that it's a point-to-point trail, often making transportation to each end a logistical challenge. But in some cases other trails can be used to create a loop with a portion of the NCT such as the Manistee River Trail. On other segments locals can help in arranging drop-offs or shuttling vehicles. If nothing else, hike in and spend the night and then hike out. In most cases the NCT is such a beautiful walk, you probably won't mind repeating it.

The best source of information on any segment of the NCT is the North Country Trail Association (866-445-3628; *www.northcountrytrail.org*). You can gather information or purchase maps online or by calling. Even better is stopping at the NCTA headquarters on the corner of Monroe Street and Main Street in Lowell. The office is open Monday through Friday from 8:30 a.m. to 4:30 p.m. and is well stocked with books, maps, displays and the latest trail information.

Built in the late 1870s as a one-room school, the North Country Trail Schoolhouse is now a comfortable lodge for backpackers walking the NCT.

North Country Trail
White Cloud to Nichols Lake

County: Newaygo
Nearest Town: White Cloud
Distance: 24.8 miles
Hiking Time: Two days
Highest Elevation Gain: 80 feet
Difficulty: Moderate to challenging
Highlights: White River, small isolated lakes, schoolhouse lodging

What began as a one-room schoolhouse in the late 1870s and later served as the national headquarters of the North Country Trail Association is now a great way for backpackers to lighten their load for an overnight hike on the NCT. With a car spotted at Nichols Lake National Forest Campground, you can use the historic NCTA Schoolhouse for lodging at the halfway point of a 24.8-mile trek and skip carrying a tent, sleeping pad, and stove.

The first day would begin just west of White Cloud and would be a 12.1-mile walk, followed by a 12.7-mile trek on the next day. At night you can bunk up at the Schoolhouse, which offers cooking facilities, mattresses, and even showers.

Although the mileage will have some people looking elsewhere for shorter walks, keep in mind that there is no significant elevation gain along most of this segment. That and the lighter load in your pack will result in a much quicker pace on the trail. Or you can easily reduce the mileage by beginning at the NCT trailhead along M-20 and spotting a car at Benton Lake National Forest Campground. That would make for a 9.1-mile hike the first day and 9.3 miles on the second, with the final 2 miles along gravel Pierce Road to reach the rustic campground.

Trip Planner

Maps: USGS topos do not show the NCT. The best map is the *North Country Trail Map: M-37 to Freesoil Trailhead* (Map MI-04) published and sold by the North Country Trail Association (866-445-3628; *www.northcountrytrail.org*).
Getting There: From M-37 in White Cloud, head west on Wilcox Avenue, past the White Cloud City Campground. Wilcox Avenue turns into Echo Drive and within 2.5 miles you'll reach where the NCT crosses Echo Drive. To reach Nichols Lake National Forest Campground, head north of White Cloud on M-37 for 13 miles and then west on 11 Mile road for 4.5 miles. For assistance in dropping off a car, contact Ginny Wunsch (231-689-6876; *wunschee@mail.riverview.net*) of the West Michigan Chapter of the NCTA.
Fees & Reservations: The Schoolhouse is $7.50 per night for NCTA

members and $10 per night for non-members. You need to reserve a bed in advance by contacting Ginny Wunsch (231-689-6876; *wunschee@mail. riverview.net*). A campsite at Nichols Lake is $12 a night.

Information: Updates on the trail are available from North Country Trail Association (866-445-3628; *www.northcountrytrail.org*) or the Baldwin Ranger District of the Manistee National Forest (231-745-4631).

Trail Guide

Day One (12.1 miles) The NCT crosses Echo Drive a mile east of Alley Lake Wayside Picnic Area and from there heads due north. Within a half mile you reach the White River and the impressive 40-foot-long foot bridge across it. Too bad you just started the hike; otherwise, this scenic bridge would be an ideal spot for an extended break.

From the White River the NCT begins curving to the west and 1.5 miles from Echo Drive crosses Rattlesnake Creek. The trail swings close to Ferris Road at one point and finally crosses the dirt road 2.2 miles from the start. On the other side you continue along a two-track before blue blazes lead you away and 3.7 miles from Echo Drive you arrive at the trailhead and parking area on the south side of busy M-20. The state highway serves as the boundary for mountain bikers as they are not permitted to ride the trail south of it, but they are to the north all the way to Nichols Lake.

North of M-20 the NCT crosses a number of two-tracks and logging roads but is always well marked. The first such road is crossed within a third of a mile of M-20 and another a half mile later. A mile from M-20 you use a narrow bridge to cross Second Cole Creek and then climb its steep bank on the other side to enter a rolling stand of red pine.

You cross a few more two-tracks, and then 3 miles from M-20 or 6.7 miles from the start you break out at paved 3 Mile Road. To the north the NCT crosses five two-tracks in the next 2 miles, but again it is always well marked. After the fifth one, the NCT climbs a ridge and then skirts a series of interesting bogs and swampy ponds.

Sandy and rutted 5 Mile Road is reached 6.9 miles from M-20 or 10.6 miles from the start. The quickest way to the NCT Schoolhouse is to head east on Five Mile Road, and within a half mile it swings south and changes from a rough two-track to a graded dirt road. Continue another mile and just south of the corner of 5 Mile Road and Felch Avenue is the Schoolhouse.

The Schoolhouse, which at one time also served as a hostel, sleeps 12. It has mattresses and cots and features an indoor bathroom with showers as well as a kitchen with a refrigerator, stove, and oven.

Day Two (12.7 miles) Begin the second day by backtracking 5 Mile Road, but this time continue north on the two-track that is occasionally listed as Ferris Avenue to save some time. The NCT will merge into Ferris Avenue within a quarter mile. Follow the two-track as it descends sharply to cross a bridge over Mena Creek. On the other side, the NCT climbs 80 feet out of

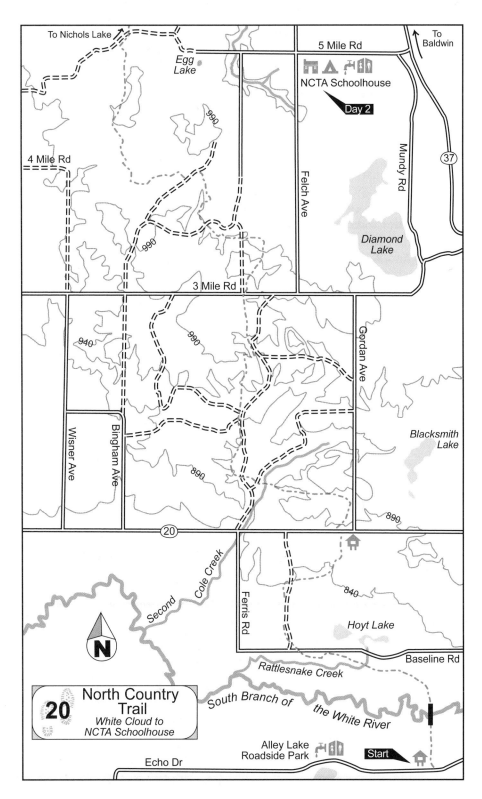

To Nichols Lake

Egg Lake

5 Mile Rd

To Baldwin

NCTA Schoolhouse

Day 2

4 Mile Rd

990

Felch Ave

Mundy Rd

37

Diamond Lake

3 Mile Rd

940

990

Gordan Ave

Wisner Ave

Bingham Ave

890

Blacksmith Lake

890

20

Second Cole Creek

Ferris Rd

840

N

Hoyt Lake

Baseline Rd

Rattlesnake Creek

20 North Country Trail
White Cloud to NCTA Schoolhouse

South Branch of the White River

Alley Lake Roadside Park

Start

Echo Dr

the ravine, the steepest climb of the hike, before breaking out at 6 Mile Road, less than a half mile from Mena Creek or 2.3 miles from the Schoolhouse. Head east 200 feet on 6 Mile Road to pick up the NCT on the north side of the dirt road.

Side Trip: A mile to the east on 6 Mile Road is the entrance to Loda Lake Wildflower Sanctuary in Newaygo County. Originally part of a 1,000-acre private reserve, much of the sanctuary was farmed before the U.S. Forest Service invited the Federated Garden Clubs of Michigan in 1938 to help them create a sanctuary for native plants, including endangered and protected species.

Today the sanctuary is a noted destination for botanists, who are attracted to the wide variety of habitats that are found in such a small area. The sanctuary's 1.5-mile trail winds through oak-maple woodlands, alongside a stream and floodplain, through old pine plantations, and on a boardwalk through a shrub swamp and emergent wetland. Lining the trail are 39 posts that correspond to an interpretive guide with each one identifying a plant or wildflower.

From 6 Mile Road the NCT swings east, crosses Ferris Avenue, and then continues as a high, dry ribbon of trail around one swampy area after another. You cross a series of two-tracks with one of them being 7 Mile Road, a sandy two-track reached 2.4 miles from 6 Mile Road or 4.7 miles from the Schoolhouse. Eventually you enjoy the longest portion of the trail without access roads or two-tracks, more than 2 miles of rolling forest that for the first time that day gives you a sense of being "out in the woods."

The NCT merges into a two-track labeled Taylor Drive on some maps, 2.6 miles from 7 Mile Road, follows it briefly, and then swings back into the woods to the east. In less than a half mile or 10 miles from the Schoolhouse, you arrive at Pierce Drive (also known as 8 Mile Road). Two miles to the west on Pierce Drive is Benton Lake National Forest Campground.

North of Pierce Drive the NCT follows an old two-track and in a half mile descends to cross Bear Creek using a foot bridge. The trail immediately crosses Parson Road, a gravel road, and then 1.7 miles from Pierce Drive reaches West Michigan Creek. This is a scenic spot, and one that is occasionally used as a backcountry campsite. The creek here flows through a grove of large cedar trees and is crossed by a long bridge. In another mile you cross Tank Creek and then arrive at Croswell Avenue, a dirt road reached 11.7 miles from the Schoolhouse.

In a little more than a half mile the NCT breaks out at 11 Mile Road, a paved road where the entrance to Nichols Lake National Forest Campground is on the north side. The rustic campground is a half mile north on the access road and has drinking water, vault toilets, a picnic area and even a small beach where you can soak your tired toes. Ahhhh!

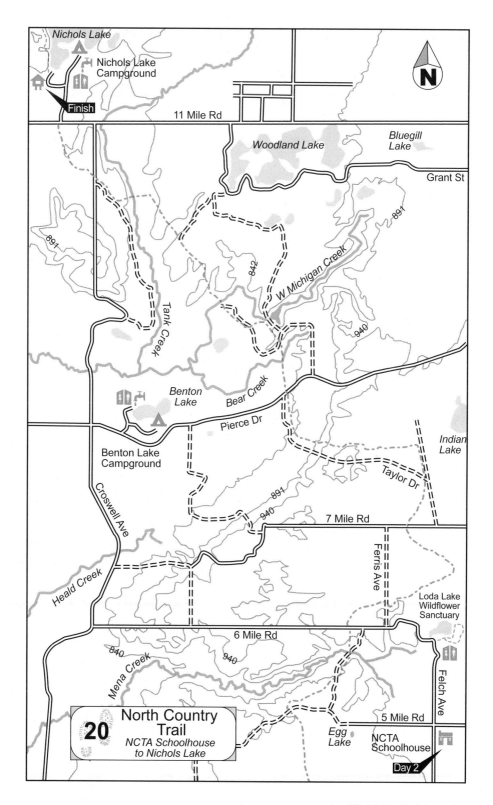

Nichols Lake

Nichols Lake
Campground

Finish

11 Mile Rd

Woodland Lake

Bluegill
Lake

Grant St

891

842

W Michigan Creek

940

891

Tank Creek

Benton
Lake

Bear Creek

Pierce Dr

Indian
Lake

Taylor Dr

Benton Lake
Campground

Croswell Ave

891

940

7 Mile Rd

Ferris Ave

Heald Creek

Loda Lake
Wildflower
Sanctuary

6 Mile Rd

940

840

Mena Creek

Felch Ave

5 Mile Rd

20 North Country
Trail
*NCTA Schoolhouse
to Nichols Lake*

Egg
Lake

NCTA
Schoolhouse

Day 2

N

A Schoolhouse for Backpackers

It's been around for more than 120 years and has served as a place of learning, a national headquarters, comfortable lodging for sore-footed backpackers, an unusual hostel for travelers from around the world.

It has also been the answer to a trivia question: Where is the halfway point of the North Country Trail, the country's longest foot path that someday will extend from North Dakota to New York? The answer is the North Country Trail Schoolhouse.

For many the old schoolhouse is as much a symbol of the trail as anything else. The classic one-room schoolhouse was built in the late 1870s in what was then Park City, a logging town on the north shores of Diamond Lake. When the loggers left, Park City became a ghost city and in 1906 local farmers moved the building to its present location seven miles north of White Cloud.

Renamed Birch Grove School, the building served rural students for more than 70 years until the White Cloud School District was consolidated in the 1950s. Then, a century after it was built the empty, in-the-middle-of-nowhere schoolhouse was given a new lease on life. In 1979 it was donated to the then fledging North Country Trail Association, an organization trying to build a trail across seven states.

Even though at the time most of the North Country Trail was a vision, not a path, organizers hung a mileage sign on the Schoolhouse; head west and you'll reach Lake Sakakawea, North Dakota in 1,633 miles. Head east and you'll arrive at Crown Point, New York, in 1,603 miles. The length of the trail is now estimated at more than 4,600 miles, but the sign is still there.

Right from the beginning the NTCA headquarters was also a place of lodging for volunteers building the trail in Newaygo County and for travelers as part of the American Youth Hostel system. Eventually the NTCA headquarters was relocated in Lowell. In 1995 the Schoolhouse dropped out of the world-wide system of hostels as it did not meet new, stricter requirements.

But it's still a comfortable bed at night for Boy Scout troops, youth groups, outdoor clubs and especially backpackers looking for a scenic, two-day trek only an hour from Grand Rapids. At long last, the perfect use of the Schoolhouse, easing the load of backpackers on the North Country Trail.

North County Trail
Nichols Lake to Highbank Lake

County: Newaygo
Nearest Town: Baldwin
Distance: 12 miles
Hiking Time: Overnight
Highest Elevation Gain: 90 feet
Difficulty: Moderate
Highlights: A series of small, isolated lakes

This segment of the North Country Trail is actually a continuation of the previous trek but is covered as a separate hike due to the lack of accommodations. While the NCTA Schoolhouse is available for the White Cloud-to-Nichols Lake walk, on this overnight adventure you'll need a tent and anything else (sleeping pad, stove) required for a comfortable evening in the backcountry.

But the extra weight is well worth it as the 8-mile segment between 11 Mile Road and 16 Mile Road in Newaygo County is extremely scenic. Here the NCT winds past a series of small isolated lakes set among ridges and rolling hills. Two of the lakes, Condon and another that is unnamed, make great settings for an off-trail campsite.

If you don't have the time to arrange transportation or the desire to trek a lot of miles, this is a great last-minute alternative. By starting at the trailhead in the south Nichols Lake boat launch, Condon Lake is only 4.7 miles away. The unnamed lake is a 6-mile walk, and from there, a half-mile spur trail descends to Highbank Lake National Forest Campground. Begin from the north Nichols Lake boat launch, and Condon Lake is only a 3-mile walk and the unnamed lake 4.3 miles.

Trip Planner

Maps: This walk is split between USGS topos Big Star Lake and Walkup Lake and neither shows the NCT. The best map is the *North Country Trail Map: M-37 to Freesoil Trailhead* (Map MI-04) published and sold by the North Country Trail Association (866-445-3628; *www.northcountrytrail.org*).
Getting There: To reach Nichols Lake National Forest Campground, head north of White Cloud on M-37 for 13 miles and then west on 11 Mile Road for 4.5 miles. To reach the North Nichols Lake boat launch continue along 11 Mile Road for 1.5 miles. Turn north on Warner Avenue and then east on Cleveland Drive to reach the boat launch in 2 miles.
Fees & Reservations: A National Forest vehicle permit ($3 daily, $5 weekly) is required to park at the Nichols Lake boat launch while a campsite at

Nichols Lake or Highbank Lake is $12 a night.

Information: Updates on the trail are available from North Country Trail Association (866-445-3628; *www.northcountrytrail.org*) or the Baldwin Ranger District of the Manistee National Forest (231-745-4631).

Trail Guide

Day One (6 miles) In the sorth Nichols Lake boat launch a large information display marks the NCT. From there the trail heads north, follows the bluff along the lake's west shore for good views of the water, and then swings away. You hike past Atodd Lake and 1.7 miles from the start arrive at the Nichols Lake north boat launch and picnic area, an alternative trailhead to begin this hike.

Here the NCT crosses paved Cleveland Drive. Across Cleveland Drive the NCT hugs Alger Avenue (also known as Forest Road 5311) briefly and then swings east and skirts a small marshy meadow. Your only glimpse of Walkup Lake is seen 2.2 miles from the start, and then the NCT swings to the northwest and descends into an interesting meadow. Ringed by hardwoods, this spot can be stunning in early October, when its golden grass is often framed by fiery autumn colors.

You climb out of the meadow, cross Forest Road 5312 and then from the dirt road descend to the west end of Leaf Lake where you're greeted with an unobstructed view of the entire length of the lake. Reached 3.2 miles from the start, this is a pretty spot to take a break. The views remain good for the next half mile however as the trail climbs above Leaf Lake and then hugs its north shore.

From Leaf Lake the NCT heads north where it follows the edge of a bluff that borders an open meadow and marshy area. This is an intriguing segment. You remain hidden in the foliage, yet are able to look down and spot any wildlife attracted to the area. The trail descends to cross a vehicle track, then returns to its ridge to skirt the upper half of a marsh that is a paradise for migrating waterfowl in the spring and fall.

Beyond the marsh the NCT merges into a two-track that skirts the south end of Condon Lake and then climbs the bluff that runs along its east shore and follows the high bank, providing watery views below. Reached 4.7 miles from the south Nichols Lake boat launch, the bluff above Condon is as level and isolated as anywhere along the trail. In other words, a great place to pitch a tent.

After leaving Condon Lake, the NCT continues north and then curves around a small pond connected to Sawkaw Lake. Through most of the summer, however, foliage makes it difficult to spot either body of water through the trees. You cross a dirt road and the trail levels out and remains in the woods until you break out to the edge of a bluff. Below you is Highbank Lake, a well-named body of water. You have a good view of the lake and can easily spot a few cottages, and the USFS campground located on it.

Nearby is the posted spur, reached 5.7 miles from the start, that will

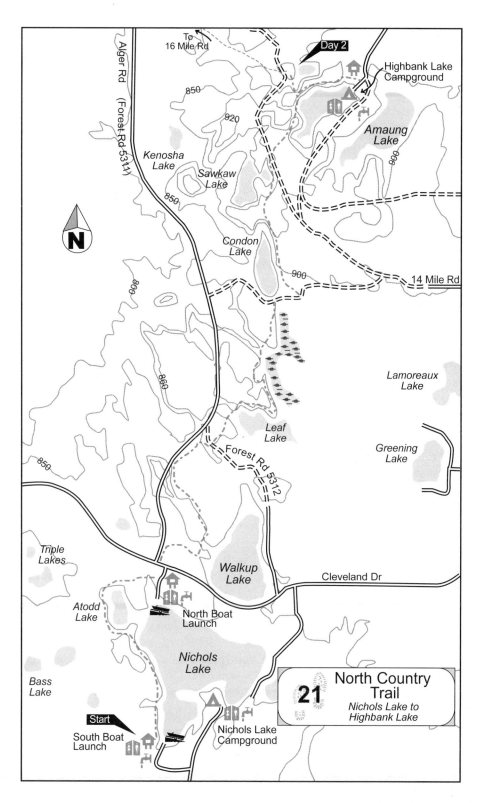

To
16 Mile Rd

Day 2

Alger Rd
(Forest Rd 5311)

Highbank Lake
Campground

850

920

Amaung
Lake

Kenosha
Lake

Sawkaw
Lake

N

Condon
Lake

800

900

14 Mile Rd

860

Lamoreaux
Lake

Leaf
Lake

Greening
Lake

Forest Rd 5312

850

Triple
Lakes

Walkup
Lake

Cleveland Dr

Atodd
Lake

North Boat
Launch

Nichols
Lake

Bass
Lake

North Country
Trail

21

Nichols Lake to
Highbank Lake

Start

South Boat
Launch

Nichols Lake
Campground

lead you a half mile along the north shore of the lake to the campground. Highbank Lake Campground is a small and delightful place to spend the night. The rustic facility has nine drive-in sites and two walk-in ones – perfect for backpackers – along with fire rings, vault toilets, and drinking water.

Within a third of a mile from the junction with the campground spur, the NCT climbs over the crest of the ridge and descends to a small, unnamed pothole lake hemmed in by hardwoods. It's another scenic and remote spot along the trail and makes an ideal place to set up camp for the night.

Day Two Your choices for the second day are either backtrack to one of the boat launches on Nichols Lake or shuttle a vehicle at Highbank Lake that would result in a walk of less than a mile. To park at Highbank Lake head north of White Cloud on M-37 for 17 miles and then turn west (left) on 15 Mile Road in Lilley. Within a mile turn north (right) on Roosevelt Drive and you'll reach the campground in 1.5 miles.

North Country Trail
Ward Hills and McCarthy Lake

County: Newaygo
Nearest Town: Baldwin
Distance: 21.6 miles
Hiking Time: Three days
Highest Elevation Gain: 140 feet
Difficulty: Moderate
Highlights: Scenic overlook in Ward Hills, remote McCarthy Lake

Bowman Lake Foot Travel Area is the destination for an easy overnight trek (see Hike 11, page 87), but also the start of a three-day adventure on the North Country Trail for those looking for more mileage and a greater variety of scenery.

The 21.6-mile hike winds through the Manistee National Forest in the heart of Lake County, beginning at the main trailhead for Bowman Lake and ending at a pizzeria on the shores of Sauble Lake (how convenient!). The first night is spent at the Timber Creek National Forest Campground, which the NCT passes through. The second night is spent at McCarthy Lake, a small, undeveloped body of water that makes for a great place to spend an evening deep in the woods.

There's an interesting variety of terrain along this walk. You begin by passing through the Bowman Lake Area, a geologically unique tract with its small kames and kettle holes, and then climb through Ward Hills past a scenic overlook. You skirt a number of wetlands during the three days as well as cross the Pere Marquette and Big Sable rivers.

The entire route is open to mountain biking and does attract a string of

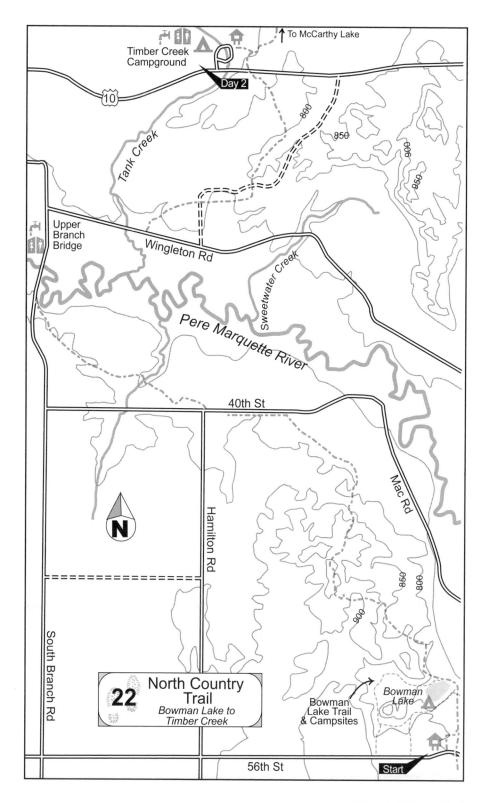

To McCarthy Lake

Timber Creek
Campground

Day 2

10

Tank Creek

800

850

900

950

Upper
Branch
Bridge

Wingleton Rd

Sweetwater Creek

Pere Marquette River

40th St

Mac Rd

N

Hamilton Rd

850

800

900

South Branch Rd

22 North Country
Trail
*Bowman Lake to
Timber Creek*

Bowman Lake Trail
& Campsites

Bowman
Lake

56th St

Start

bikers on most summer and fall weekends, particularly from Timber Creek Campground to Centerline Road. But overall, this stretch of the NCT is not as heavily used as the Manistee River Trail loop (see Hike 23) or the sections south of Traverse City in the Pere Marquette State Forest. Be prepared to filter your water at McCarthy Lake.

Trip Planner

Maps: This walk is covered by the USGS topos *Townsend Lake, Tallman,* and *Peacock* and none of them shows the NCT. Once again the best map is the *North Country Trail Map: M-37 to Freesoil Trailhead* (Map MI-04) published and sold by the North Country Trail Association (866-445-3628; *www. northcountrytrail.org*).

Getting There: To reach Bowman Lake from M-37 in Baldwin head west on Seventh Street and follow it as it curves and becomes 56th Street (also labeled Carrs Road). Within 6 miles you pass the entrance to Bowman Bridge Campground and in another 1.5 miles you arrive at the main trailhead and parking lot for the Bowman Foot Travel Area.

At the north end, this hike terminates at Sauble Lake Emporium (231-266-5641), a trail-friendly pizzeria and store whose owners allow hikers to leave a car at its large parking lot if they call in advance. They also assist hikers in finding someone to shuttle them to Bowman Lake for the start of the walk. To reach the Sauble Lake Emporium from M-37, head west on 4 Mile Road, which swings north and then west again to become 5 Mile Road. Within 6.5 miles of M-37, right across from beautiful Sauble Lake is the store.

Fees & Reservations: A National Forest vehicle permit ($3 daily, $5 weekly) is required to park at Bowman Lake Foot Travel Area. There are no fees for camping at Timber Creek or McCarthy Lake.

Information: Updates on the trail are available from North Country Trail Association (866-445-3628; *www.northcountrytrail.org*) or the Baldwin Ranger District of the Manistee National Forest (231-745-4631).

Trail Guide

Day One (8.5 miles) At the main trailhead for the Bowman Lake Foot Travel Area, next to a large display, is an access spur to North Country Trail, marked by both gray diamonds for the NCT and blue diamonds for the Bowman Lake Trail. The trail quickly arrives at a junction with the NCT. Head north (left) and you'll immediately be skirting the base of a steep ridge. Within a half mile from the start, you come to a second junction.

To the west (left) is Bowman Lake Trail, which quickly leads to four walk-in campsites, a scenic place to spend the night if you arrive late (see Hike 11). The NCT continues north (right) to climb a ridge for a nice overview of the lake and then descends the back side of it, bottoming out in a pleasant wooded bowl a little more than a mile from the trailhead.

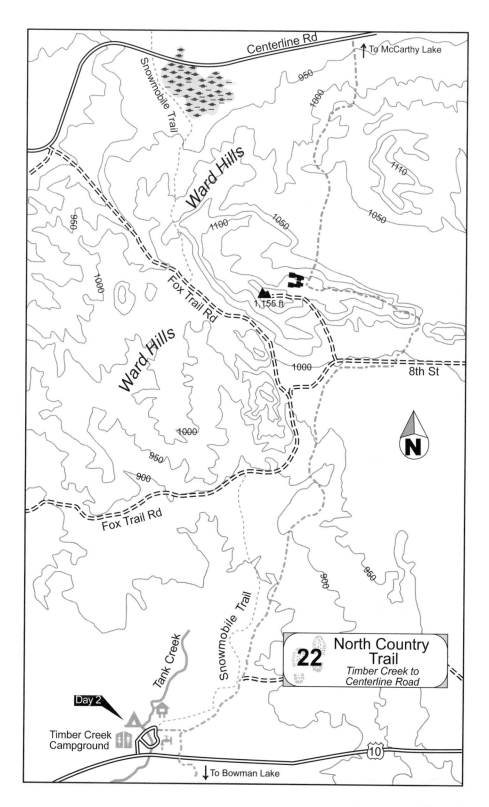

Centerline Rd

↑ To McCarthy Lake

Snowmobile Trail

950

1000

Ward Hills

950

1110

1050

1100

1050

1050

Fox Trail Rd

▲ 1,155 ft

1000

Ward Hills

8th St

1000

N

950

900

Fox Trail Rd

950

900

Snowmobile Trail

Tank Creek

Snowmobile Trail

22 North Country Trail
Timber Creek to Centerline Road

Day 2

Timber Creek Campground

10

↓ To Bowman Lake

You resume climbing, gaining 140 feet at one point, before the trail descends sharply and eventually swings west. You parallel 40th Street briefly before merging onto the dirt road 3 miles from the trailhead. Gray diamonds lead you west along 40th Street for a half mile to the intersection with Hamilton Road. At this point the NCT angles back into the woods to the north (right) but quickly emerges from the trees to cross a power line right-a-way and descends to a small creek with a bridge, a scenic area reached 4 miles from the start.

After climbing the opposite bank of the creek, the trail levels out, crosses an old two-track within a half mile and then arrives at Sulak Landing Road, a dirt road. The gray diamonds lead you around a gate and then along an overgrown two-track that descends towards the Pere Marquette River. But before reaching the river, the trail reaches paved South Branch Road within sight of Upper Branch Bridge. The bridge is used to cross the Pere Marquette River, while on its south side is a boaters' access site with vault toilets and drinking water.

The NCT continues north along South Branch Road. At 5.7 miles from Bowman Lake you head east (right) onto Wingleton Road and follow the dirt road for 0.7 mile. When the NCT departs from Wingleton Road and heads northeast (left), it first winds through a pine plantation and then moves into a much more interesting hardwood forest along a trail that remains level and easy to follow. Within a half mile of US-10, or 8 miles from Bowman Lake, you skirt a low lying wet area and then begin a gradual climb. The trail crosses a gas line right-a-way, marked by bright yellow and red posts, resumes climbing and breaks out at the edge of a bank above US-10. The NCT resumes on the other side of this busy U.S. highway where it quickly arrives at a spur to Timber Creek Campground.

The national forest campground, an 8.5-mile walk from Bowman Lake, is a pleasant, nine-site rustic facility. Although called Timber Creek Campground, the stream running through it is actually Tank Creek, which forms a small pond in the middle of the sites. Amenities include vault toilets, drinking water, tables, and fire rings. Because it is accessed from US-10, it is not unusual for this campground to be filled on the weekends.

Day Two (9 miles) This is the longest day of the trek, one that includes climbing the rugged Ward Hills. From Timber Creek, backtrack the short spur to the NCT and head north (left). Here the NCT begins as a narrow path that moves through a rolling terrain of hardwoods and pine plantations. You cross a number of snowmobile and ORV trails and abandoned logging roads before reaching 8th Street, a well established dirt road, 3.7 miles from Timber Creek. The trial is well marked on the opposite side of the road and continues north with an immediate climb.

Within a half mile you climb more than 100 feet, topping off at the crest of a ridge. Welcome to Ward Hills! The NCT swings west to follow the ridge, and the next half mile is easy and scenic. You're rewarded with several

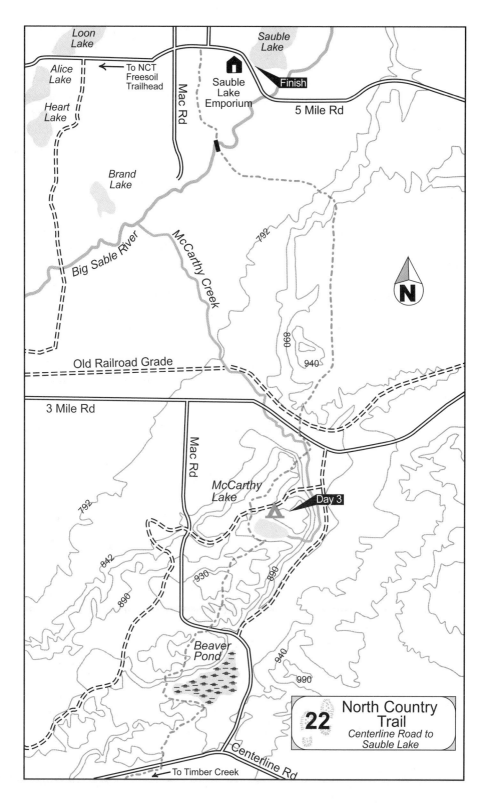

Loon Lake
Sauble Lake
Alice Lake
To NCT Freesoil Trailhead
Sauble Lake Emporium
Finish
5 Mile Rd
Heart Lake
Mac Rd
Brand Lake
Big Sable River
McCarthy Creek
792
890
940
N
Old Railroad Grade
3 Mile Rd
Mac Rd
McCarthy Lake
Day 3
792
842
890
930
890
Beaver Pond
940
990

North Country Trail
22
Centerline Road to Sauble Lake

Centerline Rd
To Timber Creek

nice views to the south and west, especially in the early spring and late fall when there is little foliage. On a clear day you can see Lake Michigan near Ludington to the west.

After reaching the high point of 1,130 feet, the NCT swings north and starts a 200-foot descent covered in 1.3 miles. Some portions are steep enough to require switchbacks. At 6.2 miles from Timber Creek you break out at Centerline Road, where the NCT is well marked on both sides by blue blazes.

From Centerline you head northeast and within a mile arrive at a vast area of standing water and wetlands labeled on USGS topos as Beaver Pond and no doubt supports a family or two. Stay and search for them if the bugs don't send you running down the trail. The NCT heads northwest to skirt the wetlands and climbs to higher ground. Within 8 miles of Timber Creek you cross Mac Road, a well-graded dirt road, and then in another mile descend to McCarthy Lake.

Also referred to by locals as Lake in the Hills, McCarthy is a beautiful body of water surrounded by low ridges. The only man-made intrusion here is a wood duck nesting box on a dead tree in the water; otherwise, McCarthy is pristine north woods. The trail emerges at the lake's south shore and then follows the shoreline around its marshy west end before crossing an access road to the lake from Mac Road. To reach the campsites on the north shore, head east on the access road for a few hundred feet. There are no amenities here except a nice view. Treat all water from the lake.

Day Three (4 miles) From the campsites, return to the NCT where it crosses the access road. Head north (right) to climb a low ridge and then proceed northeast through the maples and cottonwoods that forest the top of it. In the beginning you can catch a glimpse of McCarthy Lake but eventually it disappears in the trees. Within a half mile you descend to cross McCarthy Creek on a small bridge and then break out at 3 Mile Road, a well-graded dirt road.

On the other side of the road, the NCT heads northeast and then north to skirt private property. Within 2.5 miles from McCarthy Lake the trail swings sharply to the west, and a mile from the end, uses a bridge to cross Big Sable River. In the final stretch the NCT heads due north and within 0.7 mile arrives at paved 5 Mile Road, almost across from the junction with Utter Road.

The NCT then heads west to follow 5 Mile Road for more than 2 miles before angling north for the Freesoil Trailhead on Freesoil Road. Head east instead, and you arrive at the Sauble Lake Emporium. The store is open until 9 p.m. Monday through Saturday and 7 p.m. on Sunday. Order its Super Sauble pizza, which includes pepperoni, ham, Italian sausage, and just about anything else they can find to put on it. Don't worry about the calories. You've earned it.

North Country Trail
Manistee River Trail

Counties: Manistee and Wexford
Nearest Town: Mesick
Distance: 21.5 miles
Hiking Time: Two to three days
Highest Elevation Gain: 276 feet
Difficulty: Moderate to challenging

Highlights: The Manistee River, a waterfall, walk-in campsites

In the end all it took to create one of the best backpacking routes in the Lower Peninsula was a foot bridge, an impressive foot bridge to say the least but still just a way to keep your boots dry while crossing the Manistee River.

Built in 1996 just below Hodenpyl Dam Pond, the suspension bridge stretches 245 feet across the river with a price tag of $125,000 that was shared by the U.S. Forest Service and Consumer's Power. The steel and cable structure is for foot traffic only – bikes and horses are banned – and serves as the cornerstone for a 21.5-mile backpacking route that loops along both sides of the Manistee River.

The bridge links a rugged, 10-mile segment of the North Country Trail (NCT) on the west side of the river with one of the state's newest paths, the 11-mile Manistee River Trail, on the east side. The two routes can be combined for a two to three-day trek that is as scenic and wilderness like as the Jordan River Pathway or North Manitou Island.

The Manistee River Trail was completed in 1992 and is an interesting contrast to the rugged NCT on the opposite bank. While the NCT climbs hills and ridges to overlooks, the Manistee River Trail is relatively flat and provides views of the river from the edge of a high river bank. The NCT is open to mountain bikes; the Manistee River Trail is not.

Starting at Seaton Creek National Forest Campground, many backpackers cover this route in two days, tackling 10.5 miles the first day, 11 miles the second, and overnighting at the dispersed campsites at Red Bridge where there is water and vault toilets. The hike is described here as a three-day weekend walk, with a short hike the day you arrive at Seaton Creek and longer hikes on Saturday and Sunday. Both nights are spent in a backcountry setting along the NCT and the Manistee River Trail.

Backcountry camping is permitted along both trails as long as you do not pitch a tent closer than 200 feet to the trail or any source of water. The U.S. Forest Service has also set up nine dispersed campsites along the Manistee River Trail, most of which can only be reached by paddling or hiking in. The sites are free and posted along the trail.

Trip Planner

Maps: The route is covered by the USGS topo, *Yuma*, which includes the NCT but not the Manistee River Trail. There is also the Manistee River Trail brochure from the U.S. Forest Service and the *North Country Trail Map: Freesoil Trailhead to Cedar Creek Road* (Map MI-05) published and sold by the North Country Trail Association (866-445-3628; *www.northcountrytrail.org*).

Getting There: To reach Seaton Creek Campground head north on M-37 9 miles from its intersection with M-55 and then turn left on 26 Mile Road for 1.7 miles. Turn right on O'Rourke Drive for 1.3 miles then right on Forest Road 5993 and follow it a half mile to the campground.

If beginning from the Red Bridge river access site, turn west on 30 Mile Road from M-37. Follow 30 Mile Road to its end and then bear left at the curve onto Warfield Road. Drive south for 1.5 miles and watch for Coates Highway. Turn right on Coates Highway to Red Bridge over the Manistee River.

Fees & Reservations: You need a National Forest vehicle permit ($3 daily, $5 weekly) to park at Seaton Creek Campground. Dispersed campsites along the Manistee River Trail are free while a site at Seaton Creek is $12 a night

Information: Maps and brochures on both trails are available from the Manistee Ranger District of the Manistee Forest (231-723-2211; *www.fs.fed. us/r9/hmnf*) and the North Country Trail Association (866-445-3628; *www. northcountrytrail.org*).

Trail Guide

Day One (3 miles) Seaton Creek Campground has 17 rustic sites well spread out on a bluff above the backwaters of the Hodenpyl Dam Pond. Amenities include tables, vault toilets, drinking water, and a small picnic area with a series of steps to the water below.

The Manistee River Trail is posted in the picnic area parking lot, and from there leads you along bluffs above the sluggish Seaton Creek. There is a great view of Hodenpyl Dam Pond from its south end just before the trail swings away and crosses O'Rourke Road a half mile from the trailhead, followed by No. 1 Road, an overhead power line, and Milepost 1.

The trail, an old two-track at this point, swings north and within a quarter mile reaches the suspension bridge that spans across the Manistee River, linking the Manistee River Trail with a mile-long spur to the NCT. The Manistee River Trail swings south here, and 1.5 miles from the campground returns to the edge of the Manistee River and begins a very scenic stretch. You stay in view of the water as you skirt the flat river bluffs along a trail that is a surprisingly easy hike.

Just before Milepost 3, you pass dispersed campsites No. 3 and No. 4, both posted along the trail and near a small stream. Beyond the milepost are

A backpacker heads south along the Manistee River Trail. The trail is often combined with a portion of the NCT to form a two- to three-day loop along the Manistee River.

the famed waterfalls of Manistee River Trail, discovered when the trail was being flagged. It's a spot where a spring-fed brook is leaping its way down the bluff to the river. If it's raining, the stream might even live up to its billing as an eight-foot high cascade. If not, then you're assured of a pleasant evening and great views from the campsites.

Day Two (10 miles) This is your longest day and that's by design for a weekend backpack. Cross your fingers for good weather and get an early start.

The day begins with easy trekking, and good views of the river continue as the trail cuts across Flower Flats past Milepost 4 and Milepost 5. Just beyond Milepost 5 is perhaps the best vista of the day, a view from the edge of a 50-foot bluff where you can watch the Manistee River sweep through a long oxbow bend. Nearby is dispersed campsite No. 6.

The grand view is followed by the longest descent of the day where the trail drops more than 70 feet to finally reach the edge of the Manistee only to begin immediately climbing the bluff again, topping off at dispersed campsite No. 7. You swing out of view of the Manistee, past Milepost 6, and in less than a half mile arrive at Slagle Creek. The creek flows through a beautiful cedar-filled ravine and is crossed by a unique arch-timber bridge.

Just beyond the stream the trail climbs out of the ravine and crosses Slagle Creek Road, a dirt forest road, where nearby are dispersed campsites No. 8 and No. 9. This makes Slagle Creek a scenic place to spend the first night for those looking for a longer first day. But keep in mind that occasionally people, mostly trout fisherman looking to hook a brookie, will drive into a parking area at the end of Slagle Creek Road.

From Slagle Creek Road, the Manistee River Trail heads south and within a half mile climbs in and out of the Cedar Creek ravine and then passes Milepost 7. Just beyond the milepost you cross Cottage Road, a dirt road, and eventually the trail merges with a two-track for a half mile, passing a private cabin along the way. Keep an eye out for the gray diamond markers as the trail swings away from the two-track near Milepost 8, a spot that is easy to miss.

You descend back to the river where it forms an oxbow curve. This stretch is marshy but the trail uses a floating boardwalk to cross it before ascending back to the edge of the bluffs and another great view of the valley near Milepost 9. After crossing Arquilla Creek, the trail returns to the river bluff at a spot where you can see Red Bridge downstream though you're still a mile away. The trail stays at the edge of the bluff, passing Milepost 10 just before you begin a long climb to Coates Highway.

You emerge at the pavement a quarter mile from Red Bridge at a spot that is posted "Hiker's Trail." Head west and the trail will cross the vehicle bridge and descend to Red Bridge boat access. Located here, besides a boat ramp, are vault toilets, drinking water, dispersed campsites No. 10–14, and a trailhead for the spur to the NCT. If you're planning to spend the night at

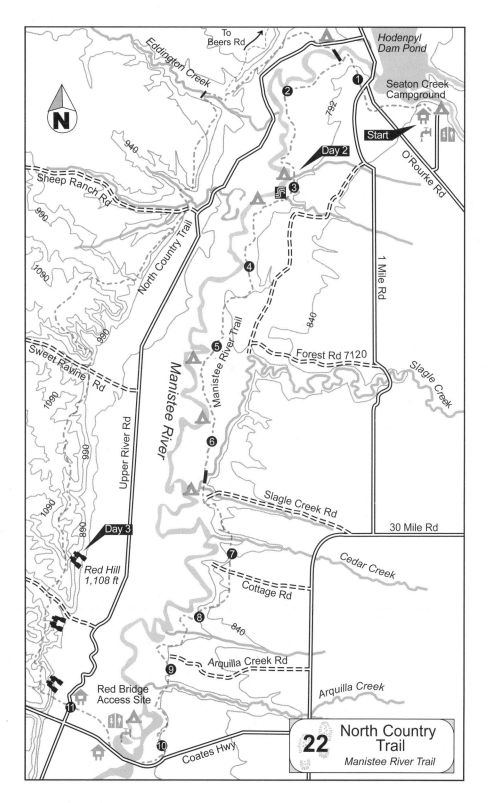

Red Hill, make sure your water bottles are filled and you're carrying enough to make it through dinner and breakfast.

Continue west on the spur and within a half mile you arrive at Milepost 11, the Upper River Road and a trailhead with parking and an information display for the North Country Trail. The spur continues west and a mile from the Red Bridge climbs almost 200 feet before arriving at a junction with the NCT. Welcome to the North Country! Get ready for a little uphill hiking.

Heading north, the NCT climbs a bit more and then quickly breaks out to your first overlook along this portion of the NCT. Beyond the view the trail follows the rugged contour of the ridge, and in less than a mile from the spur trail junction, you arrive at a second vista, a small clearing from which you can see ridges and the river to the southeast. The overlook is followed by a steady descent that bottoms out at Pole Road (Forest Road 5344), more of a two-track than a dirt road.

On the other side of the road you undertake the longest uphill march of the trek. It's a 276-foot climb in roughly a half mile as the NCT returns to the crest of the ridge and then swings around Red Hill to a junction with a spur trail posted "Red Hill Overlook." The spur is reached 2.5 miles from Red

Michigan's Undiscovered Waterfall

The two hikers in front of me on the Manistee River Trail paused on a small bridge, stared down at the stream, and then asked for my opinion when I caught up. "Think that's it?"

None of us were expecting Tahquamenon Falls. But we weren't too sure that this little leap was the "spectacular discovery" news reports proclaimed in 1990 when U.S. Forest Service rangers flagging the trail stumbled on only the second waterfall in the Lower Peninsula.

"Maybe they saw it during a flash flood," I said.

The only other natural waterfall in the Lower Peninsula is Ocqueoc Falls in Presque County. There's no question those are waterfalls. The Manistee River Trail falls (no one has named them yet) is where a spring-fed brook is leaping its way down the bluff to the river. More of a gush than a cascade.

But take note, the cascade may be ho-hum but that's it. With or without a thunder of whitewater, the rest of this 11-mile trail is nothing short of spectacular. Anywhere along the Manistee River Trail you might spot a variety of wildlife, canoers silently floating the current, or possibly a brook trout fisher working the deep pools of Slagle Creek.

What you won't see is a lot of development. There's not a strip mall for miles around and only one cottage is passed along the entire trail. To those of us who have hiked the trail, this is the "spectacular discovery"; not a waterfall, but a remote stretch of hills, rivers, and streams so close to home.

Bridge and 10 miles from the waterfall. There are spots to pitch a tent near the junction or head 200 yards farther up the spur trail. This short side trail ends at Red Hill, a 1,108-foot high point where you can see for miles to the southeast. It's hard to spot the Manistee River, but looming in front are the rugged ridges you've just hiked across. Pitch a small tent here and you can spend the evening studying what led to your sore feet.

Day Three (8.5 miles) From the junction at the overlook spur, the NCT follows the crest of the ridge to the north, paralleling a dirt road briefly and putting you 376 feet above the Manistee River. Eventually you begin an almost mile-long descent to Sweets Ravine along a rugged stretch of the NCT that makes for the most interesting hiking of the day. Several times the trail swings west into a small gulch before climbing out and over the next slope. It's impressive country, and it makes you feel like you're deep in a wilderness that's somewhere remote and exotic.

The trail bottoms out in steep-sided Sweets Ravine and crosses Sweet Ravine Road (Forest Road 8060) 2.3 miles from Red Hill and then swings west and begins a long climb back out. You ascend 270 feet in just 0.7 mile before the trail tops off and swings to the north. In the next mile the NCT hugs the edge of the ridge that is so steep you catch glimpses of the Manistee River Valley through the trees.

At 4.6 miles from Red Hill, the trail descends to cross a junction of three two-tracks, the main one being Sheep Ranch Road (Forest Road 8020). There is also a small stream here, but it can be hard to spot at times during the summer. You have to climb out this ravine, an uphill trudge of almost 90 feet, before the trail levels out along the ridge for a spell. The NCT then descends to Eddington Creek. Reached 6 miles from Red Hill, the creek is a beautiful spot where you head upstream into a wooded hollow briefly to reach a foot bridge across the creek.

Within a quarter mile of Eddington Creek, you reach a signposted junction that marks the spur to the Manistee River Trail. Head northeast (right) on the spur and within a mile you'll cross Upper River Road, pass dispersed campsites No. 1 and No. 2 and arrive at the suspension bridge across the Manistee River. On the other side of that impressive foot bridge you climb up to the Manistee River Trail and head left to backtrack the 1.3 miles to Seaton Creek Campground.

Members of the Grand Traverse Hiking Club measure the trunk of a tree in the Valley of the Giants. The NCT passes through the stand of old growth trees.

North Country Trail
Pere Marquette State Forest

Counties: Grand Traverse and Kalkaska
Nearest Towns: Traverse City and Kalkaska
Distance: 19.6 miles
Hiking Time: Two to three days
Highest Elevation Gain: 109 feet
Difficulty: Moderate
Highlights: Old growth forest, numerous lakes, walk-in campsites

The North Country Trail is more than just segments of a proposed national trail that someday will span halfway across the country. It's a network of local hikers and clubs pitching in to build, post, and maintain the NCT in their backyard. Nowhere is this more evident than in the Pere Marquette State Forest between Traverse City and Kalkaska where the Grand Traverse Hiking Club has lovingly turned the NCT into another great backpacking route in the Lower Peninsula.

When completed, this segment will extend 26 miles from Cedar Creek Road to Kalkaska's Kaliseum, a public recreation facility with showers, a pool and parking. From the west a spur will also connect the NCT to the VASA trail on the edge of Traverse City. But why wait? What is already finished is an amazing walk; a 19.6 trek from Cedar Creek Road to the Guernsey Lake State Forest Campground.

Along the way you pass seven lakes, skirt 3 miles of the Boardman River, and walk beneath the lofty boughs of an old growth forest. You have the choice of spending nights in two walk-in camping areas or two state forest campgrounds. You also get to enjoy scenic sections of two other trail systems; the Muncie Lakes Pathway and the Sand Lakes Quiet Area (see Hike 13).

A strong hiker can cover this route as an overnight adventure with a 10.8-mile walk the first day to camp at Dollar Lake and 8.8 miles the second to Guernsey Lake. But here it is broken into a three-day trek with shorter walks the first and third day to accommodate backpackers driving in for the weekend. The first day is a 6.2-mile walk to Scheck's Place State Forest Campground. The second day is a 10.6-mile trek to the walk-in sites in the Sand Lakes Quiet Area. On Sunday you'd enjoy a 2.8-mile hike to Guernsey Lake before heading back. If transportation is a problem, the 9.8-mile hike from the Muncie Lakes Pathway trailhead to the Sand Lakes walk-in campsites is such a scenic segment that most people don't mind backtracking the second day.

It's important to remember that this slice of the Pere Marquette State Forest is crisscrossed with forest roads, old two-tracks, gas pipeline corridors, power lines and snowmobile trails. Passing through the same general area is the Shore-to-Shore Trail, a route that crosses the Lower Peninsula from Lake Michigan to Lake Huron and used primarily by equestrians. At times, you will also cross all-terrain vehicle trails. Then there are the occasional logging trucks that go rumbling by and a few pumping stations for natural gas wells, a sore sight for anybody hoping to escape into the woods for the weekend.

But the beauty of this NCT segment is how well it's posted – there's never a question of where to go – and how well it's been laid out. Stay on the trail and you'll rarely see those other obtrusions. For that you can thank the Grand Traverse Hiking Club, and everyone who enjoys this trek should.

Trip Planner

Maps: The USGS topos do not show the trails or a lot of the two-tracks and pipeline corridors. The best map by far is the *North Country Trail Map: Cedar Creek Road to Charlevoix County* (Map MI-06) published and sold by the North Country Trail Association (866-445-3628; *www.northcountrytrail.org*).

Getting There: From US-131 in Fife Lake head west on M-186 and continue west on M-113. Within 4 miles of Fife Lake turn north on Hodges Road and then east on Cedar Creek Road in 2 miles. The trailhead is posted within a mile on Cedar Creek Road. To reach Guernsey Lake State Forest Campground, see Sand Lakes Quiet Area (Hike 13).

This area of the Pere Marquette State Forest can be confusing at times when trying to find roads and trailheads. For a detailed map of the forest roads in the area contact the Traverse City Convention and Visitors Bureau (800-872-8377; *www.mytraversecity.com*).

Fees & Reservations: There are no fees for hiking or camping at the walk-in sites but there are donation boxes at the trailheads for Muncie Lakes Pathway and Sand Lakes Quiet Area. Please give. Camping in the state forest campgrounds is $15 a night.

Information: For trail conditions there's the North Country Trail Association (866-445-3628; *www.northcountrytrail.org*) or the Grand Traverse Hiking Club (*www.northcountrytrail.org/gtr*).

Trail Guide

Day One (6.2 miles) The NCT is well marked where it crosses Cedar Creek Road and near the trailhead there are places to pull off the dirt road and park a car. At Cedar Creek Road the NCT begins by crossing the Shore-to-Shore Trail and then heads north along a gas pipeline corridor that resembles a well used two-track. The corridor doubles as a snowmobile route in the winter, the reason for the abundance of signage, and passes through a jack pine forest. Within 0.6 mile you can spot a gas pumping facility through the trees and a half mile later you arrive at Mayfield Road.

On the north side of Mayfield Road the NCT remains on the corridor for another half mile and then leaves the two-track to the north (right) and crosses an ATV trail at a junction that is well posted. Within a half mile, or 2.5 miles from Cedar Creek Road, you arrive at John's Campsite. John has

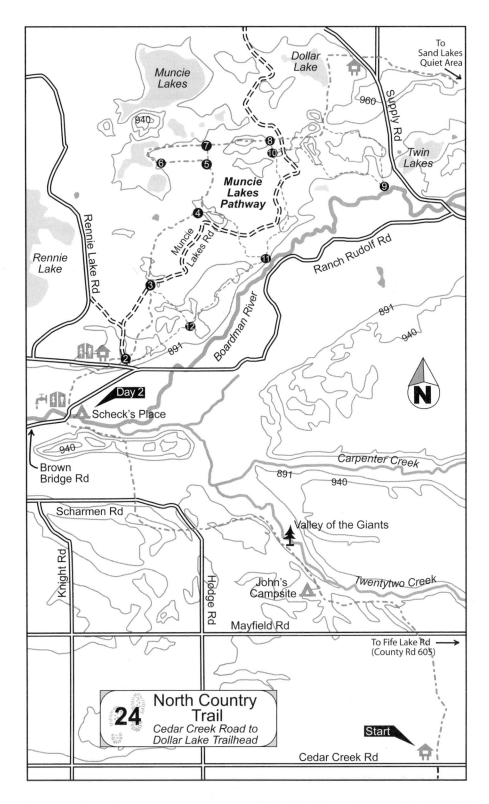

Muncie Lakes

Dollar Lake

To Sand Lakes Quiet Area

960

Supply Rd

Twin Lakes

940

7

8

10

6

5

9

Muncie Lakes Pathway

4

Rennie Lake Rd

Muncie Lakes Rd

11

Ranch Rudolf Rd

Rennie Lake

3

12

891

940

891

Boardman River

2

N

Day 2

Scheck's Place

940

Brown Bridge Rd

Carpenter Creek

891

940

Scharmen Rd

Valley of the Giants

Knight Rd

Hodge Rd

John's Campsite

Twentytwo Creek

Mayfield Rd

To Fife Lake Rd (County Rd 605)

24 North Country Trail
Cedar Creek Road to Dollar Lake Trailhead

Start

Cedar Creek Rd

a nice campsite. It's located on a small plateau above a beaver pond and includes a fire ring and space for a half dozen tents.

Beyond the campsite, the NCT descends sharply into a valley created by Twentytwo Creek. At the bottom you pass a series of beaver dams then skirt the creek itself, a beautiful stream that gurgles and swirls its way southeast. Within a half mile from John's Campsite you enter the Valley of the Giants. Twentytwo Creek valley is so steep here that this stand of trees escaped earlier logging operations. Today the old growth hemlocks, white pines and oaks are indeed giants. The massive trunk of one oak is 12 feet in circumference and the tree is estimated to be more than 300 years old.

The grove of giant trees is signposted on the north side just before you pass a posted spur to a spring. The spring is bubbling out of the ground from a pipe and can be used to refill your water bottles. Beyond it, you climb steadily out of the valley and emerge at Hodge Road, a forest road, 2.5 miles from Mayfield Road. On the west side you dip into the woods but quickly emerge at Scharmen Road. Both roads are posted with trail signs.

On the north side of Scharmen Road, the NCT follows another pipeline corridor for 0.3 mile then veers west (left) into the pine forest and climbs a ridge. You descend the north side of the ridge to a bluff above the Boardman River and follow the river briefly, a beautiful stretch of trail. Eventually you descend away from the river, cross the Shore-to-Shore Trail and breakout at Brown Bridge Road, well posted here. Head east (right) on the road to cross the Boardman River and arrive at Scheck's Place State Forest Campground, 5.1 miles from Mayfield Road or 6.2 miles from Cedar Creek Road.

The rustic campground is large, and its 30 sites are spread out on both sides of Brown Bridge Road. Many are on the banks of the Boardman River, making this a pleasant spot to spend the night. Amenities include drinking water, vault toilets, picnic tables, and fire rings.

Day Two (10.6 miles) This is a 10-mile-plus day, but the steepest climb occurs right at the beginning, long before shoulders are burning from the straps of your backpack. Just east of the state forest campground, the NCT is posted on the north side of Brown Bridge Road and from there you sidle a high ridge. It's a 109-foot gain in elevation before you break out at paved Ranch Rudolf Road and can catch your breath. Across the road is the trailhead for the Muncie Lakes Pathway, reached less than a mile from Scheck's Place and featuring a large parking area, vault toilet and a display board with maps.

Muncie Lakes Pathway is an 8.5-mile loop, with four cross-over spurs, that is used by both hikers and mountain bikers. The NCT follows the west half of the loop and begins in meadows and an old clearcut before reaching post No. 3 along Muncie Lakes Road 1.6 miles from Scheck's Place. At the junction head north (right) through the rolling terrain, you pass post No. 4 at 2.5 miles, cross a rough two-track and arrive at post No. 5 at 2.9 miles.

Here the NCT continues straight 200 yards to post No. 7. But for an interesting side trip head west (left) as the pathway winds past the largest of the Muncie Lakes and then more ponds before looping back to post No. 7.

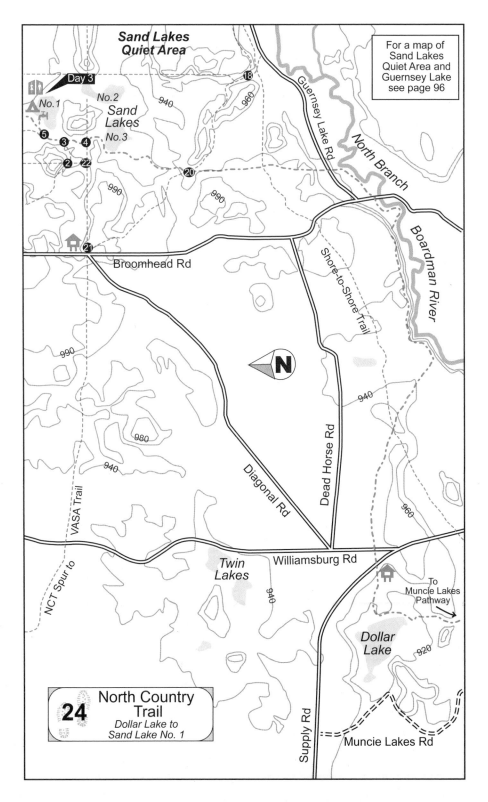

Sand Lakes
Quiet Area

For a map of
Sand Lakes
Quiet Area and
Guernsey Lake
see page 96

Day 3

No.1　No.2
Sand
Lakes
No.3

Guernsey Lake Rd

North Branch

Boardman River

Broomhead Rd

Shore-to-Shore Trail

N

Diagonal Rd

Dead Horse Rd

VASA Trail

NCT Spur to

Williamsburg Rd

Twin
Lakes

To
Muncie Lakes
Pathway

Dollar
Lake

24 North Country
Trail
*Dollar Lake to
Sand Lake No. 1*

Supply Rd

Muncie Lakes Rd

Add a mile to your day if you include this segment, which is by far the most scenic stretch of the entire pathway. Many hikers choose to camp where the trail skirts the shore of Muncie Lake, the reason for the vault toilet.

At post No. 7 the NCT swings east (right) and levels out in a predominately oak forest before quickly descending to post No. 8. Continue straight as the NCT re-crosses Muncie Lakes Road and within a third of a mile or 3.7 miles from Scheck's Place departs the Muncie Lakes Pathway for good at a well-posted junction. You head north (left) and follow an old two-track to reach Dollar Lake in a mile. This beautiful lake is totally surrounded by the state forest and thus free of cottages or any other development. It's a popular place for backpackers on the NCT to set up camp when covering the Cedar Creek Road-Guernsey Lake route as an overnight trek. Even if you're not ready to pitch a tent, Dollar Lake is close to the halfway point of the day, making it a nice place for an extended break.

The NCT departs from the east shore of the lake and in 0.4 mile arrives at the Dollar Lake Trailhead on Supply Road where there is a large parking lot. You cross Supply Road and then Williamson Road in quick succession and then dip back into the woods and head southeast. The trail crosses the Shore-to-Shore and then descends to a bluff above the North Branch of the Boardman River, reached 2 miles from Dollar Lake.

The next stretch is another scenic gem of this route. For the next 2 miles, the NCT skirts the trout stream, first from above along the river bluff, then right along it for a third of a mile until you break out at Broomhead Road, reached 8.1 miles from Scheck's Place. On the east side of the dirt road you continue to stay close to the North Branch for another half mile until the trail swings north for the Sand Lakes Quiet Area. At times along this stretch of the Boardman River you can sit quietly and watch the dissipating rings of trout feeding on hatches of insects.

You quickly cross Guernsey Lake Road (dirt) after the NCT leaves the North Branch and then in a half mile arrive at a junction with the Shore-to-Shore Trail. Continue north, and a mile from the Boardman River, you reach the trail system in the Sand Lakes Quiet Area at post No. 20. The NCT continues north towards post No. 4, reaching it in 0.7 mile after skirting Sand Lake No. 3. Continue north at this junction and in less than a half mile, you reach post No. 5 where nearby are the walk-in campsites overlooking Sand Lake No. 1, reached 2.5 miles from Broomhead Road or 10.6 miles from Scheck's place. Your long day is over.

This beautiful and quiet camping area is well shaded and has a pair of vault toilets and a water pump near the lake.

Day Three (2.8 miles) The final day is a 2.8-mile walk through the Sand Lakes Quiet Area to post No. 15 at Guernsey Lake State Forest Campground (see Hike 13 for full description.) For those continuing onto Kalkaska, the NCT leaves the Sand Lakes Quiet Area trail at post No. 14 where it heads east and in 0.6 mile breaks out at Guernsey Lake Road just north of the campground entrance.

North Country Trail
Wilderness State Park

County: Emmet
Nearest Town: Mackinaw City
Distance: 23.4 miles
Hiking Time: Three days
Highest Elevation Gain: 66 feet
Difficulty: Moderate
Highlights: Wetlands, French Farm Lake, rental cabins

When wolves returned to Michigan's Lower Peninsula in the mid-1990s, their doorstep, to no one's surprise, was Wilderness State Park. They no doubt felt at home in this 10,500-acre park that includes Sturgeon Bay, 26 miles of Lake Michigan shoreline, and a rugged and isolated interior that ranges from mature hardwood forests and wooded sand dunes to vast wetlands and a high point called Mt. Nebo.

The state park is the largest piece of contingent, undeveloped land in the Lower Peninsula, a place where a wolf can find solitude even on the busiest weekend of the summer, and the reason why a 4,492-acre slice of it has been proposed for wilderness status. Even better for backpackers, winding across the state park, from Sturgeon Bay to the Straits of Mackinac, is the North Country Trail (NCT).

At the tip of the Mitt, the NCT has been lovingly built, marked, and maintained by the Harbor Springs Chapter whose volunteer efforts include building 11 foot bridges so you can keep your boots dry in a vast wetland just west of French Farm Lake. The heart of this three-day trek, however, is the 11.4 miles of the NCT that begins in the southwest corner of Wilderness and doesn't leave the state park until the second day.

In all, the route from a trailhead on Sturgeon Bay Trail, an access road, to Mackinaw City is a 23.4-mile walk...or more depending on where you choose to camp the first night. One of the nicest aspects of Wilderness State Park is the variety of accommodations available to hikers. You can rent a rustic cabin, stay at a modern campground with showers and restrooms, or reserve one of the park's new backcountry campsites. There is even a bunkhouse available for groups, and every accommodation is accessible from the trail system. A water filter is necessary for this trip as there is no source of safe drinking water at the French Farm Lake campsites, the second-night destination. You also want to be packing along inspect repellent for any outing that occurs from late May through August. The numerous wetlands and small ponds you encounter are literally bug factories during the summer.

For a unique backpacking experience and to avoid the hassles of a point-to-point trail, hike in for an overnight stay at either the Sturgeon or

A member of the Harbor Springs Chapter of the North Country Trail Association posts a sign along a boardwalk in the wetlands west of French Farm Lake.

Nebo cabins. The Nebo Cabin is an 8-mile walk from Sturgeon Bay Trail; the Sturgeon Cabin is a 7.3-mile trek. At either one you have water pumps, bunks with mattresses, protection from bugs, and guaranteed solitude at night.

Trip Planner

Maps: The USGS topos that cover the area are *Bliss*, *Levering*, and *St. Ignace*, and show more than half the trails. A better map is the *North Country Trail Map: Charlevoix County to the Mackinac Bridge* (Map MI-07) published and sold by the North Country Trail Association (866-445-3628; *www.northcountrytrail. org*).

Getting There: The trailhead on Sturgeon Bay Trail is a quarter mile east of Lakeshore Drive, reached 5 miles north of Cross Village and the north end of M-119. The Mackinaw City trailhead is in the heart of the tourist town across from the Baymount Inn at 109 S. Nicolet Street.

One possibility for shuttle transportation is Straits Regional Ride (231-597-9262 or 866-731-1204), a four-county regional transit system that provides on-demand service between Cheboygan, Mackinaw City and Petoskey. Call for rates and possible drop-off locations.

Fees & Reservations: Wilderness State Park's six rustic cabins, including Nebo and Sturgeon, are $60 a night while a site in the modern campground is $16 to $27. Both can be reserved online (*www.midnrreservations.com*) or by phone (800-447-2757). The park's backcountry campsites are $10 a night and are reserved through the park. Campsites at French Farm Lake are free.

Information: Wilderness State Park (231-436-5381) is the best source of information on trail conditions and the status of the backcountry campsites.. Trail updates are also available from the North Country Trail Association (866-445-3628; *www.northcountrytrail.org*).

Trail Guide

Day One (8.3 miles) On the south side of Sturgeon Bay Trail is a small pullover to leave a vehicle, on the north side is post No. 7 marking the NCT. The trail winds into the woods but immediately breakes out at a telephone line. You return to the pines and balsams and soon are following the rolling contour of the dunes. These dunes are well forested, but just beneath the thin layer of needles that covers the path is the stuff beaches are made of.

Within a half mile you make a noticeable climb, level out briefly, then climb again, this time topping out at a 780-foot high point to end the first mile of the hike. Here you can gaze inland towards Bliss. If enough leaves have dropped you can also catch a glimpse of Lake Michigan to the west. You descend and then continue hiking across the dunes, reaching a second viewing point of Lake Michigan in less than a mile and finally breaking out at paved Lakeview Road 2.8 miles from the start.

Across the road is post No. 8, a major trailhead. Beautiful Sturgeon Bay is just west on Lakeview Road, the reason for the large parking area, vault toilets, and hand pump for drinking water. In the back of the parking area the NCT heads north into the forest where it continues to traverse the rolling dunes. Within a half mile you top off on the edge of a steep sided, wooded hollow and then descend into a cedar wetland reached 3.8 miles from the start. This area can be wet and buggy at times.

The trail moves onto a drier forest setting, and then in less than a mile passes two ponds followed by a small lake. You remain on a low forested ridge that borders this marshy area for a dry and very scenic walk before arriving at post No. 9, marking where the NCT merges with the park's Sturgeon Bay Trail. It's a 5.3-mile walk from the start on Sturgeon Bay Trail (the road) to Sturgeon Bay Trail (the trail) and at the junction you have to make a decision.

If you've reserved the Sturgeon Cabin, head north (left) and in 2 miles you will reach the five-bunk structure that features a wood burning stove, hand pump for water, and a view of the bay. Head south (right) on a snowmobile trail and in 3 miles you'll arrive at one of the park's three walk-in campsites, this one located on a small point along the north shore of O'Neal Lake. The site must be reserved in advance and is a delightful place to spend the evening.

Straight ahead is the NCT. The national trail follows the Sturgeon Bay Trail east, passing through a wet area in a half mile and then arriving at a second walk-in backcountry site. In another half mile or 6.3 miles from the start, Sturgeon Bay Trail ends at a junction. Those who have managed to reserve the delightful Nebo Cabin would follow the South Boundary Trail south (right) to Nebo Trail. This classic log cabin sits on a pine-covered knoll overlooking Nebo Trail and is an 8-mile walk from where you left your vehicle.

North (left) from the junction is Swamp Line Road, now a trail that will lead you to Pines Campground in 2 miles. The modern campground, located near the trailhead for Pondside Trail, has 100 sites, restrooms, drinking water and showers. A short walk away is the park's delightful Lakeshore Campground with 150 modern sites overlooking Big Stone Bay and its fine beaches.

Day Two (9.6 miles) If you've camped on the shores of O'Neal Lake, begin the second day following the snowmobile trail east 1.5 miles to the junction of South Boundary and Nebo trails. Head north on Nebo Trail, past Nebo Cabin, to arrive at the posted west end of the East Ridge Trail within a mile. East Ridge Trail doubles up as the North Country Trail.

If you stayed at one of the modern campgrounds, the second day begins by following a series of trails east, the first three short interpretive trails. From the Goose Pond Trailhead just south of the Pines Campground, you follow Pondside Trail briefly to interpretive post No. 7 and then continue east on Red Pine Trail.

This path begins by skirting Big Stone Pond and then leading you

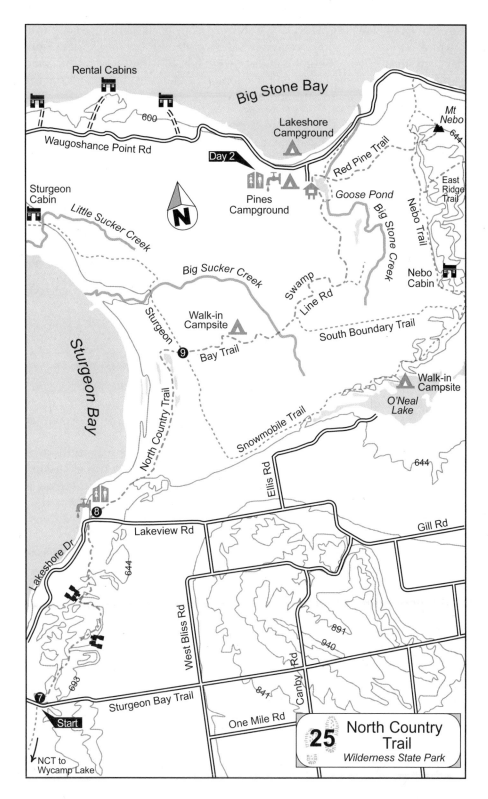

Rental Cabins

Big Stone Bay

600

Waugoshance Point Rd

Day 2

Lakeshore
Campground

Mt
Nebo
644

Red Pine Trail

East
Ridge
Trail

Sturgeon
Cabin

Little Sucker Creek

Pines
Campground

Goose Pond

Big Stone Creek

Nebo Trail

Nebo
Cabin

Big Sucker Creek

Swamp

Line Rd

Walk-in
Campsite

Sturgeon

9

Bay Trail

South Boundary Trail

Sturgeon Bay

North Country Trail

Walk-in
Campsite

O'Neal
Lake

Snowmobile Trail

644

Ellis Rd

8

Lakeview Rd

Gill Rd

Lakeshore Dr

644

West Bliss Rd

891

940

Canby Rd

693

7

Start

Sturgeon Bay Trail

841

One Mile Rd

NCT to
Wycamp Lake

25 **North Country
Trail**
Wilderness State Park

through a cedar swamp. The wettest sections have been planked, and within a half mile the soggy trail becomes a sandy path; the terrain changes from flat to rolling ridges, the habitat from wetlands to a red pine forest. Soon you're standing on the crest of a ridge looking down into the woods on one side and at a small pond on the other.

Side Trip: Within 1.3 miles from Goose Pond Red Pine Trail ends at Nebo Trail and here the NCT heads south (right). But for an interesting side trip, drop the packs and head north briefly to the junction with Hemlock Trail. This short loop will lead you on a steady but short ascent to the top of 720-foot Mt. Nebo. This "peak" is marked by a set of large stone blocks, the remains of a firetower that Civilian Conservation Corps built in the mid-1930s and used until 1949. If enough leaves have fallen, you can catch a glimpse of the Straits of Mackinac. Continue along the loop and you'll make a descent into a stand of hemlocks where some of the pines are more than 200 years old and at times more impressive than the mountain-top view. Head south on Nebo Trail to return to the NCT and add a mile to your day's total.

In less than a half mile south the NCT leaves Nebo Trail and swings northeast (left) on East Ridge Trail at a well-marked junction. You follow this trail for a half mile and then 2.1 miles from Goose Pond arrive at the junction where the NCT continues east, departing the state park for good within a mile. Along the way you cross East Boundary Trail and then quickly come to a small pond where on the east end is a third walk-in backcountry campsite.

Beyond Wilderness State Park, the NCT continues as a level path through the woods until it pops out at paved Cecil Bay Road (also known as County Road C-81) 4.5 miles from Goose Pond. On the other side of the road is post No. 10, marking the start of another interesting segment of this trek. It is also one of the wettest as you begin with a 2.5-mile stretch through wetlands, the reason for all the bridges and boardwalks here.

From the Cecil Bay Road you enter the woods and in less than a half mile come to the first bridge, an impressive wooden structure that arches across Carp Lake River. In the next mile the trail passes through a low-lying forest of balsams, cedars, and birch and you cross 10 more bridges. The wooden structures range from a pair of six-foot planks that cross a small stream to the final one, a 150-foot long boardwalk that zigzags through a cedar swamp.

You get to travel through a wetland without having to don hip boots. If the deer flies aren't zeroing in on you, you can pause along the way to look at wildflowers, including rare orchids. The wetlands also teams with wildlife. Volunteer trail workers spotted bears, coyotes, and even a bobcat while building the bridges.

Beyond the final boardwalk the NCT merges into an old two-track and follows it to the south end of French Farm Lake, an undeveloped lake reached 7.6 miles from Goose Pond. Once at the lake, the NCT winds over a series

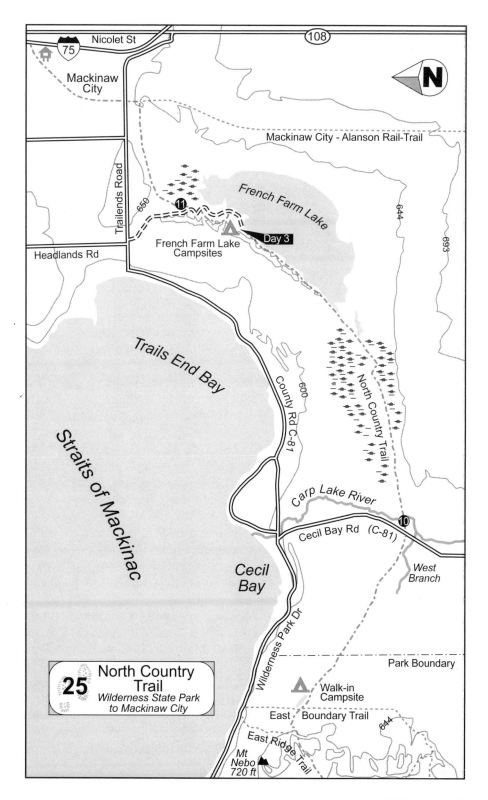

Mackinaw City - Alanson Rail-Trail

French Farm Lake

Day 3

French Farm Lake Campsites

Trailends Road

Headlands Rd

650

644

693

Trails End Bay

Straits of Mackinac

County Rd C-81

600

North Country Trail

Carp Lake River

Cecil Bay Rd (C-81)

Cecil Bay

West Branch

Wilderness Park Dr

Nicolet St

Mackinaw City

108

75

Park Boundary

Walk-in Campsite

East Boundary Trail

644

East Ridge Trail

Mt Nebo 720 ft

25 North Country Trail
Wilderness State Park to Mackinaw City

11

10

N

The NCT passes through wetlands west of French Farm Lake where hikers often spot a variety of orchids, including lady's-slippers.

of low wooded dunes along the west shore of the lake for more than a mile. You enjoy near-constant views of the water and several times reach elevated viewing points where you can sit and search for the myriad waterfowl that the large body of water attracts.

Eventually, you arrive at an unimproved boat access and a dirt road. Nearby are two of the six campsites located on the lake, all marked with numbered posts. For the remaining mile, the NCT weaves across the access road as it follows either the shoreline of the lake or climbs more dunes on the other side. Eventually you pop out at post No. 11, reached 9.6 miles from Goose Pond. Across the road is campsite No. 1. There is no charge for staying at the French Farm Lake campsites nor are there any facilities other than fire rings. All of the campsites are well spread apart along the access road.

Day Three (2.7 miles) This is a short and easy day, one that strong backpackers can combine with day two to reduce the outing to an overnight walk. From post No. 11 you leave the access road for good along a newly re-routed section. The NCT no longer follows Trailsend Road. Instead, you head north through another wetland area and curve east.

Within 1.5 miles from post No. 11 the NCT arrives at the former Michigan Northern Railroad, now a rail-trail between Mackinaw City and Alanson. In the winter this trail hums with snowmobiles, but in the summer backpackers can follow it north to reach Mackinaw City in 1.2 miles. The rail-trail quickly crosses paved Trailsend Road and continues north to end up at a large staging area beneath an I-75 overpass. After three days of walking through a park named Wilderness, you now find yourself standing under an interstate humming with traffic, while across Nicolet Street is a large collection of stores, fudge shops, and restaurants called Mackinaw Crossings.

Welcome back to civilization.

Pigeon River Country State Forest

The Pigeon River Country State Forest is a rugged 105,049-acre tract located 20 miles north of Gaylord and occupying the high central plateau of the Lower Peninsula. The forest is an outdoor playground crisscrossed with dirt roads, old two-tracks, and trails and dotted with lakes, trout streams, and rustic campgrounds. It's best known as the home of the Michigan elk herd, an animal that was reintroduced here in 1918.

Beginning and ending in the state forest is the High Country Pathway, a 70-mile loop that passes through four counties and the heart of Michigan's northern Lower Peninsula. Most backpackers need five to seven days to hike the entire circuit.

But for those who don't have the time or the inclination to hike that far, there are two other backpacking treks here, just as scenic but much shorter. Green Timbers is the site of an overnight hike to a wonderful, free-use cabin perched on the edge of a ridge overlooking the Sturgeon River valley. Shingle Mill Pathway is a two-day loop that includes a walk-in campsite on Grass Lake. Both are ideal weekend outings.

For additional information or a place to learn more about the elk herd stop at the Pigeon River Country State Forest Headquarters, an impressive log lodge on Twin Lakes Road. The headquarters (989-983-4101) is open 8 a.m. to 5 p.m. Monday through Friday.

One of the highlights of hiking Green Timbers Recreation Area in the fall is the possibility of hearing a bull elk calling his harem.

Green Timbers Recreation Area
Pigeon River Country State Forest

26

County: Otsego
Nearest Town: Vanderbilt
Distance: 8 miles
Hiking Time: Overnight
Highest Elevation Gain: 120 feet
Difficulty: Moderate
Highlights: Spectacular Sturgeon River Valley, free-use shelters

What began as an exclusive company retreat is now a unique destination for backpackers looking for an overnight adventure in the Lower Peninsula. Green Timbers is a rugged 6,300-acre slice of the Pigeon River Country State Forest that originally was logged, burned, and then used for grazing.

But in the 1950s the tract was purchased by Don McLouth, who named it Green Timbers and turned the area into a hunting-and-fishing retreat for McLouth Steel employees. Among the amenities the company added was a series of log cabins near the Sturgeon River. After the state took over the property in 1982, all the cabins were removed with the exception of two. On the banks of the Sturgeon River is Green Timbers Cabin, while perched on the edge of a ridge overlooking Sturgeon River Valley is Honeymoon Cabin. A wall in both structures was removed by the DNR to turn them into three-sided shelters, and they are now available to anybody exploring this non-motorized recreation area.

Pigeon River Country State Forest and Green Timbers in particular are best known as a haven for Michigan's elk herd. Green Timbers is just 1.5 miles north of the site where the seven elk from Yellowstone National Park were released in 1918. Today, the state's herd is the largest east of the Mississippi River, numbering more than 1,200 with the bulk of it living in the Pigeon River Country State Forest.

Thanks to the large expanse of open fields that are planted with rye, clover, and alfalfa, Green Timbers attracts a healthy portion of the herd. The elk are tough to spot in the summer as they retreat into the thick underbush of the forest to escape the heat. The prime time to view the animals and to enjoy an overnight trek in this area is early September through mid-October, when the bulls bugle to form their harems. A huge, 600-pound bull making its high-pitched call to cows in the middle of a field is one of the most unusual wildlife sounds in Michigan.

Green Timbers boasts a trail system of more than 20 miles, most of it two-tracks and old forest roads, some well established and easy to follow, many little more than overgrown trails used mainly by elk and deer. The trails are poorly marked, if at all, and do not necessarily correspond to USGS topos or the map available at the Pigeon River Country headquarters. This overnight adventure is a one-way trek of 4 miles to Honeymoon Cabin along a well-defined route. Keep in mind that Green Timbers is also open to mountain bikers, hunters, and equestrians. Plan to carry in a tent on any weekend outing, then use the shelters for cooking or as a place to gather at night. Also carry in a water filter or be prepared to boil water as there are no sources of safe drinking water at either shelter.

Trip Planner

Maps: The USGS topo, *Green Timbers*, covers this trek, and because the route is old two-tracks, it's easy to recognize it on the map. The DNR's Forest Management Division also publishes a Green Timbers map which is more than adequate.

Getting There: From I-75, depart at exit 290 and head south for Vanderbilt. In town turn left (east) on Sturgeon Valley Road and follow it for seven miles. The main entry to Green Timbers is the stonegate trailhead on Sturgeon Valley Road, reached just before crossing the Sturgeon River. To reach the Pigeon River Country State Forest headquarters continue east on Sturgeon Valley Road for 5 miles and then turn left (north) on Twin Lakes Road.

Fees & Reservations: There are no entry fees for Green Timbers or for using the cabins. The cabins are used on a first-come-first-serve basis.

Information: For maps or more information on elk viewing, call the Pigeon River Country State Forest headquarters (989-983-4101).

Trail Guide

Day One (4 miles) The major trailhead in Green Timbers is marked by a stonegate entrance and a locked yellow gate that prevents motorized users from entering the area. The trail to Green Timbers Cabin is an old two-track and probably the easiest to follow in this tract. It leads north through the forested valley with the Sturgeon River just to the east though you rarely see the water itself in the beginning. To the west the trail skirts the base of a ridge that rises almost 100 feet above you for a mile or more.

Within 2 miles of the trailhead, you arrive at a T junction. Just to the west (left) is Club Stream and the marked boundary for Fontinalis Club, a private hunting club. To the east (right) the trail quickly descends to a wide bridge across the Sturgeon River. Just on the other side, or a half mile from the junction, is Green Timbers Cabin, a classic one-room log structure.

The cabin is just upstream from the confluence between Sturgeon River and Pickerel Creek, a favorite stretch for anglers trying to entice a trout with flies or spinners. Inside the cabin are benches, a stash of wood, and a stone fireplace. If you stay for the night, good campsites abound in the semi-open grassy area around the old cabin and along the Sturgeon River. Poke around farther to the east and you'll find the stone foundation of other cabins that were once part of the McLouth Steel Company retreat.

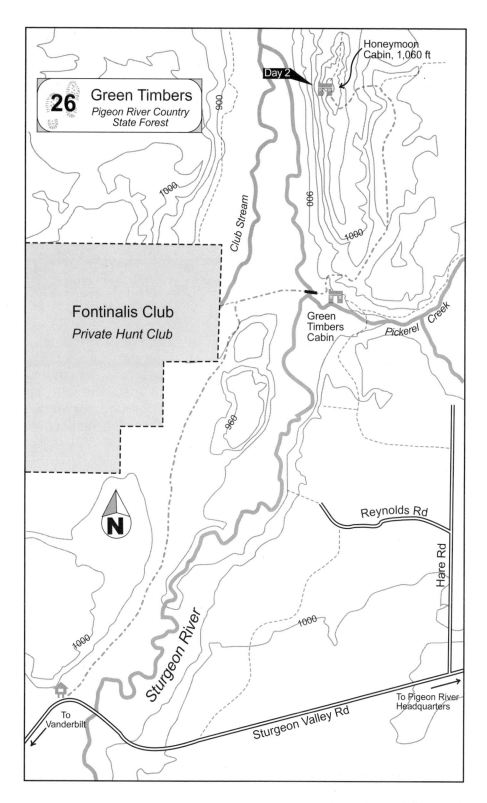

26 Green Timbers
*Pigeon River Country
State Forest*

Honeymoon
Cabin, 1,060 ft

Day 2

Fontinalis Club
Private Hunt Club

Club Stream

Green
Timbers
Cabin

Pickerel Creek

900

1000

960

1000

1000

N

Reynolds Rd

Hare Rd

Sturgeon River

To
Vanderbilt

Sturgeon Valley Rd

To Pigeon River
Headquarters

The Green Timbers Cabin is a free-use shelter in the Green Timbers Recreation Area.

The second half of this trek to Honeymoon Cabin is another two-track that departs from the east side of Green Timbers Cabin and climbs into the nearby hills. You break out in a narrow valley bordered on the west side by a very noticeable 1,060-foot ridge. At this point the trail heads north through an open clear-cut area for a mile and then forks. This junction, reached 3.5 miles from Sturgeon Valley Road, is unposted and, depending on the time of year, is easy to miss. Follow the spur west as it steadily climbs 120 feet in less than a half mile.

Your reward for the climb is at the crest. Looking all the world like a mountain-top chalet is Honeymoon Cabin. On one side of this log structure is a large stone fireplace. On the other, where a wall has been knocked out, the one-room cabin opens up to a deck perched over the edge of the ridge. Look down and see a slope that drops suddenly for more than 100 feet. Look out and you can see the entire Sturgeon River Valley, which in the fall has to be one of the most stunning panoramas in the Lower Peninsula, especially during a sunset.

If you plan to spend the night in the shelter, bring a tarp to cover the missing wall. The opening faces the west, and the ridge-top cabin is fully exposed to the weather and wind. You might also want to haul in as much water as you can. It's a long climb up that ridge from the Sturgeon River.

Day Two (4 miles) To return you simply backtrack the 4 miles to Sturgeon Valley Road. If you have a spare morning follow the trail that heads north from Honeymoon Cabin. Within a half mile a trail descends the west wide of the ridge to a foot bridge over the Sturgeon River. On the west side of the river are large meadows and grasslands, making them the best areas to look for elk in the spring and fall.

Shingle Mill Pathway
Pigeon River Country State Forest

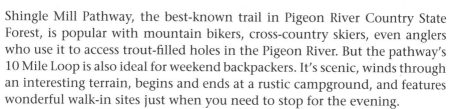

County: Otsego
Nearest Town: Vanderbilt
Distance: 10 miles
Hiking Time: Two days
Highest Elevation Gain: 114 feet
Difficulty: Moderate
Highlights: Pigeon River, overlooks, walk-in campsites

Shingle Mill Pathway, the best-known trail in Pigeon River Country State Forest, is popular with mountain bikers, cross-country skiers, even anglers who use it to access trout-filled holes in the Pigeon River. But the pathway's 10 Mile Loop is also ideal for weekend backpackers. It's scenic, winds through an interesting terrain, begins and ends at a rustic campground, and features wonderful walk-in sites just when you need to stop for the evening.

What more could you want? How about a location that's only 20 minutes from an I-75 exit? Drive up Friday after work, be home by Sunday evening.

The Shingle Mill Pathway is a system of five loops with a trailhead located in Pigeon Bridge Campground and part of the High Country Pathway. The first three loops – .75, 1.25, and 6 miles – make them best suited as dayhikes. The 11 Mile Loop has the mileage for an overnight trek and even its own walk-in campsite. But the 10 Mile Loop has scenery that is hard to pass up. Both of the longer loops follow the Pigeon River and pass through Pigeon River Campground but the 10 Mile Loop skirts three small lakes and features walk-in campsites on one of them, Grass Lake.

You can also pick up the trail at several other locations in the state forest, including the Pigeon River Campground. By beginning here you would turn the northern half of the pathway into an easier overnight hike of 6 miles with a night still spent at Grass Lake.

Trip Planner

Maps: The USGS topo, *Hardwood Lake*, covers this area and includes the eastern half of the trail, labeled on the map as the High Country Pathway. The DNR also publishes a Shingle Mill Pathway map which is adequate.

Getting There: From I-75, depart at exit 290 and head south for Vanderbilt. In town turn left (east) on Sturgeon Valley Road and follow it for 11 miles. The Pigeon Bridge State Forest Campground is reached just after crossing the Pigeon River. To reach the state forest headquarters continue east on Sturgeon Valley Road another 3 miles and then turn north (left)on Twin Lakes Road. The headquarters is passed in a mile, and Pigeon River State Forest Campground is reached in 2 miles.

Fees & Reservations: There are no fees for hiking or camping along the Shingle Mill Pathway. Campsites at Pigeon Bridge and Pigeon River State Forest Campgrounds are $15 a night.

Information: For maps or more information, call the Pigeon River Country State Forest headquarters (989-983-4101).

Trail Guide

Day One (5.2 miles) Parking is available at Pigeon Bridge Campground, a small facility with 10 sites, drinking water, and vault toilets near its namesake trout stream. The trailhead for the Shingle Mill Pathway is post No. 1 erected in the back of the campground. From here you head north but quickly reach post No. 2, marking the return for the 0.75-mile loop, and then in a half mile post No. 3, the junction where the 1.25-mile loop heads back to the campground. For the next half mile, the pathway skirts the Pigeon River and then leaves the scenic trout stream to climb a wooded ridge.

It's an uphill climb of almost 50 feet, but once on top you follow the edge of the ridge for more than a half mile, a scenic stretch of hiking in the fall, before descending to the Pigeon River Country State Forest headquarters, reached 2.2 miles from the campground. If the headquarters, an impressive log lodge, is open drop the packs and head inside to view the lobby displays on the elk herd and an impressive collection of wildlife mounts. Outside are benches, vault toilets, and drinking water.

From the headquarters, the pathway climbs in and out of the river valley before finally descending to Pigeon River State Forest Campground, reached 3 miles from the trailhead or less than a mile from the headquarters. The state forest campground has 13 rustic sites with many of them overlooking the trout stream. There are also vault toilets, picnic tables, and cold, clear drinking water from an artesian well.

Pigeon Bridge Road crosses the river near the campground and at the vehicle bridge you can soak your feet in a pool that campers have dammed with rocks. Shingle Mill Pathway also uses the bridge to cross the river and then hugs the west bank to quickly reach post No. 6. At this junction the 6 Mile Loop heads southwest (left) to cross Pigeon Bridge Road.

You head northwest (right) as the 10 Mile Loop immediately climbs a ridge bordering the west bank of the Pigeon River and then follows the crest of it for more than a half mile. Eventually you descend into a stand of red pine and reach post No. 7 a little more than 4 miles from Pigeon Bridge State Forest Campground. This junction marks the split between the pathway's 10 Mile Loop (west to the left) and 11 Mile Loop (due north to the right).

In less than a half mile the 10 Mile Loop passes beautiful Section Four Lake. This steep-sided, almost perfectly round body of water is an excellent example of the many "sinkhole lakes" found throughout this region of the Lower Peninsula. It's easy to stand on the edge of it and envision a hollowed limestone cave suddenly collapsing. Unfortunately, you are not allowed to camp along the lake or fish it as it is being used for research purposes.

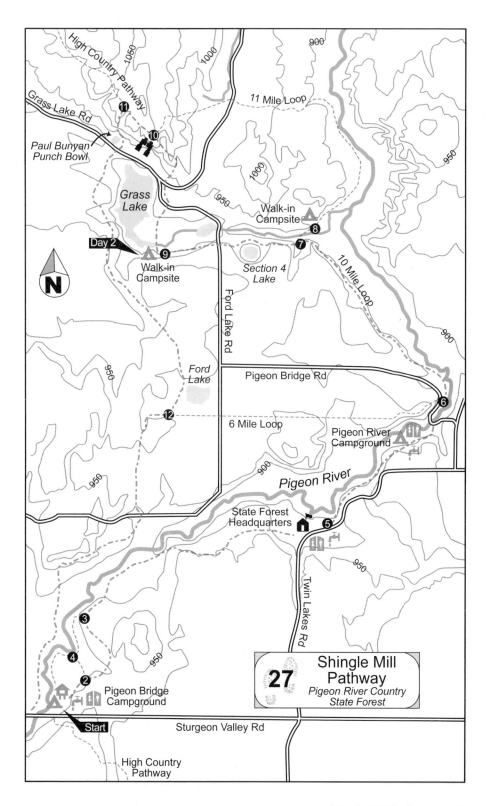

You continue west and in a quarter mile cross Ford Lake Road. On the other side of the sandy road a blue-tipped post alerts you to where the trail resumes in a pine and hardwood forest. In less than a half mile, or 5.2 miles from the trailhead, you reach the backcountry campsite on Grass Lake.

The campsite is situated in a stand of red pine, a spot where you can pitch the tent on a golden carpet of needles. In the evening you can stroll the pathway to the north for a view of Grass Lake and to wait for beavers, deer, or any other visitors that might show up at dusk.

Day Two (4.8 miles) The second day begins with the pathway skirting the south end of the lake and then crossing Ford Lake Road and Grass Lake Road, both sandy, rutted roads. On the other side you pass through a clearcut and then climb through a hardwood forest to post No. 10, reached in a little more than a half mile from the walk-in campsite. It's the steepest climb of the trek, 114 feet in a quarter mile.

The post marks the junction where the pathway's 11 Mile Loop rejoins the 10 Mile Loop while nearby is a short side trail to a fine overlook. A firetower once stood here and today you can still see its foundation. But even more impressive is the view. From this 1,040-foot perch, you can gaze down on Grass Lake, the Pigeon River Valley or look southwest and see more than 20 miles of rolling northern forest.

At the posted junction you head northwest (left) and in less than a quarter mile come to post No. 11. This junction is where the High Country Pathway merges into the Shingle Mill Pathway from the north. Head south (left) to remain on the 10 Mile Loop. The trail descends sharply and then breaks out of the woods to skirt another sinkhole lake. On some maps this lake is labeled Devil's Soup Bowl. On the USGS topo it's called Paul Bunyan Punch Bowl. I like the latter, preferring to think that the giant lumberjack sipped out of it rather than the devil.

The first mile of the day ends when you re-cross Grass Lake Road immediately after Paul Bunyan Punch Bowl. On the other side, the terrain levels out considerably. Within a half mile the pathway crosses a foot bridge as it passes within sight of Grass Lake and then, 2.5 miles from the walk-in campsite, comes into view of Ford Lake, a scenic little body of water. Keep an eye out for blue pathway markers as logging operations in the past have laced this area with two-tracks.

From Ford Lake, you climb to post No. 12, where the 10 Mile Loop merges with the 6 Mile Loop. Head west (right) through more old clearcuts and 3.8 miles from the walk-in campsite, the pathway will cross Ford Lake Road for the third time in two days. In the final mile of the trek, you climb a ridge along the river, top off at 960 feet, and descend into a wetland area.

After crossing the small marsh, you're a quarter mile from Sturgeon Valley Road and will probably hear the traffic rumbling by. Eventually you emerge at the paved road and follow it east to cross Pigeon River and return to the Pigeon Bridge State Forest Campground.

Upper Peninsula

A young backpacker works hard to attach the rainfly to his tent at Horseshoe Bay Wilderness. The mile-long hike into the lakeshore wilderness makes it ideal for families with young children. The 3,790 acres tract in the Hiawatha National Forest features 7 miles of undeveloped Lake Huron shoreline.

Horseshoe Bay Wilderness
Hiawatha National Forest

County: Mackinac
Nearest Town: St. Ignace
Distance: 2.5 to 6 miles round trip
Hiking Time: Overnight
Highest Elevation Gain: 20 feet
Difficulty: Easy
Highlights: Lake Huron beach, wildlife

The 1987 Michigan Wilderness Act created 12 wilderness tracts in the Upper Peninsula, including Horseshoe Bay. Despite spanning across 3,790 acres and featuring 7 miles of undeveloped Lake Huron shoreline, Horseshoe Bay is best known by many as the Interstate Wilderness.

In some places I-75 is less than 100 yards from the tract's western border. Just 3 miles to the south are the hotels and fast food restaurants of St. Ignace, a casino is even closer, and you can see the towers of the Mackinac Bridge from the shoreline. On summer weekends the traffic and the trucks rumbling past are so loud, you have to work hard to escape the noise.

Man's heavy handprint surrounds Horseshoe Bay. But the tract itself has changed little since loggers passed through at the turn of the century and left behind cut stumps and a few roadways that have slowly disappeared over time. Remarkably, Horseshoe Bay looks today like it did when Native Americans used the bay for fishing and voyageurs paddled fur-laden canoes past it on their way to Mackinac Island.

The vast majority of the wilderness is a series of low forested ridges separated by narrow, shallow swamps, whose dense cedar stands are especially attractive to deer. Wetland-loving species such as beaver, otter, mink, muskrat, a variety of waterfowl, and great blue herons inhabit the coastal wetlands and ponds just inland from the shoreline. Often perched on towering pines bordering the bay are bald eagles and ospreys, eyeing the water for a wayward fish.

The outstanding feature of this wilderness, however, is the undeveloped shoreline along Horseshoe and St. Martins bays. A good portion of Horseshoe Bay is a beautiful beach, where the sand is smooth and the water turquoise in color as if you were in the tropics. Eventually, the beach disappears, replaced by a marshy or rocky shoreline bordering the bays.

The Horseshoe Bay Trail is a 1.2-mile walk to the bay that leads you through the cedar swamps while keeping your boots dry. Once at the bay, you can switch to beach walking to extend the outing. Backcountry camping is allowed anywhere in the wilderness but isn't practical throughout most of it. The vast majority of backpackers set up camp close to the beach in the southern third of Horseshoe Bay. Either pack in a filter to treat your water or plan to carry enough from the Foley Creek National Forest Campground.

Trip Planner

Maps: The area is covered by the USGS topo *Evergreen Shores* but the trail is not shown. The *Horseshoe Bay Trail* handout from the Hiawatha National Forest is more than adequate.

Getting There: The Horseshoe Bay trailhead is in Foley Creek National Forest Campground. To reach the USFS campground from I-75, depart at exit 348 and head east. Follow campground signs that will lead you north along H-63 (also known as Old Mackinac Trail) to the entrance of Foley Creek. There is limited parking at the trailhead in the campground.

Fees & Reservations: There is no vehicle entry fee to hike or camp in Horseshoe Bay. A site at Foley Creek is $12 a night.

Information: Call the St. Ignace Ranger District (906-643-7900) or check the Hiawatha National Forest web site (*www.fs.fed.us/r9/hiawatha*).

Trail Guide

Foley Creek Campground is a pleasant facility with 54 rustic sites spread out in a red pine forest. Within the campground are vault toilets, drinking water, and the Horseshoe Bay trailhead at the north end of the loop. From here the trail heads north as a sandy path and quickly passes a sign announcing you're entering a designated wilderness.

You begin in a birch-maple forest, but within a half mile, the trail swings to the east through a series of cedar swamps. You cross them on planking or thick beams, and if it has been raining, you will be tip-toeing through mud and standing water. Unless insects have you running down the trail for the breezes off the bay, the swamps are interesting, a cool and shaded world even on the hottest day where you can see pitcher plants and other insect-hungry vegetation.

Within a mile you return to the drier maple forest and then 1.2 miles from the trailhead emerge from the trees at the sandy shoreline of Horseshoe Bay. The southern end of the bay lies outside the Hiawatha National Forest and you can see the end of Ingalsbe Road and a small cabin.

To the north all you see is sand and surf stretching towards a series of points and the pines that border the shoreline.

The trail ends near a small creek that empties into the bay. Bordering the beach on both sides of the creek is a series of low dunes with stately pines that make the best places to set up camp.

To continue hiking, cross the creek and stay on the beach. It's a 2-mile trek along the crescent moon beach of Horseshoe Bay. The sand eventually gives way to a more rocky footing before the shoreline swings east and you arrive at the small points that enclose the bay at the north end. Beyond them is the next small bay formed to the north where Martineau Creek, the largest stream in the wilderness, empties into Lake Huron.

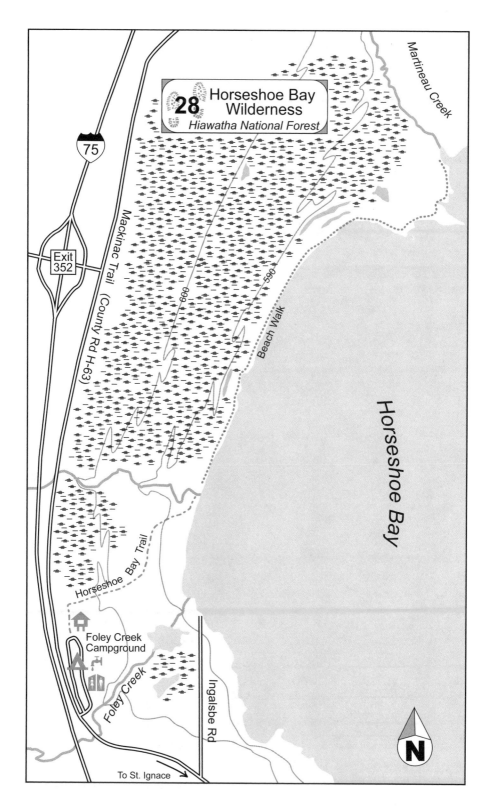

Horseshoe Bay

28 Horseshoe Bay Wilderness
Hiawatha National Forest

Martineau Creek

75

Exit 352

Mackinac Trail (County Rd H-63)

690

590

Beach Walk

Horseshoe Bay Trail

Foley Creek Campground

Foley Creek

Ingalsbe Rd

To St. Ignace

N

Along with lakes and stretches of the Indian River, backpackers hiking Bruno's Run pass the Hemlock Cathedral, a stand of old-growth pines.

Bruno's Run
Hiawatha National Forest

County: Schoolcraft
Nearest Town: Munising
Distance: 10 miles
Hiking Time: Two days
Highest Elevation Gain: 120 feet
Difficulty: Moderate
Highlights: Numerous lakes, old-growth hemlock; walk-in campsite and rental cabin

Forest Highway 13 (H-13) that connects M-28 and Lake Superior with US-2 and Lake Michigan is an avenue of outdoor recreation. Within this strip of the Hiawatha National Forest are six campgrounds, chains of lakes to paddle, wilderness areas to explore, many hiking trails and opportunities to heft a backpack and sneak into the woods for a night or two.

For those equipped with boots, instead of a paddle, the best avenue to escape into the backcountry is Bruno's Run, a 9.7-mile trail that crosses H-13 twice. Although also used by mountain bikers and dayhikers, Bruno's Run is an excellent backpacking route for a two-day walk. For starters it's a loop, conveniently ending where your car is parked. It also passes through an interesting topography, a rolling terrain of woods – even a stand of century-old hemlocks – marsh areas, numerous lakes and streams.

Finding a place to stop for the night is easy. The trail winds through two national forest campgrounds, Widewaters and Pete's Lake. Both are popular rustic facilities and Pete's Lake features a handful of walk-in campsites that put some distance between you and the rest of the campers. You can also backcountry camp along the trail without a permit.

But the best way to enjoy Bruno's Run is to plan your trek in advance and reserve either McKeever Cabin or the single walk-in site on Ewing Point. Off by themselves, away from the traffic on H-13 or the popular campgrounds, either the cabin or the campsite will assure you a quiet evening in the woods. That is, after all, why we go backpacking, isn't it?

The route described here begins at Moccasin Lake, follows the trail in a counter-clockwise direction and takes advantage of either the cabin or the campsite. This would make the first day a trek of 7 miles and the second only 3 miles.

Trip Planner

Maps: Bruno's Run is well marked and easy to follow. Most people are satisfied with the Hiawatha National Forest's *Bruno's Run* handout even though the map on it lacks contour lines and the exact location of McKeever Cabin. The USGS quads that cover the area are *Corner Lake* and *Tie Lakes,* and most of the current trail is shown.

Getting There: From M-28, east of the city of Munising, head south on H-13 for 11 miles. Trailheads for Bruno's Run easily accessed from H-13 are Moccasin Lake Roadside Rest Area opposite the entrance drive to Pete's Lake, Pete's Lake Campground off Forest Road 2173, and Widewaters Campground on Forest Road 2262. There's limited parking available at each site.

Fees: McKeever Cabin is $35 per night. You need to reserve it in order to get the key to the cabin and can do so 12 months in advance. The Ewing Point walk-in site is $10 for 1–3 nights or $20 for 4–7 nights and can be reserved for up to 7 days. Contact the Munising District Ranger to reserve or obtain a permit for either one.

Information: Call the Pictured Rocks National Lakeshore/Hiawatha National Forest Visitor Center (906-387-3700).

Trail Guide

Day One (7 miles) Park in the Moccasin Lake Roadside Rest Area and pick up the trailhead overlooking the lake. From here the trail heads southwest and within a third of a mile veers to the left. You climb a steep hill, topping off on a ridge of hardwoods, pines and a view of Moccasin Lake, only the first of many lakeside views you will enjoy along this route.

The trail skirts the south end of the lake with a bit more climbing before swinging away from the shoreline and descending into a meadow sprinkled with wildflowers in early summer. At Mile 0.8 you'll come to an intersection with a snowmobile trail, continue straight.

Eventually a sign appears, announcing that this portion of the trail was part of the Nahma & Northern Railroad, a rail line constructed by a lumber company in 1903. At first it's hard to believe railroad cars could fit through here, but soon the trail is following a wider railroad grade.

After winding and weaving over numerous hills, ridgelines, and ripples in the geography, Bruno's Run reaches the posted Hemlock Cathedral 1.6 miles from the start. The pines are passed through as you descend a ridge and are estimated to be 200 to 400 years old. Indeed, the hemlocks tower high above you, forming something of a spiritual sanctuary where it is almost impossible not to stop and reflect on why we have so few tracts of old-growth forests standing today.

After leaving the cathedral, you'll quickly cross a bridge and then encounter a rather steep downhill that uses a couple of switchbacks to descend 120 feet. Near the bottom, the trail crosses Forest Road 2262 and then 1.8 miles from Moccasin Lake comes to a long foot bridge that spans the channel connecting Fish Lake to the north with the Widewaters portion of Indian River to the south.

Side Trip: You can follow FR-2262 a quarter mile south to reach Widewaters

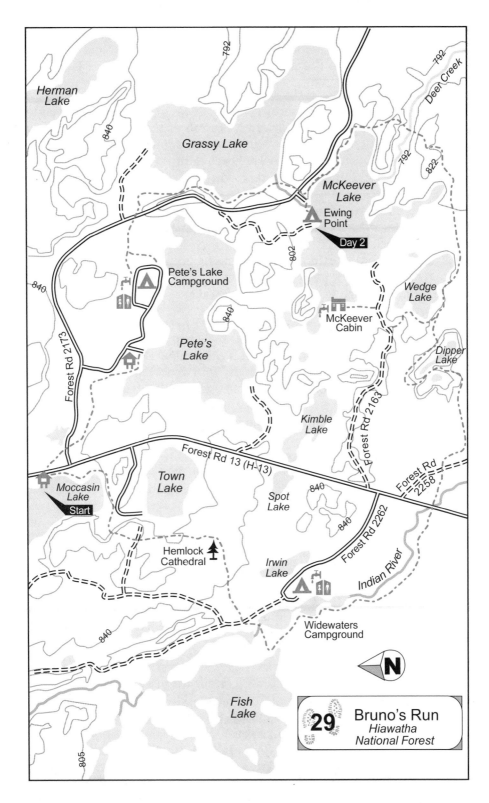

Herman Lake

792

Grassy Lake

Deer Creek

792

McKeever Lake

840

Ewing Point

Day 2

802

792

822

Wedge Lake

840

Pete's Lake Campground

McKeever Cabin

Forest Rd 2173

Pete's Lake

840

Dipper Lake

Kimble Lake

Forest Rd 2163

Forest Rd 13 (H-13)

Forest Rd 2258

Town Lake

Moccasin Lake

Start

Spot Lake

840

840

Forest Rd 2262

Hemlock Cathedral

Irwin Lake

Indian River

Widewaters Campground

N

Fish Lake

805

840

29 Bruno's Run
Hiawatha National Forest

Campground, a scenic facility that lies between Irwin Lake and Indian River. The national forest campground has 34 sites, vault toilets, and drinking water. Almost a mile to the north, FR-2262 leads to one end of Red Buck Trail (see Hike 30, page 203).

Bruno's Run crosses the channel and heads south to begin a very scenic stretch where you skirt the Widewaters portion of the Indian River under a canopy of mature pines. When you're 3.3 miles from Moccasin Lake, the trail climbs the embankment to H-13, heads north to cross Indian River on the road bridge and then departs the road to the east. After briefly skirting Indian River, you're back in the woods, climbing a ridge before crossing FR-2258, a dirt road. More climbing follows until you reach a bench on a ridge 4.3 miles from the start where there is a great view of Dipper Lake to the south. Snack time!

The terrain continues its rolling topography, and after a lengthy downhill, the trail merges into the posted C Loop of the McKeever Hills Ski Trail within a mile from the bench with view of Dipper Lake.

Side Trip: For those who have booked the McKeever Cabin, this is where you leave Bruno's Run. Turn left (north) on C Loop and follow it 0.6 mile to Forest Road 2163, a two-track open to vehicles. Follow FR-2163 east for a half mile, being guided along by brown signs with yellow arrows to a parking area at the end. Near the parking area is a posted trail to the cabin that heads north and within 300 yards the cabin appears on the right. The McKeever Cabin is a 6.4-mile trek from Moccasin Lake.

The cabin sleeps six on wood platforms and has a pit toilet, a hand pump for water, a table with stools, and a wood stove in case the night gets chilly. The cabin does not have mattresses nor lanterns or any source of light other than what remains of the candles people leave behind. It's on a small knoll above the west end of a lake, a scenic spot in a grove of pines and hardwoods. Best of all, it's yours for the evening, a great way to spend a night on the trail. To resume this trek backtrack the 1.2 miles to Bruno's Run.

Head right at the junction as Bruno's Run and the C Loop of McKeever Hills Ski Trail merged together to climb the ridges that form the southwest shore of Wedge Lake. On one of them you are rewarded with another bench overlooking a marshy meadow.

The two trails split at 5.5 miles from Moccasin Lake. Bruno's Run is the fork that heads due east (right) to pass near (but not in view of) the southern arm of McKeever Lake. You then cross a bridge over Deer Creek in another half mile in a marshy area that can be buggy during much of the summer. Beyond the creek McKeever Lake quickly comes into view and for the next half mile you enjoy a wide shoreline path.

The trail splits 6.8 miles from Moccasin Lake. Continue straight to reach a boat launch on McKeever Lake. From its parking area a trail extends west

200 yards to the Ewing Point, making the walk-in campsite a 7-mile day. The point is a grassy, open area allowing campers to enjoy a sweeping view of McKeever Lake. There is a fire grill, lantern post, and picnic tables but no source of safe drinking water. Nor is there a pit toilet.

The main attraction is the sandy lake bottom found here that provides an excellent area for swimming or just dipping tired toes. McKeever Lake is also a good place for anglers to toss a line. The 132-acre lake was stocked with northern muskie in 1990 and also supports good populations of northern pike, largemouth bass, smallmouth bass and bluegill.

Day Two (3 miles) Retreat to the junction used to reach the boat launch and follow Bruno's Run as it heads left to cross paved Forest Road 2173. Within a quarter mile you arrive at the outlet stream of Grassy Lake and then begin climbing the ridge that forms the west shore. You top off on a bluff right above Grassy Lake and follow the edge of it to a scenic viewing area a mile from Ewing Point.

Even if it's early in the day, Grassy Lake Overlook is worth a pause for the views of the lake below. The area is a pull-off for FR-2173, but most likely you will still have the place to yourself. From the rest area, Bruno's Run re-enters the woods and crosses FR-2173 again at 1.4 miles from Ewing Point. Look for the Bruno's Run bear sign and blue diamonds to re-enter the trail on the other side of the paved road.

You briefly follow a snowmobile trail, then veer left with the blue diamonds to emerge at Pete's Lake Campground at 1.8 miles from Ewing Point. The trail passes through the middle of this 41-site campground and then into the day-use areas where there are picnic tables, vault toilets, drinking water, and a sandy beach. Even if you're not up for a swim, the grassy, open area bordering the beach is a great place to soak up the sun. Pete's Lake also has two walk-in campsites, both on the shoreline of the lake.

From the day-use area Bruno's Run briefly re-enters the woods before breaking out at the boat launch. You return to the woods once again for the final stretch. You'll cross FR-2173 for a third time 2.9 miles from Ewing Point and H-13 soon follows with the Moccasin Lake trailhead just across the road.

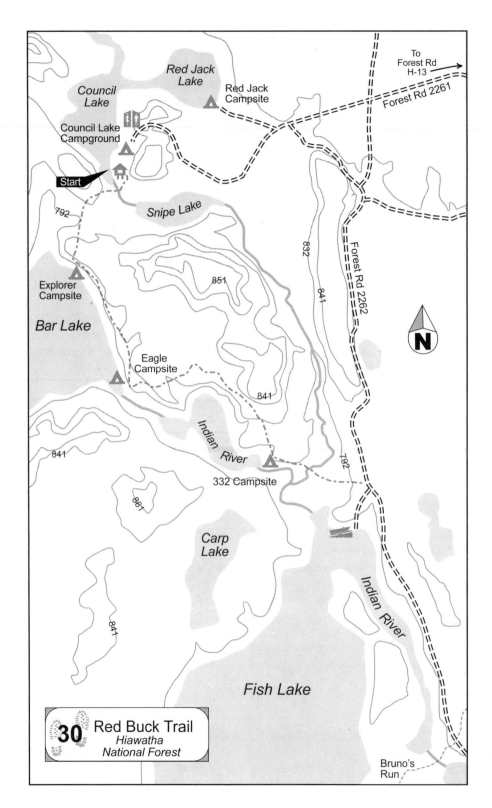

Red Jack Lake

Council Lake

Red Jack Campsite

To Forest Rd H-13

Forest Rd 2261

Council Lake Campground

Start

792

Snipe Lake

832

841

Forest Rd 2262

Explorer Campsite

851

N

Bar Lake

Eagle Campsite

841

Indian River

841

332 Campsite

792

861

Carp Lake

841

Indian River

Fish Lake

30 **Red Buck Trail**
Hiawatha National Forest

Bruno's Run

Red Buck Trail
Hiawatha National Forest

County: Alger
Nearest Town: Munising
Distance: 2 miles
Hiking Time: Overnight
Highest Elevation Gain: 40 feet
Difficulty: Easy
Highlights: Scenic shoreline campsites

Council Lake in the Hiawatha National Forest is a small, six-site campground half hidden at the end of an obscured dirt road. Still too many campers for you? Then grab your backpack and leave your car behind.

Within the campground is one end of the Red Buck Trail, a two-mile, point-to-point path from Council Lake to Fish Lake that includes a series of walk-in campsites and, in August, loads of ripe blueberries. At night you can be camped on a lake of your own eating blueberries like they're M&Ms. How sweet is that?

The first walk-in campsite is the best and the easiest to reach, only a half mile from the trailhead. This makes Red Buck Trail an ideal overnight getaway for hikers who don't want to spend a day hauling gear several miles down a trail and for families wanting to expose young children to backpacking for the first time.

Trip Planner

Maps: You can pick up a simple map of the trail at the Pictured Rocks National Lakeshore/Hiawatha National Forest Visitor Center on M-28 in Munising, which is more than adequate for this hike.

Getting There: The north end of the trail begins in Council Lake Campground. From M-28, just east of Munising, you head south on H-13 for 10 miles and then turn west on Forest Road 2661. It's a dirt road that is poorly marked but ends at Council Lake within 1.5 miles.

The south end of the trail is on Forest Road 2262, a mile north of where Bruno's Run (see Hike 29, page 197) crosses it and 1.5 miles north of Widewaters National Forest Campground.

Fees: None.

Information: Contact the Pictured Rocks National Lakeshore/Hiawatha National Forest Visitor Center (906-387-3700).

Trail Guide

If you get in late or intend to extend your adventure, spend a night camping on Council Lake, a scenic campground of six sites with three of them along the shoreline. This facility is a "dispersed camping area," meaning there are pit toilets and fire rings in this campground but no source of drinking water and more importantly no toilet paper. Most backpackers, however, are already packing a water filter and toilet paper.

Just before you reach Council Lake, Forest Road 2216A is marked and veers off to the northwest and in a quarter mile reaches Red Jack Lake. This 12-acre lake is connected to the slightly larger Council Lake by a small channel and has a single dispersed camping site and a primitive boat launch. Camping at either lake is by permit only and costs $10 for one to three nights and $20 for four to seven nights. For a permit call the Pictured Rocks National Lakeshore/Hiawatha National Forest Visitor Center (906-387-3700).

Red Buck Trail is posted at the back of the campground and begins by crossing a stream that links Council Lake to Snipe Lake and then climbs through an impressive stand of trees. The largest is a white pine that would rival anything seen at Hartwick Pines State Park. This is the longest climb of the route but in only a half mile from Council Lake the trail tops off at Explorer Campsite, the first of three along the trail.

The site has enough flat space for only two small tents and its lone amenity is a fire ring with a grill. But its location is outstanding on the edge of a high bluff overlooking Bar Lake. In the evening you can gaze down at the 60-acre lake, listen to the loons that nest on it and enjoy just enough breeze to keep most of the bugs at bay.

Red Buck Trail continues by skirting the east shore of Bar Lake, staying within view of the water, and at 1.0 mile reaches the second site. At Eagle Campsite you can pitch your tent in a stand of birch trees just above the shoreline where Bar Lake flows into Indian River.

At this point the trail swings away from the river and climbs two open hillsides where you hike through the jagged stumps from trees loggers cut a century ago. Keep an eye on the ground and a tin cup handy; this is blueberry country!

Eventually, you come to where the Indian River is so wide and sluggish it looks like a small lake and then, 1.5 miles from Council Lake, reach the final walk-in site, 332 Campsite.

The remaining half mile of the trail is overgrown from lack of use but well marked with blue diamonds.

It crosses a sluggish stream and then ends at Forest Road 2262. Head right for a quarter mile and you can end the hike at a small public access on the north end of Fish Lake.

Or keep trekking.

By continuing south on Forest Road 2262, you reach Bruno's Run in less than a mile. This trail is a nine-mile loop that will lead you past 11 lakes and two national forest campgrounds (see Hike 29, page 197).

Pine Marten Run
Hiawatha National Forest

County: Schoolcraft
Nearest Town: Manistique
Distance: 16.5 miles
Hiking Time: Three days
Highest Elevation Gain: 133 feet
Difficulty: Moderate
Highlights: Numerous lakes, backcountry fishing, free-use shelters

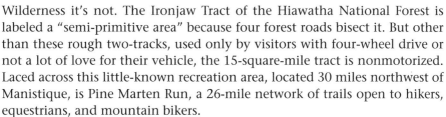

Wilderness it's not. The Ironjaw Tract of the Hiawatha National Forest is labeled a "semi-primitive area" because four forest roads bisect it. But other than these rough two-tracks, used only by visitors with four-wheel drive or not a lot of love for their vehicle, the 15-square-mile tract is nonmotorized. Laced across this little-known recreation area, located 30 miles northwest of Manistique, is Pine Marten Run, a 26-mile network of trails open to hikers, equestrians, and mountain bikers.

Wilderness or not, the scenery is excellent. The trails pass through a wide variety of vegetative communities that include a dozen lakes, a portion of the Indian River, gently rolling hills, bogs, and wildlife openings. Wildlife encounters range from deer, beavers, and waterfowl to possibly sighting an eagle or a black bear.

Pine Marten Run is composed of five loops with inter-connecting spurs and is accessed from four main trailheads off of County Roads 440 and 437, and Forest Road 2258. The area features three Adirondack-type shelters and a handful of primitive drive-in campsites on Swan Lake, Triangle Lake, Ironjaw Lake, and Nineteen Lake that can be reserved in advance through the Manistique Ranger District. Called "dispersed campsites," these isolated sites are where you can pitch a tent overlooking a lake and directly access portions of Pine Marten Run.

The hiking here is moderate, with only a few steady climbs encountered, along a mix of wide paths and two-tracks that are well posted. You do have to share the trails with equestrians and mountain bikers and watch for motorized vehicles when crossing forest roads. But overall you will encounter few other visitors in this area except during the summer weekends. Arrive mid-week in late September and you might have the entire tract to yourself.

The route described here is the perimeter of the loops that makes for a 16.5-mile, three-day trek. Both nights are spent camping at a lakeside shelter with the first one less than 2 miles from the trailhead, conveniently close for those faced with a long drive from southern Michigan that day.

Many other trail combinations are possible. The best family outing, for even children as young as five years, is a 1.7-mile walk into the Rumble

Lake Shelter. If a second day of more than 10 miles is too long, then plan an overnight 9.4-mile trek along parts of the Rumble and Ironjaw loops. Within a half mile south of Verdant Lake is a dispersed campsite on the east shore of Nineteen Lake or continue south to arrive at the Rim Lake Shelter within 1.2 miles. Either is a great spot to set up for the night.

Trip Planner

Maps: The USGS *Corner Lake* topo is detailed but does not show the entire trail system. The Hiawatha National Forest's Pine Marten Run Trail handout has a simple map of the trail system on it.

Getting There: From M-28 near Munising, head south on H-13 for 17 miles, past the trailhead to Bruno's Run and the posted entrance to Pete's Lake Campground. Head east on County Road 440 for almost 4 miles and then north on Forest Road 2258 for 2 miles. Just before crossing the bridge over Indian River is one of the four trailheads with a parking area and vault toilet on the west side of the road.

Fees & Reservations: There are no fees for using the three trail shelters. The dispersed campsites are $10 for 1–3 days. Reserve them in advance through the Manistique Ranger District (906-341-5666).

Information: Call the Manistique Ranger District (906-341-5666) or the Pictured Rocks/Hiawatha National Forest Visitor Center (906-387-3700).

Trail Guide

Day One (1.7 miles) The trailhead parking area is on the west side of FR-2258; the Rumble Loop is on the east and begins as a two-track open to motorized vehicles. Follow the rough road as it cuts through an open area that briefly comes within view of the Indian River. Within a mile you enter a pine plantation and arrive at a barrier gate that, hopefully, keeps anything motorized from going any further.

Beyond the gate, the trail is a wide path that quickly swings south into a hardwoods forest and in 1.3 miles from FR-2258 arrives at the junction with a spur to Rumble Lake. The spur is less than a half-mile long and ends at one of the three Adirondack-type shelters. These log shelters are open on one side, meaning in June and July you're still going to want to pitch a tent for bug protection at night. But in the fall it's the only shelter you'll need, and if its raining, you'll be grateful for the slanted roof overhead during dinner.

Rumble Lake is 22 acres and 24 feet at its deepest point. Walk-in anglers have a mixed bag to target, ranging from bluegills and crappies to both largemouth and smallmouth bass. The shelter is on a low rise above the lake with a fire ring that makes for a serene place to spend an evening.

Day Two (10.7 miles) Backtrack 0.4 mile to the Rumble Loop and follow the main trail southeast. You immediately begin a long climb and descent over the rolling ridge that separates Rumble Lake from Dinner Lake before arriving at a junction with the Ironjaw Loop 1.5 miles from the shelter. Head

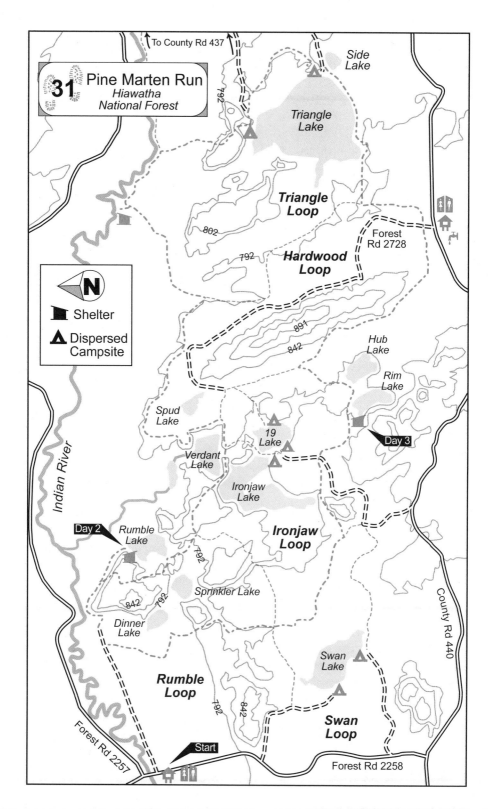

31 Pine Marten Run
Hiawatha National Forest

To County Rd 437

Side Lake

Triangle Lake

Triangle Loop

802

Forest Rd 2728

792

Hardwood Loop

891

842

Hub Lake

Rim Lake

Spud Lake

19 Lake

Verdant Lake

Ironjaw Lake

Ironjaw Loop

Day 3

Day 2

Rumble Lake

792

Sprinkler Lake

842

792

Dinner Lake

Swan Lake

Rumble Loop

792

842

Swan Loop

Start

Forest Rd 2257

Forest Rd 2258

County Rd 440

Indian River

N

◼ Shelter

▲ Dispersed Campsite

east (left) and follow the loop as it quickly climbs a narrow ridge between Ironjaw and Verdant lakes.

At one point from the crest of the ridge you can view both lakes through the trees before descending to the next junction within a half mile. To the right, a trail leads to a primitive campsite with a beautiful location overlooking both Ironjaw and Nineteen lakes from a small hill between them. The side trail connects to FR-2733, a two-track that leads a mile south to County Road 440 and is open to motorized vehicles.

Ironjaw is the second largest lake in the tract at 62 acres and the best one for anglers. Crappie fishing is excellent in the spring while the lake also contains populations of northern pike, largemouth bass, and bluegill.

The longer route described here continues east (left) at the junction. You skirt Verdant Lake's east end, a segment that can be very muddy in early summer, before climbing away from the shoreline to the next junction at 2.7 miles from Rumble Lake. Head north (left) to begin the Hardwood Loop with a scenic stretch that leads north along Verdant Lake and then climbs a ridge before swinging east. Within 1.8 miles or 4.5 miles from Rumble Lake you arrive at a junction with the west half of Triangle Loop.

Continue to the north (left) and soon you'll be traversing a cedar swamp that can be muddy at times but often is a good place to spot wildlife. Within 5.3 miles of the first shelter, you pass a posted side trail that leads a short way to the second one. This Adirondack shelter overlooks the Indian River, a noted brook and brown trout fishery. The main trail heads southeast (right) to stay close to the river and in a half mile reaches another junction.

To the east (left) the trail parallels the Indian River for a mile before emerging at a trailhead and parking area on County Road 437. The main route heads due south (right) and makes the longest climb of the day before making a quick descent to FR-2452 and two primitive campsites at the north end on Triangle Lake.

Continue along the trail and within a half mile you'll reach another dispersed campsite at the end of FR-2734, a two-track that leads east to County Road 437. Reached 6.6 miles from Rumble Lake, this site is a gem, one of the nicest places to pitch a tent along the route. It's located on a sandy strip between Triangle Lake and the large pond known as Side Lake. There is excellent swimming here while Triangle Lake can be fished for northern pike, smallmouth bass, bluegills, crappie, and perch.

As you approach the campsite, a white triangle on the left marks where you dip back into the woods and continue along Triangle Loop. The next stretch is one of the most scenic. For 0.7 mile as you skirt the southern shoreline of this 169-acre lake, the largest in the tract.

Eight miles from Rumble Lake you return to Hardwood Loop and head south (left). Within a half mile you cross FR-2728 just north of County Road 440. This is one of the main trailheads to Pine Marten Run, the reason for the parking area, toilets and drinking water.

Return to the Hardwood Loop on the west side of FR-2728 and within a third of a mile the trail will swing more northerly before reaching a junction

The Rumble Lake Shelter, one of three found along the Pine Marten Run.

with the Ironjaw Loop 10 miles from the start of the day. Head southwest (left). The trail passes within view of Hub Lake and then Rim Lake and then arrives at the short spur to the Rim Lake Shelter. A 10.7-mile trek from Rumble Lake, this shelter sits on the northwest corner of the 10-acre lake that at one time was stocked with brown trout.

Day Three (4.1 miles) Depart the shelter and head west along the Ironjaw Loop. Within a third of a mile from Rim Lake the trail crosses FR-2733, a gravel road used by vehicles to reach the campsite on Ironjaw Lake. On the other side Ironjaw Loop remains a narrow trail in the woods but in a third of a mile breaks out to a nice view of the south end of Ironjaw Lake.

The first mile of the day ends at a junction with Swan Loop. Veer to the north (right) here along a wider trail that is often marred by hoof prints. Continue straight at the next junction reached 1.8 miles from Rim Lake.

This segment of Rumble Loop begins as an easy to follow trail for the first mile but then is more difficult to spot after it enters a red pine plantation. The two-track you started out on two days ago is reached 3.4 miles from Rim Lake. Head west (left) on the two-track and in 0.7 mile you'll be back at FR-2258 and the trailhead parking area on the west side of the road.

Like Pictured Rocks National Lakeshore, Grand Island features lighthouses, as well as colorful sandstone cliffs, stretches of beach bordering Lake Superior, an extensive trail system, and a string of backcountry campsites. Unlike the national park, it's not necessary to reserve Grand Island's campsites in advance.

The Rim Trail
Grand Island National Recreation Area

32

County: Alger
Nearest Town: Munising
Distance: 21.8 miles
Hiking Time: Two to three days
Highest Elevation Gain: 148 feet
Difficulty: Moderate
Highlights: Views of Pictured Rocks, colorful sandstone cliffs, sandy beaches, walk-in campsites

Grand Island is not part of Pictured Rocks National Lakeshore but it might as well be. Lying only a half mile off shore from Munising, this 13,500-acre island is administered by the U.S. Forest Service as part of the Hiawatha National Forest. But like the nearby national park, Grand Island features colorful sandstone cliffs, intriguing sea arches and other rock formations, and stretches of sandy beach bordering the cold waters of Lake Superior. It is also a mecca for sea kayakers, hikers and backpackers, offering trails, interesting paddling, and a string of backcountry campsites in one of the most scenic regions of the U.P.

Grand Island was already a traditional camp for the Ojibway Indians when the American Fur Company arrived in the early 1800s to set up a trading post. In 1840, Illinois farmer Abraham Williams stepped ashore to become the first European to settle on Grand Island. He moved his family into the abandoned American Fur Trading cabins and began clearing the land. Williams was 81 when he died on the island in 1873. By then, his extended family had enjoyed a long and prosperous life on the homestead farm. Today, there are more than 30 members of the family buried in a cemetery near Murray Bay.

In 1900, the Cleveland-Cliffs Iron Company acquired most of the island. Although the original intentions were to use Grand Island as a corporate retreat, in 1953 CCI began selectively harvesting the forest and eventually logged nearly 8,000 of the 13,500 acres. The end result is the island is covered by mostly second-growth forest and laced by a network of logging roads. Those roads became the basis for a 40-mile trail system after the federal government purchased the island in 1990 and designated it a National Recreation Area.

Grand Island is 8 miles long and almost 4 miles at its widest point. It has an interior of rugged hills, a pair of lakes, wetlands and a healthy population of black bears. Most hikers, however, stay near the edge of the island where the best views and most dramatic scenery await them. The route along the perimeter of the island, most of it known as the West and East Rim Trails, is a 22-mile trek that begins and ends where the ferry pulls in at Williams Landing.

Along the way you pass 18 backcountry campsites, several nice beaches, and a dozen designated overlooks with views that are as stunning as anything you'll see backpacking in Pictured Rocks. For the most part the trails lie on old roadbeds and are well posted with directional signs marking junctions and campsites. On Grand Island, hikers share most trails with mountain bikers while several of the interior roads are also open to a limited amount of vehicle traffic, including a mini-bus that offers a two-hour tour on the southern half of the island. But overall, the visitation, particularly the number of backcountry users pales in comparison to what the Lakeshore Trail receives in Pictured Rocks.

A strong hiker can easily cover this route in two days, but this description of the walk is broken down into three days with the third day being a leisurely morning at Trout Bay and then a short hike to catch the ferry back to Munising. For an easier trek, spend the first night at Mather Beach, a 4-mile walk from Williams Landing. On the second day you can cut across the interior of the island to the Trout Bay campsites and then finish this 12-mile loop by walking to Williams Landing on the third day.

Drinking water is available in several places on the southern half of the island, but you will need a filter in the northern half. All campsites are equipped with either food storage lockers or bear poles to prevent any curious bruins from raiding your supplies. Be prepared for bugs, especially from mid-May through June when mosquitoes can be as thick as thieves.

Trip Planner

Maps: Two USGS topos, *Munising* and *Wood Island*, cover this hike with most of the trails displayed on the maps as former roads. Hiawatha National Forest also has a handout with a map on it that is available from its web site.

Getting There: Munising, a two-hour drive from the Mackinac Bridge, serves as the departure point for Grand Island. Most visitors arrive at the island through Grand Island Ferry Service (906-387-3503), which departs from the mainland at Grand Island Landing located on M-28, about 4 miles west of the County Road H58 and M-28 intersection in Munising.

The ferry operates from late Memorial Day to early October, departing the mainland at 9 a.m., noon, and 3:30 p.m. From July 1 through Labor Day the ferry also departs Munising at 10 a.m., 11 a.m., 4:30 p.m., 5:30 p.m., and 6:30 p.m. At Williams Landing it merely unloads and heads back. Always call and double check the ferry schedule when planning your trip. The round trip fare is $15 for adults and $10 for children.

Fees & Reservations: There is a $2 entrance fee to Grand Island that is collected by the ferry operator. You can not reserve the individual backcountry campsites, but group sites at Murray Bay and Juniper Flats can be booked in

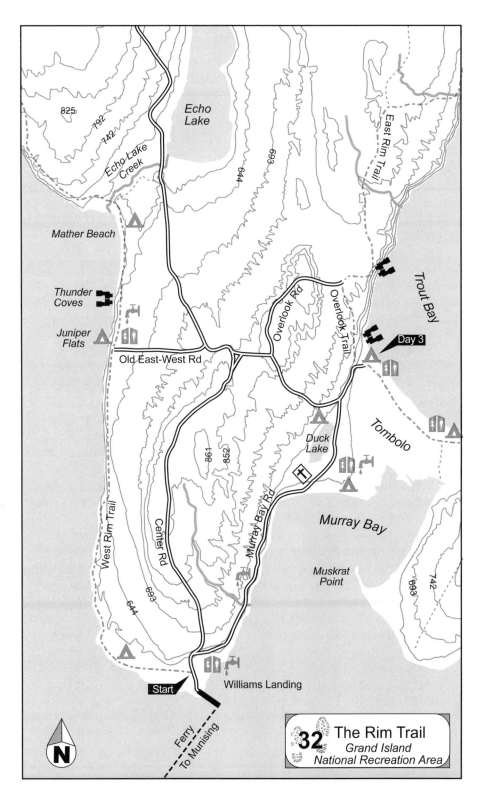

825
792
742

Echo
Lake

Echo Lake
Creek

693
644

East Rim Trail

Mather Beach

Thunder
Coves

Juniper
Flats

Old East-West Rd

Overlook Rd

Overlook Trail

Trout Bay

Day 3

Duck
Lake

Tombolo

861
852

Center Rd

West Rim Trail

Murray Bay Rd

Murray Bay

Muskrat
Point

693
742

693
644

Start

Williams Landing

Ferry
To Munising

N

32 The Rim Trail
Grand Island
National Recreation Area

advance beginning in mid-February. Call the Munising Ranger District (906-387-3700) for reservations.

Information: Contact the Munising Ranger District of the Hiawatha National Forest (906-387-3700; *www.fs.fed.us/r9/hiawatha*) for additional information or maps. For more information on the Grand Island bus tours contract ALTRAN Transportation Company (906-387-4845) from 7 a.m. to 5 p.m., Monday through Friday.

Trail Guide

Day One (9.8 miles) The mainland ferry puts you ashore at Williams Landing, where you'll find an emergency phone, information display, and a vault toilet nearby. Head north on Center Road and within 200 yards turn west (left) at the posted junction for the West Rim Trail.

The trail is an old road, the reason for the locked gate. It begins in a hardwood and hemlock forest and within a half mile passes the first of many campsites. A mile from Williams Landing you break out at Merchandise Beach, where you're rewarded with sand and a scenic view of Lake Superior. Here the trail swings north and within a mile you can see dramatic shoreline cliffs to the north.

At this point Rim Trail begins a gentle climb before descending slightly 3 miles from Williams Lansing to arrive at a posted junction. To the east (right) is the Old East-West Road that cuts through the interior for Trout Bay. Continue north as West Rim Trail widens into a two-track and quickly reaches the Juniper Flats group camping sites, where you'll find drinking water and vault toilets. A quarter mile beyond the camping area you pass Thunder Coves Trail, a 0.3 mile spur that leads to an overlook of Lake Superior and a small beach.

Continuing north, you reach Mather Beach 4 miles from Williams Landing and less than a mile from Juniper Flats. To the west, the trail passes three access points to the beach; to the east three campsites, each providing a vault toilet and a bear pole. The nearest source of safe drinking water is down the trail at Juniper Flats.

From Mather Beach, the trail veers inland to cross Echo Lake Creek and bypass a few private residences and then begins a steady climb as it returns to the shoreline bluffs. You're near the edge, but mature hardwoods block the watery views most of the time. Thus the reason for a series of overlooks, many with benches, that have been set up between Mather Beach and North Light Creek.

The first overlook is reached a mile north of Mather Beach, the second in another mile, and both provide wonderful views of shoreline cliffs that rise almost 300 feet above Lake Superior. Standing on the craggy western edge of Grand Island, you can gaze at the great lake in front of you and see Wood and Williams islands to the southwest.

Just beyond the second overlook, West Rim Trail swings inland and follows an old road that leads you past a rocky escarpment to the east.

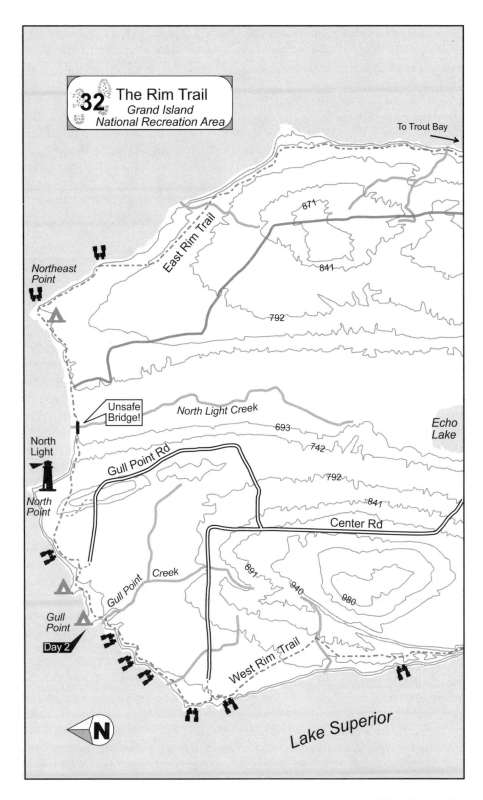

32 The Rim Trail
Grand Island
National Recreation Area

To Trout Bay

East Rim Trail

871

841

792

Northeast
Point

Unsafe
Bridge!

North Light Creek

693

742

Echo
Lake

North
Light

Gull Point Rd

792

North
Point

841

Center Rd

Gull Point Creek

891

940

980

Gull
Point

Day 2

West Rim Trail

Lake Superior

N

Eventually you cross a small stream and swing sharply to the northwest. The trail steadily descends for a mile until you are back at the shoreline cliffs, peering over the edge of them at the third overlook, reached 3.5 miles from Mather Beach.

In the next mile you pass three more overlooks with the trail staying near the edge of the shoreline cliffs in between them. At each one you can see coves where the towering sandstone has been carved out by a pounding Lake Superior and those storm-laden northwesterlies blowing down from Canada. Stone stacks and sea arches are visible in one of them. It's impressive scenery.

You then cross Gull Point Creek and cut across Gull Point to arrive at a campsite. A second campsite is located just up the trail at the next point. Reached 5.8 miles from Mather Beach or 9.8 miles from Williams Landing, these make for great spots to spend the night. Treat any water taken from Gulf Point Creek. In the evening, return to those overlooks to watch the sun dissolve into Lake Superior.

Day Two (8.7 miles) You begin the day with another overlook and then the trail swings inland to avoid the privately-owned North Light lighthouse. Within a half mile you pass the junction with Gull Point Road that heads south (right) for the center of the island. You continue east (left) past a private road to the lighthouse and arrive at North Light Creek 1.2 miles from Gull Point. The bridge over the creek is signposted unsafe to use because of erosion in the gorge that it crosses. Ford the creek and climb back up to the trail where you quickly pass a spur to North Light Beach. This mile-long beach is perhaps the most stunning one on the island. Enclosed by high sandstone cliffs, the beach offers soft sand and a view of the lighthouse to the west. You've barely hiked a mile but it's hard not to take an extended break here.

Within a third of a mile from the bridge, you pass a junction with an overgrown trail that heads south (right). You continue straight along East Rim Trail, which climbs towards the lake and 1.8 miles from Gull Point reaches an overlook at Northeast Point. From the viewing point you can gaze towards North Light Beach or straight down a sandstone wall. On the other side of the trail is a campsite.

At this point the East Rim Trail swings south and within 0.7 mile arrives at another overlook. Here you can peer down and spot a sea cave that on a windy day devours the rushing surf of Lake Superior. This is the last watery view for a mile as the trail meanders inland briefly through a rolling forest. You return to the edge of the cliffs 3.7 miles from Gull Point and hug them while enjoying views of the famed Pictured Rocks across the bay to the northeast.

You also cross three small streams before East Rim Trail swings sharply inland and ascends for more than a half mile to reach a second junction with the overgrown trail. The East Rim Trail swings south (left) here and winds through a rolling woods, passing a campsite and reaching Trout Bay Overlook 7.7 miles from Gull Point. This is the best viewing point of Pictured Rocks across the bay and includes Miner's Castle and Miner's Beach. During the summer you can sit here and watch a parade of tour boats cruising towards those famous cliffs.

Continue west on Overlook Road for a quarter mile and then head south (left) on Overlook Trail at a well posted junction. This trail gently descends 0.8 mile through a hemlock forest to a dirt road. Head east (left) on the road and in a quarter mile you'll arrive at the west end of Trout Bay, a walk of 8.7 miles from Gull Point.

Trout Bay is another beautiful beach that features a pair of campsites at its western end and another pair at its eastern end. In between them is a trail that passes through the "tombolo," a land bridge of dune swales that connects the Grand Island's thumb to the rest of the island. It's a 1.3-mile walk from the campsites at the western end of the bay to those at the eastern end. All of them feature vault toilets, picnic areas, and lots of places to soak in the sun.

Day Three (3.3 miles) This day is short by design. If you need to catch a morning ferry back to the mainland, it's only a 90-minute walk to Williams Landing. If not, then there's plenty of time to linger on the beach and enjoy the views at Trout Bay.

Return to the dirt road and a quarter mile past the junction with the Overlook Trail turn south (left) on Murray Bay Road at the next posted junction. Duck Lake quickly comes into view and within a half mile you're standing along the shoreline of this 20-acre lake searching for waterfowl and other wildlife. Continue south and 1.4 miles from Trout Bay you arrive at Murray Bay, where you'll find two campsites, a picnic area, toilets, and drinking water, all set back in a fringe of pine overlooking a beach.

Just beyond Murray Bay is the island's cemetery, well worth a visit. A short road leads back to the old gravesites that include more than 30 from the Williams family. An interesting historical display here details life on the island in the early 1800s, including how residents occasionally found drowned sailors washed up on shore.

From the cemetery Murray Bay Road swings almost due south and passes historic Stone Quarry Cabin overlooking Lake Superior and then hugs the shoreline. You hike past several private residences and then 1.6 miles from Murray Bay or 3 miles from Trout Bay arrive at the junction with Center Road. Turn south (left) on Center Road and you'll be back waiting for the ferry at Williams Landing in 0.3 mile.

A backpacker enjoys the extensive view from the top of the escarpment at Rocking Chair Lakes.

Rocking Chair Lakes
Escanaba River State Forest

County: Marquette
Nearest Town: Ishpeming
Distance: 2 miles
Hiking Time: Overnight
Highest Elevation Gain: 178 feet
Difficulty: Moderate
Highlights: Remote wilderness lakes and stunning views

Lightly used and hard to find, Rocking Chair Lakes is a 240-acre natural area in a rugged, almost inaccessible part of Marquette County. Those that do find their way to them discover stunning views from the edge of a high escarpment and one of Michigan's best wilderness fishing experiences.

The pair of small lakes, 16 miles north of Ishpeming, is nestled in the middle of a 1,672-foot-high ridge that is part of the Huron Mountains. Numerous rocky bluffs and sheer faces give the ridge an appearance as dramatic as the famous Lake of the Clouds escarpment in the Porcupine Mountains. The difference is there is no road to the top of the Rocking Chair escarpment, no paved parking lot and observation deck at the edge, no tourists snapping photos of the stunning panorama.

The ridge, with cliffs and outcroppings that tower 100 to 200 feet above Mulligan Plains, extends for more than 3 miles from north to south with a fourth of it lying in the proposed Rocking Chair Lakes Natural Area. Red and white pine and northern hardwood forests, some of it old growth, cover much of the rugged terrain and surround the two lakes. After heavy rains and during spring runoff, the lakes overflow and send a powerful waterfall cascading over the cliffs to Mulligan Creek below.

This is a place worth searching for.

Most people visiting the area are seeking a unique walk-in fishing experience. The lakes have been stocked with brook trout with the majority of them being released in North Rocking Chair Lake. The terrain is so rugged that fingerlings are either brought in by helicopter or in buckets that are carried up the ridge by hand.

But Rocking Chair Lakes is also a great place to spend a night or two in the wilderness. The hike in is not long, but it is steep. The challenge, like so many other backcountry adventures in the Upper Peninsula, is negotiating a maze of unmarked county roads and obscured logging roads to find the trail.

In ideal conditions and with a four-wheel-drive vehicle you could reach Mulligan Creek, putting you only a half mile from the lakes. But most people value their cars too much to take them through the jarring potholes of County Road AKC and often stop a half mile or more from the creek. Thus this round-trip hike is listed as a 2-mile trek. When you think about it, that's still an incredibly short distance to travel for such a unique mountain-top adventure in Michigan.

Trip Planner

Maps: Keep in mind that CR-573, the main road in, is not marked much beyond Deer Lake nor are there any directional signs. Thus the best map for the driving to the area is the *Marquette County Road and Recreation Map* produced by the Marquette Country Visitors Bureau.

Once you have arrived, you'll need the USGS topo, *Silver Lake Basin*, which doesn't show the trail but will give you the overview you'll need to traverse the ridge and reach the lakes.

Getting There: From US-41/M-28 in Ishpeming, head north on Cooper Lake Road, which will merge into County Road 573 at Deer Lake. Continue north as CR-573 becomes a forest road that crosses Dead River in several miles and swings northwest. After crossing the river, turn due north on the first two-track, labeled on some maps as AKC Road. Drive or walk to Mulligan Creek. The trail begins on the other side of Mulligan Creek.

Fees & Reservations: None.

Information: Call the Department of Natural Resources office in Marquette at (906) 228-6561. For a free Marquette County map contact the Marquette County Visitors Bureau at 800-544-4321; *www.marquettecountry.org.*

Trail Guide

It's 2 miles to Mulligan Creek along AKC Road, which is little more than a sandy two-track with foot-high weeds growing in the middle. Be careful navigating this 'road' in your vehicle. Break down out here and it's going to be a very expensive tow back to Ishpeming to get your car fixed. Most people stop way short of the creek; some never leave County Road 573 and simply hike AKC Road, turning this overnight adventure into a 5-mile trek.

Although AKC Road swings close to Mulligan Creek several times, it only crosses the stream once. There is no bridge here, but there is also no question what you have to do to continue...get your boots wet. Most of the time the ford is knee-high, a relatively easy one. But if there has been a recent downpour, you might have little choice but to turn back.

On the other side of Mulligan Creek AKC Road turns into a foot trail that continues north skirting the base of the ridge. You need to head downstream for 30 yards, looking for a path that has been described at times as a "fisherman's trail" departing from the creek. It heads into the trees and then immediately begins climbing.

In the heavy brush, the short trail to the top is easy to miss but take the time to locate it. This is by far the easiest way to reach the lakes. The

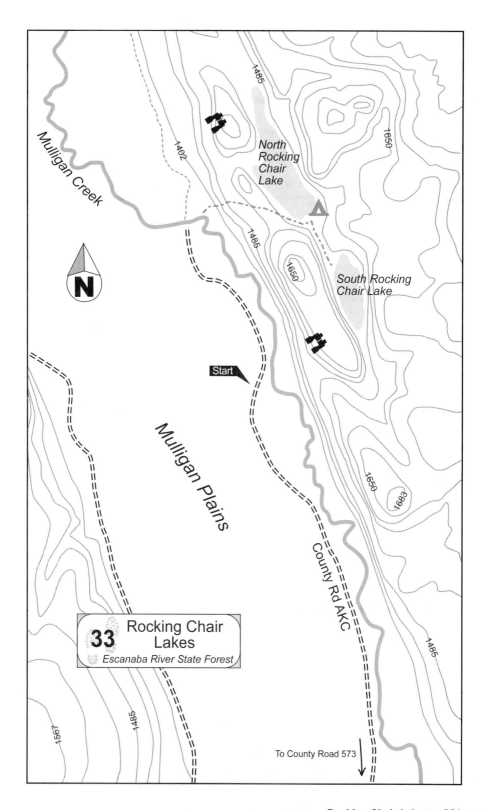

33 Rocking Chair Lakes
Escanaba River State Forest

path climbs 178 feet in a quarter mile to reach a gap in the ridge and then descends to a natural camping area at the south end of North Rocking Chair Lake.

You can pitch your tent here, one of the few places flat enough to do so, and then stand at the edge of the water and admire the steep shoreline ridges that encircle the lake like a fortress. South Rocking Chair Lake, smaller and not as impressive, is just a couple hundred yards away from the camping area via another trail. Both bodies of water can be fished for brook trout.

The best thing to do, however, is to return to the top of the escarpment and follow the ridgeline south. Hiking through the pines along the edge of it is easy and the views are spectacular. You'll be able to gaze down at the Mulligan Plains, miles of forests, hills, and streams, with not a single strip mall in sight.

McCormick Wilderness
Ottawa National Forest

34

County: Marquette
Nearest Town: Champion
Distance: 6 miles
Hiking Time: Overnight
Highest Elevation Gain: 86 feet
Difficulty: Moderate
Highlights: Granite bluffs and wilderness lakes

Michigan's Upper Peninsula is where millionaires shopped for a wilderness. Craig Lake State Park, Sylvania Wilderness, the Huron Mountain Club were all remote, primitive tracts that were purchased as private retreats by those who had the money to do so.

So was McCormick Wilderness. Tucked away on the edge of Marquette County, 12 miles north of Champion, the McCormick tract is spread over 16,850 acres and serves as the divide between the Lake Michigan and Lake Superior watersheds. It is also the birthplace of four rivers, Huron, Yellow Dog, Dead and Peshekee, while scattered between them are 18 lakes.

After loggers cleared most of the white pine in the early 1900s, the tract drew the attention of Cyrus McCormick and Cyrus Bentley. McCormick invented the reaping machine and made a fortune with International Harvester. Bentley was the chief attorney for the company. Together they purchased the area after a Harvard University professor told McCormick it was one of the greatest watersheds in the country.

The wilderness was the family retreat for the next three generations of

McCormicks. They maintained five camps here but the most impressive lodge was at White Deer Lake, built on a small island 100 yards offshore. They also maintained more than 100 miles of trail that reached every corner of their tract and beyond. The most famous was the Bentley Trail. The pathway was completed in 1905 from White Deer Lake north to the Huron Mountain Club, an equally exclusive wilderness retreat that was organized in 1899 along Lake Superior.

The last owner was Cyrus McCormick's grandson, Gordan McCormick, who willed the family estate to the U.S. Forest Service upon his death in 1967 as a way to preserve it. Twenty years later the tract was included in the National Wilderness Preservation System when Congress passed the Michigan Wilderness Act.

And wilderness it is. Adventurers can still locate segments of the original network of trails but this country is too rugged to be headed cross-country without solid map and compass skills. The terrain ranges from impressive rocky cliffs and outcrops to glacier-scoured hills with one topping off at 1,890 feet. Some of the most impressive and hardest-to-reach waterfalls in the state are on the Yellow Dog and are rarely seen.

In between the hills and bluffs are swamps, bogs, and muskegs that rim the lakes and streams.

There is also a wide variety of wildlife that thrives here. But the most stunning sight for many exploring the tract is not a bear or a moose but stumbling across one of the small pockets of virgin white pine. The 300-year-old trees are located among rugged rock outcrops and were too much trouble for the loggers to harvest. Today, they are small remnants of what Michigan looked like before Europeans arrived. A rare sight indeed.

There are few amenities here other than a parking lot with a vault toilet and a bridge over the Peshekee River. The tract's only developed and marked trail is an 8.5-mile segment of the North Country Trail that runs from west to east. The main access into the wilderness is a 3-mile, unmarked trail to White Deer Lake with a spur to Lower Baraga Lake. Although backcountry camping is allowed anywhere in the tract, White Deer Lake is the traditional destination for backpackers looking to set up camp for a day or two.

The 6-mile round-trip hike is a beautiful trek during fall colors from late September to early October but the wilderness sees more hikers in the summer. Keep in mind, however, that bugs can be blood-thirsty and relentless here from late May through much of June.

Trip Planner

Maps: The trail to White Deer Lake is an old road that is clearly shown on the USGS topo, *Summit Lake*.

Getting There: The McCormick Wilderness is 50 miles west of Marquette and reached from US-41/M-28. Two miles west of Champion turn north from US-41/M-28 onto County Road 607 and follow the former old Huron Bay railroad grade 9.3 miles to a posted parking area in the southeast corner of the wilderness.

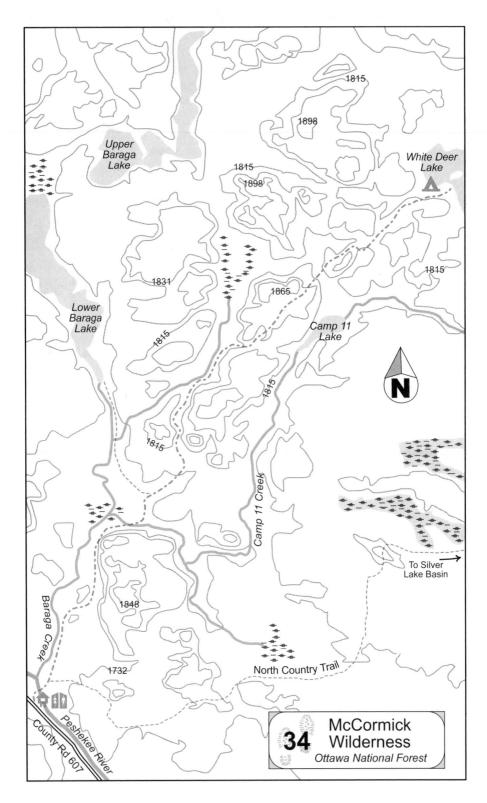

1815

1898

Upper
Baraga
Lake

1815

1898

White Deer
Lake

1831

1865

1815

Lower
Baraga
Lake

1815

Camp 11
Lake

1815

N

1815

Camp 11 Creek

Baraga Creek

1848

To Silver
Lake Basin

1732

North Country Trail

County Rd 607

Peshekee River

McCormick
34 Wilderness
Ottawa National Forest

Fees & Reservations: There are no fees for hiking and camping in McCormick Wilderness.

Information: Contact the Kenton Ranger District (906-852-3501) of the Ottawa National Forest.

Trail Guide

From the information display in the parking area, the hike to White Deer Lake begins by crossing the bridge over the Peshekee River just downstream from its confluence with Baraga Creek. On the other side is the old road, overgrown in spots but still a distinguishable route, that was built to provide access to the main McCormick estate. You quickly pass a junction where the NCT heads east (right).

In less than a half mile from the parking area you are hiking past views of Bargara Creek on one side and a small rock outcrop on the other. Within a quarter mile the scenery gets even more impressive as the trail winds beneath a series of rocky bluffs that towered 50 to 60 feet above you and then descends into the forest for the first time, passing several impressive white pines along the way.

You bottom out to cross Camp 11 Creek and then 1.2 miles from the start pass an unmarked junction with the spur to Lower Baraga Lake (left). It's a one-way walk of 0.6 mile to the outlet of the narrow lake. The main trail continues north (right) to begin its steepest climb of the day. You gain 86 feet in a third of a mile, then descend to where the trail hugs another escarpment to stay away from a marshy stream.

Beyond the wetlands the trail climbs over three ridges before descending into a meadow where scattered among the scrubs are the century-old foundations of the McCormick estate. From here it's a short walk across the meadow where you descend to the shores of White Deer Lake, reached 3 miles from the parking area. On a small island just 100 yards offshore is where the main McCormick lodge once stood.

Most backpackers set up camp in the meadow but often retreat back to the lake in the evening to watch resident loons and listen to their eerie call break the silence of the northwoods.

A backpacker with a fresh walleye dinner, so fresh it was just caught that morning in Craig Lake.

Craig Lake Trail
Craig Lake State Park

County: Baraga
Nearest Town: Champion
Distance: 8 miles
Hiking Time: Two days
Highest Elevation Gain: 80 feet
Difficulty: Moderate to challenging
Highlights: Remote wilderness lakes, backcountry fishing

Most backpackers find Craig Lake Trail a straightforward route to follow and not an overly hard hike. It's reaching the state park that is challenging. Better double check your muffler before heading in.

Once you leave the pavement of US-41/M-28, Michigan's most remote state park is a 7-mile drive along rough logging roads that can easily consume a muffler or a tire and are often impassable after heavy rains. Drivers will find themselves clutching their steering wheel and worrying about the next jarring pothole; passengers will be searching for the next park sign – or any sign, even a divine one – that they're still on course. But the effort is worth every rock ricocheting off your tail pipe.

A rugged and very special area, Craig Lake State Park is a 6,983-acre state designated wilderness with its centerpiece being Craig Lake itself, a 374-acre body of water featuring six islands and high granite bluffs along its shoreline. Scattered across the park's landscape are seven other lakes, the West Branch of the Peshekee River and steep ridges often separated by ponds and marshes and crowned by rocky outcropping.

The only amenities at the entrance are a parking area and a metal gate to prevent any motorized activity – vehicles, ORVs and even outboard motors – in the park. To explore the heart of this park, you either paddle or hike in. A network of portages provide strong-shouldered paddlers access to six lakes and canoes, preferably light ones, are the most popular way to travel through this wilderness.

But the park also has a 14-mile trail system with 7.5 miles designated the North Country Trail. Craig Lake Trail is generally referred to as the route that encircles the large lake and connects to portages to Crooked Lake and Clair Lake. The trail, plus the portages for a peak at Clair and Crooked lakes, makes for an 8-mile trek with a night in the backcountry.

You can camp anywhere in the state park, but scattered along Craig and Crooked lakes are a dozen walk-in or paddle-in campsites. The sites are first-come-first-to-pitch-a-tent and are equipped with only a tent pad and a fire ring. You'll need to pack in everything else including a water filter.

A backpacker's rod-and-reel is also handy as Craig Lake is renowned for its backcountry fishing opportunities for walleyes, northern pike, and smallmouth bass. Due to the park's unique populations of large predator fish and its wilderness state, there are a number of special rules in effect, including a ban on live bait and catch-and-release for all northern pike and smallmouth bass.

Trip Planner

Maps: A good portion of the trail system is old logging roads that appear on the USGS topo *Three Lakes*. The rest are on the Craig Lake State Park map available at Van Riper State Park.

Getting There: Lake Keewaydin Road, the main road into the park, is 7.9

A Night with Beer Baron Frederick Miller

If you're not up for carrying a tent, you can stay in a wilderness cabin overlooking Craig Lake, courtesy of Frederick Miller of the Miller Brewing Company fame.

The wealthy sportsman was president of the family brewery in Milwaukee when in 1950 he purchased most of what is now Craig Lake State Park as his private wilderness retreat. The first thing Miller did was to name Craig and nearby Teddy lakes for his sons and Clair Lake in honor of his daughter. There's also a High Life Lake, possibly the only lake in Michigan named after a beer.

Then Miller built his retreat. On a bay along the west side he had a small six-bunk cabin constructed for his caretaker and other hired help. On a point nearby he built Miller Lodge, sparing no expense despite its remote location. It included huge single-pane picture windows that overlooked the lake, hardwood floors, and a huge fieldstone fireplace. Most of the time Miller, an accomplished pilot, would arrive in his floatplane, taxiing right up to the lodge to spend a few quiet days in the splendor of Craig Lake...miles from nowhere.

The personal wilderness did not last long, however. In 1954, Miller and one of his sons died when the corporate plane they were traveling in went down. Eventually the State of Michigan ended up with the Miller estate and in 1967 the Department of Natural Resources dedicated the wilderness as its newest state park. Today, you can reserve and rent either one of the Miller cabins.

The cabins are a 2-mile walk from the Craig Lake parking area and feature bunks, drinking water, and row boats. As you can imagine, they are in very heavy demand and need to be reserved a year in advance through the state park reservation system (800-447-2757; *www.midnrreservations.com*). The large cabin is $80 a night and the smaller caretaker's cabin is $60.

The Miller Cabin in Craig Lake State Park was built by Frederick Miller of the Miller Brewing Company in Milwaukee.

miles west of the Van Riper State Park entrance on US-41/M-28 and is posted. Follow the rough dirt road north of US-41/M-28 for 2.7 miles and then turn northwest (left) on Craig Lake Road. The Craig Lake parking area is reached within 4 miles. It's imperative that you first obtain a map of the park from the Van Riper State Park headquarters and ask about road conditions. Following the lightly marked network of logging roads is extremely difficult.

Fees & Reservations: A state park vehicle pass ($6 daily, $24 annual) is required to enter Craig Lake. The park's backcountry campsites are $10 a night and fees are paid at the self register site in the Craig Lake parking area.

Information: For more information or maps contact Van Riper State Park (906-339-4461).

Trail Guide

Day One (3 miles) On the other side of the metal gate is a well-graded two-track that heads northeast. Within a quarter mile you pass a posted junction with the return of the Craig Lake Trail that also doubles up as the North Country Trail. Head north (left) and you'll quickly arrive at the Landing Site, a grassy bank where paddlers launch their canoes into Craig Lake. The spot is beautiful and includes several backcountry campsites and vault toilets. Late arrivals to the park will often camp here.

Continue north and a half mile from the parking area you arrive at another junction where the NCT merges with the Craig Lake Trail from the west. Continue north (right) on the two-track that doubles as a service road to the cabins for the Van Riper State Park staff. The trail cuts through a marsh and 1.5 miles from the parking area crosses a sluggish stream on a one-lane vehicle bridge.

Within 2 miles from the start you arrive at the Caretaker's Cabin, a six-bunk structure with a wood burning stove. The road continues north and quickly arrives at Miller's Lodge, an impressive cabin that sleeps 14 and has a large recreation room, dining area, and original fireplace. Both cabins can be rented through the state park reservation system (800-447-2757; *www. midnrreservations.com*) while outside are a pump for drinking water and a vault toilet.

At this point the two-track is replaced by a true foot path that departs just north of Miller's Lodge and enters the woods. It winds through a pine forest and quickly passes a pair of giant erratic boulders left behind by the last glacier. You catch glimpses of Craig Lake through the trees and then make an 80-foot ascent to top off at Clair Lake Portage Campsite, reached 3 miles from the parking area. There is only a fire ring and a tent pad here but the location is stunning. From this ridge-top site you can set up camp and then look down almost the entire length of Craig Lake.

The portage itself is a 10-minute walk away, reached by descending the ridge to the west. This half mile portage provides access to both Craig and Clair lakes.

Day Two (5 miles) Begin the day by descending to the Craig Lake Portage, where a trail sign says you're a mile from the cabins. You use a bridge to cross the outlet stream from Clair Lake and then climb over three ridges in the next mile with the first topping off on a rocky knob where there is a magnificent view of the northern half of Craig Lake. The third ridge has a long descent that ends with the trail sidling around a rocky bluff and arriving at the West Branch of the Peshekee River. The outlet for Craig Lake is reached a mile from the Clair Lake portage or 4 miles from the parking area and is crossed by carefully tip-toeing over a huge log.

On the south side of the river you pass the junction where the NCT splits off and heads east (left) for the McCormick Wilderness (Hike 34). Craig Lake Trail heads south through a rolling terrain and then arrives at a posted junction 2.5 miles from the Clair Lake portage. Heading due south (left) is the NCT and the shortest route to the Eagle Nest campsites on Crooked Lake. Each of the two sites overlooks the lake from a small point of its own,

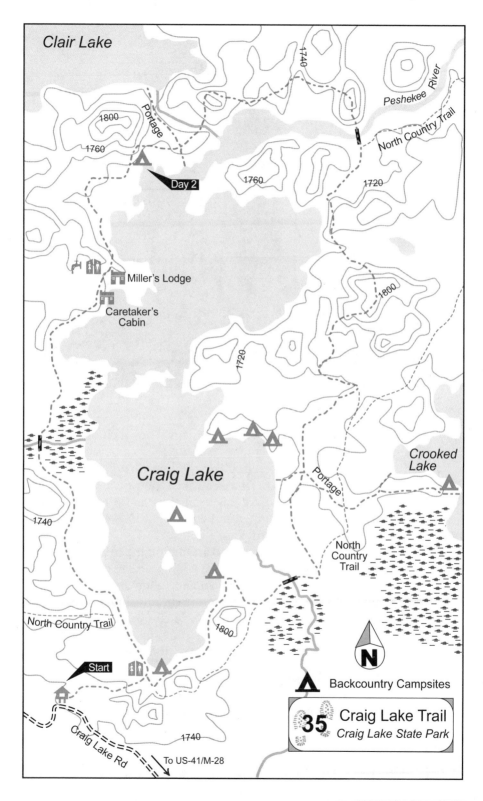

Clair Lake

1740

Peshekee River

1800

Portage

1760

North Country Trail

Day 2

1760

1720

1800

Miller's Lodge

Caretaker's Cabin

1720

Crooked Lake

Craig Lake

Portage

North Country Trail

1740

1800

North Country Trail

N

Start

Backcountry Campsites

Craig Lake Rd

1740

To US-41/M-28

35 Craig Lake Trail
Craig Lake State Park

Craig Lake is a 374-acre body of water featuring six islands and high granite bluffs along its shoreline.

making them very scenic places to pitch your tent. They include tent pads, fire rings and wilderness toilets.

Craig Lake Trail heads southwest (right) and 3.1 miles from the Clair Lake portage reaches a posted portage to Crooked Lake. This one is impossible to miss as the steep bank of Craig Lake has been terraced and a canoe drag installed to prevent further erosion. From here Crooked Lake is 0.7 mile to the east, and the Eagle Nest Campsites are a mile.

Craig Lake Trail heads south (right), skirts the high banks above Craig Lake and then a half mile from Crooked Lake Portage arrives at the junction where the NCT splits off. Head south (right) and follow the trail as it uses a bridge to bypass a beaver dam and then arrives at a junction with the trail to the Sandy Beach Campsites 4 miles from the start of the day. The campsite spur is a bit longer and involves more climbing, but I found it more interesting as at times it places you on the edge of a lakeshore ridge for a view of the water from above.

Within a quarter mile you pass a short spur to the two Sandy Beach Campsites which overlook Craig Lake and have wilderness toilets and tent pads. You return to the main trail within a half mile, where you head west (right) and quickly come to the first junction you passed in the hike. Turn southwest (left) and you'll be back the parking lot in a quarter mile or 5 miles from the Clair Lake portage.

Norway Lake Nature Trail
Ottawa National Forest

36

County: Iron
Nearest Town: Sidnaw
Distance: 1.2 miles
Hiking Time: Two days
Highest Elevation Gain: None
Difficulty: Easy
Highlights: Walk-in campsites on Nesbit Lake and Norway Lake

For your child's first backpacking trip, especially if they are under the age of six, think light, short, and interesting. Keep whatever you put in their backpack light. Select a trail that is short. But most importantly make sure wherever you set up the tent, it's an interesting location. You want to lead them away from the car to a spot where it's fun to spend the night without any facilities...not even a bathroom.

Norway Lake Nature Trail fits the criteria perfectly. Part of the Ottawa National Forest in Iron County, Norway Trail is located on the narrow strip of land that separates its namesake lake to the east from Nesbit Lake to the west. On Norway Lake there is a delightful national forest campground, on Nesbit Lake there is the youth camp and in between the two this 1.2-mile nature trail.

Best of all, this loop features a pair of walk-in sites, making it a perfect backpacking destination for young children. Mine were three and six years old when we tackled this trail with me carrying the tent, food, a water filter and three sleeping bags. My kids did fine. I was the one glad the trail was short.

Trip Planner

Maps: The lakes are covered by the USGS topo *Marten Lake* but the trail isn't shown. A map is posted at the trailhead and that's all you really need for this hike.

Getting There: From M-28 in Sidnaw, head south on Sidnaw Road for 6 miles. Turn west on Forest Road 2400, and Norway Lake Campground is reached in 2 miles.

Fee & Reservations: There are no vehicle entry fees to hike or camp on this trail. Camping at Norway Lake Campground is $10 a night.

Information: Call the Kenton Ranger District office (906-852-3500) between 8 a.m. and 4 p.m. Monday through Friday or check the Ottawa National Forest web site (*www.fs.fed.us/r9/ottawa*).

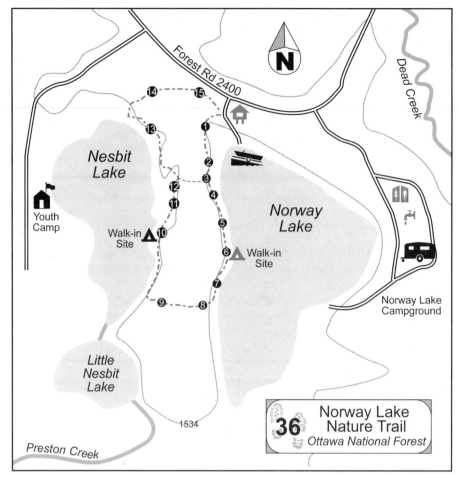

Trail Guide

On the east side of Norway Lake is the national forest campground. Norway Lake has 26 sites spread out on two loops on a bluff above the water. The first loop has 18 sites, and half of them feature an incredible view of the lake below. Within the rustic campground you'll find vault toilets, drinking water, a log shelter, and even a small sandy beach.

The trailhead is located in the Norway Lake Campground boat launch at the north end of the lake. In a clockwise direction, the first half of the loop skirts the shoreline of Norway Lake. Quickly popping up are some of the 15 interpretive posts along the trail that examine everything from deer trails and a bog where you can look for pitcher plants to a huge pine that was snapped in half by a single bolt of lighting.

But the charming aspect of this short trail is the pair of walk-in campsites, one on each lake. The first is less than a half mile from the trailhead. Absolutely no facilities here but the site is in a stand of red pine overlooking the lake. The half-mile walk in makes it ideal for children or others who just want to escape the campground for a quiet evening on the lake.

At this point the trail swings away from Norway Lake and cuts over to Nesbit Lake. Heading north you reach the second campsite 0.7 mile from the trailhead. This one is a classic. It's located on a small peninsula on the east side of the lake, a spot that usually catches enough wind to keep the bugs at bay.

The site is not very big and it's not very level but there is more than enough room for a small tent that can be pitched only a few feet from the water. If there is no group at the youth camp, you'll have the lake to yourself.

From the campsite, the trail continues north and swings slightly inland away from the shore of Nesbit Lake. You return to a view of the water within 0.3 mile and then the trail swings to the east, passing the last two interpretive signs and arriving at the boat launch to complete the 1.2-mile loop.

Hitting the Trails with Your Children

People are often amazed when I tell them that my children began backpacking when they were three- and four-year-olds, and my son was only 11 years the first time I took him backpacking in Alaska. If a child under the age of six can undertake a 2-mile dayhike, then a mile walk into a backcountry campsite, like the Norway Lake Nature Trail or the sites on Reid Lake, should be no problem...as long as the parents are willing to carry the gear.

It's been my experience that children in the range of six to eight years of age can begin carrying much of their own gear – rain parka, water bottle, and their sleeping bag – as long as their packs don't exceed twenty-five percent of their body weight.

At the ages of nine to ten, children should be able to carry all their own gear, plus a small portion of group equipment. They should also be able to handle some simple camp tasks on their own, such as gathering firewood, filtering the drinking water, or inserting the stakes in a freestanding tent.

In many ways children are like adults when it comes to backpacking. After hiking 4 miles in the woods, kids are going to be as hungry as you are. The biggest mistake I make with my son is underestimating how much his appetite increases while backpacking. We're forever fighting over the last serving of macaroni-and-cheese, and he usually wins.

Wildlife in Sylvania Wilderness includes bald eagles, beavers, river otters, black bears, and big bucks.

Sylvania Wilderness
Ottawa National Forest

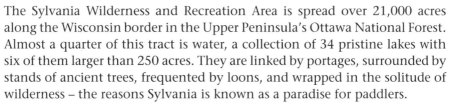

County: Gogebic
Nearest Town: Watersmeet
Distance: 9.2 miles
Hiking Time: Two days
Highest Elevation Gain: 58 feet
Difficulty: Easy to moderate
Highlights: Clark Lake, old-growth hemlock, walk-in campsites

The Sylvania Wilderness and Recreation Area is spread over 21,000 acres along the Wisconsin border in the Upper Peninsula's Ottawa National Forest. Almost a quarter of this tract is water, a collection of 34 pristine lakes with six of them larger than 250 acres. They are linked by portages, surrounded by stands of ancient trees, frequented by loons, and wrapped in the solitude of wilderness – the reasons Sylvania is known as a paradise for paddlers.

But backpackers shouldn't pass it up.

Sylvania is laced by 25 miles of trails, many of them old two-tracks that nature is slowly converting back to foot paths. They wind from one lake to the next and lead to half of the 29 backcountry campsites. These are sites that can be reserved in advance to ensure you have a place to drop your pack...even on the busiest summer weekend. The most popular loop by far is the Clark Lake Trail, described here as an overnight trek of 9.2 miles that leads you around the largest lake and deep into the heart of this wilderness.

Even for the Upper Peninsula, Sylvania is a wild and very special place. Like much of Michigan, glaciers were responsible for the area's topography, shaping its rolling hills and leaving depressions that became lakes and ponds. In 1895, A.D. Johnston, a lumberman from Wisconsin, purchased 80 acres near the south end of Clark Lake with plans to harvest the large, old-growth pines. But the trees were so impressive, he decided they were too beautiful to cut. Instead of logging the land, he invited friends to visit his forest and fish the lakes. They in turn purchased their own personal retreats and eventually the wealthy landowners became known as the Sylvania Club.

It was a common occurrence throughout the U.P.; if you had the wealth, you could own a wilderness.

Thus the tract entered the 1960s with virgin stands of timber: trees that were more than 200 years old and some that botanists believed date back to the 1500s. There are a few patches of white pine and they easily tower above the treeline. But most of the forest is northern hardwoods: sugar maple, yellow birch, hemlock, and basswood that come mid to late September turn brilliant shades of autumn colors. In between these trees, the wildlife is abundant. Whitetail deer are plentiful; so are beavers, otters, fishers, and porcupine. Campers are advised to string their food bags high in the trees to bear proof their camps because black bears roam the tract. Many visitors pack along a pair of binoculars and then search the lakeshores for bald eagles, loons, ospreys or a variety of waterfowl.

In 1966, Sylvania was purchased under the Land and Water Conservation Fund and became part of the Ottawa National Forest as Sylvania Recreation Area. Rangers immediately put in a large vehicle campground at the north end of Clark Lake along with a picnic area and a developed beach. But the rest of the tract was so devoid of roads and so isolated that it was decided small backcountry campsites scattered around the larger lakes would be best.

In 1987, Sylvania was one of 10 Michigan areas added to the National Wilderness Preservation System. Sylvania Wilderness is actually 18,327 acres while the rest of the tract, which includes the developed campground and dayuse beach, remained the recreation area.

This trek is described as a two-day walk with 3.2 miles the first day and 6 miles the second. But if very young backpackers are involved you can easily shorten the second day by passing up a trip to Loon Lake and spending the night at Birch Campsite, a 4.5-mile walk from the boat launch. Even better is to plan three days with your children to cover the route.

Trip Planner

Maps: Due to its status as a federally designated wilderness, Sylvania's trails are for the most part, unmarked but are fairly easy to follow. The exception to a lack of signage is an occasional confidence marker at junctions and blue blazes that hikers had placed on trees. A good map is a necessity and the best is USGS topo *Black Oak Lake*, which covers the entire Clark Lake Trail.

Getting There: At the corner of US-2 and US-45, just south of Watersmeet, is the Ottawa National Forest Visitor Center that has maps, information, and an interpretive display area devoted to the wilderness. From the visitor center head west on US-2 for 4 miles and then south on Country Road 535. The entrance into Sylvania is off Country Road 535 and near it is the Wilderness Entrance Station (906-358-4404) where you pick up backcountry permits.

Fees & Reservations: There are 29 backcountry campsites in Sylvania, each with two sites that require a permit to use and can be reserved. In 2007, Ottawa National Forest changed its reservation system and now Sylvania's campites are booked through the National Recreation Reservation Service (877-444-6777; *www.recreation.gov*), a national reservation center. Sites can be reserved 240 days in advance, and reservations are strongly recommended for any trip from June through August. Although 25 percent of the sites are saved for walk-in registrations, this drive is too long to arrive to find out you can't spend the night in the backcountry. If you don't have a reservation, stop at the Wilderness Entrance Station to see if sites are still available.

Camping is $10 per site per night plus a $10 reservation fee. There is also a fee ($5 per vehicle per day or a $20 annual pass) to use the Clark Lake Dayuse Area, which includes restrooms, hot showers, boat launches, picnic areas and a beach at the north end of the lake. Nearby is Clark Lake Campground, a 48-site, rustic facility that is $12 per night.

Information: Ottawa National Forest Visitor Center (906-358-4724) is open 9 a.m. to 5 p.m. daily and is the best place for additional information on the wilderness. The Wilderness Entrance Station (906-358-4404) is open May 15 to September 30 from 8:30 a.m. to 5 p.m. Saturday to Thursday and 8:30 a.m. to 6 p.m. on Friday. There is also information about Sylvania on the Ottawa National Forest website (*www.fs.fed.us/r9/ottawa*).

Trail Guide

Day One (3.2 miles) The Clark Lake Trail is posted in the southeast corner of the boat launch where it enters the pines but stays close to the shoreline. Within a half mile you ascend to Ash Campsites, a pair of sites located on top of a small wooded point jutting out into the lake. The trail descends to quickly reach Balsam Campsites 0.8 mile from the start and then climbs to an overlook of the lake.

You reach a second view of Clark Lake within 0.3 mile and then descend to skirt the shores of Golden Silence Lake, a small but appropriately named lake that lies within a stone's throw of Sylvania's largest lake. Just beyond the lake you arrive at Pines Campsite, two scenic sites within view of Clark Lake. You are only 1.7 miles from the boat launch but this is a great spot to spend a night if you plan to arrive at Sylvania late in the day.

Trophy Fishing in Sylvania Wilderness

The cold, clear lakes of Sylvania Wilderness and special fishing regulations placed on them have resulted in some of the best trophy fishing in the Upper Peninsula. Species that are caught vary from lake to lake, but include lake trout, walleye, and northern pike. Bass fishing is outstanding and catching an 18- to 20-inch smallmouth is not uncommon.

Paddlers have a leg up on backpackers as they are able to reach and fish the entire lake. But hikers who are also anglers should pack a rod and spinning reel as well to fish from shore. Often in the evening bass move into shallow areas and begin feeding aggressively. Sylvania's special regulations include:

• Only artificial lures with barbless hooks may be used for fishing. Live, dead, or preserved bait or scented material may not be used when fishing.

• It's catch and release for largemouth and smallmouth bass, regardless of their size or which lake they were caught in.

• You may keep only one northern pike, walleye and lake trout per day. Pike and lake trout have to be at least 30 inches long and walleye at least 20 inches in length.

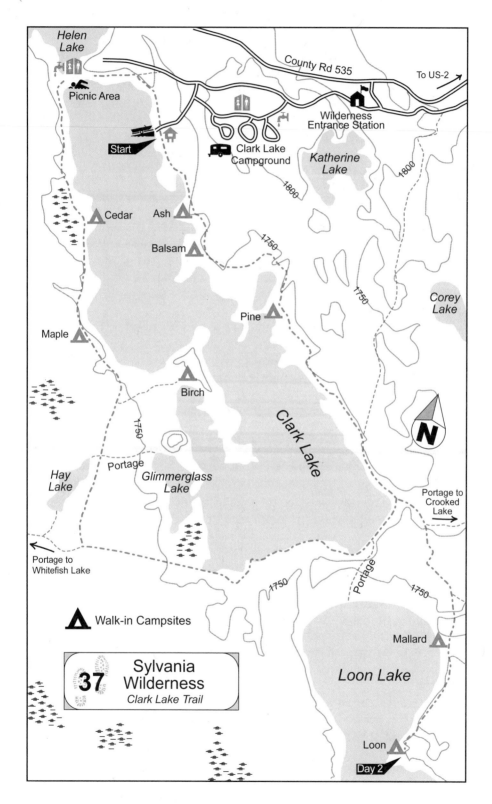

Helen Lake

Picnic Area

Start

County Rd 535

To US-2 →

Wilderness Entrance Station

Clark Lake Campground

Katherine Lake

1800

1800

Cedar

Ash

Balsam

1750

1750

Corey Lake

Pine

Maple

N

1750

Birch

Hay Lake

Portage

Glimmerglass Lake

Clark Lake

Portage to Crooked Lake →

← Portage to Whitefish Lake

1750

Portage

1750

▲ Walk-in Campsites

37 Sylvania Wilderness
Clark Lake Trail

Mallard

Loon Lake

Loon

Day 2

From Pines Campsite you enter the ancient forest of towering trees and in a quarter mile pass a small bay where views of Clark Lake are possible. You return to the rolling woods and 2.2 miles from the start you break out in a meadow and a small sandy beach in the southeast corner of Clark Lake. Located here is the junction with the trail to Loon Lake.

To spend the night even deeper into the solitude of Sylvania, take the left-hand fork at the junction and follow the path to Loon Lake, a 375-acre lake that reaches depths of up to 55 feet. The trail is an old two-track that climbs away from the beach and quickly reaches a junction with the portage to Crooked Lake to the east (left). Stay to the right at this junction and the next one where an old two-track heads left east (left) for Deer Island Lake.

The path to the right descends to Mallard Campsite on the shoreline in the northeast corner of Loon Lake and a 2.7-mile walk from the boat launch. From here a trail skirts the shoreline another half mile to Loon Campsite. This is another scenic, and popular, spot to spend a night where you'll be camped on a small peninsula in the middle of Loon Lake.

Day Two (6 miles) Back track to Clark Lake, a walk of a mile from Loon Campsite, and head left (west) at the junction. You enter the woods to pick up another old two-track that follows a low ridge southwest along the shoreline. Within 0.3 mile you pass the portage that paddlers use to move from Clark Lake to Loon Lake.

Beyond it, the two-track continues to skirt Clark Lake, which at 820 acres makes for an impressive sight to plop down and study. The lake reaches depths of up to 75 feet, allowing it to support a mix bag of fisheries including smallmouth and largemouth bass, perch and lake trout.

Less than a mile after arriving at Clark Lake, the two-track veers away from its southwest corner along a ruler-straight route that heads due west. Within 0.7 mile is a posted junction where you head north (right) to continue along Clark Lake Trail. Here the trail resembles a foot path and 3 miles from Loon Campsite, you reach the portage to Glimmerglass Lake. To the west (left) the portage quickly emerges at Hay Lake, a small, 14-acre lake. In less than 0.3 mile to the east (right) is Glimmerglass Lake, larger at 34 acres. Either one can be fished for largemouth bass or bluegill, even from shore.

Clark Lake Trail continues heading north and in a third of a mile passes a path that heads west for Birch Campsite. These two campsites are on a well-protected bay that features a small sandy beach. At night you can listen to the loons laugh while huddled around your campfire.

From the junction Clark Lake Trail ascends a low ridge and skirts it briefly before dropping to the shoreline and reaching Maple Campsite. You continue north, climbing once to a view of Clark Lake but for the most part staying close to the shoreline. Within a half mile of Maple Campsite you pass through Cedar Campsite and then emerge in the picnic area and beach at the north end of the lake, 5.5 miles from Loon Campsite.

Either stop for a hot shower or continue along the lakeshore to reach the boat launch within another half mile.

Pictured Rocks National Lakeshore

The towering sandstone cliffs, known as the Pictured Rocks, rarely fail to impress whoever passes through this far north. First it was Ojibway tribes, who would honor the spirits of such a grand creation by leaving behind tobacco. Then French voyageurs paddling canoes laden with furs and early scholars like Henry Rowe Schoolcraft, who wrote in 1820 that the bluffs were "some of the most sublime and commanding views in nature."

And finally a nation. In 1966, President Lyndon B. Johnson signed landmark legislation that made Pictured Rocks America's first National Lakeshore. They are that stunning.

Towering 200 feet above the world's largest freshwater lake, the multicolored cliffs extend along 12 of the 42 miles of shoreline within the park. The wind, waves, and fury of Lake Superior have subsequently sculptured the soft sandstone into caves, arches, pinnacles, and pillars with such fine detail they resemble castle turrets, battleships, and Indian warriors. Seeping minerals have stained this stone canvas with a palette of colors: reds and oranges from iron, black from manganese, green from traces of copper, while the sun and the seasons allow you to return again and again and never see the same painting twice.

Where the sandstone escarpment swings inland, miles of unspoiled beaches continue, and finally the lakeshore comes to a crescendo with Grand Sable Banks, towering sand dunes perched high above the blue and turquoise-colored waters of Lake Superior. It's impressive scenery, and winding along most of it are foot trails.

True to its name, the Lakeshore Trail stretches along Lake Superior the length of the park between Grand Marais and Munising. This 42-mile path is not only the crowning jewel of the North County Trail, but one of the great walks in America. Almost equally long is the Fox River Pathway, a four-day walk that begins in the town of Seney and ends on the shores of Lake Superior in Pictured Rocks National Lakeshore. Although not nearly as scenic as the Lakeshore Trail, the pathway is rich in logging history and wrapped in the myth of author Ernest Hemingway.

Two shorter treks are also covered in this section. The Chapel Loop and the Beaver Lake Loop both include a segment of the Lakeshore Trail and a stretch of the shoreline that visitors – from voyageurs to backpackers – have marveled at for so long.

The west entrance of Pictured Rocks National Lakeshore is Munising, a two-hour drive from the Mackinac Bridge via US-2, M-77 and M-28. The east entrance is Grand Marais, 25 miles north of Seney at the end of M-77. In between the two is County Road H-58. The 50-mile road skirts the boundary of the park, providing access to a handful of roads that head into its interior. H-58 is paved from Munising to Little Beaver Lake Road; after that it's a rugged, twisty dirt road. Plan on two hours for the drive from Grand Marais to Munising.

The best source of information while planning a trip is the Pictured Rocks National Lakeshore web site (*www.nps.gov/piro*) or the Pictured Rocks National Lakeshore/Hiawatha National Forest Visitor Center (906-387-3700) in Munising.

A backpacker pauses to admire the Pictured Rocks during his four-day trek along the Lakeshore Trail.

Lakeshore Trail
Pictured Rocks National Lakeshore

County: Alger
Nearest Town: Munising
Distance: 42.4 miles
Hiking Time: Four to five days
Highest Elevation Gain: 145 feet
Difficulty: Moderate to challenging
Highlights: Pictured Rocks, Grand Sable Dunes, shipwrecks

In one of the most spectacular regions of the state, Pictured Rocks National Lakeshore, you have one of the most spectacular paths to hike, the Lakeshore Trail. One couldn't be without the other.

For many, the only way to view and appreciate Pictured Rocks' dramatic scenery is to strap on a pack and hike the 42.4-mile trail that doubles as part of the North Country Trail. This is unquestionably one of Michigan's classic hikes. The trek is a walk between two towns, Grand Marais and Munising, past lighthouses and shipwrecks, giant sand dunes and towering sandstone cliffs, beaches on Lake Superior and beaches 200 feet above it. And except for a five-mile stretch from the Grand Sable Visitor Center, the eastern trailhead, you're almost never out of sight of the largest Great Lake of them all.

The scenery is so amazing and at times so exhilarating that the Lakeshore Trail is often considered the crowning jewel of the NCT's 4,600 miles.

Most backpackers first utilize the ALTRAN Public Transit buses to be dropped off at the Grand Sable Visitor Center and then hike from east to west, ending back at their vehicle at the Munising Falls parking area. Once past the Log Slide on the first day, the scenery improves dramatically with every step west.

This trek is laid out as a four-day walk with nights spent at Benchmark, Beaver Creek, and Mosquito River. These are some of the most scenic backcountry campgrounds along the trail but it does require you to hike between 9 and 12 miles a day. If that is too much mileage, then cover the route in five days with nights spent at Au Sable Point East, Trappers Lake, Chapel, and Potato Patch, a hike in which the longest day is 10.9 miles and the rest are 8-mile days.

The park's 13 backcountry campgrounds are scattered along the trail at 2- to 5-mile intervals and overlook Lake Superior. These 84 walk-in sites, the only places backcountry camping is allowed, are also used by sea kayakers, whose numbers have increased dramatically in recent years. So has the number of hikers, resulting in a backcountry reservation system being installed in the late 1990s. It is now wise to book your campsites in advance for weekends in July and August or risk a No Vacancy sign when you arrive.

Along with a backcountry reservation system, the park also began charging an "administrative fee" to help defray the cost of maintaining an increasingly popular trail. But the $4 per night fee shouldn't deter anybody. The Lakeshore Trail is a classic well worth the price of admission.

Trip Planner

Maps: The park sells *Pictured Rocks National Lakeshore*, a topo that is printed on waterproof paper and is ideal for this hike. You can purchase it at the Pictured Rocks National Lakeshore/Hiawatha National Forest Visitor Center (906-387-3700) in Munising for $7.

Getting There: Munising Falls Interpretive Center is on Sand Point Road, just east of M-28 in Munising and across from Munising Memorial Hospital. At Munising Falls an ALTRAN Public Transit bus stops at 10 a.m. on Monday, Thursday, and Saturday from mid-June through September and arrives at Grand Sable Visitor Center at 11:30 a.m. It then departs at 11:45 a.m. and returns to Munising Falls at 1 p.m. The fare is $20 per person.

You must call ALTRAN (906-387-4845) and reserve a seat on the bus at least a week in advance. The bus won't make the trip if nobody has reserved a seat. They will also make special runs, including trips to the Chapel Falls area of the park, but these must also be set up in advance. Call ALTRAN for options and prices.

Fees & Reservations: It is best to reserve all your backcountry campsites in advance. Reservations are accepted beginning January 1 for that year and a lottery-type drawing is held on the third Thursday in January. Reservation requests received after that will be filled on a first-come-first-serve basis.

A *Backcountry Reservation* form can be obtained by calling a visitor center or downloading it from the park web site (www.nps.gov/piro). You can either mail it in (Backcountry Reservations, Pictured Rocks National Lakeshore, P.O. Box 40, Munising, MI 49862-0040) or fax it (906-387-4457). There is a $15 fee for each reservation request that can be paid by credit card (Visa or Mastercard), checks, or money orders. All reservations must be postmarked or faxed at least 14 days prior to the first day listed on the backcountry itinerary.

The first day your hike starts or one day prior, you must then obtain a backcountry permit from either the Pictured Rocks National Lakeshore/ Hiawatha National Forest Visitor Center in Munising or the Grand Sable Visitor Center in Grand Marais. Permits are $4 per person per night.

Keep in mind that reservations are not accepted for the drive-in campgrounds reached from the trail, Little Beaver Lake, Twelvemile Beach, and Hurricane River. There sites are first-come-first-serve and $12 a night.

Information: You'll find most information available on the Pictured Rocks National Lakeshore web site (*www.nps.gov/piro*). The main center is Pictured Rocks National Lakeshore/Hiawatha National Forest Visitor Center (906-387-3700) on M-28 in Munising, which is open daily in the summer from 9 a.m. to 6 p.m. The Grand Sable Visitor Center (906-494-2660), on

Campers relax on Twelvemile Beach, the high point for many in the first half of the Lakeshore Trail.

County Road H-58 a mile west of Grand Marais, is open from 9:30 a.m. to 6 p.m. daily from late May through Labor Day. The Munising Falls Interpretive Center (906-387-4310) is open 9:30 a.m. to 6 p.m. daily from Memorial Day through Labor Day.

Trail Guide

Day One (11.2 miles) This is a long day, especially if you're not arriving until 11:30 a.m. on the ALTRAN bus. There are two ways to get around this. One is to shorten the hike by requesting the ALTRAN driver to drop you off at the Log Slide. This reduces the first day to 5.9 miles by bypassing the only section of the trail not along the Lake Superior shoreline. The other solution is to lengthen your day by spending the night at Woodland Park in Grand Marais. So many backpackers do, that the township campground has 20 walk-in sites designated for them. This would allow you to get an early start the next morning.

The Lakeshore Trail officially begins at the Grand Sable Visitor Center, where it crosses County Road H-58 and heads southwest through a mix of fields and forests. The trail passes through a picnic area at the north end of Grand Sable Lake and then follows Country Road H-58 west. On one side of you is beautiful Grand Sable Lake, on the other the towering Grand Sable Dunes spilling sand across the pavement. In 1.2 miles from the visitor center, you arrive at a scenic pullover for motorists. The trail leaves H-58 and heads southwest to continue along Grand Sable Lake. Eventually it swings sharply west, leaves the shorelines and re-crosses the county road 3 miles from the visitor center.

On the north side of H-58, the Lakeshore Trail is an old two-track. It remains in the woods but skirts the base of the dunes, and from time to time, the sandy slopes are visible through the trees. Within a mile you pass Masse Homestead Campsites, a handful of sites in a wooded setting, and then emerge at Log Slide Road, 5.3 miles from the visitor center. The Log Slide is one of the most stunning views in Michigan. In the late 1800s, loggers built a 500-foot-long wooden chute to send timber down the steep bank to Lake Superior below where the logs were rafted up and floated to sawmills. Today it's a viewing deck where to the east you can see the dramatic arc of the Grand Sable Banks, dunes that rise more than 300 feet above the Great Lake. To the west is the Au Sable Light Station while on the horizon is the deep blue of Lake Superior.

The Lakeshore Trail heads west from the viewing point and follows the high bluffs above Lake Superior. Though well forested in hardwoods, there are numerous openings for views of the the lake and the shoreline. In less than a mile you begin a long descent, losing 230 feet in less than a half mile. Eventually you bottom out, and 1.8 miles from the Log Slide or 7.1 miles from the start you reach Au Sable East Campsites, nine sites overlooking Lake Superior from a low bluff. This is often the stop for backpackers walking the trail in five days.

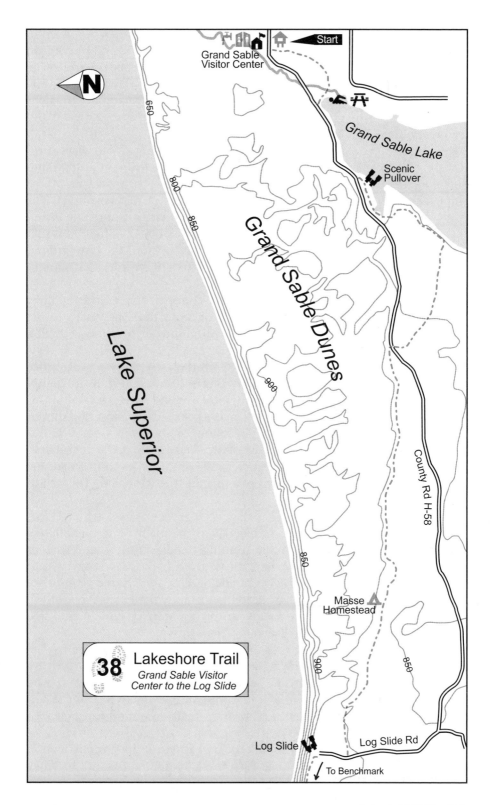

Grand Sable
Visitor Center

Start

N

650

800

850

Grand Sable Lake

Scenic
Pullover

Grand Sable Dunes

Lake Superior

900

County Rd H-58

850

Masse
Homestead

900

850

38 Lakeshore Trail
*Grand Sable Visitor
Center to the Log Slide*

Log Slide

Log Slide Rd

To Benchmark

Less than a half mile away is the Au Sable Light Station. Completed in 1874, the lighthouse has since been renovated by the park, and in 2007 an information center with displays was added to the lightkeeper's quarters. The center is open from 10 a.m. to 6 p.m. July through Labor Day and staffed by a ranger who leads tours through the complex, including climbing the light tower. Needless to say, the view from the top of the tower is magnificent and well worth the $2 fee for the tour.

From the light station the trail heads west, following an old access road just above Lake Superior. It's an easy 1.5 miles to Hurricane River Campground and along the way there are posted spurs that descend to the lake and three shipwrecks that are either half-buried in the beach or just beyond it. The first two are 150 yards west of the light station, where onshore you'll find the mangled pieces of the *Sitka* and *Gale Staples*, wooden bulk freighters that sank in 1904 and 1918. Just in the water 100 yards east of the campground are the remains of the *Mary Jarecki*, a wooden freight steamer that sank in 1884.

Reached 8.7 miles from the Grand Sable Visitor Center, Hurricane River Campground has 21 rustic sites on a pair of loops near the mouth of its namesake river. It's a very scenic spot, and within the campground are tables, vault toilets, and drinking water.

To continue onto the Benchmark Campsites, you cross a foot bridge over Hurricane River and head west, arriving within a half mile at County Road H-58, a dirt road at this point. The trail actually swings inland at this point but, being the end of a long day, many backpackers chose the shorter and more scenic alternative of simply following the county road. In 1.7 miles H-58 swings south and the Lakeshore Trail continues west reaching the six Benchmark campites in a quarter mile or 2.5 miles from Hurricane River. Drinking water is only a third of a mile further west along the trail in Twelvemile Beach Campground.

Day Two (9.2 miles) This a beach day with much of it spent along Twelvemile Beach, either hiking that seemingly endless line of sand itself or just above it on a low bluff. From Benchmark the trail heads west and within a third of a mile passes through Twelvemile Beach Campground. This drive-in campground has 36 rustic sites located on a sandy bluff above a beautiful Lake Superior beach. There are toilets, drinking water, a dayuse picnic area and steps down to Twelvemile Beach.

Follow the campground road west to pick up the trail again. The Lakeshore Trail skirts the bank right above Twelvemile Beach for an easy hike past numerous views of Lake Superior. The alternative here is to drop down to the beach itself and follow that west all the way to Beaver Creek if you are so inclined. Keep in mind, however, that loose sand can make for tired legs after awhile.

Within 2.8 miles from Benchmark the trail arrives at the posted junction with the north end of the Fox River Pathway, a 30-mile walk south to Seney

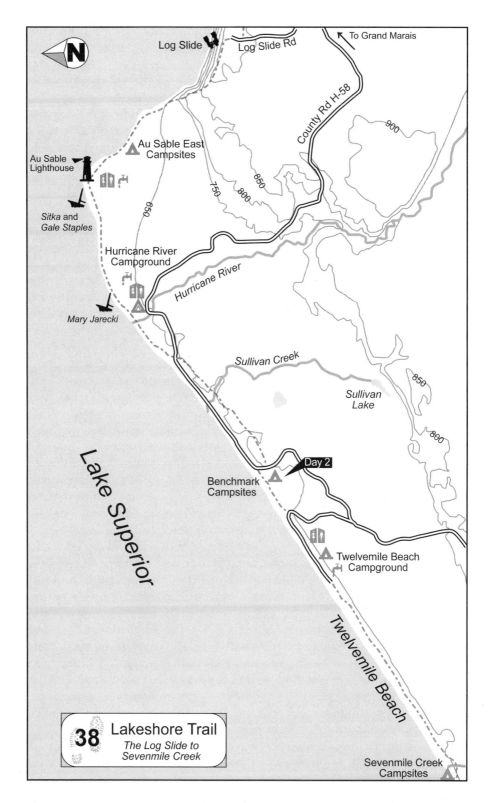

N

Log Slide
Log Slide Rd
To Grand Marais

County Rd H-58

900

Au Sable East
Campsites

Au Sable
Lighthouse

Sitka and
Gale Staples

750
800
850
650

Hurricane River
Campground

Hurricane River

Mary Jarecki

Sullivan Creek

Sullivan
Lake

850

800

Day 2

Benchmark
Campsites

Lake Superior

Twelvemile Beach
Campground

Twelvemile Beach

38 Lakeshore Trail
*The Log Slide to
Sevenmile Creek*

Sevenmile Creek
Campsites

(see Hike 41, page 267). The Lakeshore Trail continues west (right) and in less than a half mile swings inland to cross a bridge over Sevenmile Creek. On the other side of the creek are the Sevenmile Creek campsites. Beyond Sevenmile Creek the trail remains level but stays in the forest and out of view of Lake Superior. Again the alternative is to follow the beach.

On a bluff overlooking Twelvemile Beach and 6.8 miles from Benchmark, you reach the second of two junctions for Trappers Lake. This one is for Trappers Lake Trail, which heads almost due south (left) and in a half mile arrives at the five walk-in sites on the lake. The Lakeshore Trail continues west (right) and in a mile or 7.7 miles from Benchmark passes Pine Bluff Campsites. True to its name, the five sites are scattered among the pines that line the bluff.

The Lakeshore Trail continues west, remaining an easy and level walk and arriving at the Beaver Creek Campsites within 1.5 miles or 9.2 miles from Benchmark. This final stretch, from Pine Bluff to Beaver Creek, is a particularly scenic stretch to walk on the beach as you'll be able to view Grand Portal Point for much of the way. Beaver Creek has six sites on another pine-covered bluff and is a pleasant spot to spend the night with both Lake Superior and the small creek below you.

Day Three (10 miles) This day is the highpoint of the trek for most backpackers. Once past Beaver Creek, you begin viewing the Pictured Rocks, layers of colored sandstone that have been carved into caves, arches, and monoliths as tall as a nine-story building.

The morning begins by descending to a foot bridge across Beaver Creek and then continues along a trail that at first follows the west bank of the creek and then passes a junction to Beaver Lake. The Lakeshore Trail continues west (right) and resumes skirting Twelvemile Beach through an aspen and birch forest until it reaches a junction with a trail that heads south (left) to Little Beaver Lake 1.1 miles from Beaver Creek. This side trail reaches Little Beaver Lake Campground, a source of drinking water, in 1.5 miles.

Near the junction seemingly endless Twelvemile Beach finally ends and within a quarter mile the Lakeshore Trail passes Coves Campground, five sites in the hardwood forest above Lake Superior. The trail swings more inland and in 1.5 miles or 2.8 miles from Beaver Creek passes Coves Group Campsite. From here it's just 0.7 mile to Spray Falls, reached by a short spur before the Lakeshore Trail crosses a foot bridge over Spray Creek. This cascade is one of the most impressive in a park filled with impressive waterfalls. Spray Falls makes a 70-foot leap from the sandstone cliffs that make up the Pictured Rocks directly into Lake Superior. No tour buses here. Spray Falls can only be reached on foot or by kayak.

The trail continues to skirt the cliffs above Lake Superior and 1.6 miles from Spray Falls or 5.3 miles from Beaver Creek reaches Chapel Rock. The standstone formation is posted but you couldn't miss if you tried. Located right along the trail, the rock is a striking pair of sandstone pillars with a

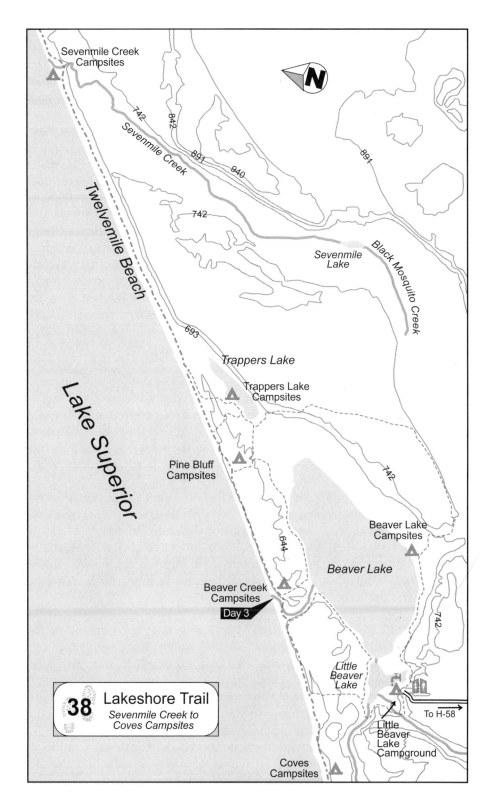

Sevenmile Creek
Campsites

N

742

842

Sevenmile Creek

891

940

891

742

Sevenmile
Lake

Black Mosquito Creek

Twelvemile Beach

693

Lake Superior

Trappers Lake

Trappers Lake
Campsites

Pine Bluff
Campsites

742

Beaver Lake
Campsites

644

Beaver Lake

Beaver Creek
Campsites

Day 3

742

Little
Beaver
Lake

Little
Beaver
Lake
Campground

To H-58

38 Lakeshore Trail
*Sevenmile Creek to
Coves Campsites*

Coves
Campsites

large pine growing on the top of them. Just a third of a mile to the west you use a foot bridge to cross Chapel Creek and then follow the bluff past Chapel Beach Campsites, 15 sites with a backcountry toilet. Below you, and accessible from several stairways, is Chapel Beach, a half mile long stretch of sand framed in at one end by colorful sandstone cliffs and at the other by a waterfall where Chapel Creek leaps into Lake Superior.

For many the most impressive section of this four-day walk is the next 4 miles, where the Lakeshore Trail skirts Lake Superior and passes numerous overlooks of the promontories, caves, arches and other formations that make up the Grand Portal cliffs. There is no shoreline in Michigan more beautiful than this stretch where the orange-reddish sandstone contrasts vividly with the deep blue of Lake Superior.

Within a mile you reach a promontory that gives way to views of Grand Portal Point to the west. Then you reach the point itself in another half mile or 6 miles from Beaver Creek. This sandy ledge is lightly forested and extends far enough into Lake Superior to allow you to gaze at miles of Pictured Rocks in both directions. Just past the point is another interesting spot: a sandy beach on top of the cliffs, almost 200 feet above the cold waters of Lake Superior. Glaciers originally created this unusual phenomenon, but today it's the strong northern winds that maintain it as they erode the face of the cliffs and then push the sand on top of them.

From this "beach" the trail continues along Lake Superior, passing more views of the Pictured Rocks and breaking out at another cliff-top beach within 0.3 mile. Here you can look back at a rock formation that most agree looks like an Indian's head with a Mohawk. The Lakeshore Trail has now swung to the southwest and dips in and out of the trees near Lake Superior along sandstone cliffs that gradually descend towards the mouth of Mosquito River.

You reach the river 4.7 miles from Chapel Rock or 3.2 miles from Grand Portal Point just after passing a junction with a trail to the Chapel trailhead parking area (see Hike 39, page 259). Part of the shoreline here is layers of flat, reddish rock where you can stretch out and relax after a 10-mile day. Just above them, tucked away in the pines, are 10 sites and a backcountry toilet. Mosquito River is a scenic and popular area to camp, especially with kayakers who put in at Miners Beach.

Day Four (12 miles) The final day is a 12-mile trek, but hopefully your pack is lighter without a bulging food bag and your walking legs are strong. Just the thought of a whitefish sandwich and a rootbeer float at the A&W in Munising is more than enough to motivate most backpackers down the trail.

You begin by crossing Mosquito River on a foot bridge and quickly arrive at a junction. One trail heads south (left), heads for Mosquito Falls, and then the Chapel trailhead. The Lakeshore Trail continues southwest

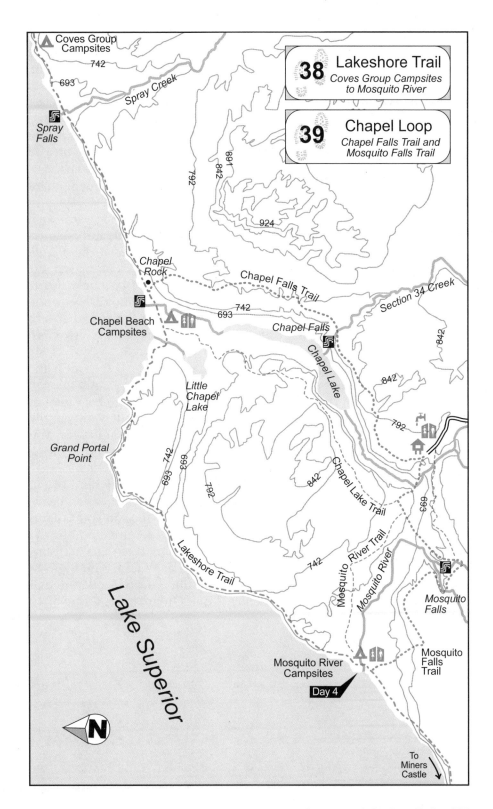

Coves Group
Campsites

742

693

Spray Creek

Spray
Falls

38 Lakeshore Trail
*Coves Group Campsites
to Mosquito River*

39 Chapel Loop
*Chapel Falls Trail and
Mosquito Falls Trail*

891
842
792

924

Chapel
Rock

Chapel Falls Trail

Section 34 Creek

742
693

Chapel Falls

842

Chapel Beach
Campsites

Little
Chapel
Lake

Chapel Lake

792

Grand Portal
Point

742

693

693

792

842

Chapel Lake Trail

693

Lakeshore Trail

742

Mosquito River Trail

Mosquito River

Mosquito
Falls

Lake Superior

Mosquito River
Campsites

Day 4

Mosquito
Falls
Trail

N

To
Miners
Castle

(right) and stays on the cliffs above Lake Superior, where there are numerous opportunities to view the Pictured Rocks in both directions. Within 3 miles you reach Potato Patch, three walk-in sites. If you plan to spend the night, keep in mind there is no quick access to Lake Superior for water.

Beyond Potato Patch, the Lakeshore Trail crosses a field and then makes its steepest ascent, dropping 142 feet to Miners Basin Escarpment to beautiful Miners Beach. The wide, sandy beach is almost a mile long and features a picnic area in a stand of pines, drinking water, and toilets. It's often busy in the summer with kayakers, brave (foolhardy?) swimmers, and backpackers. This is a good spot to take a break because you're about to face the sharpest climb of your trip.

The Lakeshore Trail crosses Miners River on a foot bridge and then ascends 145 feet in a series of switchbacks before breaking out at the Miners Castle dayuse area at the top of the escarpment. Reached 5 miles from Mosquito River, Miners Castle is the park's most famous rock formation, the only one accessible by road. The castle is composed of a soft, crumbly, quartz sandstone and in April, 2006 its northeast turret collapsed into Lake Superior. Although only one turret remains, Miners Castle is still the busiest area of the park during the summer. Facilities include viewing decks, restrooms, drinking water and picnic area and interpretive displays.

Continuing its southwest direction, the Lakeshore Trail stays near the edge of the sheer sandstone cliffs, on a level route through lightly forested hardwoods. There are numerous opportunities to look at Miners Castle to the northeast or Grand Island to the west. Within 0.6 mile you pass the Cliffs Group Campsite and in 2 miles or 7 miles from Mosquito River you arrive at Cliffs Campsites, the last backcountry campground before reaching Munising.

Within 4 miles from Miners Castle you reach a viewing point of Sand Point extending into Lake Superior and can spot the park headquarters below adjacent to a marshy area. A junction with a side trail to Sand Point (right) is then quickly passed while the Lakeshore Trail (left) continues to hug the edge of the Pictured Rocks escarpment. After crossing three small streams and passing an open field that at one time was a dairy farm, you begin to make a gentle descent off the escarpment. Within a quarter mile the trail ends at the Munising Falls Visitor Center, 7 miles from Miners Castle or 12 miles from the start of your day.

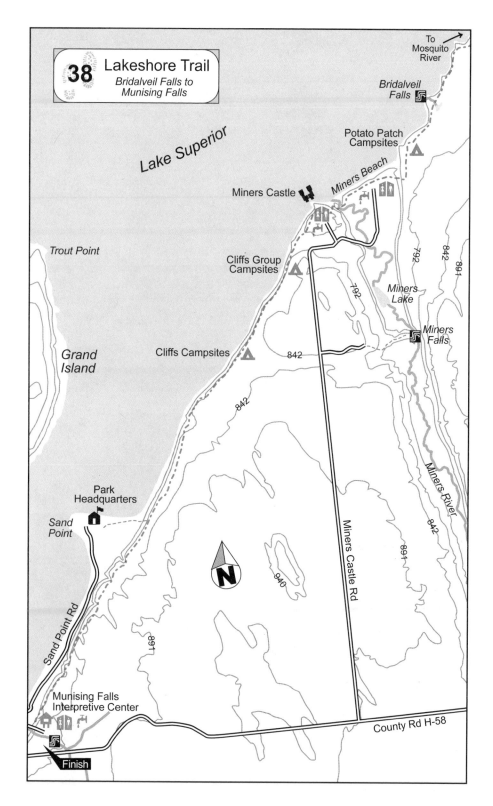

Lakeshore Trail
38 Bridalveil Falls to Munising Falls

To Mosquito River

Bridalveil Falls

Lake Superior

Potato Patch Campsites

Miners Beach

Miners Castle

Trout Point

Cliffs Group Campsites

Miners Lake

792

842

891

Miners Falls

Grand Island

Cliffs Campsites

842

842

Park Headquarters

Sand Point

Miners Castle Rd

891

842

N

940

Miners River

Sand Point Rd

891

Munising Falls Interpretive Center

County Rd H-58

Finish

A backpacker stands at the edge of the Pictured Rocks to soak in the scenery. The Chapel Loop is a two-day trek with much of it along the top of the famous sandstone cliffs.

Chapel Loop
Pictured Rocks National Lakeshore

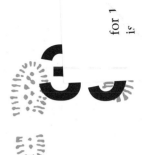

County: Alger
Nearest Town: Munising
Distance: 10.4 miles
Hiking Time: Two days
Highest Elevation Gain: 150 feet
Difficulty: Easy to moderate
Highlights: Pictured Rocks, waterfalls, Chapel Beach

The Lakeshore Trail is one of Michigan's classic backpacking treks, a 42.4-mile walk from Grand Marais to Munising. But if you don't have four to five days to spare or the desire to haul a backpack for 40-plus miles, the Chapel Loop is the perfect alternative.

The hike begins and, more importantly, ends at Chapel trailhead parking lot, 14 miles east of Munising. The entire loop is a 10.4-mile walk over generally level terrain, making it either a long dayhike or an easy overnight outing. There are also several ways to shorten this trek, but in doing so you'll miss the extraordinary scenery that has made this national park so famous and the loop such an exceptional walk.

The first leg of the loop is a hike to Lake Superior followed by a 4.7-mile segment of the Lakeshore Trail. You complete the loop and return to your vehicle via Mosquito Falls. Along the way you enjoy the most stunning stretches of the Pictured Rocks and pass five waterfalls.

There are also two backcountry campgrounds along this route to set up camp for the night. If you arrive in the morning, you can easily hike to the Mosquito River campsites, a trek of 7.8 miles. If you arrive in the afternoon or even the early evening, you can stop at Chapel Beach campsites, making the first day a walk of only 3.4 miles.

Both campgrounds have backcountry toilets but neither has safe drinking water. Bring a filter. These are also two of the most popular backcountry camping areas in the park. Reserve your site well in advance during the summer.

Trip Planner

Maps: The park's *Pictured Rocks National Lakeshore*, a topo that is printed on waterproof paper, is the best map for this loop. You can purchase it at the Pictured Rocks National Lakeshore/Hiawatha National Forest Visitor Center (906-387-3700) in Munising for $7.

Getting There: From the Pictured Rocks National Lakeshore/Hiawatha National Forest Visitor Center in Munising head east on County Road H-58

4 miles and then turn north on Chapel Road. The trailhead parking lot at the end of Chapel Road, reached in 6 miles from H-58.

Fees & Reservations: It is best to reserve a site in advance in either Chapel Beach or Mosquito River backcountry campgrounds. See the Fees & Reservations section of the Lakeshore Trail for reservation procedure. All the fees are the same for the Chapel Loop as they are for the Lakeshore Trail.

Information: The main information center is the Pictured Rocks National Lakeshore/Hiawatha National Forest Visitor Center (906-387-3700) on M-28 in Munising which is open daily in the summer from 9 a.m. to 6 p.m. Most information you need for this hike is also available on the Pictured Rocks National Lakeshore web site (*www.nps.gov/piro*).

Trail Guide

Day One (7.8 miles) The map for this hike has been combined with the fourth map of the Lakeshore Trail (see Hike 38, page 255). From the trailhead parking area you have a choice on how to reach Lake Superior and the Lakeshore Trail: Chapel Falls Trail or Chapel Lake Trail. The vast majority of people choose the latter, the trail that passes the falls.

Chapel Falls Trail begins as an old road that heads north into the woods and makes a gentle but steady half-mile climb through a dense woods. In less than a mile from the trailhead you reach an overlook where you can gaze at Chapel Lake below and in 1.3 miles you arrive at Chapel Falls, one of the most impressive in the park. Two observation decks provide a good view of the 60-foot waterfall that hurls itself over the sharp edge of a cliff into a steep-sided canyon.

From the second observation deck at the falls, the trail swings north as a narrow path that uses planking to cross wet areas. In less than 2 miles from the falls or 3.1 miles from the trailhead, you descend sharply to Chapel Rock and a view of Lake Superior. The sandstone pillar is impressive while just 0.3 mile to the west are the Chapel Beach campsites.

For backpackers arriving late in the afternoon at the trailhead, this is the ideal place to camp. Reached 3.4 miles from the parking lot, the 15 campsites are located on a wooded bluff above Chapel Beach, a half mile of beautiful sand with colorful sandstone cliffs at one end and a waterfall leaping into Lake Superior at the other. Along with a backcountry toilet and bear poles, there are several stairways to access the beach.

From Chapel Beach it is a 1.5-mile walk to Grand Portal Point and from there another 2.9 miles to Mosquito River. For a complete description of the route see Day Three of the Lakeshore Trail (Hike 38, page 252). You reach Mosquito River backcountry campground 7.8 miles from the Chapel trailhead, where there are 10 sites in the woods above the reddish rocky shoreline of Lake Superior along with a backcountry toilet. This is a beautiful place to spend the night as you can view towering Pictured Rocks in both directions of the shoreline.

A weary hiker soaks her feet in Chapel Falls at the east end of Chapel Beach. Chapel Beach is one of the most popular backcountry campgrounds in Pictured Rocks.

Campers at Mosquito River Backcountry Campground gather at the Lake Superior shoreline in the evening.

Day Two (2.6 miles) There are two routes back to the Chapel parking lot with Mosquito River Trail being the shortest, a walk of less than 2 miles. Mosquito Falls Trail, one of the newest trails in the park, is longer at 2.7 miles but the extra mileage is worth it. This trail is much more interesting as it passes three cascades along the way, including its namesake waterfall.

From the campsites descend to cross the foot bridge over Mosquito River and then follow the Lakeshore Trail briefly west as it skirts a small beach strewn with glacial boulders. The well-posted junction of the Mosquito Falls Trail is quickly reached, and you head south (left) on it. The trail begins with a steady climb as you gain more than 150 feet in the first half mile. When you top off, the trail swings east for a spell and then resumes heading south.

Within 1.6 miles from the campsites, the trail descends a small ravine to cross a branch of the Mosquito River, climbs out.and then quickly reaches the main branch. You actually hike south past Mosquito Falls to cross the river further upstream and then hike north past them again. The main cascade is where the river slides and drops 10 feet over layers of black rock. Continue along the trail and you'll spot two more smaller falls in the next 200 yards. Overall it's a scenic spot to linger if mosquitos aren't too thick. Unfortunately, the river is named after the pesky insect for a reason.

The trail continues north but eventually swings away from the river and in a half mile or 2.2 miles from the campsites arrives at a junction with Mosquito River Trail. Head east (right) and within 200 yards you'll arrive at a junction with Chapel Lake Trail. Head south (right) here and you'll be back at your vehicle in a third of a mile.

Beaver Lake Loop
Pictured Rocks National Lakeshore

County: Alger
Nearest Town: Munising
Distance: 11.5 miles
Hiking Time: Two days
Highest Elevation Gain: 142 feet
Difficulty: Moderate
Highlights: Twelvemile Beach, inland lakes, backcountry fishing

Like that lanky uncle that has gone soft over the years, Beaver Basin is the bulging waistline of a long, skinny park. Much of Pictured Rocks National Lakeshore is less than a mile wide. But the basin is a 3-mile-wide bowl, large enough to contain three inland lakes, numerous streams, and extensive wetlands. To the south it's bordered by the park's famed sandstone escarpment that swings inland near Spray Falls; to the north by seemingly endless Twelvemile Beach. Located in the heart of the park, Beaver Basin can be reached only by a pair of winding dirt roads, making it as quiet, remote, and wilderness-like a spot as you can find in this national park.

That alone should be enough reason to hike and spend the night along the Beaver Lake Loop, described here as a two-day trek. But the area also contains the most abundant wildlife in the park, from loons on the lakes and bald eagles in the tallest trees to river otters and beavers in obscured ponds and streams. Then there is the opportunity for backcountry fishing. Boaters can reach Beaver and Little Beaver lakes but are limited to electric motors only. Trappers Lake is for walk-in anglers only. At all three you can end the day casting a line from your campsite in waters that receive minimal fishing pressure.

There are four sets of backcountry campsites along this route that can and should be reserved in advance. There is also Little Beaver Lake Campground, a drive-in facility where the trailhead is located and the only source of safe drinking water in the area. You can also begin from a trail that departs Beaver Basin Overlook but that adds almost 3 miles to the total distance of the walk as you end up backtracking the initial 1.4 miles required to reach the loop.

Trip Planner

Maps: Once again the best map is the park's waterproof *Pictured Rocks National Lakeshore* topo ($7).
Getting There: From the Pictured Rocks National Lakeshore/Hiawatha National Forest Visitor Center in Munising, head east on County Road H-58 for 19 miles and then turn north on Little Beaver Lake Road. Within 3 miles

the road ends at Little Beaver Lake Campground, where the trailhead is located.

Fees & Reservations: It is best to reserve in advance any backcountry campsite along the loop. See the Fees & Reservations section of the Lakeshore Trail for the booking procedure. Reservations are not accepted for sites in Little Beaver Lake Campground. All other fees are the same for the Beaver Lake Loop as they are for the Lakeshore Trail.

Information: The main information center is the Pictured Rocks National Lakeshore/Hiawatha National Forest Visitor Center (906-387-3700) on M-28 in Munising, which is open daily in the summer from 9 a.m. to 6 p.m.

Trail Guide

Day One (5.5 miles) Posted in the campground is the Beaver Lake Trail which quickly crosses Bills Creek and then heads east for Beaver Lake. You reach the large lake in 0.7 mile and closely follow its shoreline for the next half mile. Eventually the trail swings inland to a stretch of open meadows, once the site of a resort, and then uses a bridge to cross Lowery Creek. Just before the creek are Beaver Lake Campsites, 10 individual sites and a group site reached 1.4 miles from Little Beaver Lake. Spread across 767 acres, Beaver Lake is the largest in the park and supports smallmouth bass, northern pike, and perch. It was also stocked with walleye in the past and remnants of that fishery are still around.

At Lowery Creek the trail heads south and begins climbing. You gain 142 feet in less than a half mile before topping off at a junction, reached 2 miles from Little Beaver Lake. To the south (right) a trail climbs to Beaver Basin Overlook, reaching it in 1.4 miles. To the northeast (left) is the trail to Trappers Lake. This trail begins as an old road skirting a forested plateau and then in a mile swings due north and cuts across it.

After passing a junction with an unmarked trail departing east (right), you descend from the plateau and 5.4 miles from Little Beaver Creek arrive at a junction near the west end of Trappers Lake. Head northeast (right) and you'll shortly arrive at Trappers Lake Campsites.

The five individual sites and one group sites are well spread out along the wooded shoreline of the lake. Because most backpackers prefer to stay near Lake Superior, these sites are not as heavily in demand as most backcountry campsites. Yet they are scenic and quiet on a lake that never sees a boat. Trappers Lake is 45.5 acres in size and supports rock bass and perch.

Day Two (6 miles) Begin the day at the junction within Trappers Lake Campsites and head north on Trappers Lake Trail for Lake Superior. Within a half mile you're at a junction with the Lakeshore Trail (see Hike 38) on a bluff overlooking Twelvemile Beach. You now have options. You can head west (left) on the Lakeshore Trail to remain on the bluff, passing through Pine Bluff Campsites in less than a mile and Beaver Creek Campsites in 2.4

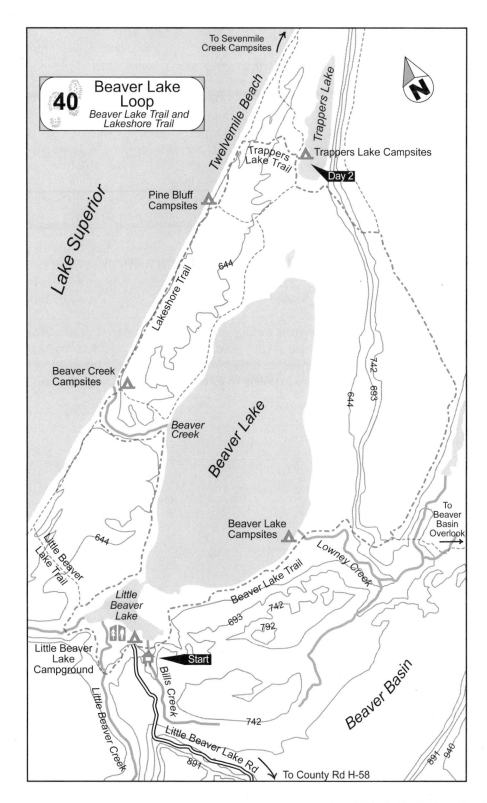

40 Beaver Lake Loop

Beaver Lake Trail and Lakeshore Trail

To Sevenmile Creek Campsites

Twelvemile Beach

Trappers Lake

Trappers Lake Trail

Trappers Lake Campsites

Day 2

Lake Superior

Pine Bluff Campsites

Lakeshore Trail

644

Beaver Creek Campsites

Beaver Creek

Beaver Lake

742

693

644

To Beaver Basin Overlook

Beaver Lake Campsites

Lowney Creek

Little Beaver Lake Trail

644

Beaver Lake Trail

693

742

792

Little Beaver Lake

Little Beaver Lake Campground

Bills Creek

Start

Beaver Basin

Little Beaver Creek

742

Little Beaver Lake Rd

891

891

940

To County Rd H-58

miles (for full description see Day Two of Hike 38, page 250).

Your other option, of course, is to descend to the beach at the junction with Trappers Lake Trail and follow Twelvemile Beach west. This is a particularly nice stretch of beach to walk as you'll be able to view Grand Portal Point for much of the way. When you arrive at the mouth of Beaver Creek head upstream a short ways to a trail bridge across it.

The bridge puts you back on the Lakeshore Trail but within a quarter mile you arrive at a junction. More options. You can stay on the Lakeshore Trail for another 1.1 miles to reach Little Beaver Lake Trail that will lead you south to the campground and the start of this loop.

Or you can head south (left) on a trail that will return you to the shores of Beaver Lake. Within a half mile you reach the south end of Beaver Creek where it drains into the big lake. The trail then swings southwest and follows the shoreline for almost a mile to a sandy beach at the west end. From here you continue west to Little Beaver Lake and follow its north shore in an area that is often populated by waterfowl and other wildlife. Within 2 miles of Beaver Creek Campsites or 5 miles from Trappers Lake, you reach a junction with Little Beaver Lake Trail.

Head west (left) and within a mile this trail will lead you around the marshy end of Little Beaver Lake, with boardwalks to keep your feet dry, and then across Little Beaver Creek via a foot bridge. Just beyond the creek is a junction with a spur leading east (left) to Little Beaver Lake Campground.

Fox River Pathway

Lake Superior State Forest and
Pictured Rocks National Lakeshore

Counties: Schoolcraft and Alger
Nearest Town: Seney
Distance: 34.7 miles
Hiking Time: Four days
Highest Elevation Gain: 40 feet
Difficulty: Challenging
Highlights: Backcountry fishing, Kingston Plains stump fields, Lake Superior

In 1919, Ernest Hemingway and two old high school friends from Chicago traveled to Seney, a logging town well past its peak, for a late summer fishing and camping trip. Five years later the adventure became the basis of Hemingway's short story, *Big Two-Hearted River*, in which his character, Nick Adams, also heads to the Upper Peninsula to ease the pain and shell-shock trauma he suffered from World War I.

The story is one of Hemingway's best known in Michigan, but ironically the author probably never laid eyes on the Big Two-Hearted, much less pulled a trout from it. Most literary scholars agree that he merely borrowed its romantic name for his Nick Adams tale. The river he and his friends fished was the Fox, which today is still a great trout stream and one of the principal features of this 34-mile walk from Seney to Lake Superior.

Seney is only a 90-minute drive from the Mackinac Bridge, yet the Fox River and its branches wind through an incredibly remote and isolated slice of the Upper Peninsula. The river begins in swamps and wetlands of the Deadman Lake, 10 miles southwest of Grand Marais, and flows 35 miles to the Manistique River near the village of Germfask. In 1988, the Fox and its East Branch were designated a Wild and Scenic River by the Michigan's Natural Rivers Program. It has also been crowned a Michigan Blue Ribbon Trout Stream, thanks in part to the two- and three-pound brook trout that some anglers reportedly catch every summer.

The Fox River Pathway is actually a 27.5-mile walk to Kingston Lake Campground, where, at times, you're standing on the banks of the main branch, the West Branch, or the Little Fox River. In between, you hike past meadows that are loaded with blueberries in August, dark and damp black spruce bogs, a series of kettle lakes, and the eerie stump fields leftover from the cut-and-run logging practices of the 19th century.

You will also hike through areas that have been recently logged, and that's the source of discontent for this trail by many backpackers. The numerous open areas and clearcuts are not something you'll be stopping to take pictures of and there are times when it is hard to follow the trail due to a lack of standing trees for blue blazes. If coming down from a hike in the spectacular Pictured Rocks National Lakeshore, you'll most likely be disappointed with this pathway.

But in recent years, the pathway has been extensively remarked and even re-routed in places, making it easier to hike through what is still an isolated and wild area. There have been times when I have followed the tracks of wolves for 2 miles along a sandy stretch of this trail or spotted bear scat so fresh it was still steaming. This described trek also adds another day to the pathway: the 6.5-mile connector trail from Kingston Lake to Lake Superior, ending at Twelvemile Campground in Pictured Rocks National Lakeshore. Suddenly emerging at the endless blue that is the world's largest freshwater lake and then spending a night along it is as a climactic a finish as there is on any trail in this book.

The pathway is rated challenging, but not because of rugged terrain; there isn't any. The challenge is a pair of 10-mile-plus days and finding the next blue blaze in a constant attempt to stay on course. This is not a trail you want to hike in May or early June due to wet conditions and overwhelming numbers of mosquitoes and black flies. Late August through September is by far the best time.

With the first and third nights spent at state forest campgrounds, the only time you're without a source of drinking water is at Stanley Lake. Either pack a filter or, to save weight, plan on boiling water that evening. Backpacking anglers will also need to bring fishing equipment, while blueberry pickers will want to pack along a frypan and fixings for pancakes. Both brook trout and blueberries can be plentiful during certain times of the summer and a welcome treat for anybody spending four days enduring clearcuts.

Trip Planner

Maps: Unfortunately, the Fox River Pathway is split over five USGS topos; *AuSable Point SW, Driggs Lake, Suken Lake, Seney NW and Seney*, and none of them has the trail on them. The *Pictured Rocks National Lakeshore* topo ($7) that the park sells only covers the pathway in detail from Kingston Lake to Lake Superior.

Make sure to pick up a copy of the brochure, *The Fox River Pathway*, produced by the DNR Forest Management Division. The brochure contains a map of the trail and text for the numbered posts along it. Even though many of the 24 posts are missing, anybody hiking the trail will find the background information interesting. The three maps in this section will show the position of all the posts, whether they are still there or not.

Getting There: This is a point-to-point hike with the southern trailhead at Seney Township Park on Fox River Road (also known as County Road 450), a half mile north of M-28 in Seney. The finish is at Twelvemile Campground

In the Kingston Plains backpackers pass through a stump museum while hiking the Fox River Pathway.

on H-58 in the Pictured Rocks National Lakeshore, 17 miles west of Grand Marais.

There is usually somebody in Seney willing, for a fee of course, to help backpackers drop off a car at Twelvemile Campground. Contact the Seney Field Office or the Fox River Motel (906-499-3332; *www.foxrivermotel.com*) for help in arranging such transportation.

Fees & Reservations: Fox River and Kingston Lake State Forest Campgrounds are $15 a night, Twelvemile Campground is $12, and Seney Township Park is $10. Sites can not be reserved in any of them. Backcountry camping is free at Stanley Lake but you need to first pick up a Dispersed Camping Permit from any DNR office.

Information: For trail conditions call the Seney DNR Field Office (906-499-3346) but be forewarned, the office is small and often there is nobody around to answer the phone.

Trail Guide

Day One (6 miles) For a place to pitch the tent the night before, there's Seney Township Park, a pleasant campground overlooking the Fox River, with drinking water, toilets, even hook-ups for RVers. The trailhead with post No. 1 and a small parking area is just north of the campground on Fox River Road.

You begin on a dirt two-track but quickly leave it to follow a narrow path through the woods. You skirt the famous trout stream for a mile but only see it twice, much to the disappointment of anybody packing along a rod-and-reel. A mile from the trailhead, the pathway pops out at Fox River Road and crosses it at Two Mile Ditch. This ditch and many others were dug in 1914 to drain the logged-out forests in a developer's scheme to sell the tracts as agricultural land. Farmers who purchased the land, usually immigrants, quickly discovered the sandy soil would grow little, if anything, and eventually walked away.

At 1.3 miles from the Seney trailhead the pathway merges into a sandy two-track that doubles as a snowmobile route in the winter. For more than 3 miles you'll be following this two-track past orange snowmobile signs and clearcuts. Some of the most extensive clearcuts, where nothing is left standing, are reached within a mile. The DNR brochure works hard to explain that such logging practices are necessary and even beneficial to certain species of trees and wildlife. Still a clearcut is a clearcut and it can be depressing for any backpacker hiking this section of the trail.

The snowmobile trail reaches a "V" junction with another two-track 4.7 miles from the start. Just before that, the pathway departs the snowmobile trail and heads northeast (right). If you miss the pathway, and many hikers do, just follow the two-track that also heads northeast (right) rather than the well marked snowmobile trail that heads northwest (left). In less than a half mile on either the pathway or the two-track you will arrive at Fox River Road, where just across the dirt road are the blue blazes leading to the state

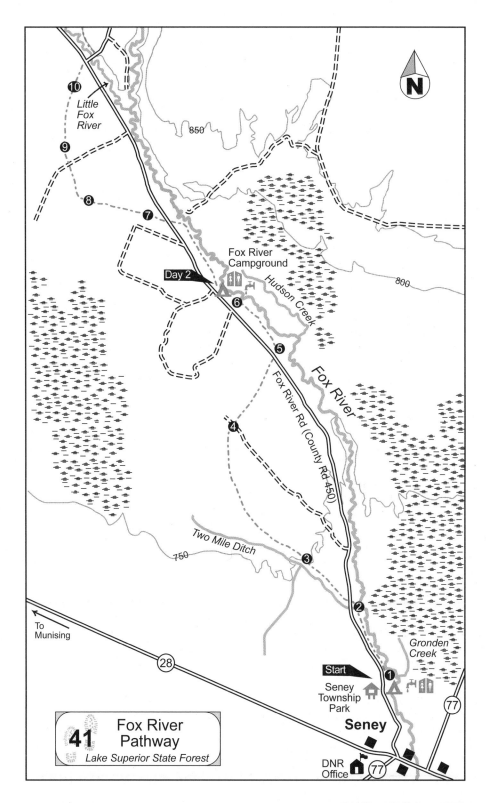

Fox River Campground

Day 2

Hudson Creek

Fox River

Fox River Rd (County Rd 450)

Little Fox River

850

800

750

Two Mile Ditch

To Munising

28

Start

Seney Township Park

Gronden Creek

Seney

DNR Office

77

77

41 Fox River Pathway
Lake Superior State Forest

forest campground.

On the east side of Fox River Road, the pathway is extremely hard to spot and a complete contrast to what you just experienced with the snowmobile trail. But the blue blazes are frequent and within a few yards of the road you pass post No. 5. You quickly move into a more mature pine forest (thank goodness!) and closer to the river, but again rarely see water. After a mile from Fox River Road or 6 miles from the Seney trailhead, you arrive at the Fox River State Forest Campground.

The rustic campground has seven sites, most of them in the lightly forested area on a bluff above the Fox River. Trees block any view of the water from your site, but numerous stairways provide quick access to the riverbank. The campground features drinking water and vault toilets.

Day Two (11.4 miles) This is a long day on a trail that is hard to spot at times. Start early, slow your pace, and always keep an eye out for a faded blue blaze. Many of them will be painted on stumps.

From the state forest campground the pathway descends closer to the river and begins one of the most pleasant stretches of the day. For the next mile you're treated to numerous views of the Fox River, the best is only 0.3 mile from the campground, and a handful of big white pines. This scenic segment ends when the trail arrives at Fox River Road and crosses it to the west side. The trail is not as well defined here while the big pines are replaced by scrawny jack pine. Within 1.5 miles from the campground you cross a snowmobile trail and then in a quarter mile reach post No. 8, marking the location of a logging camp from the 1880s. There's not much left of the foundations but there's enough rusted iron scattered around that it's easy to believe there was a work camp here.

At this point the pathway swings to the northeast, crosses a pair of sandy two-tracks in the next mile and then winds through a field of ancient stumps where the blazes will be hard to spot at times. Finally 3.6 miles from the state forest campground you arrive at Fox River Road again. The trail crosses the road and continues on Wagner-Taylor Dam Road briefly, using the dirt road's one-lane bridge to cross the Little Fox River. Pause and take a good look of this branch of the Fox River. You hardly see it the rest of the day.

Just beyond the bridge, you leave Wagner-Taylor Dam Road to the north (left) at a well-marked spot. For the next 2 miles the trail parallels the river but stays out of view of it then swings to the east to climb a low bluff. It skirts a pond 6.8 miles from the state forest campground and then moves into a wetland area. The trail uses a series of low sandy ridges to keep your boots dry.

The day comes to a close when you ascend into semi-open, rolling ridges 10 miles from the start that lead you through a wild blueberry management area. If it's late July through August keep one eye on the ground for blue dots and the other on trees for blue blazes. You follow the ridges for a half mile and then descend to a small area of black spruce. Finally, 11 miles from the Fox River Campground, you break out at a two-track where just to the left is

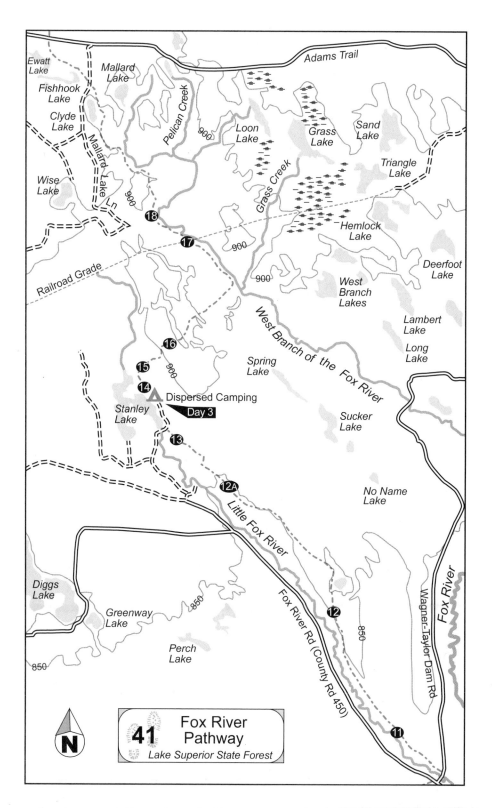

the Stanley Lake Dam and the beautiful body of water it created.

Simply follow the two-track to the right as it skirts the east side of Stanley Lake. The best camping areas are at the north end of the lake, a half mile from the dam, where there was once a state forest campground. Here you can pitch your tent beneath towering red pines on a carpet of pine needles with a clear view of the water. The lake attracts a healthy population of waterfowl, while anglers can cast here for northern pike.

Day Three (10.8 miles) The pathway leaves the two-track at the north end of the lake and briefly follows a loggers railroad grade from the 1890s as it moves into the forest. In less than a half mile from Stanley Lake you pass some impressive white pines before the trail swings east and tops a bluff with a noticeable 40-foot climb.

The pathway continues in an easterly direction and 2 miles from Stanley Lake swings north to follow the West Branch of the Fox River. You stay near the river for the next 1.5 miles and spot it often. Within 3 miles from Stanley Lake you cross the Lake Superior and Ishpeming Railroad grade, built in 1958 for hardwood logging in this area but discontinued only five years later. You'll know when you cross it, in the winter it's a snowmobile trail.

Eventually the West Branch swings east, while the pathway heads north to follow a series of low forested ridges. The ridges keep you above the wetlands to the east while the trees hide the stump fields of the Kingston Plains to the west. Within a half mile you begin skirting the fields of jagged stumps, and depending on your point of view, it's either an amazing scene or a shocking sight. Some stumps are several feet across and so large they leave you wondering how big the entire trees must have been.

The Kingston Plains are the result of fires that swept through the area after logging companies had removed most of the timber in 1890s. As was the practice of the day, the loggers left behind treetops and limbs known as slash that, when dried, was easily ignited by lightning. These intense wild fires burned not only the slash but much of the organic matter in the topsoil, markedly decreasing its fertility. Because the plains were never replanted with trees, what remains is a "stump museum," infertile sandy ground covered with mostly grass and lichens, and dotted with the stumps of the original forest. Brush and small pines are now popping up but the plains are still very much a field of charred stumps that late in the day can appear ghostly and even sinister.

When you're 4.6 miles from Stanley Lake, the trail passes a view of the headwaters of the West Branch to the east, a large pond with the small river snaking its way south. Then the pathway drops into the forest, and after briefly following a two-track, you depart the two-track to the west (left). Within a quarter mile you arrive on a low bluff overlooking Clyde Lake. The lake's high banks, lightly forested by tall red pine, offer plenty of spots to pitch a tent if you're so inclined to stop for the day.

The pathway skirts the north end of Clyde Lake and then crosses Mallard

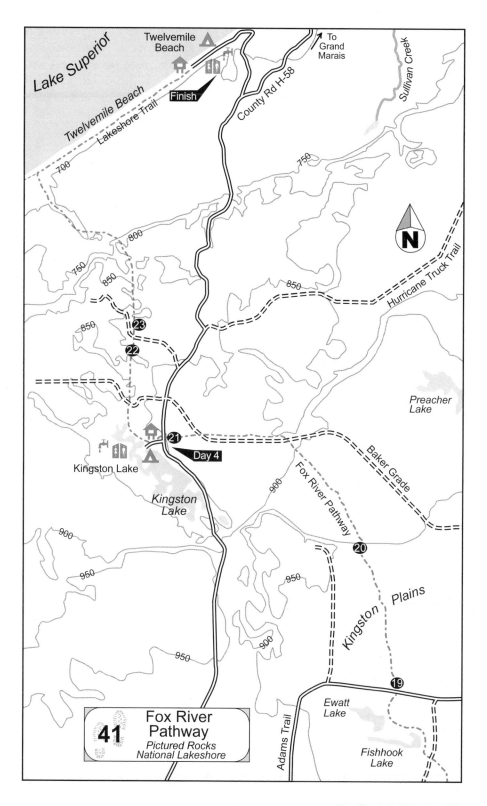

Lake Superior

Twelvemile Beach

To Grand Marais

County Rd H-58

Twelvemile Beach Lakeshore Trail

Finish

700

800

750

850

850

23

22

Hurricane Truck Trail

N

Sullivan Creek

Preacher Lake

21

Day 4

Kingston Lake

Kingston Lake

Baker Grade

Fox River Pathway

900

20

900

950

950

Kingston Plains

950

900

19

Adams Trail

Ewatt Lake

Fishhook Lake

41 Fox River Pathway
Pictured Rocks National Lakeshore

Lake Lane, a sandy two-track, to re-enter the Kingston Plain. You wind through more grayish stumps for 0.3 mile and then arrive at Fishhook Lake. The lake is really a series of ponds that are almost covered by lily pads and surrounded by wetlands. It does, however, resemble a fishhook with the trail skirting its point before moving onto Ewatt Lake. From this lake it's a quick walk to Adams Trail, a major dirt road reached 6.6 miles from Stanley Lake.

On the other side of Adams Trail you enter the heart of the Kingston Plains and for more than a mile will be hiking through an open field of stumps. Plans call for a ban on reseeding in this area so we can preserve this as a visual record of the amazing size and density of the pines that provided so much of Michigan's wealth at the turn of the century. Eventually you enter a living forest covering the stumps and then climb a pair of bluffs within a half mile of each other.

The pathway crosses Baker Grade 2.5 miles from Adams Trail, and then swings northwest and for the next 1.2 miles skirts the two-track. You cross Baker Grade a second time and within a half mile break out at County Road H-58. On the other side the pathway quickly reaches Kingston State Forest Campground, 4.2 miles from Adams Trail or 10.8 miles from Stanley Lake.

This a beautiful campground, located on a small peninsula in the middle of the lake. Along with drinking water and vault toilets, there are 16 well-shaded sites with most of them facing the water.

Day Four (6.5 miles) The Fox River Pathway resumes north from near the boat access site as a well-defined path in a pine forest. On your final day you are spared massive clearcuts (only small ones) and hard-to-find trails. For almost a half mile the pathway skirts Kingston Lake and then departs from its north end to quickly cross a two-track. It remains as a level trail in the woods and 1.5 miles from Kingston Lake passes post No. 22, marking a kettle, a small lake created by the leftover ice of a retreating glacier.

The trail continues north, crosses another two-track and then in less than a half mile enters perhaps the most rugged stretch of the entire trek. You endure a bit of up-and-down hiking for the next 1.5 miles, including a pair of 40-foot descents, until the pathway drops into a tight ravine. For the most part you remain in the forest, and where other trails and two-tracks are encountered, the pathway is well posted.

The ravine briefly closes in on you but within 0.3 mile the terrain opens up and 4 miles from Kingston Lake you reach a junction with the Lakeshore Trail. There on the other side of the trail is Lake Superior and what a beautiful sight it is. If the day is clear, that deep blue lake will be framed at the top by even a bluer horizon and on the bottom by a white sandy strip that is Twelvemile Beach. If you're not in a rush to get back to your car and race home, drop the pack and soak your tired toes. You've earned it.

At the junction with the Lakeshore Trail, head east (right) and in 2.5 miles you'll reach Twelvemile Campground, one of three drive-in campgrounds in Pictured Rocks National Lakeshore. For a full trail description see Day Two of the Lakeshore Trail (Hike 38, page 250).

North Country Trail

Spanning across the Upper Peninsula, 575 miles from near Ironwood to the Mackinac Bridge, is the North Country Trail. It is not only the longest trail in the U.P., but it also serves as a link between the region's greatest parks; Porcupine Mountains Wilderness State Park, McCormick Wilderness, Craig Lake State Park, and Pictured Rocks National Lakeshore to name but just a few. It's hard to imagine another region of the country that the NCT passes through that is as dramatic, wilderness-like, or scenic as the areas it touches in the Upper Peninsula.

The NCT offers an almost limitless number of backpacking opportunities in the U.P. Anywhere it crosses a road is an opportunity to park the car and sneak off into the woods for a night or more. Segments of it in the Porcupine Mountains and Pictured Rocks are covered in other sections of this book.

This section covers the NCT in Tahquamenon Falls State Park, a two-day loop with a night spent at the park's new backcountry campsites. Also included is the easy, overnight hike to the Oren Krumm Shelter on the Sturgeon River and the rugged two-day walk along the Norwich Bluff, where you can pitch your tent in a mountain-top-like setting. The camping is free on Norwich Bluff; the view from your tent priceless.

As is the case in the Lower Peninsula, the best source of information is the North Country Trail Association (866-445-3628; *www.northcountrytrail. org*) or one of its chapters. You can gather information or purchase maps online or by calling.

A hiker climbs a stairway along the Tahquamenon River Trail that spans the Lower Falls to the Upper Falls in Tahquamenon Falls State Park.

North Country Trail
Tahquamenon Falls State Park

County: Luce
Nearest Town: Paradise
Distance: 15 miles
Hiking Time: Two days
Highest Elevation Gain: 80 feet
Difficulty: Moderate
Highlights: Waterfalls, old-growth pines, walk-in campsites

To travel across the heart of Tahquamenon Falls State Park, the second largest in Michigan at 46,179 acres, you either have to paddle or hike. Winding 25 miles through the park and plunging repeatedly to form some of the largest and most impressive waterfalls in the state is the Tahquamenon River.

But also traversing the park is 22 miles of the North Country Trail, extending from County Road 500 on the west side and ending in the Rivermouth Unit on Lake Superior. Ironically, for all its underdeveloped acreage, including the 19,000-acre Tahquamenon Natural Area, there were no places to pitch a tent for the night other than next to monster motorhomes in the park's large campgrounds. Backpackers would pass a brewpub along the way, but not any walk-in sites and off-trail camping wasn't allowed.

All that changed in 2008 when the park began to implement a plan to build seven cluster groups of backcountry campsites. Each group will feature three sites, a fire ring, and a wilderness toilet. The first group to be built was on Clark Lake, while others are to follow, including four along the NCT and two on the Tahquamenon River for paddlers. After all these years, backcountry visitors finally have the opportunity to spend a quiet evening in the remote corners of one of Michigan's most noteworthy state parks.

This 2-day trek begins in the Upper Falls dayuse area and combines almost 8 miles of the NCT with portions of the Wilderness Loop and the Clark Lake Loop in the Tahquamenon Natural Area. You spend the night on remote Clark Lake, hike past all the park's waterfalls, and can end the 15-mile trek enjoying a frosty mug of Porcupine Pale Ale at Tahquamenon Falls Brewery.

For the most part this loop is easy to follow and well posted with trail markers and numbered junctions with maps. In late spring and early summer parts of the route can be wet and extremely buggy. Always pack along insect repellent and a filter as there is no source of drinking water at Clark Lake.

Trip Planner

Maps: The loop is split between two USGS topos, *Betsy Lake South* and *Timberlost*, and neither shows the trails. The route is shown in limited detail on the *North Country Trail Map: Curley Lewis Road to Grand Marais* (Map MI-09) published and sold by the North Country Trail Association (866-445-3628; *www.northcountrytrail.org*). The state park also has a map of its trail system.

Getting There: From the Mackinac Bridge, continue 8 miles north on I-75 and depart at exit 352. Turn left onto M-123 and follow the state highway 55 miles to Paradise. Tahquamenon Falls State Park is 12 miles west of Paradise on M-123.

Fees & Reservations: A state park vehicle permit ($6 daily, $24 annual) is required while backcountry campsites are $10 a night and need to be reserved through the park. In Tahquamenon Lower Falls Campground modern sites are $16 to $21 per night, in Rivermouth Campground rustic sites are $10, semi-modern are $16 and modern $19 to $21. Reserve campground sites online (*www.midnrreservations.com*) or by phone (800-447-2757).

Information: For the status of the backcountry campsites or to reserve one call Tahquamenon Falls State Park headquarters (906-492-3415).

Trail Guide

Day One (7 miles) Leave your vehicle at the Upper Falls dayuse area, pass up the urge for a final meal at the Tahquamenon Falls Brewery, and head south on the Old Growth Forest Nature Trail in the southeast corner of the parking area. For almost a half mile you pass interpretive displays and old growth trees, including maples, beech, and eastern hemlock before arriving at a paved path. Turn west (left) at post No. 10 and join the crowds to marvel at the Upper Tahquamenon Falls. In the next quarter mile, until you reach the trailhead for the Giant Pines Loop, you pass a handful of viewing points of the giant cascade as well as two sets of stairways that will lead you down into the gorge of the river.

Often cited as the third largest cascade east of the Mississippi River, the Upper Falls is a powerful sight. It tumbles over a sandstone shelf that spans 200 feet across the gorge and then drops with a roar 50 feet into the river below. More than 50,000 gallons per second of root-beer-colored water has been recorded cascading over these falls. If you have never seen the Upper Falls before, drop the packs and at the very least descend the second stairway, a series of almost 100 steps to an observation platform right above the edge of its drop.

Back at the top of the gorge, the path from the second stairway quickly arrives at post No. 1, the start of the Giant Pines Loop. Giant maples and beech will surround you as you head north. The trail crosses paved M-123 within 0.3 mile, re-enters the forest on the north side and 1.1 miles from the start arrives at the reason for the loop; a pair of giant white pines, 120 feet high and with trunks more than five feet in diameter, so thick two people can't link their arms around them. Reflect on what it must have looked like when most of the Upper Peninsula was covered with a forest like this, and then move on.

The most remote corners of Tahquamenon Falls State Park are part of the Tahquamenon Natural Area, a non-motorized, 19,000-acre tract that includes three lakes, old growth white pines, and one of the largest northern peatlands in the eastern Upper Peninsula.

You remain in the forest along a trail that can be wet at times and 1.9 miles from the Upper Falls parking area arrive at post No. 2. Head west (left) to leave the Giant Pines Loop and to continue with the NCT. The trail follows a series of low, sandy ridges forested in red pine to keep you out of the water. You pass Wolf Lake, not visible from the trail, and in less than a mile from post No. 2 pass the location for a proposed cluster of backcountry sites.

At this point the trail swings to the north and 2.2 miles from the start reaches post No. 3. To the west (left) the NCT continues to County Road 500, a route that can be very wet and hard to locate at times. You head north (right) to leave the NCT behind and continue on the Wilderness Loop deeper into the Tahquamenon Natural Area.

Although the natural area does include land around the Upper and Lower Falls, the majority of it surrounds Clark, Betsy, and Sheephead lakes and features one of the largest northern peatlands in the eastern Upper Peninsula. Such peatlands include black spruce forests, open muskeg with stunted spruce and tamarack trees, and bogs with no trees at all. Wildlife can be plentiful where you're about to hike. Keep an eye out for bald eagles, sandhill cranes, river otters in the lakes, beaver, and, if you're extremely lucky, possibly a moose or a black bear.

From the junction the trail quickly skirts a bog and small pond and then swings to the northeast. Vast peatlands dominate the west side of Betsy Lake, but here the terrain has just enough elevations for the next mile so that it's somewhat dry by mid-July. A small sandy knoll with a stand of tall red pine is reached 1.1 miles from post No. 3 and then you drop into a wet area of black spruce and cedar. In the wettest parts there are moss-covered logs that you can tip-toe carefully across; otherwise, just accept the fact your boots are going to get muddy. Hopefully they're not new.

In the middle of the tip-toeing or 1.5 miles from post No. 3, the trail suddenly climbs a 20-foot-high ridge and you top off in an impressive stand of hemlock and maple. If you're lucky enough to be here in early October, the size of the pines and the color of the hardwoods will be stunning. The trail quickly drops back into the wet area and even uses a series of rotting logs to cross a sluggish stream.

Within 2.5 miles from post No. 3 you cross another stream on a solid foot bridge and then climb the bank to a view of the Beaver Pond, surrounded by wetlands and featuring a huge lodge on the shore closest to you. The trail skirts the wetlands along dry ground and 6 miles from the Upper Falls parking area reaches Clark Lake Loop at post No. 4.

Head north (left) at the post to follow a dry rolling path through woods and meadows. Within a mile the trail swings due north and you climb a bluff to your first view of Clark Lake. It's a memorable sight for most backpackers partly because it comes at the end of the day and partly because this wilderness lake has no development on it, no cabins, no boats, no signs that anybody else is out here but you. On the bluff a trail leads west (left) to the Clark Lake backcountry sites, reached 7 miles from the Upper Falls.

Day Two (8 miles) You begin the day following the south shore of Clark Lake. At one point you descend away briefly to cross a wet area on planking but quickly return to those top-of-the-bluff views that allow you to gaze over almost the entire lake. Within 0.3 mile you arrive at post No. 5, and here the trail descends away from the lake and becomes a wide sandy path past bogs and wetlands. You pop out at the parking area at the end of Clark Lake Road and continue along the rough two-track, reaching post No. 6 a mile from the campsite.

Although the road is open to vehicle traffic, it is a tight, winding two-track with lots of bottomless potholes. In other words, there's generally not too much traffic on it if there is any at all. You remain mostly in the woods until you arrive at M-123, 2.3 miles from the campsite. Directly across the paved road is a trail that leads to the Lower Falls area of the park. Follow this trail into the Overlook Campground, a large modern facility of almost 100 sites where at the end of one of the loops is the Overlook Trail. Head west (right) on the trail and within a half mile you descend to the massive boardwalk and a return to the NCT. To the west (right) the boardwalk quickly

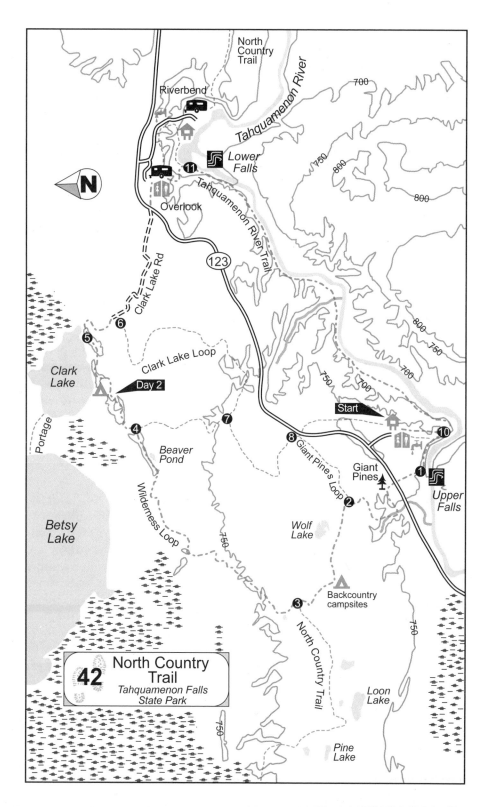

North
Country
Trail

Tahquamenon River

700

Riverbend

Tahquamenon River

750

800

800

Lower
Falls

⑪

Tahquamenon River Trail

Overlook

800

750

123

700

Clark Lake Rd

⑥

⑤

Clark Lake Loop

750

700

700

Clark
Lake

△ Day 2

Start

750

Portage

④

⑦

⑧

Giant Pines Loop

⑩

Beaver
Pond

Giant
Pines

①

Wilderness Loop

②

Upper
Falls

Betsy
Lake

750

Wolf
Lake

③

Backcountry
campsites

750

North Country Trail

42 North Country
Trail
*Tahquamenon Falls
State Park*

750

Loon
Lake

750

Pine
Lake

reaches a large observation deck overlooking two of the eight cascades that make up the Lower Falls.

Although not nearly as big or powerful as the Upper Falls, the Lower Falls are still scenic and interesting. Here the Tahquamenon River drops 22 feet through a series of waterfalls scattered around a small island. A park concessionaire rents row boats so visitors can reach the island and hike a mile loop around it to see all the cascades.

The boardwalk ends near post No. 11, marking the beginning of the Tahquamenon River Trail. First constructed in the early 1950s, the trail fell into disarray in the late 1970s and was even closed for a few years during the state park budget cuts of the 1980s. Eventually the route was re-opened and in 1995 the state park received a grant to substantially upgrade it with bridges, boardwalks, and benches. Today, park officials estimate more than 30,000 people hike it every summer.

What workers didn't alter was the trail's most endearing feature, the way it practically hugs the Tahquamenon River much of the way. From the boardwalk, the trail continues as a root-covered foot path and within a quarter mile climbs a bluff and stays high to give you a different perspective of the river and the whitewater below.

You return to the river and hug the edge of it for almost a mile, passing a bench at the 2 Mile marker along the way. Have a seat and enjoy the view. Rising from springs north of McMillan, the Tahquamenon River heads northeast and drains a watershed that covers more than 790 square miles before ending its 94-mile journey at Whitefish Bay. The root beer color of the water is caused by tannins leached from the cedar, spruce, and hemlock in the vast swamps the Tahquamenon flows through. The frothy root beer foam you see floating by along this trail is the result of the extremely soft water being churned by the Upper Falls upstream.

You pass beneath a huge Douglas fir 2.8 miles from post No. 11 or 5.8 miles from the Clark Lake campsites and then use a pair of stairways to climb away from the river. Within a quarter mile the trail passes a classic bench made out of logs, from which there is a view of the river below, and then skirts the bluff briefly. The steepest descent of the day follows, but a stairway makes it easy on the knees, especially for those who overloaded their backpacks.

The next half mile is flat but an interesting stretch as you hug the river while hiking beneath giant pines and beech. Another stairway greets you 4 miles from post No. 11 and tops off on the edge of a steep buff above the Tahquamenon River. You follow the bluff, and if it's a windless day, will hear the Upper Falls before you break out at the paved path, reached 4.5 miles from post No. 11 or 7.5 miles from the Clark Lake campsites. In the final half mile you pass a stairway down to the river gorge and then head north (right) on the Old Growth Forest Nature Trail to return to your vehicle. There, on the edge of the parking lot, is the Tahquamenon Falls Brewery.

Anybody up for a mug of Lumberjack lager?

North Country Trail
Tibbets Falls/Oren Krumm Shelter

County: Baraga
Nearest Town: Covington
Distance: 3.6 miles
Hiking Time: Overnight
Highest Elevation Gain: 50 feet
Difficulty: Easy
Highlights: Tibbets Falls, walk-in shelter

Not every trek on the North Country Trail is long and challenging. This overnight hike to the Oren Krumm Shelter is relatively level and easy along a trail that is well marked. Little effort is expended to reach the shelter, yet you're rewarded with the wilderness-like setting of the Sturgeon River, a beautiful waterfall, and a scenic place to spend a quiet evening.

Located in the Copper Country State Forest, the walk in is less than 2 miles and for the most part stays within view of the Sturgeon River. Despite a forest fire that occurred in the area in 2007, the hike is still a beautiful walk and an ideal get-away adventure for backpackers with limited time in the area or passing through on their way to places like Porcupine Mountains Wilderness State Park.

The shelter is free and open to all trail users. You don't need a tent but should be packing along a sleeping pad as the bunks are wooden platforms. There is also no safe source of drinking water at the shelter or the trailhead.

Trip Planner

Maps: The USGU topo, *Covington*, covers the area but does not show the trail or the shelter. There is also *North Country Trail Map: Alberta to Cascade Falls* (Map MI-13) published and sold by the North Country Trail Association (866-445-3628; *www.northcountrytrail.org*).

Getting There: From M-28 turn north on Plains Road 2 miles west of Covington and the US-141 intersection. Within 3 miles you'll cross a bridge over the Sturgeon River and the trail, marked by white blazes, will immediately be seen on the west side of the road.

Fees & Reservations: There are no fees for hiking the NCT or using Oren Krumm Shelter.

Information: The best source of information is the North Country Trail Association (866-445-3628) and the website of its Peter Wolfe Chapter (*www.northcountrytrail.org/pwf*).

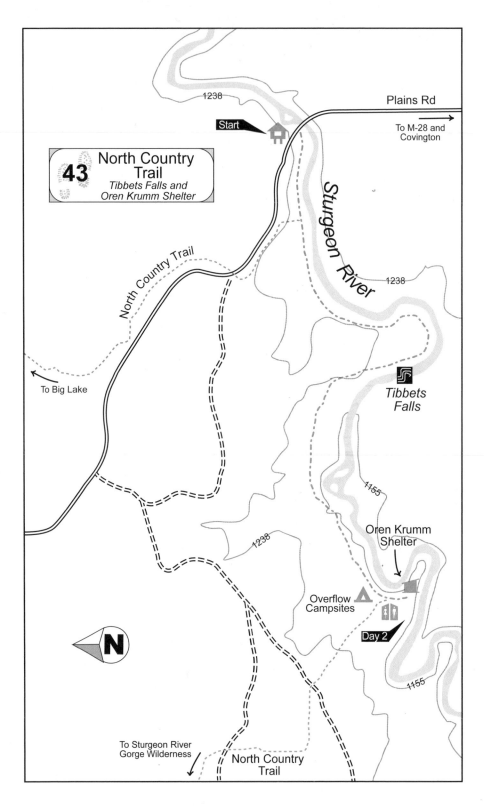

43 North Country Trail
*Tibbets Falls and
Oren Krumm Shelter*

1238

Start

Plains Rd

To M-28 and
Covington

Sturgeon River

1238

North Country Trail

To Big Lake

Tibbets
Falls

1155

Oren Krumm
Shelter

1238

Overflow
Campsites

Day 2

N

1155

To Sturgeon River
Gorge Wilderness

North Country
Trail

Trail Guide

The trail that begins just north of the Sturgeon River Bridge is the original segment of the NCT before it was re-routed north to Big Lake. The foot trail heads west from Plains Road and enters a forest of mostly aspen, pine, and spruce. Within a third of a mile you arrive at the NCT (marked by blue blazes) at a junction which may or may not be posted as this segment has yet to be certified. To the north (right) the NCT reaches Plains Road in a half mile.

To reach Oren Krumm Shelter continue west (straight) on the NCT. The trail swings south to skirt the Sturgeon River as its flows through a large oxbow and reaches whitewater halfway through it. You swing north and arrive at Tibbets Falls just over a mile from Plains Road.

The cascade is beautiful and well worth dropping your pack to explore. It's a series of ledges that extend from the banks to a 40-foot stretch of drops, ranging from a few inches to almost five feet depending on the water level. From the NCT a side trail descends downstream to a series of ledges that allow you to sit near the river and enjoy a view of the falls.

The NCT climbs the bluff above Tibbets Falls and then leaves the whitewater for good as it enters a floodplain. Keep in mind that this area of the Sturgeon River is prone to flooding in high water. Within 0.7 mile from the falls you arrive at the junction to Oren Krumm Shelter, located just 400 feet south (left) on the spur.

The original shelter was built in 1999 and was a gift from the Krumm family in memory of their son who died from an illness while at college. That structure burned down during the forest fire that scorched the area in April, 2007. The Peter Wolfe Chapter of the NCT replaced it that summer, building another three-side shelter with screens on the open side to keep bugs out. Inside are platform bunks and hooks to hang backpacks.

Outside is a fire pit near the edge of the bluff overlooking the Sturgeon. The shelter also has a backcountry toilet and two overflow tent sites. Overall, this is a great spot to spend the night as in the evening you can often hear the howls of wolves, whose numbers are expanding across the Upper Peninsula. Members of the Peter Wolfe Chapter have occasionally even seen wolves while working on the shelter and on sections of the NCT in the Baraga Plains.

To see the results of the forest fire and to witness how fast a forest regenerates, hike another mile west on the NCT.

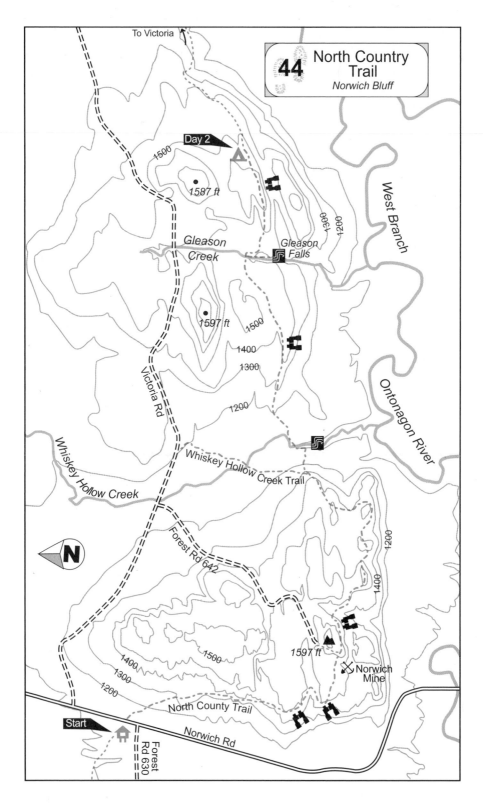

To Victoria

44 North Country Trail
Norwich Bluff

Day 2

1500

1587 ft

West Branch

1300

1200

Gleason Creek

Gleason Falls

1597 ft

1500

1400

1300

Ontonagon River

Victoria Rd

1200

Whiskey Hollow Creek Trail

Whiskey Hollow Creek

N

Forest Rd 642

1200

1400

1597 ft

1500

Norwich Mine

1400

1300

1200

North County Trail

Start

Norwich Rd

Forest Rd 630

North Country Trail
Norwich Bluff

County: Ontonagon
Nearest Town: Rockland
Distance: 12.9 miles
Hiking Time: Two days
Highest Elevation Gain: 380 feet
Difficulty: Challenging
Highlights: High rock bluffs with spectacular views

The 14 miles of the NCT between Norwich Road and Victoria in the Ottawa National Forest is one of the most spectacular segments of the national trail in the western Upper Peninsula, a region loaded with waterfalls and high vistas. This segment, often referred to as Norwich Bluff, features almost a dozen overlooks from high rocky bluffs, a waterfall and the historic remains of old copper mines.

It is a challenging route because of the rugged, up-and-down contour of the ridges. And while the Peter Wolfe Chapter of the NCTA has done a wonderful job maintaining and marking the trail, at times you will find yourself pausing to search for the next cairn or blue diamond. It is also, like most of the NCT, a point-to-point trail that requires special transportation arrangements.

This trek is an exception, however. By combining the first leg of the NCT with the Whiskey Hollow Creek Trail and a portion of the lightly used Victoria Road you create a two-day loop that begins and ends at a trailhead on Norwich Road. You have to backtrack 3 miles of the NCT, but it's the segment with the best overlooks from the ridge. At night you can set up a backcountry camp high on a ridge with a million-dollar view.

The trail wind across both the Ottawa National Forest and private land. It's important to camp only on public land, areas where the NCT is marked by blue diamonds. White blazed trails or blue rectangular paint blazes indicate private property. While you can hike the trails, you should not camp near them.

Whisky Hollow Creek is the only dependable year-round water source along this described route. You may pass other streams but during the height of a dry summer they could easily be dry. It's important to carry enough water to reach the camping area and to last you until you return to Whiskey Hollow Creek the next day. As always filter all water.

Trip Planner

Maps: The route is split between the USGU topos *Oak Bluff* and *Matchwood*

NW, and neither shows the trails. You'll find the route in limited detail on the *North Country Trail Map: Alberta to Cascade Falls* (Map MI-13) published and sold by the North Country Trail Association (866-445-3628; *www. northcountrytrail.org*). You can also download some handy maps from the web site of the Peter Wolfe Chapter.

Getting There: Head west on M-64 from Ontonagon and within 1.5 miles turn south on Norwich Road. The NCT trailhead will be reached within 13 miles and is on the west side of Norwich Road, just north of the junction with Forest Road 630.

It's important to remember that Victoria Road from Victoria to Norwich can be a difficult, if not impossible, drive in a 2WD vehicle in late spring or just after a hard rainstorm as it can be extensively washed out and rutted in places. One of the worst spots is 2 miles east of Norwich Road near where Whiskey Hollow Creek Trail begins.

Fees & Reservations: There are no fees for hiking or camping on the NCT.

Information: The best source of information is the North Country Trail Association (866-445-3628) and the website of its Peter Wolfe Chapter (*www. northcountrytrail.org/pwf*).

Trail Guide

Day One (6.7 miles) From the parking area at the NCT trailhead, cross Norwich Road and pick up the trail as it heads southeast into the woods. The NCT immediately begins a steady ascent of Norwich Bluff and 1.3 miles from the trailhead reaches the first of many views. From this overlook and the next half mile down the trail the Trap Hills are spotted to the west, while Lake Superior is seen to the north.

Eventually the NCT swings east and within 2 miles from the trailhead you arrive at a junction with an unmarked spur heading north (left). The spur climbs a hill that was once the site of the Norwich Lookout Tower (still labeled on topos) that was built at the 1,567 foot peak. Just below the peak, the spur merges with Forest Road 642 that leads 1.8 miles to Victoria Road.

Near the junction are remnants of Norwich Mine. The rich vein of copper was discovered in 1846 and work on the underground mine was started in 1850 by the American Mining Co. of Vermont. The mine was closed in 1865 after producing a total of 993,000 lbs. of refined copper. None of the tailings or shafts is seen from the NCT and you have to be extremely careful if going off trail to look for them. Eventually the U.S. Forest Service would like to build a Norwich Mine Interpretive Trail here.

The NCT continues east (right) and within a quarter mile descends into a narrow valley where it merges onto an old two-track road and heads south briefly. You need to watch where the NCT departs east (left) from the two-track and not go to the bottom of the hollow. The trail climbs out of the valley and 3 miles from the trailhead reaches another great view in an area of scattered red pines. You then head north and within a half mile climb another ridgeline to more great views before the NCT swings east and descends towards Whiskey Hollow Creek.

Less than a quarter mile before reaching the creek in an area of scattered hardwoods you reach the junction with Whiskey Hollow Creek Trail. The trail, an old road actually, is marked by white blazes as it crosses private property and can be easily missed from the NCT. It is 3.8 miles from Norwich Road and you'll want to note its location for the return trip. Just east (right), the junction trail markers become blue rectangular paint blazes, indicating camping is not allowed in this area.

From the junction you continue to drop into the ravine before arriving at Whisky Hollow Creek, where the NCT heads left. Just downstream from here this beautiful stream forms a small waterfall where it leaps over a series of basalt ledges. The trail follows the west bank of the creek and then 4.2 miles from the trailhead crosses the stream. Before climbing out of the hollow, make sure your water bottles are topped off for the evening.

The ascent back up Norwich Ridge follows a long rocky ridge where the views improve with every step up and are among the best of this trek. It's a climb of almost 400 feet from the creek to where the NCT briefly joins an old two-track before beginning its descent to Gleason Creek.

The creek is reached 5.5 miles from the trailhead and here the Gleason Falls Trail heads south (right) to follow the east side of the gorge briefly downstream to the cascade. When there is water, usually late spring, Gleason Falls is described as a 20-foot cascade. Throughout most of the summer, it's a trickle if that. Nearby is an old exploration shaft made by miners exploring for copper in the mid-1800s.

From Gleason Creek, the NTC climbs the ridge to the east and within a mile reaches yet another stunning overlook to the south. From here to a quarter mile east, the NCT is on National Forest land and camping is permitted. The panoramic view from this fairly open stretch of the ridge makes most nights a memorable one.

Day Two (6.2 miles) Backtrack to Whiskey Hollow Creek and then keep a watchful eye out for the junction to Whiskey Hollow Creek Trail. This side trail should be roughly 300 to 400 yards west of the creek and heads north (right) for Victoria Road.

The side trail cuts back northeast (right) towards the creek, crossing it in about 0.3 mile. You then continue in a northeast direction until reaching Victoria Road 0.8 mile from the junction on the NCT. Head west on Victoria Road, a dirt road that at times can be impassable by vehicles, and within 2 miles or 5.7 miles from the start of the day, you reach Norwich Road. Less than a half mile to the south is the NCT trailhead where your vehicle is parked.

Porcupine Mountains Wilderness State Park

orcupine Mountains Wilderness State Park, the beloved Porkies to many backpackers, is not only Michigan's largest state park at 59,020 acres, but it is also the most rugged and the wildest. In the Porkies you have the state's third highest peak, a healthy population of black bears, and an area large enough to contain entire rivers, 25 miles of Lake Superior shoreline, and the only ridges in Michigan we can possibly call mountains.

There are also more than 90 miles of foot paths that wind through the heart of this wilderness. The trail system includes three backpacking adventures covered here. The Lake Superior Trail is the park's longest path, stretching 17 miles along the lakeshore. The Big and Little Carp River Trails are combined for a four-day loop in which it's possible to hike from cabin to cabin if you plan your trip in advance. And the final one is an easy, overnight trek to a mountain-top campsite along the spectacular Escarpment Trail.

The Porkies are big, rugged, and unmerciful on the unprepared. This is one of the few places in Michigan that backpackers have to know where and when to ford unbridged streams and be bear-wise to avoid any unpleasant encounters with a bruin. There is a reason why the vast majority of the park's backcountry campsites have bear poles to hang your food at night.

There are more than 60 backcountry sites scattered across the park with most of them marked along the trail. Some are in clusters of two to four sites but most are single sites. A few have wilderness toilets, but the vast majority are just a fire ring, a bear pole, and a flat space to pitch a tent. You can also camp off trail anywhere in the backcountry as long as you are a quarter mile from a cabin, yurt, road, or scenic area.

One of the most unusual aspects of the park, however, is its 23 rustic cabins and yurts, the vast majority of which can only be reached on foot. Some of the cabins date back to 1945 when the park was created. The yurts, Mongolian-style wall tents, are relatively new. Any of them can be reserved and rented to lighten your pack and make for a memorable evening on the trail.

The east entrance to the state park is reached from M-107, 16 miles west of Ontonagan and 3 miles west of Silver City. The west entrance is reached by County Road 519 that departs US-2 at Wakefield and in 15 miles ends at Presque Isle Campground on Lake Superior. In between the two is South Boundary Road that skirts the southern edge of the park to provide access to campgrounds, trailheads, and scenic areas.

All vehicles entering the park must have either a $6 daily pass or a $24 annual state park pass. All cabins, yurts, and sites in Presque Isle and Union Bay campgrounds can be reserved through the Michigan State Park Central Reservation Service (800-447-2757; *www.midnrreservations.com*). Cabins and yurts are $60 a night, modern campsites $16–25, and rustic sites $14.

Backcountry campsites are $14 a night for up to four people. You can not reserve these in advance. You pay for the sites when you pick up your backcountry permit at the park's Wilderness Visitor Center on South Boundary Road just south of M-107.

For information in advance of your trip or to receive park brochures, call the park headquarters (906-885-5275) or check the DNR web site (*www.michigan.gov/porkies*).

A backpacker enjoys the view of Lake Superior at the mouth of the Big Carp River, one of the most scenic spots in Porcupine Mountains Wilderness State Park.

Lake Superior Trail
Porcupine Mountains Wilderness State Park

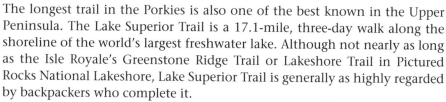

Counties: Ontonagon and Gogebic
Nearest Town: Silver City
Distance: 17.1 miles
Hiking Time: Two to three days
Highest Elevation Gain: 82 feet
Difficulty: Moderate to challenging
Highlights: Lake Superior shoreline, waterfalls, rental cabins

The longest trail in the Porkies is also one of the best known in the Upper Peninsula. The Lake Superior Trail is a 17.1-mile, three-day walk along the shoreline of the world's largest freshwater lake. Although not nearly as long as the Isle Royale's Greenstone Ridge Trail or Lakeshore Trail in Pictured Rocks National Lakeshore, Lake Superior Trail is generally as highly regarded by backpackers who complete it.

The trail begins near one of the park's most stunning settings, the Lake of the Clouds overlook, and ends at another, the point at which the Presque Isle River thunders into Lake Superior as a fury of waterfalls and whitewater. In between you tread along the lake, pausing at the scenic mouths of the Big Carp and Little Carp rivers. The trail is also a link to six rustic cabins that can be reserved in advance and 20 backcountry campsites, making it easy to break up the walk into as many different stages as you wish.

That's important because the Lake Superior Trail may look easy on a map, but it can be a tedious and even a challenging walk at times. This is especially true in the west end where you have to climb in and out of several steep ravines to cross streams. Nor should you expect a watery view every step of the way. Despite being close to the lake the trail is often a path in the woods.

The most common itinerary is to begin at the M-107 trailhead and to return to the Lake of the Clouds overlook along the Big Carp River Trail, a three-day, 19.3-mile loop. Others return along Little Carp River Trail or via the Correction Line and North Mirror Lake trails for a longer trek into the park.

But I'm a traditionalist who loves hiking trails in their entirety, from one trailhead to the other. In the past that was a problem with the Lake Superior Trail due to a lack of transportation, but now there is a shuttle service in the state park. And when hiked from end to end, the Lake Superior Trail leaves most backpackers with a strong sense of accomplishment of having traveled from one corner of the park to the other. Much like the Greenstone and Lakeshore trails.

Trip Planner

Maps: The state park is spread across four USGS quads with *Carp River* and *Tiebel Creek* covering the Lake Superior Trail.

Getting There: The Lake Superior Trailhead is 6.5 miles west on M-107 from its intersection with South Boundary Road. Another 1.5 miles west, M-107 ends at Lake of the Clouds Scenic Area.

The other end of the trail is in Presque Isle Campground, reached from the east end of the park by heading south on South Boundary Road. Follow the road 25 miles around the park to County Road 519 and then head North on CR-519. Presque Isle can also be reached from US-2, where the campground is 15 miles north of Wakefield via CR-519.

Shuttle transport can be arranged through Porcupine Mountain Outpost (906-885-5612), a concessionaire store located near Union Bay Campground. For $80 per vehicle, the Outpost will follow you out to Presque Isle and then transport you to the start of the Lake Superior Trail on M-107.

Fees & Reservations: Above and beyond the park entrance fee, backcountry campsites are $14 a night per party for up to four people. Pay your site fees and pick up a backcountry permit at the park's Wilderness Visitor Center.

The cabins along Lake Superior are Buckshot Landing, Big Carp Four-Bunk, Big Carp Six-Bunk, Lake Superior, Little Carp and Speakers. All are $60 a night plus an $8 reservation fee and should be reserved (800-447-2757; *www.midnrreservations.com*) months in advance.

Information: Just south of M-107 on South Boundary Road is the Wilderness Visitor Center (906-885-5208) for information, maps, and backcountry permits. The center is open daily from 10 a.m. to 6 p.m. from late May through mid-October.

Trail Guide

Day One (4.9 miles) A strong backpacker could easily cover the Lake Superior Trail in two days. But most backpackers will find this trek far more enjoyable if they take three days to follow the trail. The first day is the shortest, allowing you time to shuttle a vehicle to Presque Isle Campground.

From the M-107 trailhead you depart north into old growth hemlock for 0.3 mile and then gradually ascend to the high point of 1,122 feet and your first view of Lake Superior. From the rocky outcrop you can see Lone Rock just to the west, and if the day is clear the Apostle Islands off Wisconsin. You may be in the Porkies but this is as high as the Lake Superior Trail climbs.

The route swings west, follows the ridge briefly to unveil more views of the Great Lake before beginning its descent to the shoreline. At first, the grade is gentle but then becomes a rapid, knee-bending drop when the trail swings more to the north. On the way down you pass a backcountry campsite and after a mile, you finally bottom out in an area of young hardwoods. Nearby is another walk-in site. Though you are only a few hundred yards from the lake, it is hard to spot the water through the trees.

The trail swings west, crosses a wet area on boardwalk, and within a

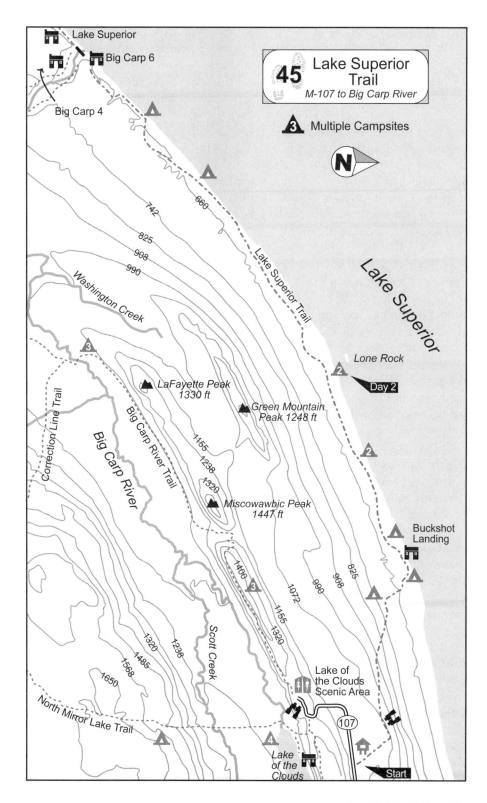

Lake Superior

Big Carp 6

Big Carp 4

45 **Lake Superior Trail**
M-107 to Big Carp River

3 Multiple Campsites

N

742
660
825
908
990

Washington Creek

Lake Superior Trail

Lake Superior

3

Correction Line Trail

Big Carp River Trail

Big Carp River

LaFayette Peak
1330 ft

Green Mountain
Peak 1248 ft

Lone Rock

2

Day 2

2

1155
1238
1320

Miscowawbic Peak
1447 ft

Buckshot
Landing

1400

3

1072

825

990

908

Scott Creek

1155

1320

1320
1238
1485
1568
1650

North Mirror Lake Trail

Lake of
the Clouds
Scenic Area

4

107

Lake
of the
Clouds

Start

quarter mile you arrive at the spur to Buckshot Landing Cabin. The four-bunk cabin is 2.5 miles from M-107 and just 30 yards from the shoreline, so close you can see the lake from its windows.

At this point the trail levels out and in fact becomes one of the most level trails in this unleveled park. For the next 2 miles it stays inland from the shoreline, far enough so you can't see the water, close enough where you can hear the surf on a windy day. The spur to Lone Rock, a solitary boulder lying a quarter mile offshore, is reached 2.4 miles from Buckshot Landing.

Scattered in between the cabin and the rock are five more backcountry sites. The first is just west of Buckshot Landing; the last two are clustered near the Lone Rock spur. The short spurs are marked along the trail and the sites are either within view of the lake or very close to it. Take your choice and pitch the tent for the night.

Day Two (5.9 miles) Continue west from Lone Rock as the Lake Superior Trail swings even further inland and away from the Great Lake. Within 1.7 miles the trail swings back towards the shoreline and arrives at a pile of rubble and rocks in a small clearing. One of the park's three Adirondack-style shelters once stood here, but eventually all of them were removed. What remains today is the short path to the lake.

To the west the remaining 3 miles to Big Carp River is one of the most delightful stretches of the long route. You quickly break out along the shoreline and stay there for a mile or more. From the middle of the path, you're rewarded with a continuous view of this sea of blue with the waves breaking only a few feet away.

There is a little climbing involved at first as the trail traverses the narrow bench that lays between the lake and a low ridge to the southeast. After passing a backcountry campsite, the trail climbs the low ridge and then descends back to the shoreline where another walk-in site is located. You're now roughly a mile from Big Carp River.

The trail climbs the low ridge once more and 4.6 miles from Lone Rock you emerge on the edge of a bluff above the Big Carp River. The trail quickly descends into a large flat area, arriving at a well-marked junction with Big Carp River Trail near Big Carp Six-Bunk Cabin. The cabin, overlooking the Big Carp River is one of the most picturesque in the park and one of the most popular to reserve. It's a great place to spend a night, but you need to plan your hike months or even a year in advance.

Lake Superior Trail continues west (right) at the junction and crosses the Big Carp River on a foot bridge that lies between two huge boulders with a bench at one end. Here you can rest those tired toes while viewing the river rippling into the surf of Lake Superior. If it's September, you can watch salmon spawn upstream.

On the other side is a junction with Cross Trail that heads south (left) to South Boundary Road. Just up the trail is the Big Carp Four-Bunk Cabin in a more secluded spot overlooking a pool in the river. Even if you're moving on, take time to drop the pack here and hike out to Lake Superior. The mouth

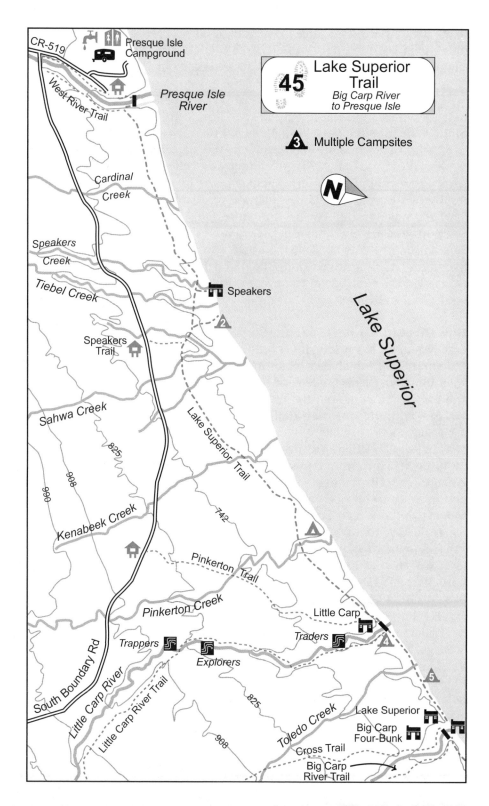

CR-519

Presque Isle
Campground

West River Trail

Presque Isle
River

45 Lake Superior
Trail
*Big Carp River
to Presque Isle*

3 Multiple Campsites

N

Cardinal
Creek

Speakers
Creek

Tiebel Creek

Speakers

2

Speakers
Trail

Sahwa Creek

825

908

990

Lake Superior Trail

742

Lake Superior

Kenabeek Creek

Pinkerton Trail

Pinkerton Creek

Little Carp

Traders

4

Trappers

Explorers

South Boundary Rd

Little Carp River

Little Carp River Trail

908

825

Toledo Creek

5

Lake Superior

Big Carp
Four-Bunk

Cross Trail

Big Carp
River Trail

of the Big Carp River is a large flat of gravel and boulders with large trunks of driftwood trees washed up during one of Lake Superior's moments of fury. If camping nearby, this is an excellent spot to drag out the sleeping pad on a clear evening to watch the sunset.

Continuing west, you quickly reach Lake Superior Cabin, a four-bunk unit tucked away in the trees, and then you begin another scenic stretch of the Lake Superior Trail. In the final 1.3 miles to Little Carp River, you're so close to Lake Superior that on a windy day the surf will be crashing only a few yards away. Halfway there, you cross a bridge over Toledo Creek, so named to remind us what little Michigan gave up to get the Porkies and the rest of the Upper Peninsula. A wilderness in exchange for urban sprawl.

Lake Superior Trail reaches the Little Carp River 5.9 miles from Lone Rock, arriving at a cluster of four backcountry campsites within view of Lake Superior on the east bank of the gorge. Camp here or stop earlier at the five sites that are scattered along the trail between Big Carp and Little Carp rivers. On the west side of the gorge is the Little Carp River Cabin, a four-bunk that can be reserved in advance.

Day Three (6.3 miles) The Little Carp River is a major crossing in the park's trail system with a posted junction on each side. On the east side is Little Carp River Trail, which departs south (left) and then east for Mirror Lake (see Hike 46). From there you descend into the steep gorge via a massive stairway and bridge and climb out the other side where on the west bank there's a junction with the Pinkerton Trail and a spur to Little Carp Cabin.

Lake Superior Trail continues its westward journey by traversing the top of a low ridge and then crossing a small creek to arrive at another backcountry campsite. In a mile from Little Carp River, you arrive at another major gorge, Pinkerton Creek. You descend more than 80 feet to reach the creek at the bottom only to be faced with a climb just as steep to get back out. After topping out at a high point of 707 feet, you swing close to Lake Superior where it's easy to leave the trail briefly for a view of the water.

From here the trail swings more than a half mile inland for a somewhat level stretch that includes crossing Kenabeek Creek 2.4 miles from Little Carp River and then two branches of Sahwa Creek. These are not deep gorges like Pinkerton Creek nor is it difficult to keep your boots dry while hopping across the streams unless you're in the middle of a downpour.

At 3.5 miles from Little Carp River, you arrive at the posted junction with Speakers Trail. This short trail heads south (left) to reach South Boundary Road in a half mile. Lake Superior Trail heads west (right), merging into old forest road, and quickly crosses the third branch of Sahwa Creek with the help of a narrow vehicle bridge built when there were eight summer cabins along the lakeshore to the north.

On the other side a spur splits off to the north (right) from the main trail and leads 0.3 mile to a pair of backcountry campsites now located where the summer cabins used to be. Lake Superior Trail heads west (left) and within a half mile crosses Teibel Creek and then arrives at the short spur to Speakers

Backpackers cross a dry channel of the Presque Isle River at the west end of the Lake Superior Trail, the longest trail in Porcupine Mountains Wilderness State Park.

Cabin just before you cross Speakers Creek. Speakers Cabin is a four-bunk unit on the edge of a bluff overlooking Lake Superior and only a mile from South Boundary Road via Speakers Trail.

Beyond Speakers Creek, the Lake Superior Trail continues to stay out of view of Lake Superior and 5.2 miles from Little Carp River descends into a ravine carved by Cardinal Creek and then a second ravine a half mile later. Now you're so close to the Presque Isle River, it's almost possible to hear the thunder of its whitewater.

The final day, the entire trek in fact, comes to a dramatic finish when the Lake Superior Trail emerges at a junction on the edge of the Presque Isle Gorge. Below you is Manido Falls upstream, Manabesho Falls downstream, and wild, swirling water in between. At the junction, West River Trail heads south (left) to skirt the gorge. Lake Superior Trail descends into the gorge.

You bottom out at what is usually a dry river channel where the trail has you scrambling over layers of slate to a backdrop of tumbling whitewater just upstream. The trail then crosses a thin peninsula in the mouth of the river. A side trail here will quickly lead you to an impressive view of the Presque Isle River flowing into Lake Superior.

To the west, Lake Superior Trail uses a massive swing bridge to cross the roaring river and then a boardwalk to climb out of the gorge to its western trailhead. Nearby is Presque Isle Campground that features restrooms with showers, ideal for the final night of any trek across the Porkies.

The start of the Big Carp River Trail is a stroll along the Escarpment, a high, rocky bluff with mountain-top views.

Big & Little Carp River Trails
Porcupine Mountains Wilderness State Park

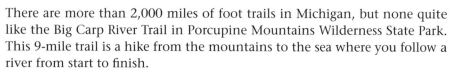

Counties: Ontonagon and Gogebic
Nearest Town: Silver City
Distance: 27 miles
Hiking Time: Four days
Highest Elevation Gain: 396 feet
Difficulty: Moderate to challenging
Highlights: Shining Cloud Falls, cabin-to-cabin hiking

There are more than 2,000 miles of foot trails in Michigan, but none quite like the Big Carp River Trail in Porcupine Mountains Wilderness State Park. This 9-mile trail is a hike from the mountains to the sea where you follow a river from start to finish.

It begins at the most popular spot in the park, the Lake of the Clouds overlook on top of the Escarpment, and ends at one of the most remote, the mouth of the Big Carp River on Lake Superior. In between, there are mountain-top views, thundering waterfalls, stands of virgin pine, a steep-sided gorge, black bears, bald eagles, and brook trout.

Once you reach Lake Superior there are several ways to return. Combining the Little Carp River Trail with the North Mirror Lake Trail not only makes for a perfect loop – thus eliminating the need for special transportation – but it's one of the most interesting backpacking treks in the Upper Peninsula. Such a route would be a 27-mile, four-day outing past six named waterfalls and a dozen more that are nameless but almost as soothing.

The loop also winds past 11 of the park's 18 wilderness cabins, offering the rare opportunity to hike from cabin-to-cabin and lighten your load a bit. You must reserve the cabins in advance, by as much as a year, depending on when you want to hike. But such an effort in planning would result in the unusual experience of spending each day walking through the glorious country that is the Porkies and each night at a different cabin, snug and safe in the middle of the wilderness.

This trip is described as a cabin-to-cabin hike but those with a tent in their backpack will also discover 37 backcountry campsites along the way. They are scattered in scenic settings along all three trails, often overlooking rivers and lakes. Some are so close to a waterfall that the cascading current is like a lullaby at night.

Trip Planner

Maps: Like the Lake Superior Trail, this route is covered on a pair of USGS quads; *Carp River* and *Tiebel Creek*.
Getting There: The Big Carp River is located at the end of M-107 in the Lake

of the Clouds Scenic Area, 8 miles west of the state highway's intersection with South Boundary Road.

Fees & Reservations: If hiking cabin-to-cabin, the best itinerary is to reserve one at the mouth of the Big Carp River for the first night (Big Carp Four-Bunk, Big Carp Six-Bunk, Lake Superior), on the Little Carp River for the second night (Section 17 or Greenstone Falls) and on Mirror Lake for the final night (Mirror Lake Two-Bunk, Mirror Lake Four-Bunk and Mirror Lake Eight-Bunk). Obtaining reservations is easier with more than one cabin in each location.

All cabins are $60 a night plus an $8 reservation fee and are reserved through the Michigan State Park Central Reservation Service (800-447-2757; *www.midnrreservations.com*). Backcountry campsites are $14 a night and can not be reserved in advance.

Information: Pay your fees and pick up a backcountry permit or the cabin keys at the park's Wilderness Visitor Center (906-885-5208), located just south of M-107 on South Boundary Road. The center is open daily from 10 a.m. to 6 p.m. from late May through mid-October.

Trail Guide

Day One (9.6 miles) This is a long day, longest of the trek in fact, but for the most part a downhill walk from the Escarpment to the shores of Lake Superior. The scenery is so good, there'll be plenty of places to stop and rest those tired feet.

The Big Carp River Trail is posted in the Lake of the Clouds parking lot and begins by heading west into the woods. You quickly break out at the first of many views. Just to the east is Lake of the Clouds and the beginning of the Big Carp River journey to Lake Superior. The trail dips back into the wood and steadily ascends 100 feet.

The next time the Escarpment opens up you follow the edge of the rocky bluff for more than a mile, passing one spectacular view after another. You reach 1,468 feet, the high point of the day, 1.5 miles from the parking lot and here you can stand on the edge of the steep-sided Escarpment and stare 400 feet down into the valley of the Big Carp River or gaze at Lake of the Clouds now in the distance to the east. To the west you can see Miscowawbic Peak in the foreground, LaFayette Peak 2 miles further away, marking one end of the Escarpment, or even more peaks outside the park. Located on the crest of the ridge nearby is the first of three backcountry campsites. If arriving late in the day any of these would be beautiful spots to pitch a tent for the evening.

The trail resumes following the bluff for 0.3 mile, then begins the long descent to the floor of the valley. It's a half mile drop, sharp at first but gentle most of the way as you lose almost 350 feet in elevation. Along the way you move from a beech/maple forest to a stand of stately hemlock.

Once on the valley floor, reached 2.5 miles from the trailhead, you continue southwest through the forest along the base of the Escarpment, where the walking remains fairly level and surprisingly dry. Even on the hottest day, it's cool and dark among the hemlocks, where the average age of the pines is 220 years old but some were, no doubt, around when the Pilgrims landed in America. The rule-of-thumb used by park naturalists is a hemlock will have 10 inches of diameter growth for every hundred years and in this stand, it's not hard to find hemlocks four feet in diameter or close to 500 years old.

At 3.5 miles you appear on the edge of a low rise, skirt it briefly, then make a quick descent from hemlock into beech and maple. The walk down the valley remains level and along the way you'll pass three more backcountry campsites. Finally, 5 miles from the Lake of the Clouds parking lot, you reach the Big Carp River. This far upstream the Big Carp is 15 to 20 yards wide and the perfect cold water habitat for brook trout.

A foot bridge provides passage to the south side of the river, and within a quarter mile is the junction with Correction Line Trail. This trail heads east (left) and makes a steady climb to Mirror Lake. Big Carp River Trail swings to the southwest (right) and begins in a low-lying wet area before climbing the bluffs above the river.

On the high ground, you follow the river for another mile as the trail weaves through pines and hemlocks and swings past views of the water. It is another scenic stretch of Big Carp River Trail, but it ends when you descend to ford the river, 6.5 miles from the start. This ford is usually easy, not much more than ankle deep, but heavy rains or a late runoff can change everything.

On the north side, you immediately climb a steep riverbank bluff and then move out of sight of the water as the Big Carp makes a big swing to the south. This stretch, muddy at times but level, is an easy stroll through

Fording Rivers in the Porkies

Not every stream in the Porkies has a bridge across it; actually the majority don't, forcing backpackers to do something they don't do a lot of in Michigan: ford a creek or a river. Most bridgeless crossings are easy. The best place to cross is usually well marked and hikers often switch from their boots to a pair of sport sandals or running shoes before splashing into the cold water.

But immediately after a heavy rainfall is a different story. You might have to search for a better spot upstream and sometimes you might not be able to ford at all.

In June of 1983 a storm dumped 13 inches of rain on the Porkies; resulting in all the park's rivers becoming dangerously swollen. The worst flooding, however, occurred along the Little Carp River below Lily Pond. The water rose to depths of 30 feet, stranding several backpacking parties, wiping out bridges, and causing mudslides on bluffs and hills bordering the Little Carp River.

another impressive stand of hemlock. Within 2 miles from Correction Line Trail, you return to the Big Carp, where you pass another backcountry campsite and then follow the edge of a steep gorge until you are standing downriver from Shining Cloud Falls.

Reached 8.2 miles from the Lake of the Clouds parking lot, Shining Cloud Falls is regarded by most as the most spectacular in the park. Actually the falls are a pair of cascades that combine for a 30- to 35-foot drop and are enclosed on one side by stone walls. You can hike down to the thundering water, but take caution as it is a very steep drop on slippery rock.

Big Carp River Trail descends from the gorge to skirt the river itself and for the next half mile you pass almost a dozen cascades and another backcountry campsite. Some of the waterfalls are small, but four of them have drops of more than 6 feet that end in deep pools. Nameless, but still stunning, even at the end of a long day. Less than a mile from departing Shining Cloud, you come to an area where Big Carp River levels out at a spot posted "Bathtub Falls." The falls are really a series of one-foot drops and pools where more than one backpacker has soaked their weary feet in this ice-cold Jacuzzi.

Eventually Big Carp River Trail leads you away from the river and makes a steep climb, via a series of switchbacks, up a river bluff. You top off at a sweeping view where far below is the river you've been following all day while for the first time on the horizon you can see the freshwater sea where it's headed.

In the remaining half mile the trail hugs the bluff and then descends to Big Carp Six-Bunk Cabin near the mouth of the river. This is one of the most scenic spots in the park and a popular place to spend the night. Across the bridge is the posted end of the Cross Trail and the Big Carp Four Bunk Cabin. Follow Lake Superior Trail west a short way and you will pass Lake Superior Cabin, a four-bunk unit. Reserve any in advance for a delightful place to spend the night. Five more backcountry campsites line the Lake Superior Trail between Big Carp River and Little Carp River.

Day Two (7.3 miles) Begin the day heading southwest on the Lake Superior Trail, skirting the Great Lake past the Lake Superior Cabin and then five backcountry campsites. Within 1.3 miles from Big Carp River, you arrive at the Little Carp River gorge with its massive stairways and bridge. But lucky you, you don't have to cross. Located on the east bank is the junction with the Little Carp River Trail that departs to the south (left).

Little Carp River Trail is the second longest trail in the park at 11.8 miles and one of the most scenic. You can begin near Lake Superior, elevation 611 feet, and for the most part, make a gradual climb to Mirror Lake, which at 1,532 feet is the one of the highest inland lakes in the state. The western half of the trail is free of any steep climbs and fords the river only twice.

From the junction with the Lake Superior Trail, the Little Carp River Trail skirts the edge of the gorge briefly before descending its steep side. You

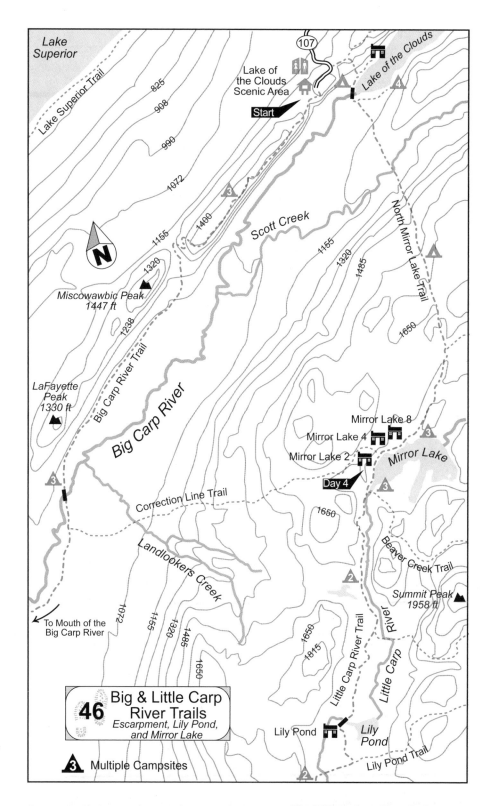

Lake Superior

Lake of the Clouds

107

Lake of the Clouds Scenic Area

Start

Lake Superior Trail

825
908
990
1072

3

Scott Creek

1155
1400

N

1155
1320

1320
1485

North Mirror Lake Trail

1650

Miscowawbic Peak
1447 ft

1238

Big Carp River Trail

LaFayette Peak
1330 ft

Big Carp River

Mirror Lake 8

Mirror Lake 4

3

Mirror Lake 2

Mirror Lake

Day 4

3

3

Correction Line Trail

1650

Landlookers Creek

Beaver Creek Trail

1072
1155
1320
1485

To Mouth of the
Big Carp River

2

Summit Peak
1958 ft

1650

Little Carp River Trail

Little Carp River

1815

1650

46 Big & Little Carp
River Trails
*Escarpment, Lily Pond,
and Mirror Lake*

Lily Pond

Lily
Pond

Lily Pond Trail

2

3 Multiple Campsites

can view Traders Falls on the descent or cut back to the small cascade once you bottom out. What follows is an extremely scenic segment of the trail as you follow the flowing river through stately stands of virgin hemlock and maples. Within 2.8 miles from Big Carp River, you make your first ford of the day at a well marked spot where it's easy to see the trail on the other side of the river.

Now on the west side of the river, you pass a backcountry campsite and then Explorers Falls, reached 3.8 miles from Big Carp River. In 0.3 mile you come to yet another display of falling water, Trappers Falls, a distinctive cascade where the river slides down a wide rock chute. Nearby is a backcountry campsite, while just beyond Trappers Falls you ford the Little Carp again.

Back on the east side the trail for the most part follows the top of the bluffs. Along the way you pass three backcountry campsites, reached 1.5 miles past Trappers Falls. Eventually you climb a low bluff to arrive at the junction with the Cross Trail, 7.3 miles from the Big Carp River. Near the junction is another backcountry campsite and a quarter mile beyond it, you pass a stairway that leads to a foot bridge across the Little Carp River to Section 17 Cabin on the south side. Originally built as a ranger patrol cabin, the four-bunk unit is well secluded from trail traffic and is located on a low bluff overlooking the Little Carp River.

A short distance from the Section 17 Bridge is the Greenstone Falls Cabin. More recently renovated, the four-bunk unit is within view of the river, but not the falls themselves, and is located right on the trail. The cascade is posted another 100 yards up the trail. Here the river has formed a veil of water the tumbles 15 feet down a rock embankment in a small gorge.

Day Three (6.3 miles) To save a day you could combine the final two for a 10-mile trek. But Mirror Lake is such a lovely and secluded spot in the middle of the park, it's hard to justify passing it up to rush back to your car.

Begin by hiking to Greenstone Falls and then pausing to savor the cascade, the last one seen on this trek. Just beyond the waterfall, Little Carp River Trail crosses a bridge over a feeder creek and arrives at a junction with the access route from Little Carp River Road. A car parking area is only half mile away from here with South Boundary Road another mile beyond it.

Little Carp River Trail heads east and immediately begins the steepest climb of the route. It is a steady ascent of 160 feet until you top off at the second junction to South Boundary Road, reached a mile from the Cross Trail junction. Here an old forest road heads south (right) to reach South Boundary Road in a mile. Little Carp River Trail continues east and in the next half mile makes a more gentle climb to 1,560 feet, the high point along the route. In all, from Greenstone Falls to here is a climb of 396 feet. Welcome to the Porkies!

You follow the ridge briefly until the trail descends to cross the Little Carp River. Nearby are a pair of backcountry campsites. The trail makes a final climb back to 1,560 feet then descends to a posted junction with Lily

The classic Eight-Bunk Mirror Lake Cabin was the first cabin built in Porcupine Mountains Wilderness State Park. You can turn your outing into a cabin-to-cabin hike by reserving in advance a string of these trailside cabins.

Pond Trail, reached 3 miles from the Cross Trail junction. To the east (right) Lily Pond Trail leads 2.5 miles to Summit Peak Road. To the north (left) Little Carp River Trail passes through an impressive stand of white pine and in a half mile reaches Lily Pond Cabin, a four-bunk unit surrounded by towering pines and overlooking the west end of the small lake.

You can admire the Little Carp River from where it flows out of the lake thanks to a huge bridge and boardwalk. The view of the river and the wilderness lake are so scenic that the bridge has a bench in the middle of it. From the bridge, the Little Carp River Trail heads northeast along a fairly level route. If it's late fall, you'll spot Summit Peak, the highest point in the park at 1,958 feet, to the southeast.

You pass the junction to Beaver Creek Trail 4.3 miles from the Cross Trail junction and here the Little Carp River Trail swings to the north and resumes skirting its namesake river in the final 1.5 miles to Mirror Lake. Along the way you pass two backcountry campsites. The beautiful lake comes into view just before you reach the junction with South Mirror Lake Trail, 5.8 miles from Cross Trail.

Mirror Lake marks the end of the Little Carp River Trail and is a favorite place to spend an evening, thus the reason for all the cabins and campsites. The lake is surrounded by rugged bluffs and ridges, many of which can be climbed for views of the area, while towering pines dominate much of the shoreline. This place is stunning in late September and very much worthy of

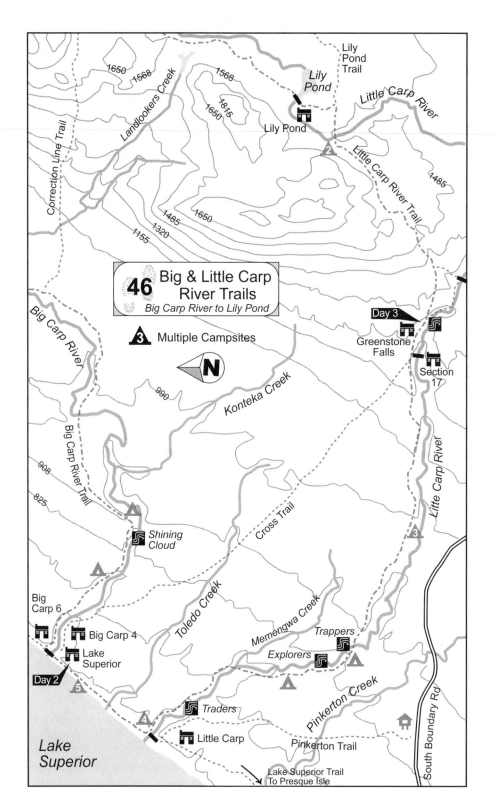

Lily Pond Trail

Lily Pond

Lily Pond

Little Carp River

1650 1568

Landlookers Creek

1568

1815

1650

Little Carp River Trail

1485

Correction Line Trail

1485

1650

1320

1155

46 Big & Little Carp River Trails
Big Carp River to Lily Pond

▲3 Multiple Campsites

Big Carp River

Day 3

Greenstone Falls

Section 17

N

990

Konteka Creek

Litte Carp River

Big Carp River Trail

908

825

Cross Trail

3

Shining Cloud

Toledo Creek

Memengwa Creek

Trappers

Big Carp 6

Big Carp 4

Explorers

Lake Superior

Day 2

5

Pinkerton Creek

South Boundary Rd

Traders

4

Little Carp

Pinkerton Trail

Lake Superior

Lake Superior Trail
To Presque Isle

its name on any calm day.

Continue east along the lake to reach the spur to the Mirror Lake Two-Bunk Cabin and then the junction to the Correction Line Trail. Just beyond the junction is the Mirror Lake Four-Bunk Cabin located near the lake in a stand of towering pine. Finally you reach the Mirror Lake Eight-Bunk Cabin, a virtual log lodge perched right above the water and the park's first cabin when it was built in 1945.

Three backcountry campsites are reached by following South Mirror Lake Trail to a small inlet at the west end of the lake, a very scenic place to pitch a tent. Three more are reached from a spur off North Mirror Lake Trail.

Day Four (3.8 miles) The North and South Mirror Lake trails provide a route that crosses the heart of the Porkies, beginning from Summit Peak Road and ending at the Lake of the Clouds overlook. The South Trail is the shortest and easiest route to popular Mirror Lake, a trek of only 2.5 miles. The harder North Mirror Lake Trail is often used as a return to M-107 and finishes off this loop.

Beginning at the shores of Mirror Lake near the classic Eight-Bunk Cabin, the North Mirror Lake Trail quickly crosses a creek and then parallels Trail Creek as it climbs a low ridge. Even though you are well above the creek, this section can be wet and muddy from heavy use. In less than a mile you come to the junction with the Government Peak Trail.

Government Peak heads east (right) to reach the 1850-foot high point in 2 miles. North Mirror Lake Trail begins a gentle descent to the north (left). Within a mile you top off at 1,640 feet. In the fall this stretch provides views of the 1,700-foot ridges that enclose the Big Carp River below. You pass a lone backcountry campsite and then begin the long descent into the valley.

The descent is gradual at first, but 2.5 miles from Mirror Lake the trek becomes a knee-bending drop. Be thankful you're heading north. If you're coming from Lake of the Clouds, this is one of the steepest climbs in the park. In a half mile, you descend from 1,640 feet to 1,160 through a gorge-like area where a tributary of Scott Creek rushes downhill.

You bottom out to cross Scott Creek, climb over a 1,200-foot ridge and at 3.3 miles from Mirror Lake arrive at the west end of Lake of the Clouds. A spur heads right to four backcountry campsites. A long boardwalk crosses a stream emptying into the lake here and provides a long view of Lake of the Clouds. On the other side is another backcountry campsite while almost straight above you is the Lake of the Clouds overlook. If the day is still, you can hear people oooing and ahhhing from the high observation area.

The trail swings to the east, skirts the shoreline of the lake and then comes to the spur that leads to the Lake of the Clouds Cabin a quarter mile away. The final half mile is a steep march uphill as the trail becomes a series of switchbacks, gaining more than 150 feet from the level of the lake until finally breaking out at the M-107 parking lot at 1,246 feet. Along the way you pass a posted junction to the west end of the Escarpment Trail.

The views are stunning along the Escarpment Trail, the most scenic hike in Porcupine Mountains Wilderness State Park.

Escarpment Trail

Porcupine Mountains Wilderness State Park

County: Ontonagon
Nearest Town: Silver City
Distance: 4.3 miles
Hiking Time: Overnight
Highest Elevation Gain: 231 feet
Difficulty: Moderate
Highlights: Lake of the Clouds, mountain-top views

Not every backpacking adventure in the Porkies has to be a three- or four-day march across its rugged interior. Scattered throughout the park are 61 backcountry campsites with many of them in locations ideal for quick adventures. In other words, scenic spots close to the road.

Among those well suited for an easy overnighter are three sites on the Escarpment of the Big Carp River Trail (see Hike 46), the Lost Lake site via Lost Lake Trail, and the four sites on the south shore of Lake of the Clouds. All these are less than 2 miles from where you pick up the trail. My favorite, however, is the Cuyahoga Peak Campsite along the Escarpment Trail.

Many believe there is no finer hike in Michigan than the Escarpment Trail. This 4.3-mile hike begins at the Lake of the Clouds overlook, ends at the Government Peak Trailhead on M-107 and combines a high rocky bluff with mountain-top views of the park's rugged interior, Big Carp River Valley and, of course, the centerpiece of the park, Lake of the Clouds. This is as close to alpine hiking as we have in Michigan.

Located just east of Cuyahoga Peak, the high point of the trail, is a backcountry campsite, perfect for those who want to spend the night at the top, gazing at the stars. There are three ways to reach it. The closest is via the Cutoff Trail, making the campsite less than a mile from M-107. From the Government Peak Trailhead, Cuyahoga Peak is a hike of 1.6 miles.

But by far the most scenic way to arrive is to begin at the Lake of the Clouds overlook and follow the Escarpment Trail from west to east, a one-way hike of 2.7 miles. To spend the day soaking in the scenery from the Escarpment and then spend the night on its rocky crest is the ultimate overnight experience in this park.

Keep in mind that there is no source of water on the Escarpment nor is drinking water available at the Lake of the Clouds overlook area. If spending the night, you'll have to pack along enough for both days.

Trip Planner

Maps: The Escarpment Trail falls on two USGS quads, *Carp River* and *Government Peak*.

Getting There: The western trailhead for the Escarpment Trail is located at the end of M-107 in the Lake of the Clouds Scenic Area, 8 miles west of the state highway's intersection with South Boundary Road.

Fees & Reservations: The park's backcountry campsites are $14 a night and can not be reserved in advance.

Information: Pay your fees and pick up a backcountry permit at the park's Wilderness Visitor Center (906-885-5208), located just south of M-107 on South Boundary Road. The center is open daily from 10 a.m. to 6 p.m. from late May through mid-October.

Trail Guide

Day One (2.7 miles) From the Lake of the Clouds parking area, the hike begins with the North Mirror Lake Trailhead. You follow a rock and boulder-strewn path for a half mile as the trail dips and climbs along the Escarpment. At a well-posted junction, North Mirror Lake Trail plummets towards Lake of the Clouds while the Escarpment Trail heads west (left) to climb through a forest of pines and young oaks. Quickly you arrive at the first overlook, staring down at the middle of the lake.

The trail resumes with a sharper climb and within a half mile you break out to a second vista that is better than even what is seen at the popular overlook at the end of M-107. At an elevation of 1,480 feet, you stand at the edge of the escarpment and look 400 feet straight down at Lake of the Clouds, painted in royal blue. To the west you can see visitors who have just stepped out of their cars and to the east is the rest of the Escarpment and the Upper Carp River winding its way into the lake.

The trail continues along the open cliff for a quarter mile where you enjoy the scenery every step of the way before dipping into the woods. After crossing two small knobs, you make a rapid descent and then begin the climb to Cloud Peak. The 1,514-foot peak is reached 2 miles from the overlook parking lot, and for the first time in the hike you are standing at the east end of the lake and viewing it to the west.

From Cloud Peak, the trail makes another rapid descent and reaches the junction with the Cutoff Trail 2.3 miles from the overlook. The spur heads north (left) to descend to M-107 in less than a half mile. To the south (right) is a trail to the site of Carp Lake Mine, a short side trip to see the twin boilers and other remains of the stamping mill. Carp Lake was the name for Lake of the Clouds when the mine was established in 1858. The operation lingered into the 1920s but reached its peak in 1865 when a company of more than 50 men used a small stamping mill to produce 13,000 pounds of copper from several shafts into the Escarpment.

The Escarpment Trail continues straight and immediately begins it ascent to Cuyahoga Peak. You climb more than 200 feet to close in on the 1,600-foot peak and in less than a half mile from the junction you arrive at another panoramic vista, this one centering on the Upper Carp River. Here the trail hugs the edge of the Escarpment while skirting the wooded top of

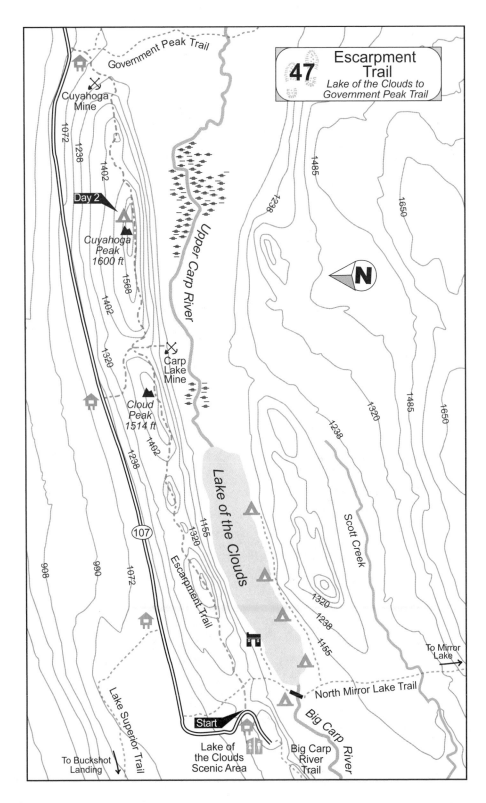

The most famous resident of the Porcupine Mountains is the black bear. To eliminate backpacker-bear encounters, the park has equipped most backcountry campsites with bear poles.

Cuyahoga Peak. A bit further, reached 2.7 miles from the overlook parking area, is the Cuyahoga Peak backcountry campsite.

The site is posted and features only a fire ring and enough flat space for one or maybe two small tents. But its location is amazing. It's set back slightly in the trees, yet three steps away is the edge of the rocky bluff where you can sit all night and watch the stars or possibly the Northern Lights reflect off Lake of the Clouds. Return in the morning and you can watch another day begin.

Day Two (1.6 miles) To finish the Escarpment Trail continue east. Quickly you'll leave the open ridge behind and begin a mile-long descent off the ridge. For the most part this is a steady drop through the forest with only an occasional view popping up in the first half mile. Eventually you pass the Cuyahoga Mine site, mostly piles of tailings, and then in a quarter mile bottom out at the junction with the Government Peak Trail. Head north (left) on that trail and you'll emerge at M-107 within minutes.

Isle Royale National Park

In the stormy northwest corner of Lake Superior there is an island without roads and thus without cars or street lights or a single set of golden arches. It is a place where the moose and the wolves live in a natural balance with each other, with little regard to humans, and where wildlife flourishes in one of Michigan's most pristine settings. People can visit, but come November, everybody has to leave.

Isle Royale is one of the most unusual national parks in the country. It is one of the smallest at only 210 square miles and has one of the lowest number of visitors, a mere 17,000. It is the only national park in the country to completely close down in the winter and is also one of the most costly to visit as special transportation is needed to reach the isolated island.

But most of all, Isle Royale has become a paradise for wilderness enthusiasts, particularly backpackers. The 45-mile-long island is laced with 165 miles of foot trails and dotted with backcountry campgrounds. The cost of getting there and the excellent opportunity for wilderness adventure are why Isle Royale has one of the longest visitation averages (the amount of time a visitor stays) in the country. At Yellowstone National Park most tourists stay only a few hours. At Isle Royale the average visit is four days.

People come to escape at Isle Royale, not to sightsee.

And more often than not they take to the trails with a backpack to escape that crush of civilization they left at home. This section covers three of the park's longest trails, each an avenue into the natural world that is Isle Royale. The Greenstone Ridge Trail is one of Michigan's classic treks, a five-day walk from one end of the island to the other. The Minong Ridge Trail is the state's toughest trail, a six-day walk along the rocky crest of the ridge. The Feldtmann Ridge Trail is a three-day walk out of Windigo where the highlight for many who follow the loop is spotting a moose.

You must come prepared and in good walking shape. This is not a place to be breaking in your new boots. All backpackers must arrive with a water filter and a small stove as fires are not allowed in most of the park. You should also arrive with a light pack and lots of moleskin for unexpected blisters. Isle Royale is not mountainous but it is composed of long ridges and on all three of these trails there will be considerable up-and-down hiking.

Small price to pay to escape the routines at home.

Getting There: Three ferries and an air service company provide transportation to the island. The 165-foot *Ranger III* is operated by the National Park Service and travels from Houghton to Rock Harbor on Tuesdays and Fridays, departing Houghton at 9:00 a.m. It returns from Isle Royale on Wednesdays and Saturdays, departing Rock Harbor at 9:00 a.m. for the six-hour trip back to Houghton.

You can cut the sailing time by 1.5 hours by departing from Copper Harbor, home to the 100-foot *Isle Royale Queen IV*. From mid-June to July the ship leaves Copper Harbor at 8 a.m. daily except Wednesday and Sunday and departs Rock Harbor the same day at 2:45 p.m. In the first two weeks of July it departs Copper Harbor daily except Wednesday and from mid-July to mid-August it makes the round-trip run to Isle Royale daily.

From mid-May to late September the 63-foot *Voyageur II* departs Grand Portage, Minnesota, Monday, Wednesday and Saturday at 8:00 a.m. (Central Daylight Time), stops at Windigo, and overnights at Rock Harbor Lodge. The following day, either Tuesday, Thursday or Sunday, it departs from Rock Harbor at 8:00 a.m. (Central Daylight Time) for Windigo and Grand Portage.

There is also floatplane service from Houghton for either Windigo or Rock Harbor Lodge. You can take the plane to Windigo, hike to Rock Harbor Lodge, and then return on the *Ranger III*.

Fees & Reservations: Isle Royale National Park has a user fee of $4 per person per day but advance reservations are not required to obtain a backcountry permit.

Advance reservations are urged for all three ferries from late June to late August. One-way fare for adults is $56 for the *Ranger III*, $62 for the *Isle Royale Queen IV* and $57 for the *Voyageur II*. Royal Air Service charges $180 per person for the flight to Isle Royale and during the height of the season will make up to five flights a day.

Information: For information on the park or reservations for the *Ranger III* contact Isle Royale National Park (906-482-0984; *www.nps.gov/isro*). You can also stop at its main visitor center at 800 E. Lakeshore Drive in Houghton, which is open 8 a.m. to 6:00 p.m. Monday through Friday and 11 a.m. to 6 p.m. Saturday June through July with reduced hours the rest of the year.

For reservations on the *Isle Royale Queen IV*, contact Isle Royale Line (906-289-4437; *www.isleroyale.com*), for the *Voyageur II*, contact Grand Portage – Isle Royale Transportation Line (651-653-5872, 888-746-2305; *www.isleroyaleboats.com*), and for seaplane transport, contact Royale Air Service (218-721-0405, 877-359-4753; *www.royaleairservice.com*).

Backpackers take a break along the Greenstone Ridge Trail to enjoy the views from Mount Franklin.

Greenstone Ridge Trail

Isle Royale National Park

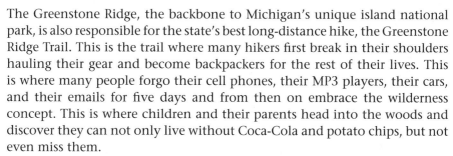

County: Keweenaw
Nearest Towns: Houghton and Copper Harbor
Distance: 42.4 miles
Hiking Time: Five days
Highest Elevation Gain: 480 feet
Difficulty: Moderate
Highlights: Michigan's best wilderness experience

The Greenstone Ridge, the backbone to Michigan's unique island national park, is also responsible for the state's best long-distance hike, the Greenstone Ridge Trail. This is the trail where many hikers first break in their shoulders hauling their gear and become backpackers for the rest of their lives. This is where many people forgo their cell phones, their MP3 players, their cars, and their emails for five days and from then on embrace the wilderness concept. This is where children and their parents head into the woods and discover they can not only live without Coca-Cola and potato chips, but not even miss them.

This trail is a Michigan classic, a beautiful and personally fulfilling hike from one end of our largest island to the other. Every backpacker should hike the Greenstone at least once. Lucky you if you get to experience it twice.

The Greenstone is technically a 40-mile trail that extends from Lookout Louise near the east end of Isle Royale to Windigo on the west end. Few hikers take the time to arrange boat transportation from Rock Harbor across Tobin Harbor to Hidden Lake, the start of the Lookout Louise Trail. Instead most hikers begin with the Rock Harbor Trail and spend their first night at Three-Mile Campground. The following day they take the Mount Franklin Trail to the Greenstone, the way this description follows.

Although the trail is rated moderate and is easy to follow, there are eight high points that exceed 1,300 feet and often knee-bending climbs between them. Experienced hikers with strong legs can cover the 40-plus miles in 3 days. But why rush? It took a bit of time and effort to get here, but you're here, in Michigan's purest wilderness. Stay awhile and take four or even five days to hike the Greenstone.

Trip Planner

Maps: Without question the best map for any hike on the island is National Geographic's Trails Illustrated Map, *Isle Royale National Park*, that covers the park and all its trails in 1:50,000 detail.

Getting There: To return to Rock Harbor from Windigo after hiking the

Greenstone most backpackers book passage on the *Voyageur II*. After arriving at Windigo from Minnestoa, the ferry circumnavigates the island clockwise and overnights at Rock Harbor Lodge. The following day, it continues with possible stops at Daisy Farm, Chippewa Harbor Campground, Malone Bay Campground, and Windigo before returning to Grand Portage. The trip not only gets you back to Rock Harbor but provides a view of Isle Royale not seen from the crest of the Greenstone Ridge.

Fees & Reservations: Intra-island passage on the *Voyageur II* ranges from $40 to $52, depending on where you are picked up and dropped off. Reservation for the ferry are strongly recommended in July and August.

Information: Once on the island, information, maps and backcountry permits can be obtained from the Rock Harbor Visitor Center at the foot of the ferry wharf. There is a small store across from the visitor center with limited and very expensive supplies.

For more information on the *Voyageur II* contact the Grand Portage – Isle Royale Transportation Line (715-392-2100 or 888-746-2305; *www.grand-isle-royale.com*).

Trail Guide

Day One (2.7 miles) The *Ranger III* arrives at Isle Royale from Houghton at 3 p.m., the reason many backpackers spend their first night in Rock Harbor. The other popular choice is to hike the Rock Harbor Trail to Three-Mile Campground, a 1.5 to two-hour walk for most people. This sets you up to reach Chickenbone Lake the next day. The alternative that leads to a shorter second day is to continue on the Rock Harbor Trail to Daisy Farm Campground. For most people, however, the four to five-hour trek to Daisy Farm is too much hiking for such a late start in the afternoon.

Pick up the Rock Habor Trail from the Rock Harbor Campground where it heads west into a spruce forest. Within a half mile you break out on a bluff above the water. From this point to Three-Mile, the Rock Harbor Trail is one of the most scenic hikes on the island. It stays within view of the water most of the time but is constantly crossing flat rock outcroppings.

Eventually, the trail dips to waterline and passes an islet just offshore before ascending to the spur to Suzy's Cave, a well-posted stop reached 1.8 miles from Rock Harbor. The cave is actually an inland sea arch carved by waves when the shoreline of Lake Superior was higher. The cave itself is small but provides an excellent viewing point of the Rock Harbor waterway.

Beyond Suzy's Cave, Rock Harbor Trail returns to edge of the shoreline and within a mile arrives at Three-Mile Campground. The campground is pleasant, situated right off the shoreline, and a quiet alternative to the busy one at Rock Harbor. Three-Mile Campground has eight shelters, group and individual campsites, pit toilets, and a dock and a one-night limit.

Day Two (11 miles) This is a long day that comes early in your trip when your pack is still loaded with food. Start early and take lots of breaks.

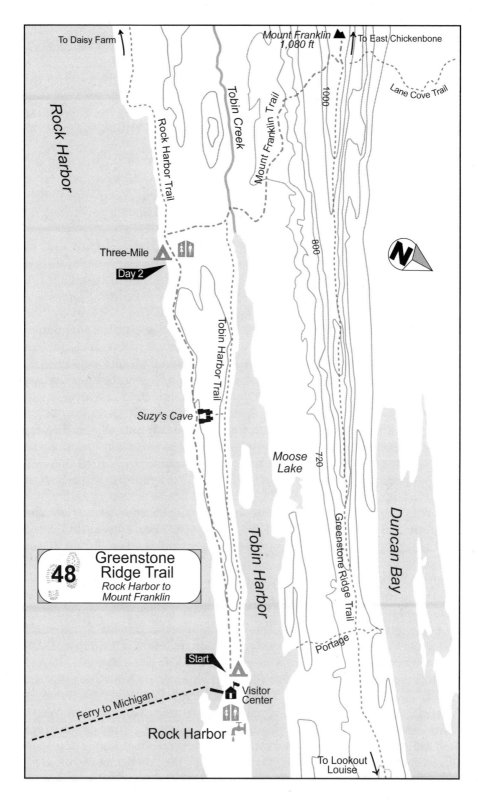

To Daisy Farm

Mount Franklin
1,080 ft

To East Chickenbone

Lane Cove Trail

Rock Harbor

Tobin Creek

Rock Harbor Trail

Mount Franklin Trail

1000

800

N

Three-Mile

Day 2

Tobin Harbor Trail

Suzy's Cave

Moose
Lake

720

Duncan Bay

48 Greenstone
Ridge Trail
*Rock Harbor to
Mount Franklin*

Tobin Harbor

Greenstone Ridge Trail

Start

Portage

Visitor
Center

Ferry to Michigan

Rock Harbor

To Lookout
Louise

Three-Mile to East Chickenbone Lake Campground is an 11-mile walk, and many backpackers push on to the more popular West Chickenbone Lake Campground for a day that is close to 13 miles. If either day is too much mileage for you, then spend your first night in Rock Harbor and the second night in Daisy Farm, reducing this day to a 7.7-mile walk to West Chickenbone. Keep in mind that there is little water on the Greenstone Ridge Trail from Mount Franklin to East Chickenbone Campground. If the day is hot and sunny, you could easily need two quarts per person.

From Three-Mile head west on Rock Harbor Trail for a quarter mile and then north (right) on Mount Franklin Trail. This 2-mile trail serves as an entry ramp to the Greenstone Ridge Trail and from its junction you immediately begin climbing a ridge. You descend the back side of the ridge to a wetland area crossed by a boardwalk and then reach Tobin Harbor Trail, a half mile from Three-Mile. To the east (right) Tobin Harbor Trail leads 3 miles to the Rock Harbor seaplane dock.

Mount Franklin Trail heads north (left), climbs another low ridge, crosses another swamp and then begins its steep climb of the Greenstone Ridge. The hike to the crest of the Greenstone Trail is a knee-bender that lasts for half mile and ascends more than 480 feet from Tobin Creek. At the well posted junction on top you head west (left) on the Greenstone Ridge Trail and in a 0.3 mile west or 2.5 miles from Three-Mile you reach Mount Franklin. The high point is not really a mountain, but rather a rock bluff that was named after Benjamin Franklin and at 1,080 feet is high enough to provide a superb view of Canada and the north side of the island.

From Mount Franklin, the trail descends quickly into a wooded area and then levels out for a mile before climbing gently back up to the rocky ridgetop for a spell. The hiking is easy along this stretch and when standing on the open crest of the Greenstone Ridge you're rewarded with views of Rock Harbor to the south.

Within 2 miles of Mount Franklin the trail descends sharply for the first time and then climbs out of the trees to the open crest again. In the final half mile to Mount Ojibway the trail remains in open terrain and is especially scenic, giving way to views of the north shore and Rock Harbor to the south.

The former fire tower at Mount Ojibway (1,136 feet) is located 2.8 miles from Mount Franklin or 5.3 miles from Three-Mile and is now used to monitor air pollution. A favorite spot among backpackers for an extended break, the tower also marks one end of the Mount Ojibway Trail from Daisy Farm Campground.

You continue west (straight) from the Ojibway Lookout Tower as the Greenstone Ridge Trail follows predominately open ridge to the next junction. Within 1.5 miles, you reach the junction with the Daisy Farm Trail, the second trail to Daisy Farm Campground. The Greenstone Ridge Trail continues west (straight) winding over several small knolls and then descending toward Angleworm Lake. Eventually the trail comes within a few

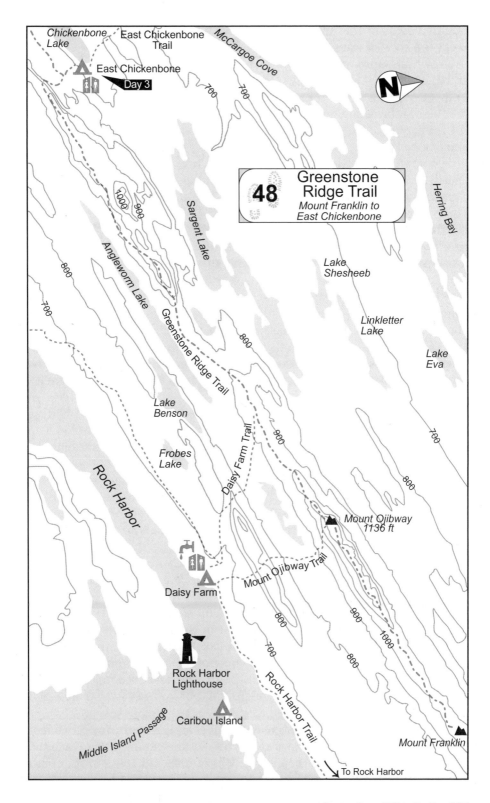

hundred yards of the Angleworm Lake to the south, although thick forest keeps the body of water hidden much of the summer.

The trail begins another climb, where it reaches a high point of 934 feet, and then descends again to dense forest with scattered bogs. The trail remains in this terrain for a spell before making a gradual ascent to an open crest on the ridge and leveling out. At one point near a rock overhang you can view the north side of Isle Royale along with Pie Island in Ontario, and the east end of Chickenbone Lake. You depart from this picturesque spot, descend a little, and then make a 90-degree turn. From here you drop quickly off the Greenstone Ridge and into a bog before reaching the junction with the East Chickenbone Trail, reached 5.7 miles from Mount Ojibway or 11 miles from Three-Mile Campground.

Head north on East Chickenbone Trail and in 300 feet you'll reach East Chickenbone Campground, located on a ridge above the east shore of the lake. The campground has individual and group campsites and pit toilets.

Day Three (9.3 miles) Backtrack to the Greenstone Ridge Trail and continue west (right). From the junction with the East Chickenbone Trail you follow the thin strip of land separating Chickenbone Lake to the north and Lake Livermore to the south. Occasionally through the trees you can catch views of both bodies of water. Within a half mile you arrive at the short portage between the two lakes and then cross a stream. From here it's another mile of easy walking to one of the park's major junctions; Indian Portage and the Greenstone Ridge trails. To the south (left) Indian Portage Trail leads to Lake Richie and eventually Chippewa Harbor. A quarter mile to the north (right) on Indian Portage Trail is the popular West Chickenbone Campground on the shores of its namesake lake.

The Greenstone Ridge Trail continues its westward journey to the other end of the island. You climb over a low hill and then after crossing a planked stream, begin a steep and steady climb. This one is a kneebender as you gain 300 feet in less than a half mile. But once you reach the top of the first knoll, you are rewarded with perhaps the best view of the inland lakes. Before you McCargoe Cove to the east, followed by Chickenbone, Livermore, and LeSage lakes. To the south, you can spot Lake Richie, Intermediate Lake, Siskiwit Lake, and Siskiwit Bay.

The fine view is followed by another scenic stretch. For the next 3 miles the trail stays high on the ridge and most of the time on the open, rocky crest of it. At times you can view Siskiwit Lake to the south and then, after climbing a 1,187-foot knob, the north shore of the Island. You begin sidling the grassy southern flank of Mount Siskiwit (1,205 feet), 4.6 miles from the junction to East Chickenbone Campground, but you never actually reach the peak.

Beyond Mount Siskiwit the trail descends sharply into the trees for a half mile and levels out along an open ridge. You resume climbing and reach the high point of 1,195 feet where the big slabs of rock and views to the south

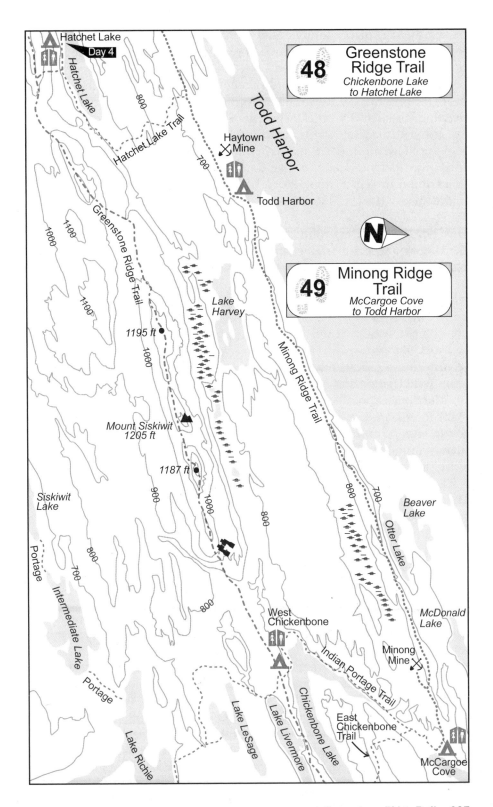

Hatchet Lake

Day 4

Hatchet Lake

800

Hatchet Lake Trail

Haytown Mine

Todd Harbor

Todd Harbor

Greenstone Ridge Trail

700

1000

1100

1100

1195 ft

Lake Harvey

1000

Mount Siskiwit
1205 ft

1187 ft

Siskiwit
Lake

900

1000

800

Portage

700

800

Intermediate Lake

Portage

Portage

Lake Richie

Lake LeSage

Lake Livermore

Chickenbone Lake

West
Chickenbone

Indian Portage Trail

East
Chickenbone
Trail

Minong Ridge Trail

800

700

Otter Lake

Beaver
Lake

McDonald
Lake

Minong
Mine

McCargoe
Cove

make it an ideal place for lunch. After lunch the trail descends and 7.3 miles from East Chickenbone arrives at a bog, where a stream, often dried at the height of the summer, is planked.

In the final 1.5 miles to the Hatchet Lake Trail, you climb a bit but never break out of the trees. The final climb is a short one to the signposted junction, reached 8.8 miles from East Chickenbone. To the north (right) the Hatchet Lake Trail winds around its namesake lake before ending at the Minong Ridge Trail in 2.6 miles. Within 0.3 mile, however, is a spur that heads west (left) to Hatchet Lake Campground, a half-mile walk from the junction on the Greenstone Ridge Trail. The campground is on a wooded hillside above the lake's south shore and has pit toilets.

Day Four (8.1 miles) You're first half mile of the day is an uphill return to the Greenstone Ridge Trail where you head west (right) and climb another quarter mile to a 1,155-foot knob. Take a breather and enjoy the fine views of Siskiwit Lake, Malone Bay, even Siskiwit Bay. Beyond the knob the trail winds between stands of birch and open patches of the ridge where you can see Siskiwit Lake in all her glory. Within 1.5 miles from Hatchet Lake Trail you climb steeply and then arrive at a unposted spur that heads north (right) to a rock bluff. Keep an eye out for it because the view from the bluff – not seen from the Greenstone Ridge Trail – is stunning and includes Hatchet Lake, Todd Harbor, and Mount Siskiwit.

The Greenstone Ridge Trail descends briefly again, levels off through birch forests, and then sharply climbs to another high point with more scenic views. From here the trail winds through open clearings for more than half mile before it begins its final 0.5-mile climb to Ishpeming Point (1,377 feet), the second highest point in the park.

For being such a lofty spot, Ishpeming Point can be rather disappointing. There are almost no views from the top as the lookout tower, a short squatty structure now used for research, is lower than the surrounding trees. If it's raining, however, the tower is a wonderful spot to have lunch as its platform doubles as a roof that will keep you dry and is located almost halfway between Lake Desor (3.8 miles) and Hatchet Lake Campground (4.3 miles). It is also the junction to the Ishpeming Trail which departs south (left) to reach the Malone Bay campground in 7 miles.

The Greenstone Ridge Trail continues west (straight) with an immediate descent from the tower and then levels out. For the next 2.0 miles you follow the rolling crest of the ridge without enduring any great climbs. But, unlike the first half of the day, there are no views either other than the trees that surround the path. After breaking out at a small pond and open bog, the trail does climb steeply, topping off at 1,245 feet, where there is an open stretch of the ridge and a rocky knob. From the knob here you're finally rewarded with your first view in the second half of the day; Lake Desor to the west.

From here you descend steadily but not sharply for 0.7 mile and shortly after bottoming out you arrive at the posted junction with the spur to South

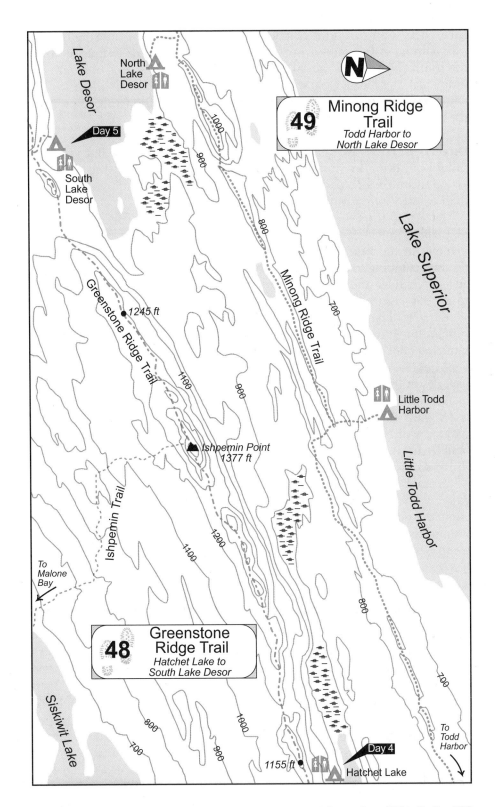

Lake Desor

North Lake Desor

Day 5

South Lake Desor

Lake Superior

N

49 Minong Ridge Trail
*Todd Harbor to
North Lake Desor*

1000

900

800

Minong Ridge Trail

700

1245 ft

Greenstone Ridge Trail

900

1100

Little Todd Harbor

Little Todd Harbor

▲ Ishpemin Point
1377 ft

Ishpemin Trail

1200

1100

To Malone Bay

800

48 Greenstone Ridge Trail
*Hatchet Lake to
South Lake Desor*

Siskiwit Lake

800

700

1000

900

1100

700

Day 4

To Todd Harbor

1155 ft

Hatchet Lake

Lake Desor Campground, reached 3.5 miles from Ishpeming Point. The campground is 0.3 mile from the Greenstone Ridge Trail, situated above the south shoreline of the lake. The campground is a scenic one with the individual sites located in a stand of birch while nearby is a small sandy cove where backpackers can watch the sun set in the evening while listening to the resident loons.

Day Five (11.3 miles) This is the longest day of the trek. But your legs should be strong by now, your food bag nearly empty and the visions of an ice cream bar or a package of Oreo cookies from the Windigo store more than enough to motivate you down the trial.

Return to the Greenstone Ridge Trail and head west (right) where you immediately makes a steep ascent to the crest of the ridge. You climb almost 170 feet in the next half mile before the trail levels out briefly and then resumes climbing to a high point of 1,239 feet. Here the trail swings near the edge of the ridge and 1.5 miles from the Lake Desor junction a side trail leads to a rocky clearing in the trees. From this spot you can see the Canadian shoreline to the north and flat-topped Pie Island in Lake Superior. Enjoy the sun and the breaks in the foliage; these are the last significant views for the remainder of the trail.

The Greenstone climbs steeply again, this time to the high point of 1,319 feet, descends briefly to a marshy area crossed by planking and then makes its final and steepest climb to the top of Mount Desor. At 1,394 feet, this is the highest point on the island, but there are no grand views as the peak is covered with sugar-maple trees. It's simply a wide spot in the trail with a boulder in the middle of it, not even a sign announcing you have reached the roof of Isle Royale.

From the mountain, the trail descends gradually for more than 1.5 miles, where it levels out and crosses a swamp on planking. From the marsh you climb the ridge again before the trail levels out for a 0.3 mile and arrives at a well-posted junction, 5.1 miles from South Lake Desor Campground. Heading south (left) is the Island Mine Trail, reaching Island Mine Campground in less than a half mile and Siskiwit Bay Campground in 4.8 miles. Island Mine Campground is often used by backpackers who want to break this long segment into two days.

The Greenstone Ridge Trail continues west by gradually climbing the remaining half mile to the top of Sugar Mountain. This is the third highest point in the park at 1,362 feet but, like Mount Desor, no sign, view, or even a break in the trees to indicate you've reached the peak. The mountain is named after the sugar-maple trees that cover it and make up the forest much of the way to Windigo. As late as the 1870s, Indians arrived at Sugar Mountain to tap the trees for their sweet sap.

From Sugar Mountain, it's 5.5 miles to Windigo along a trail that is mostly downhill. Within a half mile you drop to a cedar swamp and cross it on a boardwalk and then continue along the gradually descending Greenstone

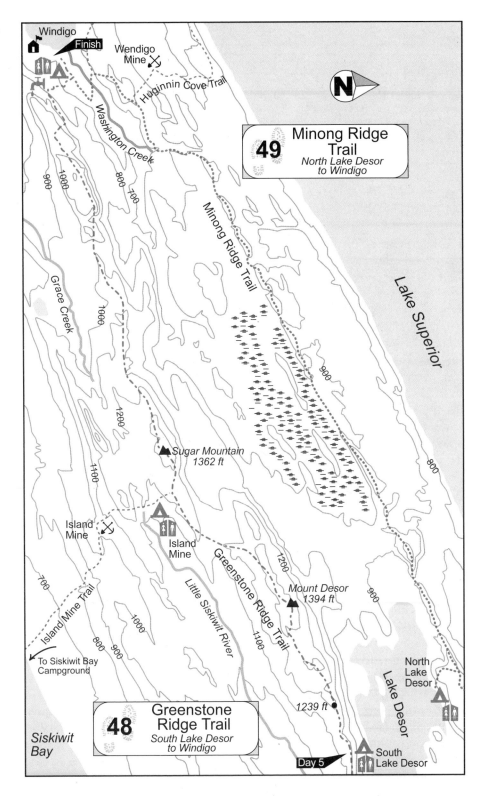

Windigo

Finish

Wendigo Mine

Huginnin Cove Trail

Washington Creek

Grace Creek

1000
900
800
700

Minong Ridge Trail

49 Minong Ridge Trail
North Lake Desor to Windigo

Lake Superior

900

800

1200

1100

Sugar Mountain
1362 ft

Island Mine

Island Mine

Island Mine Trail

700

Little Siskiwit River

Greenstone Ridge Trail

1200

Mount Desor
1394 ft

900

1100

700

800
900
1000

To Siskiwit Bay Campground

Lake Desor

North Lake Desor

48 Greenstone Ridge Trail
South Lake Desor to Windigo

1239 ft

Siskiwit Bay

Day 5

South Lake Desor

Backpackers follow the Rock Harbor Trail. The scenic trail is the most common route to the Greenstone Ridge Trail from the entry point of Rock Harbor.

Ridge for the next 3 miles. Eventually the trail swings sharply north to leave the ridge for good. It's a rapid descent as you drop from 960 feet to 631 feet in a little more than a mile. You bottom out at a junction with the Minong Ridge Trail. Head west (left) here to reach Washington Creek Campground in 0.3 mile or 11.3 miles from South Lake Desor. This is a large and busy campground with 10 shelters along the creek, toilets, tables, and piped-in water, along with individual and group campsites.

Continue west on the trail to reach Windigo in another 0.3 mile, where you'll find a comfort station that contains public showers, a small laundry facility and flush toilets. Ah, a shower for the first time in almost a week. Who knew you could last so long? Nearby there is also that store, an interesting visitor center, and the wharf where the *Voyageur II* ties up.

Minong Ridge Trail

Isle Royale National Park

County: Keweenaw
Nearest Towns: Houghton and Copper Harbor
Distance: 31.6 miles
Hiking Time: Six days
Highest Elevation Gain: 150 feet
Difficulty: Challenging
Highlights: Scenery and solitude on Michigan's toughest trail

Few backpackers who have walked the Minong Ridge Trail will argue that this 29-mile route is one tough trek. Minong Ridge is not only the most challenging stretch of the Isle Royale's 161-mile trail system, but arguably the hardest hike in Michigan.

And that's the way the park staff intends to keep it. The Minong Ridge Trail was cut in the mid-1960s as a "fire manway," a route fire fighters could use to access the isolated northern half of the island. Almost from the beginning, backpackers began following it, and eventually the National Park Service decided to maintain the route as a primitive trail with as few markers, bridges, and boardwalks as possible.

That's the appeal and the challenge of Minong Ridge.

Part of the challenge is the amount of time needed to hike it. The trail itself is a three to four-day walk from McCargoe Cove Campground to Windigo. But most backpackers also need another two days to reach McCargoe Cove from Rock Harbor. Carrying six days worth of food and fuel makes for a heavy backpack on a trail where you want to be as light as possible.

Minong Ridge is also an up-and-down hike that, at times, will have you wondering if you're headed in the right direction. Portions are a path in the woods but much of it is a route along a rocky ridge where the only indication of the trail is an occasional rock cairn. No other trail in Michigan uses cairns so extensively. Along many open stretches you are simply hiking from cairn to cairn and at times it's easy to miss the next one. If you become temporarily turned around on the ridge, pause and search for a cairn or backtrack to the last one you passed and start again.

The Minong Ridge is best hiked from east to west, leaving the long 12.6-mile portion from Lake Desor to Windigo for the end. If you're following the trail at the peak of summer from mid-July to mid-August, start the day early and carry two quarts of water per person. It can be hot on the open ridge, and water can be hard to find at times, particularly between Little Todd Harbor and North Lake Desor.

Because the Minong and the Greenstone Ridge Trail parallel each other,

The view of Todd Harbor is nice, especially after a long day on the Minong Ridge Trail.

both trails are covered in the same set of set maps used for the description of the Greenstone.

Trip Planner

Maps: The best map for this hike is National Geographic's Trails Illustrated Map, *Isle Royale National Park*, that covers the park in 1:50,000 detail.
Getting There: To reach the start of the Minong Ridge Trail on foot follow the first two days of the Greenstone Ridge Trail and then continue on the East Chickenbone Trail to McCargoe Cove, a 2.1 mile hike. Many hikers will hike to Daisy Farm the first day and then to McCargoe Cove via the East Chickenbone Trail the second day.

A far easier way to reach the start of the Minong and to save time is to book passage on the *M.V. Sandy*, the tour boat operated by Rock Harbor Lodge and Marina. Once a week the vessel makes a day-trip to McCargoe Cove from Rock Harbor and can be used by backpackers as one-way transportation.

To return to Rock Harbor from Windigo after hiking the Minong book passage on the *Voyageur II* (see Greenstone Ridge Trail).
Fees & Reservations: Contact the Rock Harbor Resort to find out current schedule and costs for the *M.V. Sandy*. In the past the boat made the trip to McCargoe Cove on Wednesday, charging $23 for one-way passage to the start of the Minong Ridge Trail.
Information: For more information on the *M. V. Sandy*, contact Rock Harbor Lodge (906-337-4993 (summer) or 866-644-2003 (winter); *www. isleroyaleresort.com*).

Trail Guide

Day Three (6.6 miles) Maps that accompany this text are included with the Greenstone Ridge Trail maps (see Hike 48). This description takes into account that most hikers need two days to reach McCargoe Cove from Rock Harbor. But whether you walked to McCargoe Cove or were just dropped off by the *M. V. Sandy*, plan on spending a night at this beautiful campground. The site has a half-dozen shelters, individual and group campsites. There is also a dock where campers gather in the evening to watch the resident moose feed across the cove.

The Minong Ridge Tail is located at the rear of the campground and begins with a gentle climb for almost a mile. You level out at the first of two junctions of side trails to Minong Mine. This spur parallels the Minong Ridge and in a half mile reaches the Minong Mine, Isle Royale's largest copper mine that operated from 1874 to 1883. The area is marked by large piles of rock tailings, rails, and ore cars from the small railroad that hauled rock from several shafts to McCargoe Cove.

The Minong Ridge Trail departs the junction to Minong Mine and ascends steeply, at one point passing an unmarked second junction to the Minong Mine. You top off at the rocky crest of the ridge 1.5 miles from McCargoe Cove and are rewarded with the first of many fine views of the north shore of Isle Royale and Canada. Cairns take over here leading you on a rugged up-and-down trek along the ridge.

Within 2.5 miles from McCargoe Cove, Otter Lake unexpectedly appears to the north as a deep blue gem in a green setting. Sharp eyes will even spot the east end of Todd Harbor from this spot. You continue along the ridge and in the next half mile pass two more views of the lake, the second time is when you're standing at the edge of a rocky cliff with Otter Lake straight below you.

Beyond Otter Lake the trail drops into the woods and stays in the forest the remaining 2 miles to Todd Harbor. Along the way, it continues to drop and climb as it passes through swamps, but this is considerably easier than the rocky ridgetop. Within 1.5 miles of Todd Harbor or 5 miles from McCargoe Cove, you cross a small stream where drinking water is easily accessible. The trail continues in the woods and then in the final half mile swings toward the lakeshore and works its way down to the shore of the harbor.

Todd Harbor is a beautiful spot to spend the night. Its protected bay is usually calm and peaceful while the view across the water can be stunning during sunsets. The campground has one shelter, group and individual campsites, pit toilets, and a dock.

From near the fire ring, a trail heads 0.2 mile west to the Haytown Mine. This mine held some of the richest copper deposits on the island but its isolated location and lack of protection from strong northerly winds made the operation unprofitable. The mine operated from 1847 to 1853 and today all that remains is a shaft that has been fenced off and a pile of rock tailings.

Day Four (6.7 miles) Strong hikers will occasionally combine this day to Little Todd Harbor with the segment to North Lake Desor Campground, a walk of 11.3 miles. That's less than what you are faced with on the final day to Windigo. But be forewarned that hike from Little Todd Harbor to Lake Desor is by far the most challenging section and an especially tough one when it comes in the second half of a long day.

The day to Little Todd Harbor begins with a brief climb and then is followed by a level walk in a birch forest for more than a mile. Within 1.6 miles from Todd Harbor you cross a footbridge over a stream and reach the junction with Hatchet Lake Trail, the path that heads south (left) for the Greenstone Ridge Trail. The Minong Ridge Trail continues west (straight) for Little Todd Harbor and for the next half mile remains as an easy walk through the woods.

Eventually you climb back to the open ridgetop. The trail now follows the up and down contour of the Minong Ridge for the next 3 miles. You never completely break out of the trees along this segment but within a mile begin treading along a narrow spine of rock where both sides of the Minong Ridge drop steeply below you. Within 5.7 miles from Todd Harbor, the Minong Ridge Trail skirts a large grassy marsh to the south. The towering bluff that borders the south side of the marsh is the Greenstone Ridge.

The trail returns to the forest and in the final mile of the day swings to the north to descend to a stream. There's no footbridge at this unnamed stream, just a series of logs to tiptoe over. You climb the bank on the other side and then begin a rapid descent, bottoming out to arrive at the junction with the spur to Little Todd Harbor. This side trail is a gradual 0.6-mile descent to the shoreline that passes a pair of bogs.

There are no shelters at Little Todd Harbor, and the individual sites, arranged in two clusters, lack privacy if more than two parties are spending the night. Still, after a tiring day on the Minong Ridge, this is a pleasant place to rest those aching muscles. Most of the campsites are close enough to the shoreline that at night you can be lulled to sleep by a gentle Lake Superior surf.

Day Five (5.7 miles) Little Todd Harbor to the North Lake Desor is the most intriguing part of the Minong Ridge. It's a trek of only 5.7 miles, but you spend almost the entire day on the open ridges hiking from cairn to cairn. The few times you won't be on the crest, you'll be climbing to the next stretch of bare rock. Such long spells on rough rock is jarring on the ankles and tough on the knees. Trekking poles are a huge help here but the best thing you can do is just take your time and stop often. And you'll want to. The day is almost a continuous panorama of the island, Lake Superior, and Canada only 14 miles to the north.

Backtrack 0.6 mile to the Minong Ridge Trail which heads west (right) at the junction and immediately climbs out of the birch and aspen forest to the rocky crest of the ridge. At the top, you should have gained enough elevation for a clear, unobstructed view of the Greenstone Ridge to the south, Lake Superior to the north, or more of the ridge straight ahead.

You'll stay on the open ridge with the exception of a few dips-and-climbs into the forest below in a pattern that will become all too familiar by the end of the day. This is where you can easily wander off the route, so keep one eye out for rock cairns or other trail markers. Within a half mile of reaching the open crest of the ridge, you arrive at another panoramic view; on the horizon is Lake Superior and the Canadian shoreline, straight below are the islets called Gull Rocks.

The best view of the day, however, arrives 2.6 miles from Little Todd Harbor. Here the Minong Ridge is a steep rocky cliff and from the edge of it you can see all the way back to Todd Harbor to the east. The trail continues to follow the crest of the ridge and in another half mile skirts the bluffs above an unnamed lake. The lake remains in view off and on for a half mile and then you finally drop into the forest, instant relief for feet tired of walking on rock.

The relief is short lived. The trail climbs back to the open ridge in the final 2.0 miles to North Lake Desor Campground. This is the most rugged stretch because twice you are faced with long climbs out of the woods back to the top of Minong's rocky backbone. But each time you top off there are views of Isle Royale's north shore and Canada to enjoy while rubbing your toes.

Eventually you descend off the rocky crest and just inside the trees arrive at the signpost that marks the side trail to North Lake Desor Campground. The half-mile trail winds through the forest as it gently descends to the campground. North Lake Desor has a pit toilet and individual campsites but no group site or, for that matter, much level ground. Along the shoreline just east of the campground is a small sandy cove ideal for soaking tired ankles and toes.

Day Six (12.6 miles) North Lake Desor to Windigo is the longest day of the trek but not as difficult as the previous segments along the Minong Ridge. Despite a natural eagerness to reach those shelves of junk food at the Windigo store, take your time, and keep your eye on the trail. This stretch can get confusing when it crosses a couple of beaver ponds.

Return a half mile to the Minong Ridge Trail where it heads west (left) by immediately climbing to the top of the ridge. You follow the crest for a half mile and then dip back into the forest only to begin a steep climb 1.5 miles from the campground. The reward at the top is a grand view of Lake Desor over your shoulder.

The trail remains on the open ridge for another half mile and then descends into a beautiful birch forest where it remains for 2 miles. Eventually you climb to the top of a thimbleberry-covered ridge. If it's late July or August, you're in luck with easy pickings of the fruit that looks like a raspberry on steroids. This break in the trees is brief as the trail descends back into a low-lying forest with a marshy stream that is crossed on a series of logs.

Beyond the stream, you make a steep climb to break out at a small clearing on Minong Ridge. This is the first of four opening you climb to in the next 2 miles that for the most part is an up-and-down walk in the woods. After the third clearing the trail descends sharply and bottoms out in a marshy area that is crossed by an extremely long stretch of planking. From the planking, you're faced with the fourth and longest climb that tops off at a stretch of rocky crest.

The trail descends to a small pond that is crossed by tiptoeing over a beaver dam, climbs again and then, 9 miles from the junction to North Lake Desor, descends to a second beaver pond. This pond is larger and thus much more challenging. Don't worry about getting your boots wet; worry about not getting your pack soaked.

On the other side, markers indicate where the trail climbs again with the steep ascent ending at a high rocky point known as Minong Trail Overlook, a popular dayhike destination from Windigo. The view is not as panoramic as others you have witnessed along the Minong Ridge Trail, but you can spot parts of Canada, Pie Island, and Washington Harbor to the southwest. You are now 3.3 miles from that package of Oreo cookies.

A pair of tired backpackers approach the North Lake Desor Campground after spending the day on the Minong Ridge Trail.

The trail descends from the overlook towards Washington Creek Basin and crosses a branch of the creek before swinging west and climbing again. You reach the posted junction of East Huginnin Cove Trail 1.8 miles from the Minong Overlook. The Minong Ridge Trail heads west (left) while East Huginnin Cove Trail departs north (right) and in 0.3 mile reaches the posted ruins of the Wendigo Mines.

From the junction, you descend the last bit of the Minong Ridge for 0.6 mile, bottoming out at the southern trailhead of the West Huginnin Cove Trail. Just to the south (left) the Minong Ridge Trail crosses Washington Creek, where near the bridge is a hydrologic benchmark station.

You climb out of the creek basin and in a half mile finally reach the end of the Minong Ridge Trail at a spot where it merges into the Greenstone Ridge Trail. Congratulations on completing the toughest trail in Michigan. Just a 0.3 mile walk to the west is Washington Creek Campground, with piped water, 10 shelters, and individual and group sites, while the ranger station, store and ferry dock at Windigo are 0.6 mile away.

The halfway point of the Feldtmann Ridge Trail, and a great spot for lunch, is the old firetower. The views from the top of the tower are the finest of the day.

Feldtmann Ridge Trail

Isle Royale National Park

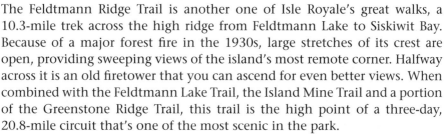

County: Keweenaw
Nearest Towns: Houghton and Copper Harbor
Distance: 29.8 miles
Hiking Time: Three days
Highest Elevation Gain: 280 feet
Difficulty: Moderate to challenging
Highlights: Feldtmann Lake and frequent moose sightings

The Feldtmann Ridge Trail is another one of Isle Royale's great walks, a 10.3-mile trek across the high ridge from Feldtmann Lake to Siskiwit Bay. Because of a major forest fire in the 1930s, large stretches of its crest are open, providing sweeping views of the island's most remote corner. Halfway across it is an old firetower that you can ascend for even better views. When combined with the Feldtmann Lake Trail, the Island Mine Trail and a portion of the Greenstone Ridge Trail, this trail is the high point of a three-day, 20.8-mile circuit that's one of the most scenic in the park.

But best of all, Feldtmann Ridge experiences far fewer hikers than the Greenstone or the trails at the east end of the island. The loop is popular with backpackers from Minnesota who arrive at Windigo, but hikers who step ashore in Rock Harbor have to make additional transportation arrangements to reach this trail. But this loop is well worth the additional costs and is the perfect choice for anybody not up for a five- to six-day traverse of the island along the Greenstone or Minong ridges.

The other alternative is to ferry to Windigo and hike this loop to the Greenstone Ridge Trail near Island Mine Campground. Here you head east, instead of west, to return to Rock Harbor. Such a grand adventure would require seven to eight days but would be unmatched by any other walk on the island in terms of scenery, wilderness solitude and the possibilities of spotting wildlife, particularly moose. Just make sure you pack plenty of gorp.

Trip Planner

Maps: Like the other two island hikes covered in this guide, the best map for Feldtmann Ridge is National Geographic's Trails Illustrated Map, *Isle Royale National Park*.

Getting There: To reach Windigo and return to Rock Harbor, book passage on the *Voyageur II* (see Greenstone Ridge Trail). Alternatively, you can book a flight to Windigo with Royale Air Service, which flies out of the Houghton County Memorial Airport. You can also arrange an inter-island flight between Windigo and Rock Harbor.

Fees & Reservations: Seaplane service between Houghton and Isle Royale is $180 one-way and $260 round-trip. An inter-island flight is $100 per person.
Information: To book the seaplane service contact Royale Air Service, Inc. (218-721-0405 or 877-359-4753; www.royaleairservice.com).

Trail Guide

Day One (8.5 miles) The first day to Feldtmann Lake Campground begins at the road in front of the Windigo ferry dock, which heads west to quickly reach the start of the Feldtmann Lake Trail. Once on the trail you continue to skirt Washington Harbor for a mile, enjoying constant views of the shoreline and Beaver Island in the middle of the harbor.

From this scenic stretch, Feldtmann Lake Trail swings sharply south to climb what remains of the Greenstone Ridge. Within a half mile you ascend 100 feet, resume heading west and 2 miles from Windigo break out on a rocky crest to views of Lake Superior, Grace Harbor, and the mouth of Grace Creek.

The trail follows the open ridgetop for another quarter mile and then descends the Greenstone Ridge. After bottoming out you reach a foot bridge across Grace Creek 3 miles from Windigo. Pause here to look for signs of moose (nugget-like scat, tracks) or even the animals themselves as they are frequent visitors to this area. Beyond Grace Creek, the trail climbs a low ridge and then swings west. You head west toward Grace Harbor for the next mile along a trail in the woods where the only views, other than trees, are an occasional swamp.

You approach Middle Point 4.5 miles from Windigo but never reach it. The trail swings south here, follows an interesting rock bluff and then descends through another swamp where again moose will occasionally be encountered. Eventually you swing southeast and hike below the old beachlines formed when glaciers kept Lake Superior at a higher level. The old beaches are an interesting formation as they create the impression you are hiking below Feldtmann Lake and are an indication you are only 1.5 miles from the campground.

Within half mile of the campground, the trail finally breaks out at a view of Feldtmann Lake, a beautiful body of water crowned in the southeast corner by Feldtmann Ridge and Sugar Mountain off in the distance. The campground is on the west end of the lake and has individual and group campsites, pit toilets, and a red sandy beach. Nearby is the east end of the Rainbow Cove Trail, a 0.8-mile walk to Lake Superior. Rainbow Cove earns its name from the stunning sunsets that can be enjoyed on a clear evening from its pebbled beach.

Day Two (10.3 miles) The hike along the Feldtmann Ridge to Siskiwit Bay Campground makes for a long day. Start early, take your time, and pack plenty of water. From Feldtmann Lake Campground the Feldtmann Ridge Trail uses a foot bridge to cross a stream, rounds the southwest corner of the

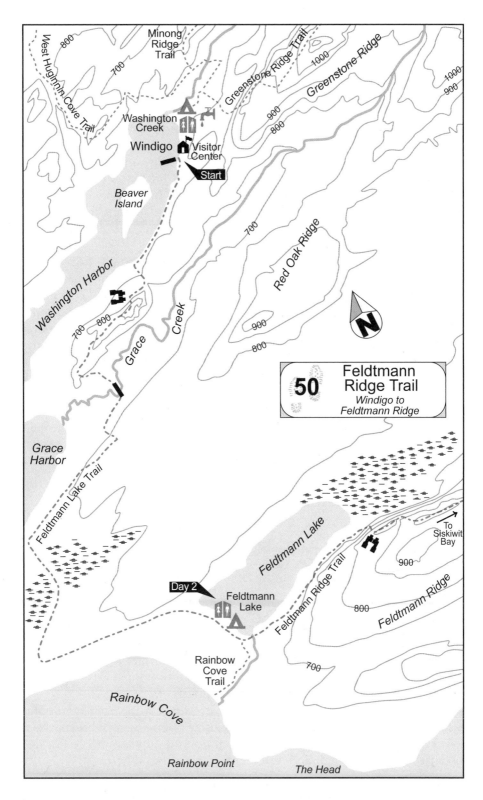

lake and then follows its south shoreline for 1.5 miles.

The easy hiking ends when the trail reaches Feldtmann Ridge, seen from below as high reddish bluffs. You begin climbing sharply and will gain 230 feet within a half mile. With rubbery knees and rapid breathing, you top off on a knoll with an incredible view and shaded by three pine trees. Below is Feldtmann Lake, including any moose feeding at its east end, while to the west are Grace Harbor and Rock of Ages Lighthouse. To the east you can see Siskiwit Bay and the Greenstone Ridge.

The trail follows the rolling contour of the ridge and more views are enjoyed to the north. You pass through stands of birch and mountain ash, then openings caused by the forest fire of 1936 and finally arrive at a swamp with signs of beaver activity around it. You skirt a small pond and then dip into a shaded cut where a stream flows out of a scenic red rock bowl as a small waterfall.

From the stream, the trail begins its ascent to the tower, gaining 273 feet in 1.8 miles. The tower is reached 4.8 miles from Feldtmann Lake Campground, making it almost the halfway point to Siskiwit Bay and the perfect place for lunch. The tower is at 1,173 feet, and puts you above the surrounding trees for one of the best views on Isle Royale. You can gaze for miles in every direction and see almost the entire western half of the island, including Big Siskiwit Swamp, Sugar Mountain, and the Greenstone Ridge; to the northeast, Siskiwit Bay, Lake Halloran, and even Malone Bay are visible.

Heading east from the lookout tower, the trail descends into the trees but quickly resumes climbing again, and in a half mile breaks out on an open ridge. The stone foundation and collapsed logs are remains of the original fire tower on the ridge. You departs the ruins and begin a mile-long descent off Feldtmann Ridge. If it's late July or August, look for ripe thimbleberries after you bottom out.

Most of the remaining route to Siskiwit Bay was originally logging roads that were built in the swamps of Big Siskiwit River in the mid-1930s. The road, and thus the trail, is remarkably level because loggers cut it along an old Lake Superior beachline. You begin paralleling Lake Halloran 3.5 miles from the tower but never see the rectangle lake that is located a half mile to the south.

The last leg of the day leaves the patches of thimbleberries and ferns, enters a forest and finally crosses a large grassy clearing just before reaching Siskiwit Bay. The large clearing was the site of the logging camp responsible for all the swamp roads and then a Civilian Conservation Corps (CCC) camp after the fire of 1936. A little farther on, just before entering the campground, you arrive at the junction with the Island Mine Trail.

Just after passing the junction with the Island Mine Trail, you enter Siskiwit Bay Campground. This campground is often a mix of backpackers, kayakers, and powerboaters and has been dubbed "Riviera of Isle Royale" because of the warmer air and water temperatures found here.

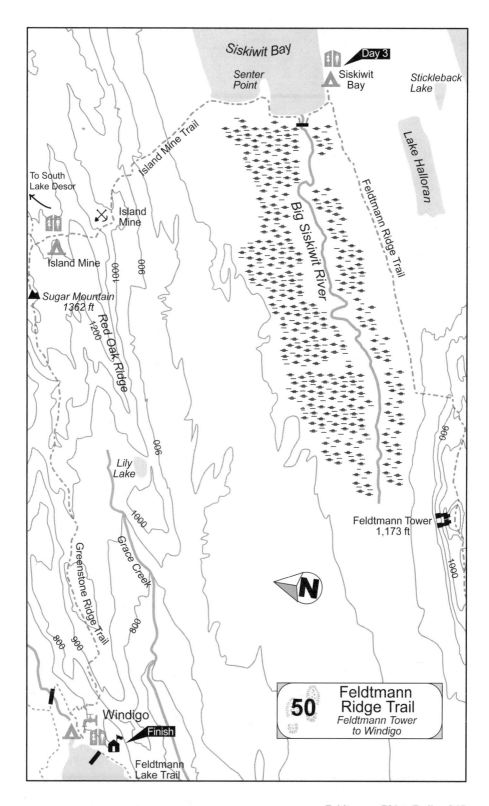

Siskiwit Bay

Senter Point

Day 3

Siskiwit Bay

Stickleback Lake

Lake Halloran

Island Mine Trail

To South Lake Desor

Island Mine

Island Mine

Feldtmann Ridge Trail

Big Siskiwit River

Sugar Mountain 1362 ft

Red Oak Ridge

1000

900

1200

Lily Lake

900

1000

Feldtmann Tower 1,173 ft

900

1000

Greenstone Ridge Trail

Grace Creek

1000

800

800

900

Windigo

Finish

Feldtmann Lake Trail

50 Feldtmann Ridge Trail
Feldtmann Tower to Windigo

A hiker sets up camp in Feldtmann Lake Campground.

Day Three (11 miles) Island Mine Trail leads you back to the Greenstone Ridge Trail, where you have three options. You can spend the night at nearby Island Mine Campground or continue on to Windigo, a mostly downhill walk of 11 miles to Washington Creek Campground. Or you can head east to South Lake Desor Campground, a trek of almost 10 miles.

Just west of the campground the Island Mine Trail departs north (right) from the Feldtmann Ridge Trail at a well posted junction and begins as a beautiful walk skirting Siskiwit Bay. For 1.5 miles you follow the west end of the bay, most of the time just inside the brush off the beach. In the middle of this, two bridges provide dry footing over a pair of forks of the Big Siskiwit River and then the trail crosses the base of Senter Point. The point was used by the Island Mine Company in the 1870s to store their explosives and just before returning to the beach you can poke around to see the remains of the stone powder house.

Beyond Senter Point, you resume following the beach to its northern end, where the trail swings northwest and moves inland. At this spot the mining company built a town to house mine workers and a wagon road from there to the shafts where 213,245 pounds of refined copper were recovered from 1873 to 1875. Thanks to that wagon road the next 2 miles to the mines are an easy walk that gently climbs in the second half.

You reach the Island Mine 3.7 miles from Siskiwit Bay Campground. What remains are large piles of rock tailings, evidence that this was the second largest mining operation on the island. Sadly, the wagon road ends here with the trail becoming a much more narrow and rugged path. You make your steepest ascent of the day, gaining 280 feet before reaching the crest of Red Oak Ridge at an elevation of 1,280 feet.

The trail then descends the ridge through a series of switchbacks and quickly bottoms out at a stream with Island Mine Campground on the other side. Your day is done if you plan to camp at Island Mine.

If not, pass through the campground and follow the trail as it ascends 80 feet to the crest of the Greenstone Ridge. The junction with the Greenstone Ridge Trail is 0.4 mile from the campground. To the west Washington Creek Campground is 6.2 miles away along a mostly downhill route. For that description or east to South Lake Desor turn to the Greenstone Ridge Trail (Hike 48).

A backpacker admires Monument Rock at Isle Royale National Park.

About the author

Jim DuFresne is an outdoor writer based in Clarkston, Michigan, and author of more than a dozen wilderness/travel guidebooks. His books cover areas from Alaska and New Zealand to Michigan's own Isle Royale National Park. He also contributes recreational outdoor and travel articles to a variety of magazines and is a regular contributor to *Michigan Blue* Magazine.

DuFresne is a journalism graduate from Michigan State University and the former outdoors and sports editor of the *Juneau Empire,* where in 1980 he became the first Alaskan sportswriter to ever win a national award from Associated Press.

Shortly after that, DuFresne spent a winter in New Zealand to backpack and write his first book, *Tramping in New Zealand* (Lonely Planet Publications). Six editions and 25 years later *Tramping in New Zealand* is the world's bestselling guidebook to backpacking in that country. DuFresne's *Isle Royale National Park: Foot Trails & Water Routes* (Mountaineer Books) has been in publication in various editions for more than 20 years.

DuFresne's other titles include *Porcupine Mountains Wilderness State Park* and *Michigan's Best Campgrounds* (Thunder Bay Press), *Glacier Bay National Park: A Guide to the Glaciers and Beyond* and *Best Hikes for Children: Michigan* (Mountaineer Books), *50 Hikes In Michigan* (Backcountry Publications), and *Road Trip: Lake Michigan, Hiking in Alaska*, and *Alaska* (Lonely Planet Publications).